Book Two (09/2018-1

The
A Chronicle of the Trump Administration—Book Two (Sept. 2018-Nov. 2019

By Charles E. Hurlburt

The Enemy Within: A Chronicle of the Trump Administration

Copyright 2019
Charles E. Hurlburt

Also by Charles E. Hurlburt

It's Time For the Truth: The JFK Cover-up

The Dawn of a New Age of Reason: Breaking Religion's Chains in the Twenty-First Century

Book One of this series

Book Two (09/2018-11/2019)

Dedication

I am dedicating this book to the brave and patriotic whistleblowers who have come forward so far and those who will come forward in the next few months. They should get a big chunk of the credit when Donald Trump is finally removed from office.

The Enemy Within: A Chronicle of the Trump Administration

Table of Contents

Section	Page
Author's Note	5
September, 2018	7
October, 2018	37
November. 2018	75
December, 2018	119
January, 2019	157
February, 2019	189
March, 2019	227
April, 2019	273
May, 2019	307
June, 2019	347
July, 2019	377
August, 2019	405
September, 2019	425
October, 2019	445
November, 2019	469
Epilog	495
Acknowledgements	498
Bibliography	499

Book Two (09/2018-11/2019)

Author's Note

For those who have not read *Book One* of the same title, a little recap is in order as background. This work was begun the day after Trump's election and soon developed into a day-by-day chronicle. It grew too large to be published as one book. *Book One* ended with August 31, 2018; a couple of months before the mid-term election. This book picks it up from there. I have altered the format from a day-to-day report to a week-to-week report, to somewhat reduce the number of pages consumed as I try to take this volume as far as the impeachment trial and verdict. I have described each week on a Monday-to-Sunday basis, with a few exceptions.

If Trump survives impeachment, Book Three will be lengthy also. If he does not, Book Three will be an addendum to this one.

The Enemy Within: A Chronicle of the Trump Administration

Book Two (09/2018-11/2019)

September, 2018

Sept. 1-9

Several days of tribute to Senator John McCain ended with his funeral on Saturday, which was attended by former Presidents George W. Bush and Barack Obama, but the uninvited President Trump was dividing his time between rallies and playing golf (again). The eulogies presented by John's friends, relatives, and dignitaries, including President Obama, were in stark contrast in eloquence, sincerity and class to what we see on a daily basis coming out of today's White House.

The race for Governor of Florida between the Democrat Andrew Gillum and the Republican Ron DeSantis has Gillum currently leading by five points in the polls (48-43 percent). All over the South, we are seeing a trend back from red to blue. It all depends now on getting people to actually vote.

Russian oligarch Oleg Deripaska has been sought for months by Christopher Steels as a possible flipper. Now he is also a target of Robert Mueller.

The tributes to, and the funeral of Senator John McCain are now behind us, but I would like to close that subject with a reminder of where he stood on the issue of our current president. Shortly after Trump's disastrous summit with Putin, McCain wrote a statement about it that contained the following words, which will forever live in US history.

"Today's press conference in Helsinki was one of the most disgraceful performances by an American president in memory. The damage inflicted by President Trump's naiveté, egotism, false equivalence and sympathy for autocrats is difficult to calculate. But it is clear that the summit in Helsinki was a tragic mistake. No prior president has ever abased himself more abjectly before a tyrant."

It is important to remember that this is one Republican evaluating another.

There were no significant events this Monday pertaining to the Trump administration, but there is a huge one coming up tomorrow, when the Senate debates the nomination of Judge Brett Kavanaugh to be our next Supreme Court Justice, which would bring that court back to a full complement of nine. It should get off to a contentious start, because the long-requested documents pertaining to this judge's past performance were dumped, en mass, at the last possible moment with no time for the Democratic opposition to go through them. Even this belated dump of the requested case file documents included only a fraction of what the Senators need, to make an informed judgement on the nominee.

By withholding so many case files they create the impression that there is something to hide. These hearings should make for very interesting TV viewing, for all who care about the future of our country. Latest polls show that Kavanaugh has the support of only 37%, while 40% oppose him, which is the lowest approval rate in history for one of these Supreme Court candidates.

One issue that the Democrat Senators are sure to raise is the fact that Kavanaugh lied about ever ruling on the US policy on torture during the Bush administration, when Kavanaugh went through a similar hearing for a lower court. He said then that he was not involved in that issue, but he is on record as supporting the Bush policy.

This Tuesday and Wednesday produced two of the most damaging salvos against the Trump presidency we have seen to date. This one-two punch is so inter-related that I have decided to combine the two under one sub-heading.

Book Two (09/2018-11/2019)

There have been a series of explosive books exposing the activities, attitudes, comments, etc. inside the Trump White House. The first blockbuster was Wolfe's *Fire & Fury inside the Trump White House.* Then we had Omarosa's book *Unhinged.* On Tuesday we learned of a new expose by a member of the duo who helped bring down Richard Nixon-- Bob Woodward, who has long been considered the very epitome of the reliable, accurate and honest journalist. His book is titled, *Fear: Trump in the White House,* and is scheduled to be released later this month. Cable news journalists have all received advance copies and have been revealing excerpts for two days now. Woodward, much like Wolfe, has somehow managed to obtain many hours of taped interviews with dozens of members of the Trump administration who have been more than willing to provide their feelings and experiences as they try to maintain some semblance of sanity in the West Wing. Here are a couple of the excerpts that we have been privileged to hear so far. Former Trump attorney John Dowd: "The White House is having a nervous breakdown", and "Mr. President, I can't help you." Every person that Woodward interviewed expressed similar negative and apprehensive views about the way things *are* going and *have been* going from day one of Trump's presidency. Then on Wednesday the second half of the one-two haymaker landed, when an anonymous high-ranking member of Trump's staff published on op-ed essay in the *New York Times.* It was titled, *I Am Part of the Resistance Inside the Trump Administration.* Here is a sample of the contents of this remarkable piece.

"The root of the problem is the President's amorality. Anyone who works with him knows he is not moored to any discernable first principles that guide his decision making. Meetings with him veer off topic and off the rails, and his impulsiveness results in half-baked, ill-informed and occasionally reckless decisions that have to be walked back. Given the instability many witnessed, there were early whispers within the cabinet of invoking the 25th Amendment, which would start a complex process for removing the President. But no one wanted to precipitate a constitutional crisis. So we will do what we can to steer the administration in the right direction until, one way or another, it is over."

One White House insider told the Washington Post that, "the sleeper cells have taken over." The op-ed writer refers to a coordinated effort among most, if not all, cabinet members and high officials to do their best to keep a rein on Trump as much as possible without incurring a tantrum. This "resistance" seems to think of themselves as saving us all from a complete disaster. But they are not yet willing to do what could *really* put an end to our nightmare, if they had the guts to walk out en mass and really blow things up, figuratively, before our crazed commander-in-chief blows us all up literally. This modern day version of "deep throat" needs to, and I believe *will*, come forth and identify him or herself sometime in the very near future, if he/she wants to really have a lasting impact. Lawrence O'Donnell has predicted that it will turn out to be DNI Dan Coats, and he may be right on target. We will see. Soon we hope.

Trump has reacted in in a way that has been described as "volcanic"—no surprise. He calls it TREASON (showing that he doesn't know the definition of that word), and says that the *Times*, who knows who it is, must "turn him over" for prosecution immediately (still no concept of freedom of the press).

Invoking the 25th Amendment may seem extreme and with the current make up of Congress would not achieve the two-thirds majority of both houses to succeed, but after the midterms it would be worth attempting, before we end up with a *Seven Days in May* scenario and see the administration end with a military coup.

Book Two (09/2018-11/2019

The other big newsworthy event during this same pair of days was the Senate hearing on judge Kavanaugh. It got off to an embarrassingly raucous start, as protester after screaming protester had to be removed by security for disrupting the proceedings. Their sentiments are very understandable but the tactic used was not a good image for the Democratic Party.

After hours of opening statements from Senator after Senator, alternating between Democrat and Republican, Kavanaugh had a chance to make his own statement. Not much in the way of questioning took place until Wednesday, when the nominee was peppered with many questions about very important issues, most of which had bearing on the situation that the President finds himself in, or may end up in shortly. In almost every case, Kavanaugh dodged or just plain refused to answer, usually because he classified it as hypothetical. There was no clarification on how he would vote on Roe v. Wade, or whether a president could be subpoenaed or could pardon himself, or on several other very important concepts that are apt to come up in the near future.

The Republicans want those disputed documents and emails to be reviewed only by Kavanagh's long-time friend, Bill Burke, a Republican lawyer who represents several White House staffers. The Democrats are having none of that idea and, of course, want a delay of these proceedings until they have had a chance to review the thousands of pages representing the judge's views on a wide variety of subjects. It is highly unlikely they will get any kind of compromise from this Senate. There is one particular email that indicates how Kavanaugh would deal with racial profiling. It is one of many that has been designated as *Senate Confidential*, which means it should not be released to the public. Senator Cory Booker (D, New Jersey) decided that the public deserved to know how the judge dealt with that issue and said he intended to release it, even if they wanted to remove him from his Senate seat. That night, the Republicans decided to free up all the emails.

The Democrat Senators repeatedly asked Kavanaugh about the fact that he had apparently lied three times during a previous confirmation hearing, but he dodged and weaved without ever actually addressing the questions.

There were a few other items of a less earth-shaking nature that arose over these two days that are worth mentioning.

Former Secretary of State John Kerry was a guest on Rachel Maddow's show and pointed out that most of the American states, as well as the other signatories to the Paris climate accord and the Iran Nuclear deal, have remained in and are working for those agreements without the US government's participation.

Michael Campuano, a ten term Representative from Massachusetts, was defeated in a primary by newcomer Ayanna Pressley by a ten point margin. The ladies continue to shine!

As the Kavanaugh hearing was about to begin, Fred Guttenberg, the father of one of the girls killed at Parkland in Florida, approached the judge and extended his hand and introduced himself. Kavanaugh looked at him, then turned his back and walked away. What a guy!

Not only has our president been mocking his Attorney General for every trait that he has, including his southern accent, he has actually been mocking the South in general, where a major portion of his support comes from, calling them "dumb southerners." Who's the dumb one Donald?

The day was completely taken up with the reactions to the blockbuster op-ed essay in the Times that has the President just about climbing the walls and talking about having AG Sessions start an investigation into who that anonymous "enemy of the state" could be.

This, of course, is another completely inappropriate use of the Justice Department, which Sessions will simply ignore and infuriate Trump even further. Two dozen (and counting) members of his staff, cabinet, etc. have denied being the author, but this is to be expected at this early point. John Kelly, who is considered by some, including by the President's daughter, to be a very likely suspect, is leading the probe into tracking down the guilty party. Whoever it was will probably come out eventually. It is almost certainly a Republican, or he/she would not be in this White House.

As to Woodward's book, *Fear*, Trump responded to the slurs about southerners that are attributed to him in the book, by claiming, "I don't talk that way." Another silly lie which was immediately rebuffed by several audio replays of his past comments.

As the hearings continue on the Kavanaugh nomination it becomes more and more controversial because of his equivocation on many important questions. His approval rating going into the hearings was at an all-time low—even lower than Bork, who was rejected, or Harriet Miers, who withdrew under extreme criticism. He has lied in several of his answers, according to the records which contradict the lies. His email records show his questionable racial attitudes and his lack of any intent to maintain Roe v. Wade. He refers to birth control as "abortion-producing drugs," an obvious extreme right-wing dog whistle.

As we reached the end of a week when the Trump administration was dealt a double-barreled shotgun blast to the gut, things were not going any better. Here are the main topics.

The Enemy Within: A Chronicle of the Trump Administration

John Dean addressed the Senators on the last day of the Kavanaugh hearings, and alluded to the Trump administration by repeating his famous quote made in the Nixon era, that there was "a cancer growing on the presidency."

He made the point that no Supreme Court nomination by a president who is now an unindicted co-conspirator in a federal crime, should be considered, let alone confirmed. He specifically warned about this nominee's views on the scope of presidential powers. Kavanaugh's lies told during these hearings should, by themselves, disqualify him. If he is confirmed, he will be vulnerable to being impeached at some future date, when the political winds have changed. The confirmation now rests in the hands of two female Senators who have defended a woman's right to choose, and who support Roe v. Wade. The pressure is really strong now on Susan Collins of Maine and Lisa Murkowski of Alaska, to buck their GOP constituents and vote NO on Kavanaugh.

A Roger Stone associate named Jarome Corsi was subpoenaed to appear before Robert Mueller's grand jury today, but failed to show up. He is subject to arrest. Mueller is closing in on Stone, and should not let the fact that we are now within sixty days of the midterm election hinder him from issuing an indictment on him or his pal, says Representative Ted Lieu, Democrat from California.

George Papadopoulus began a *two-week* sentence in jail today, for lying to federal prosecutors. Talk about a slap on the wrist!

Bloomberg News, a business and market publication, reports that the Trump Organization is under investigation by New York (Manhattan) prosecutors, for campaign finance crimes. The Trump children are very much involved.

The speculation about the identity of the author of that explosive NYT op-ed essay continues unabated, while Donald

Book Two (09/2018-11/2019)

Trump continues to rant and rave about "treason." Trump has so many assorted pressures bearing down on him at this point that he doesn't know which way to turn. Even if he *had* been intellectually able to govern this country during the first few months of his term, he would not be able to do so under the cloud he is under now.

Obama's re-entry onto the political scene has sparked a lot of debate as to whether he will help or hurt the Democrats this November. Whose base will he energize the most? I believe that all he has to do is energize both sides equally and the Democrats will come out ahead, simply because the polls show that right now they are two-thirds to one-third ahead on the raw number of voters. The polls were not wrong in the overall number in 2016—only in the state-by-state breakdown.

Over fourteen hundred children are still in custody awaiting reunification with parents that some of them might not even recognize if they ever see them again. And no solution to this problem is in sight.

Sept. 10-16

The new Woodward book comes onto the market tomorrow, and it is already as hot, if not hotter, than Wolfe's *Fire and Fury*. Trump certainly is having a bigger meltdown over it, as he tries to narrow down his list of potential suspects over that other sword in his side—the *Times* anonymous whistleblower. He doesn't know which one to curse out the loudest.

Woodward appeared on several cable news shows today, talking about his book and giving us a taste of its contents. One of the most concerning things he says, that most of us already felt, was this quote:

"I have never seen a president so detached from reality." One event described in the book, which has induced a ton of concern, is one that Woodward attributes to Gary Cohn, the former Director of the White House Economic Council. This describes Cohn removing a document from Trump's desk when the President was not around to see him do it. Cohn says he felt he *had* do this to prevent Trump from signing a tariff bill that would have been financially disastrous. Woodward says that this was a repeated theme among most of the White House staff, who felt it to be their duty to the country to try to prevent as many stupid moves as they could, by the man who has no idea about anything. Woodward also told the TV hosts that he is afraid that the country is not taking the danger of the Trump presidency seriously enough. Ron Reagan also made an appearance to back Woodward on this point.

Trump has thrown in the towel on his case against Stormy Daniels for breaking her non-disclosure agreement that she made, not to talk about her affair with him, for which he paid her $130 grand. Like most of Trump's threats to sue, down through the years, he failed to follow up. Her attorney, the now famous Michael Avenatti, predicted that this was coming, and he has no intention of letting Trump off that easy. He is planning to go ahead with his counter suit against Trump for defamation and illegalities, already admitted to on the Cohen audio tape.

Senator Patrick Leahy, Democrat from Vermont, is accusing Brett Kavanaugh of lying under oath to the Senate, both during his previous confirmation hearing for a lower court judgeship, *and* during the past week of current hearings. He and the Senate at large have the documentation to prove this accusation. Lisa Graves, formerly on the Democrat staff of the Senate Judiciary Committee during the Bush administration, says that Kavanaugh *"should be impeached and removed from his current judgeship—not promoted to the highest court in the country."*

Amongst all the historic turmoil boiling over in the Trump administration, the completely delusional president tweets, "The White House is a smooth-running machine." He also thinks that the Mueller probe has somehow swung over to investigating Clinton. He must be having a flashback to when Bill was president.

But Trump isn't the only delusional one in the White House. In an interview on *Face the Nation*, Vice President Pence said, "I think Donald Trump is the most accomplished of my lifetime, and the most successful in history." Under hypnosis, maybe? Or just the most obsequious VP ever to hold that office.

Polls show that 55% of Americans believe that Bob Woodward's book is true, while 28% don't. I guess the other 17% aren't living on this planet, or too dumb to care.

Today is the seventeenth anniversary of the terrorist attack that brought down the twin towers in New York City. President Trump commemorated the event by visiting the site and greeting the mourners with a double fist-pump of the type you might give at a rally. Empathy and sensitivity are not Donald's strong suits.

As a new category-four hurricane takes aim at the Carolinas, and people are evacuating the area, instead of talking about the danger and the preparations he is taking (or not) for dealing with the aftermath, Trump is bragging about what a great job his administration did in Puerto Rico during and after Hurricane Maria. This is the one for which he played down the damage and the death count, and then neglected the island and is still neglecting it more than a year later. He is the only one on this planet who thinks he did a *decent,* never mind *great*, job of addressing this disaster. To add insult to injury, he has transferred ten million dollars from the FEMA budget to the ICE budget, to beef up his campaign against undocumented aliens.

The Enemy Within: A Chronicle of the Trump Administration

Bob Woodward's book *Fear* came out today and was an instant sell-out, except as an e-book, so I was able to download a copy that way. I don't have time to get through one Trump expose book before another gets published. The author was a guest of Rachel Maddow tonight (she gets them all) and told us a few more interesting revelations that he was able to obtain through his numerous and very frank conversations with White House insiders. One of them pertained to what VP Pence knew and when he knew it about Flynn's correspondence with the Russians—a crucial element in the "collusion" case. He also told us of some interesting things that Secretary of Defense James Mattis told him about having to explain to the President why stationing US troops in South Korea and in Europe was essential to preventing World War Three. Trump thought it would be a good idea to save the country some money by withdrawing from the world and returning to isolationism.

The GOP is preparing to introduce yet another tax cut bill to make the rich even richer (again). Their greed knows no bounds!

The Washington Post is reporting that Paul Manafort has been discussing a possible plea deal with the Mueller team. Including cooperation?

As Hurricane Florence bears down on the South Carolina coast, we learn that FEMA is not the only organization from which Trump is pulling funds. He is reported to be planning to pull $29 million from the Coast Guard as well, to be used in the same way that he intends to use the FEMA money—ICE. Locking people up for the crime of not being a documented American is more important to him than safeguarding or saving lives. In FEMA's case, the offered excuse is that the money is coming from a part of their budget that was not intended to pay for storm recovery but is from the general operating fund. But this is ringing hollow, especially to FEMA officials.

Book Two (09/2018-11/2019

Robert Mueller is expecting Paul Manafort to provide testimony about the President if he expects to make any sentence-reducing deal with his team. At this point, with two more trials facing him, Manafort cannot expect much of a sentence reduction by just pleading guilty. The pressure to flip grows heavier by the day.

Senators have presented Brett Kavanaugh with a list of hundreds of written questions they want answered ASAP. Kavanaugh has already submitted his written answers. Some of the questions raise some surprising topics, such as possible gambling addiction and debt payoffs by others to bail him out. The judge *denies* all gambling related questions. The Senate is planning to vote on his confirmation tomorrow, and we are still guessing about how Collins and Murkowski are going to vote. Murkowski is under the most pressure because Kavanaugh has a terrible record as to the Alaskan native population. She meets today with a group of these people and will undoubtedly get an earful.

Bob Woodward's book *Fear*, and the author himself, on live cable TV, tell us about a joint defense agreement that thirty-seven witnesses who have testified before the Mueller team have signed to present a united front. Trump's former Russia-case lawyer, John Dowd, is the apparent driving force behind this group. He says he has received debriefings from each of the lawyers who represent these witnesses. This allows this group to share information about what each of them has told Mueller. Flynn was part of this agreement before he pled guilty. Trump is complaining to the Mueller team, through Dowd, that he is hampered from performing his duty as president by the Mueller investigation. Why not speed it along by agreeing to a meeting with Mueller, Donald? The more we learn about what Woodward's book, and Omarosa's book, and Michael Wolfe's book reveal about the actions and thoughts of our *unhinged* commander-in-chief, the more we must come to the conclusion that he is unwilling and/or unable to change his long-held incorrect or childish views on virtually *everything*! Facts are whatever Trump wants them to be, in his bubble-world.

The Washington Post reports that the GOP is publicly voicing their concern about a coming "shipwreck" in the November midterms, where they now fear that they could lose *both* houses of Congress. The polls certainly point that way, on a consistent basis. The latest one shows that voters in the midwest, one of Trump's strong areas, now favor Democrats over Republicans by 51 to 47 percent. In July the same poll was 43 to 42%. Another poll shows that 47% want Trump impeached right now.

Instead of addressing the current hurricane that is hitting the Carolinas right now, Trump is rambling about how the Democrats invented twenty-nine hundred and seventy-five phony deaths from hurricane Maria's devastation of Puerto Rico last year, just to make him look bad. What makes him look bad is the insane conspiracy theories he keeps dreaming up to try and shift blame onto anyone but himself. I'm sure the relatives and friends of those 2975 victims of his negligence are pretty disgusted with this dismissal of their losses. A Puerto Rican State Senator is calling for an inquiry into the lack of management over the project of restoration, and the utter lack of necessary resources to distribute supplies, etc.

Paul Manafort is reported to be on the verge of making some sort of deal with the prosecution that would involve a guilty plea to avoid the upcoming trials. It is unclear at this point whether that deal would include cooperation with the Mueller team, but it is unlikely he would be able to get very much of a sentence reduction without it. We may find out tomorrow.

Senator Dianne Feinstein came up with a new bombshell today. She unveiled a letter she has been given that was written by a woman who wanted the Senate to know, before they vote

Book Two (09/2018-11/2019)

on the confirmation of Brett Kavanaugh to be the newest Supreme Court Justice, that he was guilty of sexual misconduct of an as yet unspecified nature.

This woman wished to remain anonymous, but it is probably out of her hands because Feinstein has passed the letter on to the FBI, who passed it on to the White House. This is going to get very nasty and could turn into something akin to the Clarence Thomas/Anita Hill case. Thomas managed to get himself confirmed in spite of the slander, but this may be the last straw for a certain pair of lady Senators we are depending on for their NO vote on Kavanaugh. That vote was scheduled for tomorrow but has been postponed until September 17.

The above mentioned sexual misconduct that has been alleged by an anonymous female from Brett Kavanaugh's past, has now been specified in some detail. This unnamed woman says that when they were in high school, Kavanaugh and another teenage boy lured her into a bedroom and the second boy held her down while Kavanaugh got on top of her. She says that she somehow managed to get away from them and has never reported the incident until she wrote about it in the letter, which she gave to a Democrat Representative from California named Anno Ershoo, who passed it on to Feinstein. Kavanaugh, of course, has vehemently denied the charge, but at least it has stalled the confirmation vote for a week while the Senate decides how to handle this new situation.

We now know that Michael Cohen has been talking with the Mueller team, as part of what will become a plea deal which *will include complete cooperation with the prosecutors.* This is the worst news yet for Donald Trump and family.

At long last Paul Manafort has completely flipped against the Trump administration and will cooperate fully with Mueller. The last holdout has surrendered, and this is a major threat to Donald Trump Jr. as well as the President. Manafort was a participant in the June 9 Trump Tower meeting with Trump Jr. and knows to whom that phone call over a "blocked" phone was made (you only get one guess).

He has provided Mueller with a lengthy list of all the things he can tell about. This is the eighth person who was a part of the Trump campaign and/or administration whom Mueller has "convicted" so far. What we have here is a rerun of *All the President's Men*. Senator Swalwell, on *The Rachel Maddow Show*, says, *"The jig is up."* It's only a matter of time. It's been another very bad week for Trump.

It was beginning to look like there was not going to be anything worth mentioning on the daily Trump saga this weekend, but at about 2:00 PM on Sunday, *this* happened.

A Professor at Palo Alto University, California, named Christine Blasey Ford has come forward to identify herself as the writer of the letter that Senator Feinstein introduced Thursday to the US Senate. She tells that she and her husband had been meeting with a "couple's therapist" in 2012 when she first reported the attack by Kavanaugh and another teenaged boy named Mark Judge. She said they had both been drinking heavily. When confronted, Judge claimed that he doesn't remember any such event.

Ford has already taken and passed a polygraph test. She is also willing to testify before the Senate. If this isn't enough to at least stall the confirmation of this judge, then something is seriously wrong with the entire process.

Sept. 17-23

As we begin a new week, things are really heating up on the subject of the Kavanaugh confirmation. For the rest of the week I will be leading off with this vital issue, unless something even more vital, like a Mueller report or a Trump resignation, comes along.

Dr. Christine Blasey Ford and Judge Brett Kavanaugh have been invited by the US Senate to appear to testify before them one week from today. They should subpoena the reluctant Mark Judge to also take part.

Dr. Ford says that she will be willing to do so after the FBI has conducted their usual investigation into the matter. This requires that the President tell the FBI to look into it, but Trump makes the absurdly erroneous statement, "It seems that they (the FBI) don't do that." They did it in the Thomas vs. Hill case, *after* he had already been confirmed. As one of the Democrat Senators pointed out, "that is what the 'I' in FBI stands for." Dr. Ford has been subjected to hate-mail and death threats and has felt it necessary to move out of her home because of the reaction over her allegation.

Trump is declassifying and releasing a huge number of documents, including emails and text messages, related to the people like DOJ official Bruce Ohr, James Comey and Carter Page. This is another attempt by Trump to cast a shadow over the FBI and the Mueller probe by exposing "improper" procedures by the Justice Department, at the expense of exposing methods and contacts that would jeopardize national security. Representative Adam Schiff issues the following evaluation of this Trump move: "President Trump, in a clear abuse of power, has decided to intervene in a pending law enforcement investigation by ordering the selective release of materials he believes are helpful to his defense team and thinks will advance a false narrative. With respect to some of these materials, I have been previously informed by the FBI and Justice Department that they would consider their release a red line that must not be crossed as they may compromise sources and methods."

Schiff considers this move to be even a more egregious obstruction of justice than the firing of James Comey. It also sends a bad message to our allied nations that we have to work with on sensitive intelligence issues.

The Enemy Within: A Chronicle of the Trump Administration

FEMA Director Brock Long is facing criminal charges over his handling of the Puerto Rico recovery effort. He is also the one who gave Trump the idea that the death toll from Hurricane Maria and its aftermath was an inflated number to make Trump look bad.

Polls in the Arizona Senate race show the Democrat leading fifty to forty-three percent. In Tennessee that race shows the Democrat ahead by fifty to forty-five percent. And the shift from red to blue keeps getting stronger.

In spite of stubborn insistence by Senator Chuck Grassley, that they will proceed with a hearing on the Kavanaugh nomination next Monday, with or without Dr. Ford's appearance, she persists that she will not testify before the FBI conducts an investigation into her allegation that she was sexually assaulted by the judge when they were in high school together. The Senate would like to make this a simple case of "she said-he said", with no way to prove which one is telling the truth. It may actually come down to that choice eventually, but if it does, the Senate and the public will be left to ask itself which one is more likely to be lying: the one who is insisting on an investigation to make every effort to get at the truth, or the one who is not; the one who has a squeaky clean record, or the one who has a record of lying under oath to two separate confirmation hearings; the one who wants to have time to gather her thoughts and present a comprehensive narrative of what happened back then and whom she told about it since then, or the one who, along with his supporters, want to rush through the hearings as quickly as possible. What we are witnessing today is the ultimate in political polarization, where truth is no longer the object—political power is.

The third person in the room at the time of the alleged attack, Mark Judge, claims he doesn't remember anything about that particular party because he was too drunk, but doesn't deny that

Book Two (09/2018-11/2019

it happened. He wrote a book about their days at the elite school, and how often they were totteringly drunk.

Trump has been surprisingly controlled in his remarks about Dr. Ford's revelation, saying that "we want to hear both sides," but maintains that "it is not the FBI's thing."

Dr. Ford's lawyers have written a letter to the Senate stating that she is quite willing to testify, but needs more time to deal with the death threats, and she really wants the FBI to investigate her claim first. Senator Grassley responds that she will appear on Monday or not at all, and he wants the essentials of her testimony in writing by 10:00 am this Friday. There is absolutely no valid reason for this kind of a rush or pressure on this woman. These are the same Senators who held up the Merrick Garland nomination for months until Obama's term was up. Now they won't give an inch on *their* nominee. This is the epitome of political polarization of the type that is tearing our great country apart. *No one*, especially the GOP, comes out looking good if they proceed without Ford's testimony.

A long-time friend and classmate of hers, Samantha Gueny, has appeared on cable news and supported Dr. Ford. Kavanaugh has shown several serious signs of a credibility problem during both this current set of hearings and the previous one. An intensive FBI background check is standard procedure in cases like this, including re-checks when the situation calls for it. Yet the Senate and the President are avoiding that subject like the plague. What are they trying so desperately to hide? Senator Grassley in particular, has been very duplicitous in his statements between now and when he was involved in the case of Thomas vs. Hill, especially on the issue of an FBI probe. He has been downright bullying toward Dr. Ford. Cecile Richards, former president of *Planned Parenthood*, tweeted this on the subject: "Any woman who has been called before a Republican-led panel knows it's not about fact-finding. It's political theater masquerading as a search for the truth." This confirmation hearing has become a hoax and a sham, thanks to the desperation of the Republicans in the US Senate. The most disappointing of all is that Senators Flake and Collins, two of the very few Republicans who seemed to have a modicum of fairness in them, are now pushing for that unreasonable Monday meeting deadline, siding with Grassley and the rest of the GOP.

Donald Trump's declassification of those Mueller probe documents has been condemned by former Intelligence Director John Brennen. He says that DOJ officials should refuse to obey this dangerous and unlawful order, or resign. If they *do* get released, they must be heavily redacted to protect contacts and state secrets.

Trump says, "I don't have an Attorney General." No you *don't*, Mr. Trump, the country does. It is clear, Sessions will be fired as soon as the midterm election is over. In the meantime, he keeps trying to pressure him out, but Sessions is standing firm, making him an unlikely hero, even to those of us who despise his policies.

Trump is furious at Florida's Republican gubernatorial candidate, Ron DeSantis, because Ron disputed Trump's claim about the Puerto Rican death count being inflated. He no longer speaks in DeSantis' favor.

Trump claims tremendous progress is being made in reducing the North Korean nuclear threat. The evidence our intelligence agencies have seen disputes this claim.

Representative Beto O'Rourke now has a two point advantage in the polls over Ted Cruz for Cruz's Senate seat this November.

Doctor Christine Blasey Ford's lawyers have let the US Senate know that she is willing to testify sometime next week, but Monday is impossible. She still feels that an FBI investigation should be conducted, but will not pass up the opportunity to tell her story, if her safety can be assured and other witnesses can be heard.

The eleven Republican males on the Judiciary Committee have been seeking a female lawyer who could ask the questions of this witness and avoid what they know would be bad optics-- worse than in the Anita Hill grilling. Ford says, "No thanks" to that offer, but it won't be up to her. For the last three days, Kavanaugh has been spending most of his time at the White House, being coached and advised by ousted *Fox News* exec Bill Shine, who was fired for his own sexual misconduct.

As to any investigation into Ford's allegation, Senator Grassley proposes that his committee is prepared to conduct such a probe, rather than bother the FBI with this type of thing. This would be like allowing the parents of a rapist to look into the crime of their own child. As former tennis great John McEnroe used to like to say, "You can't be serious!"

There is no deadline for finishing this confirmation process, so it is completely unreasonable for Grassley and his committee to be pushing so hard on wrapping this issue up ASAP. As Senator Leahy from Vermont asked today, "What are they trying so hard to hide?"

The Republicans' Chief Counsel for Nominations, Mike Davis, who works for Senator Grassley, has tweeted the most blatantly partial remarks imaginable this morning, declaring in no uncertain terms that they intend to confirm this nominee, no matter what the hearings produce. His tweets caused such a backlash that they were taken down before the day was half over.

Senator Grassley and his committee are breaking every Senate rule and norm in order to ram this nominee down our throats, no matter what the cost to the image it is creating of the GOP in general, in order to advance the conservative agenda and satisfy the Religious Right's agenda as promised.

The Enemy Within: A Chronicle of the Trump Administration

A large group of women stormed the Senate Office Building to protest the way the Senate was treating the Kavanaugh/Ford controversy. Fifty-six of them were arrested.

The polls on how the public views Brett Kavanaugh have shown a clear decline in his approval. Here are the numbers. July—32% YES, 26% NO (+6); August—33% YES, 29% NO (+4); September—34% YES, 38% NO (-4).

It is worth noting that there is no statute of limitation on the crime of attempted rape in the state of Maryland. Even if Kavanaugh makes it onto the Supreme Court, he is still vulnerable to future prosecution.

The risk to his Court nominee is bad news for Trump, but the other news of the day is *very* bad news for him and his three oldest children. It is now clear that Michael Cohen has spent many hours talking with Robert Mueller about several topics in addition to conspiracy with Russia. This includes crimes committed by the entire family in their activities involving the Trump Organization and the Trump Charity. He has been spilling his guts without any cooperation deal being struck as yet.

James Comey remarked today that the Mueller probe is now into the fourth quarter. It seems like it is a lot closer than that. At this point, firing Mueller would not help Trump at all. The mountain of evidence that has been accumulated against him, his family and several members of his administration, is not going away, and neither are the many members of his team who are ready to pick up the torch if Mueller falls.

The Senate has responded to Dr. Christine Blasey Ford's offer to meet on Thursday of next week if they agreed to a few very reasonable conditions, one of which is demanding that it take place on Wednesday instead. They are quibbling over ONE DAY for no reason whatever, other than to rush things through as fast as possible on an issue this vital. Senator Collins says she is "…appalled at Trumps' attack on Dr. Ford." Senator Feinstein says "The Senate is abusing its power." Senator Barbara Boxer says, "The Senate's action is unprecedented." Dr. Ford's lawyer has responded to Grassley with a blistering letter denouncing the bully tactics and explaining the necessity of giving her client until Thursday to appear. The ball is back in Grassley's court.

Trump is backing off on his demand for the release of the aforementioned documents. It seems that he has actually allowed himself to be persuaded by none other than acting AG Rod Rosenstein. Ironically, this decision was almost immediately followed by a *New York Times* report about Rosenstein that has him discussing, right after the Comey firing, the possibility of recording Trump and preparing to invoke the twenty-fifth amendment. This caused Trump to erupt and immediately threaten to fire Rosenstein. Rosenstein responds that if he *did* say anything along those lines, he was just sounding off sarcastically. This is serious. All hell could break loose this coming week.

Rob Goldstein, who is the man who set up the Trump Tower meeting, has broken his silence and now tells the world that the Trump team "…eagerly accepted the offer of a meeting with Russians to get compromising data on Clinton." More confirmation for Mueller if he feels he needs it, which I doubt is the case.

The Senate finally smartened up and granted Dr. Ford the extra day she was requesting, so she will be testifying this Thursday. Unfortunately, no one else will be there to support her testimony, so let's hope she can provide names, phone numbers and subsequent times and places where she told about the attack upon her that she is claiming. It should make for very interesting TV viewing. On Sunday, another woman came out to accuse Kavanaugh of exposing himself to her while he was a

The Enemy Within: A Chronicle of the Trump Administration

Yale student, a few days after the Ford incident. Her name is Deborah Ramirez, a fellow student at Yale who was present at one the frequent drinking parties they liked to attend in those days. She is also willing to testify to her experience with the judge. This problem just keeps getting worse for the nominee. Will he even make it to Thursday?

Nothing else on the Trump nightmare to report. It was a quieter than usual weekend.

Sept. 24-30

Stormy Daniels' attorney, Michael Avenatti, just dropped another bomb on Trump's nominee for the highest court in the land. He has a client who will be accuser number three against Kavanaugh, sometime in the next forty-eight hours, according to Avenatti. She will not only testify to the Senate, if called, she also plans to file charges for criminal *gang rape*. Avenatti claims he has credible evidence and witnesses to support claims of what the students referred to as "trains," where the guys would line up outside the room where the "action" took place. We have seen over the past few months that Mr. Avenatti does not make claims that he cannot substantiate. He also says that it is essential that Mark Judge be subpoenaed because he is an integral part of the long-term criminal behavior that was part of that scene. It now looks like Kavanaugh is more likely to end up in prison than on the Supreme Court. Dr. Blasey Ford's lawyer has sent a letter to Senator Grassley objecting to the unfair format that has been set up for Thursday's hearing. He is especially disturbed about the use of an outside, female interrogator being used instead of the Senators themselves asking the questions. He wants to know who this person will be and what her qualifications are.

Trump summoned Deputy AG Rosenstein to the White House this morning, causing a flurry of speculation over whether this would result in his resignation or his firing. Rosenstein says he will refuse to resign. He spent a lengthy meeting with Chief-of-staff Kelly (Trump was in New York

Book Two (09/2018-11/2019)

where he spoke to the UN). When he emerged, he was escorted by Kelly and they shook hands before the Deputy AG got in his car, still holding his job (for now). He is scheduled to come back to meet with Trump on Thursday (what a momentous day that could turn out to be). Even Sean Hannity is advising Trump against firing the man who is standing in the way of Trump acting against Robert Mueller.

A new generic (non-specific) poll just out shows that the Democrats have increased their lead over the GOP to twelve points (52-40) as we approach the midterm election.

In the continuing Kavanaugh saga, the outside questioner hired by the Republicans has been identified as Rachel Mitchell, a prosecutor from Arizona. She will ask the questions submitted by each one of the eleven Judiciary Committee Republicans. We shall see if this hurts or helps the GOP with their concern about the optics of what has turned into something not far removed from a farce. They have already said that they plan to vote on Friday, no matter what they hear from the two people who will testify. In other words, except for the three previously discussed fence-sitters, they have already made up their mind to push him through no matter what they hear tomorrow.

Avenatti's new client/accuser, has come forward to identify herself. Her name is Julie Swetnick, and from what Attorney Avenatti says, I believe that she is going to be strike three—you're out, for Judge Kavanaugh, if she is even needed. We will find that out in the next couple of days, in all probability. It is notable that Kavanaugh's roommate in school, James Roach, made the following statement about him: "I would see him as he returned from nights out with his friends. It is from this experience that I concluded that although Brett was normally reserved, he was a notably heavy drinker, even by the standards of the time, and that he became aggressive and belligerent when he was very drunk."

In the Ramirez case, there are several witnesses who could be called to possibly provide corroboration, but the Senate Republicans have no interest in hearing from them. In Thursday's hearing, each Senator will have *five* minutes to have their questions asked and answered through Ms. Mitchell, alternating between Democrat and Republican Senators. This is the briefest time period to be used in a procedure like this, and is absurdly unfair. Mark Judge has been located, but is a reluctant witness and there seems to be no intention to subpoena him.

The other topic of the day is the reaction our embarrassing president received from the rest of the world, when as he spoke at the UN today and boasted that his administration had accomplished more in the first two years than almost any in US history. This produced a very audible round of laughter that was several seconds long. Trump's response to this spontaneous humiliation was, "I wasn't expecting *that,* but that's OK." No, Mr. President, it is definitely not OK for you to continuously lie to the world about how great you think you are, and make your countrymen cringe every time you speak.

One topic continues to dominate the Trump-related news. Now there is a *fourth* woman who has emerged (anonymously) to allege that she was assaulted by Kavanaugh outside a bar, where he drunkenly pinned her against a wall and forcibly kissed her. She also says she would be willing to testify. Every day seems to bring another accuser out of the shadows. All ten Democrats on the Judiciary Committee continue to push for an FBI investigation, but the GOP is stubbornly failing to see the need for one. The overriding aspect in trying to determine who is telling the truth in this case, is the fact that the person resisting any further investigation is the judge and his supporters—not the doctor. The fate of the nomination of Kavanaugh lies in the lap of these four undecided Senators:

Book Two (09/2018-11/2019)

Republicans Jeff Flake, Susan Collins, Lisa Murkowski and Democrat Joe Mancin, who is viewed as a swing vote.

Today, Sept. 27, was Confrontation Day—another day that will live in infamy—when the accused and his alleged victim sat in front of the Senate Judiciary Committee for several hours each, and presented their sides of a very consequential and partisanly-disputed issue. I watched all of Dr. Ford's testimony, and as much as I could stomach of Kavanaugh's ranting, belligerent and at times tearful defense of her allegation. Her testimony, in the opinion of everyone who watched it on both sides of the issue, was controlled and believable. It was a huge blow to the nominee's chances of being confirmed. It put tremendous pressure on Kavanaugh to be at least as convincing if he wanted to recover from the damage she did.

He did just the opposite. He was loud, belligerent and aggressive, just as he has been described when he was drunk in his younger days, which has been described by some as a "Jekyll and Hyde personality." This is not the type of temperament and presence that we expect to see in a Supreme Court Justice. When he was asked by Senator Feinstein if he would call for an FBI investigation to try to get to the truth of the matter, he was unable to respond, but reverted to his standard talking points about his innocence based on his sterling record. Among his more irrational utterances was this: "This is a circus. The consequences will extend long past my nomination. This whole two-week effort has been a calculated and orchestrated political hit for revenge on behalf of the Clintons." If this is the way he was coached by Bill Shine during those last few days at the White House, Shine certainly failed to help him.

But the blaring difference between the demeanors of the two adversaries was overshadowed by the disgustingly blatant partisanship of Senators Chuck Grassley and Lindsey Graham, chalking up the fight against Kavanaugh to a "vast left-wing conspiracy." They made a circus of the whole procedure and sunk the Republican Party even deeper into the morass of partisanship, insensitivity, unfairness, misogyny and several other unsavory traits, than they already were. The most rational person on the GOP side was the hired questioner, Mitchell, who was suddenly relieved of her services when she started displaying a more balanced side. When she was questioning Ford, she displayed quite a bit of sensitivity and friendliness, often sharing smiles with Ford. It seems the Republicans picked the right person to put some lipstick on this pig of a hearing. At the end of the day, it was pretty obvious that on the credibility scoreboard, Ford won by about a hundred to zero

The American Bar Association (ABA) sent a letter to the US Senate urging that no vote be taken on the Kavanaugh nomination until a thorough background check has been conducted by the FBI.

As the Judiciary Committee debated before voting to move the nomination on to the floor of the Senate, Senator Leahy of Vermont made the following statement: "In my time in the Senate, I have never seen such volatility, partisanship, and lack of judicial temperament from *any* nominee for *any* court, in *any* administration. ... Voting to advance and ultimately confirm Judge Kavanaugh while he is under this dark cloud of suspicion will forever change the Senate and our nation's highest court." And then came a major breakthrough event.

Senator Jeff Flake was confronted by two women protesters, Maria Gallagher and Anne Marie Archila, as he was entering an elevator. These two brave ladies gave him an impassioned earful about their own unbelieved victimization, as they propped the elevator door open while they continued speaking. Flake then proceeded to a meeting where he listened to his friend Chris Coons make a convincing argument for an FBI probe to be done before the vote on the nomination is taken. Flake voted YES to advance the issue to the main floor, *but* he let it be known that he *will not vote* to confirm, unless at least a week is devoted to an FBI probe into the Ford allegation. This was a major pivot which may have changed the course of US history. Today produced three heroines and a potential hero who will live in the history books forever. The news of this development was relayed to Trump, and this afternoon he folded under that threat of losing his nominee and issued the following statement: "I've ordered the FBI to conduct a supplemental investigation." Maybe there is still hope to stop this so-called "sure thing." Anything can happen in the coming week, if the FBI performs up to their potential of speed and fairness.

Unfortunately, almost immediately after the President announced his reluctant agreement for a quick probe, Flake let it slip that he intends to vote YES on Kavanaugh. Apparently he doesn't even care what the investigation finds—his mind is made up. If so, he will go from hero to goat very quickly.

The LA Times has reported that the FBI has already contacted one of the other women, either Ramirez or Swetnick, and asked to interview her *tonight*! That was fast!

As we end another historic week and another historic month, we face an upcoming week that could be extremely important for the fate of both Brett Kavanaugh and Donald Trump.

The FBI has contacted Ms. Ramirez who has agreed to cooperate with them. Oh, to be a fly on the wall for that meeting!

In other topics…a Washington federal judge has ruled that a group of four hundred Congressmen can proceed with their lawsuit against the President for violations of the emoluments clause.

While this country was focused on the Kavanaugh case, the Congress passed another tax cut bill that will add another 3.8

trillion dollars to our national debt. Financial experts are predicting a catastrophic crash on the horizon because of this administration's reckless greed.

Book Two (09/2018-11/2019)

October, 2018

Oct. 1-7

We begin a new month with the Brett Kavanaugh nomination issue still in a state of confusion, apprehension, and hope that all is not lost. The battle to keep Kavanaugh off the Supreme Court has become every bit as vital as the need to get Trump out of the White House as soon as possible. Kavanaugh on the court would affect the welfare of every American for decades, but Trump will almost certainly be gone in a few months at most.

Trump repeatedly claims that the FBI has "free rein" in their one-week extended background check, probably because he was in a state of euphoria over the agreement with Canada on a new trade treaty, which is really just a revision of NAFTA. But the FBI's list of approved witnesses for their interrogation contains only four names, and Julie Swetnick is not one of them. Since her allegations are the most egregious of the bunch so far, this seems like a very odd name to be omitted. We can only hope that those who are leading this new and vital probe will follow their conscience and do whatever is necessary to get to as much of the truth as possible in the time allotted to them. Things are not looking good so far. Several potential witnesses have stated that they have been unable to get through to the FBI to report that they have relevant information to give, pertaining to lies they have heard him tell in the hearings. They leave messages and don't get called back. It looks like they are getting the runaround. The question is, why? It smells like a cover-up.

Several of his classmates are telling about text messages from Kavanaugh pressing them to support him against charges he anticipated Ramirez to accuse him of, as far back as last July. If true, this is blatant witness tampering, and needs to be seriously followed up. The lack of access to the FBI by so many eager to tell their story, is very disturbing.

The Enemy Within: A Chronicle of the Trump Administration

Julie Swetnick was interviewed on NBC News tonight. She described what she saw at some of the parties that she, Kavanaugh, Judge, and several other acquaintances often attended in those days, where she would see guys lined up outside bedrooms awaiting their turn. She described occasions when a drunken Brett shoved a girl up against a wall to grope her.

Senator Barbara Boxer says about the Kavanaugh testimony at Thursday's hearing, "I have never seen any Senate witness, never mind someone up for a judgeship, act in this way." Senator Susan Collins calls for the FBI to add Swetnick's name to their list to be interviewed. Senator Flake says that if Kavanaugh is shown to have lied to the Senate, this would end his nomination. We shall see if he means it, because Kavanaugh has already been caught lying several times.

One of Kavanaugh's classmates, named Charles (Chad) Ludington, has submitted a written statement to the FBI in which he says that Brett is lying. Here is some of the text of his statement: "In recent days I have become deeply disturbed by what has been a blatant mischaracterization, by Brett himself, of his drinking at Yale. Brett was a frequent drinker, and a *heavy* drinker. I know because, especially in our first two years of college, I often drank with him. On many occasions I heard Brett slur his words and saw him staggering from alcohol consumption, not all of which was beer. When Brett got drunk, he was often belligerent and aggressive. On one of the last occasions I purposely socialized with Bret, I witnessed him respond to a semi-hostile remark, not by defusing the situation, but by throwing his beer in the man's face and starting a fight that ended with one of our mutual friends in jail." His story is backed by a police report of the incident.

Former FBI Assistant Director for Counter-Intelligence Frank Figluizzi points out that Trump's verbal OK to expand the investigation to include anyone the FBI sees fit to talk to, is meaningless unless it is put into a written order, which it apparently has not, since no such expansion seems to be taking place. Their hands are still tied. Something is very fishy! Meanwhile, Senator McConnell promises they will be taking that final vote on Friday.

Rachel Mitchel showed her true colors in her official memo to the Senate summarizing her conclusions about the testimonies she heard on Thursday. It was one-sided and irrelevant.

On a lighter note, if you need a good laugh after all this drama, consider the fact that Trump, in a recent press briefing of sorts, told us how he and Kim Jong Un have "fallen in love."

Our beleaguered president, who has already set an unbeatable record as the most corrupt in US history, on Tuesday was hit with another huge bombshell, lobbed at him by "the failing *New York Times*." It seems that their investigative reporters have been hard at work for months on a new story that today took up eight extra pages of today's issue. The myth that Trump sold to his audiences during the campaign, that he was a genius self-made billionaire, has now been exposed as the lie many of us knew it was. *The Times* managed somehow to get their hands on at least twenty years of Fred Trump's tax returns, which show that Donald was not only born with a silver spoon in his mouth, he was spoon fed with all the cash he needed all of his life, or at least while daddy was alive. It also exposed multiple cases of tax fraud by Donald over the years, which adds yet another legal woe for him to fret over. Several such suits will be waiting for him when he becomes an ex-president.

Meanwhile, Trump held another ego-rally in Mississippi today where he made a one-eighty degree turn from the reasonable-sounding admission that Ford came across as credible during the hearing, to the mean-spirited misogynist that he has always been, using the mocking tactic for which he has become notorious.

The FBI is now saying that they are ready to close their sham of an investigation as early as tomorrow (Wed.), thus truncating an already very brief period in which to track down people and leads. This is both absurd and outrageous! If this is not enough to convince Flake, Collins and Murkowski to vote NO on Kavanaugh, then they had better be prepared for a tremendous negative backlash from the public and from the voters in November. Dozens of witnesses who are practically screaming to be heard have not been contacted, and now they are saying their report will not be made public. This whole thing smells worse and worse by the day. The number of Kavanaugh's lies that have been uncovered, just since the Thursday hearing, grow each day that goes by. Any one of those lies should be enough to disqualify him. This joke of a so-called investigation should not even come close to satisfying anyone who has been on the fence.

In 2015 Judge Brett Kavanaugh made a speech in which he described the type of person who is qualified to serve on the Supreme Court. In it, he emphasized the qualities of controlled temperament and impartial approach to all questions brought before him or her. His description was *exactly the opposite* of what he showed us last Thursday in the most important presentation of himself he has ever given. The most disqualifying comment that he uttered during the hearing was his blatant threat, "what goes around, comes around." He might as well have said, "Wait until I'm on the Supreme Court and you Dems have a vital case before me."

The New York Times printed a letter today that was signed by *over six hundred and fifty Law Professors,* who urged the Senate *not* to confirm Kavanaugh because of his obvious partiality, never mind all the other reasons, such as perjury, temperament, and possible criminal sexual assault.

One of the major newspapers from Senator Collins' home state of Maine, the *Portland Times Herald*, had an editorial rejecting Kavanaugh for his partisanship and temperament. Let's hope she is listening.

Dr. Ford's attorneys issued the following statement: "An FBI supplemental background investigation that did not include an interview of Dr. Christine Blasey Ford—nor the witnesses who corroborate her testimony—cannot be called an investigation.
We are profoundly disappointed that after the tremendous sacrifice she made in coming forward, those directing the FBI investigation were not interested in seeking the truth."

Senator Grassley made a statement proclaiming that in all the previous background checks on this judge, "they never uncovered a whiff of bad behavior." This is disputed by several Democrat Senators who have seen these same reports. Nevertheless, Grassley announced that they have received the new report, lacking any interviews with *over forty people* who wanted to be heard, and it would be reviewed by each Senator tomorrow morning, starting at 10:00 am, and they will be voting on Friday.

We now have a pretty good idea of why the FBI did not push the White House harder for written permission to do a real investigation. It seems that FBI Director Wray was a classmate of Kavanaugh in law school, and Deputy Attorney General Rosenstein worked with Kavanaugh on the Ken Starr investigation. Somehow that really doesn't seem like enough of a motive to participate in a cover-up of a story this important.

The Senators are taking turns studying the FBI report today, and the comments we have heard so far from the key members are not encouraging. Senator Collins calls the report, "thorough". The report may be a thorough description of what they investigated, but the investigation itself is far from it, for the several reasons already listed.

Retired Supreme Court Justice Jon Stevens issued a statement that Kavanaugh should *not* be confirmed, because of temperament and partisanship.

Senator Heidi Heitkamp, from the red state of North Dakota, an undecided vote up to now, has declared her intent to vote NO, in spite of endangering her own chances of being reelected in November. Encouraging. Now we need two of the remaining holdouts to follow suit.

Senator Cory Booker, after reading the FBI report, says, "The fix is in."

The FBI interviewed nine witnesses in their sham probe, while ignoring over forty who were clamoring to be heard, as they truncated two days off their allotted schedule.

The Senate took a second vote, called "cloture", to advance the nomination to the final vote. This was done at 10:30 this morning, and Murkowski of Alaska voted against it, so there is one of the two we need to stop Kavanaugh. This leaves it all up to Susan Collins of Maine. The climax of this fight came at about 4:00 this afternoon. Collins made a lengthy speech in which she gave a detailed explanation of how she came to her decision. She dwelt on Kavanaugh's sterling record over his years as a jurist and she explained why she felt that Dr. Ford's allegation was not corroborated sufficiently to satisfy the more-likely-than-not test, in her mind. What she did *not* discuss was the several episodes of obvious lies about several subjects; she did *not* discuss his blatant temperament problem; she did *not* discuss his obvious partisanship with his remark about "a left-wing conspiracy for revenge on behalf of the Clintons", followed by "what goes around comes around." These are the things that, even without bad behavior in his youth, should disqualify him. Before she finished speaking, it was obvious she had decided to vote YES.

Senator Joe Manchin of West Virginia will be the lone Democrat to vote YES on Kavanaugh, so the final vote will be 51-49 when they take that vote tomorrow, unless something unexpected takes place between now and then. We needed Flake as well, and he is failing us again, as he does every time the chips are really down. This controversy amounts to reliving the Thomas/Hill case again. It seems that no progress has been made in the last two decades. Now they will have to live with the shame, if and when the law catches up to our new "Justice".

Twenty-four-hundred law professors signed a letter expressing their disapproval of the Kavanaugh confirmation. Senator Blumenthal, after reading the report called it a cover-up, and promised that the people who were not called by the FBI will get to have their stories heard eventually. I doubt that the Brett Kavanaugh saga is completely behind us yet. I have a feeling he will remain a target for quite a while to come.

Don McGahn, the White House's attorney, persuaded Trump to limit the scope of the FBI probe because "a wide-ranging inquiry like some Democrats were demanding and Trump was suggesting, would be potentially disastrous for Judge Kavanaugh's chances for confirmation."

Susan Rice has stated that she is seriously considering running for Senator from Maine, after hearing Collins' speech in favor of the judge.

The Saturday vote went exactly as expected, and Judge Kavanaugh will be sworn in as our new Supreme Court Justice. Donald Trump and Mitch McConnell both expressed their jubilation over this hard-fought victory and predicted that the Democrats' "political scheme to derail it" would light a fire under their base for the November midterms. This may be true to some extent, but it will have at least as much impact on the Democrats' base, and I predict that the independents will heavily reject the manner in which this battle was conducted.

Oct. 8-14

Well, the Kavanaugh battle is now over, and Trump won, but I feel it will turn out to be a pyrrhic victory in the long run. Time will tell. Trump presided over the White House swearing-in ceremony today, and his comments continued to fuel the divisiveness that has been his main theme since his election. He started by apologizing to Brett and his family for "the horrible way he was treated by those vengeful Democrats", during the controversy. He once again claimed that the "smear campaign was all a hoax." He is no longer referring to Dr. Ford as a sincere and credible witness. Now she is an outright liar and Kavanaugh "has been proven innocent of her accusation", which is another of his multitude of lies for which he is now infamous across the entire globe. His remarks were clearly aimed at stirring his base, with zero attempt to bring the country back together, as was done after the Clarence Thomas fight was over.

So now we can focus on other news again, which includes the following interesting items.

We have more on that two-week old story by the *New York Times* about the financial history of the Trump family. The Attorney General of New York is delving into decades of tax fraud that produced the Trump fortune, and which the President is still trying to conceal by not releasing his tax returns. This is sure to be discussed by Mueller when he issues his report.

Mueller is also reported to be investigating Rick Gates' role in working with an Israeli company named Psi-Group, which did the same type of social propagandizing as Cambridge

Analytica, working with Face Book. The object of their work was to target Trump's competition in the primaries, and then Clinton, after Trump gained the nomination. Gates has been cooperating with Mueller's team for several months now, so this could become significant.

The House Intelligence Committee is finally going to release most of the transcripts of fifty-three of the witnesses who appeared before it a while back, and Senator Swalwell says they will be starting a new investigation after the midterms.

President Donald Trump and Deputy Attorney General Rod Rosenstein (Robert Mueller's boss) met on Air Force One for a lengthy meeting, which Trump described as "a very nice talk." He also stated "I am not making any changes." So, the good news is (if you can believe Trump) that Rosenstein appears to be safe, at least until the midterms are over. The bad news is that the President and the Justice Department are supposed to stay at arms-length to maintain the independence of the two branches of government. It does not look good when a president, who is under investigation by the DOJ, hob-nobs with the guy who is in charge of that investigation.

Beto O'Rourke, the Democrat who is competing with Ted Cruz for a Senate seat in Texas, has just held the largest campaign rally Texas has ever seen. Cruz seems to be in trouble in a state that hasn't elected a Democrat Senator in decades.

Environmental scientists have reminded us that we now have an estimated *twelve years* before we encounter a global disaster, which can only be averted by immediately and drastically taking the steps necessary to reduce air pollution. Trump's repeal of several regulations in that area have only made things much worse than they already were.

The Enemy Within: A Chronicle of the Trump Administration

The hot topic of the day was the announcement that Nikki Haley is resigning her position as UN Ambassador. No reason has been given, but if she intends to run for president in 2024 this timing makes a lot of sense, before she is tainted by the expected debacle the Republicans face this November.

Although she has disagreed with Trump a few times during her two years at the UN, she maintains her devotion to him and publicly promised not to oppose him in 2020.

George Nader, adviser to the UAE's Crown Prince, has been granted immunity by Mueller for his cooperation as to his involvement with Rick Gates in the dealings with Psi Group, that false-propaganda company mentioned yesterday. Nader paid that company two million dollars for their services, acting as the Trump campaign's bagman.

The New Yorker has published an interesting story about a clandestine connection between the Trump campaign and Russia's Alfa-Bank in 2016, using a server-to-server link and coded messages. It is reported that the *New York Times* had this story back in 2016, but was persuaded by the FBI to hold off on it while their investigation was ongoing. We will probably be learning more about this later, maybe in the Mueller report. The Democrats on the Intelligence Committees wanted to pursue this lead, but were stymied by the Republican majority.

Conjecture abounds about what will take place in the first days after the midterm election, as to what Trump will do about Rosenstein, Sessions and Mueller, and what that will mean for the Russia investigation. It's a good bet that copies have been made of all relevant documents and all evidence safeguarded.

The just-released report on climate change is a dire warning. When Trump was asked what he thought about it, he said that he *will* read it but hasn't yet. Don't bet on it. He has absolutely no interest in anything scientific, or in reading in general.

Book Two (09/2018-11/2019)

The new GOP rally and scare phrase is "Mob Rule," which they fervently want their base to believe the whole Democrat Party is devoted to imposing upon our country. They are using as evidence, the numerous and wide-spread demonstrations that are taking place against the way the Republicans rammed their defective Supreme Court nominee down our throats in the most partisan manner possible.

The all-important midterm election is now exactly four weeks away. A new generic poll shows the Democrats holding a *thirteen* point lead, but it is vital not to become complacent!

While Michael, the most devastating hurricane to ever hit the Florida panhandle, was wreaking it's havoc, President Trump was holding another of his ego-rallies in Pennsylvania, where he boasted about how big a margin he won the state of Florida by in the 2016 election. He did read from his teleprompter, a few insincere commiserating remarks to the hurricane victims before beginning his usual off-the-cuff, red-meat remarks to pump up his base and get the cheers he needs to hear almost on a daily basis, at the taxpayers' expense.

Ethics complaints have already been filed against Brett Kavanaugh with the US tenth circuit court of appeals. And so begins the first in what is almost certain to be a string of legal actions that this highly unpopular Supreme Court Justice will be facing in the coming months.

FBI Director Christopher Wray was intensely questioned by Senator Kamala Harris today, about the limitations that were placed on the bureau by the White House. Wray hedged about the standards that he was forced to apply for this type of background-check supplement. The client, which is the White House, failed to provide specifics as to the limits. He as much as admitted that the system for this sort of thing is broken and needs to be more clearly defined.

The Enemy Within: A Chronicle of the Trump Administration

Flake, Collins and Murkowski missed their opportunity, when they had the pressure to force a real investigation, to convey to Trump that a sham would not satisfy them, and then stick to their threat to vote NO.

A new name has surfaced in the Mueller investigation. Richard Pinedo is a US citizen who has just been sentenced to six months in federal prison, six months house-arrest and six months of probation for his role in helping the previously-indicted thirteen Russians in hacking Clinton's emails and trolling anti-Clinton propaganda. He is the third person from the Trump campaign to be sentenced, with several more waiting to find out the length of their term.

The Associated Press reports that Georgia's Secretary-of-State, Brian Kemp, who is now running for governor of the state, has a record of suppressing 1.4 million voter registrations since 2012. Currently, over 5300 forms are being held because of "exact-match irregularities." It is estimated that seventy percent of these are from black voters. Meanwhile, Kemp has not resigned his current position, which gives him control over an election *in which he is a candidate*. How is that lawful? His Democrat opponent in the governor race, Stacy Abrams, has demanded that Kemp resign from that post, but to no avail so far.

A Saudi journalist and government dissident named Jamal Khashoggi, who has been living in the United States, wanted to marry his fiancé, who was a Turkish citizen. So he had to fly to Turkey to get the necessary documents. This required a visit to the Saudi Consulate in Istanbul. Surveillance cameras show him entering the building but never returning, while his fiancé waited for him outside. *The Washington Post* reports that they have uncovered communications between the Saudi Crown Prince and a team of assassins, ordering his death, which US Intelligence was aware of, and had a duty to warn, but failed to do so, and Trump has not commented on the story.

It is worth remembering that Jared Kushner, in his role as middle-east liaison, has become a buddy of the Saudi Crown Prince. What makes this story even more disturbing than it otherwise would have been, is the well-known intense hostility Trump displays on a daily basis toward the news media, which is not lost on foreign despots who now feel even freer to carry out whatever crimes against their detractors that they see fit, without repercussions from the American government.

The Washington Post also reports that Trump has been talking with Jeff Sessions' Chief-of-Staff, Matt Whitaker, about replacing Sessions as AG. This man is not in the line of succession for the job and is poorly qualified for it, but has one characteristic that the President finds very appealing: he is on record as believing that the Mueller investigation has overstepped its bounds.

In the case of the disappearing Saudi journalist, Jamal Khashoggi, the Turks now claim to have audio and video recordings of his gruesome murder and dismemberment inside the Saudi consulate. Trump has been besieged with questions about what the US is prepared to do about this egregious act on the part of the Saudi Arabian regime. He is not shy about revealing his reluctance to rush to condemn them, citing the financial benefits that nation provides to the US through arms deals etc., which could be lost if he was to anger them. The data he provides to back up this concern are, as usual, not based on facts. He avoids mentioning that he himself has been the beneficiary of millions of dollars from the Saudis who have provided a ton of business to his residential and office towers, as well as his son-in-law's cash-strapped property. One of the reasons Trump is so reluctant to release his tax returns is because of the deep financial morass he has created between his company and the Saudis, which are still on-going and constitute a gross violation of the Constitution's emoluments clause. Trump has publicly stated this year that "we are not here to tell other nations how to live." This gives every brutal, oppressive regime carte blanche to do whatever they want to their people without fear of repercussions from the United States.

Brian Kemp's Georgia voter-registration scandal has produced serious and immediate repercussions, as it also brought to light that he is right now withholding about 20% of the votes in the state. This is becoming a battle to watch as the midterm approaches.

Rachel Maddow tonight exposed a horror story that has been going on for decades in Waller County, Texas. There is a college there named *Prairie View A&M University* whose students have systematically had their votes nullified for one reason or another for decades. Their case went all the way to the Supreme Court in 1979 and was decided in the students' favor, but that has not deterred the county's officials from continuing to find ways to suppress the young people's voice because they tend to vote Democrat.

Not long ago the Supreme Court voted in favor of a plea from an organization known as *Citizens United,* which removed all limits on the amount any person could contribute to a political party. As a result, the Republican Party has been the beneficiary of this ruling to the tune of many *billions* of dollars in donations. One such donor is an American oligarch named Sheldon Adelson, who owns and operates Las Vegas casinos. Mr. Adelson had already contributed tens of millions of dollars to the GOP in its effort to keep control of Congress, and now he has added another fifty-five million to that kitty. This is peanuts compared to the 1.2 **billion** dollars in tax reduction he was blessed with, thanks to Trump's tax cut. A clear case of quid pro quo.

Trump also lobbied the Japanese leader for a casino that Adelson would love to build in Japan. Over the years, the GOP has become increasingly dependent on oligarchs like Adelson to finance their political campaigns and agenda, to the point where

Book Two (09/2018-11/2019)

they are now *owned* by these donors. A huge danger to democracy in our country. When you hear people rant about that awful *Citizens United* decision, this is what they are talking about.

Trump and his legal team are working on written answers to written questions submitted by Robert Mueller and his team of prosecutors, all of them focusing on the subject of conspiracy with Russia. Mueller is still negotiating on the question of a sit-down to talk about obstruction. Written answers have the advantage of letting the lawyers help Trump with the wording of his answers, but the disadvantage of not being able to spin or worm around the statements.

Paul Manafort is in prison awaiting sentencing. Meanwhile, the judge on his case has ordered the forfeiture of five of his luxury properties to pay for his mounting legal fees. He is against delaying Manafort's sentencing until Mueller is through extracting testimony from him. The judge wants to know just what Paul has had to offer.

Nearly every day now, Trump has scheduled another rally designed to stoke the passions of his brainwashed supporters and to salve his own ego. He has forty of them on the schedule during the three months leading up to the midterm election. At each rally his talks get crazier and his attacks more scatter-gun in scope, against all enemies both past and present. His mental state is becoming dangerous. Even more alarming is watching and listening to the people in his adoring crowd, who thrive on his craziness. It has reached the point where the TV ratings for Fox News' start-to-finish airing of these events have fallen off so much that they have now curtailed these shows.

John Kelly has once again displayed his blatant misogyny with emails in which he again followed Trump's lead in the

The Enemy Within: A Chronicle of the Trump Administration

attack on Elizabeth Warren. He has proven to be little more than Trump's flunky since day one of his White House job.

The US Senate has started its vacation period which will not end until after the midterm. Nice reward for doing such a great job propping up the most corrupt and inept administration in history.

Georgia's Secretary-of-State Brian Kemp is now being sued by a coalition of Civil Rights groups, over his blatant and long-term suppression of minority voters while in his current office. In particular they are appealing his use of the "exact match" to disqualify thousands of votes for things like missing hyphens.

It has now been learned that Kemp ignored warnings from FBI and US Intelligence officials that his voter data servers were wide open to hacking and needed to be safeguarded. Apparently, he wanted it that way. He was the only election official to refuse to heed these warnings. His server also includes personal data, such as social security numbers, etc.

Robert Mueller's indictment of thirteen Russian hackers singled out Georgia, Iowa and Florida as the states most vulnerable to hacking. In the recent past, Kemp arrested and charged Georgia citizens with mailing in fraudulent absentee ballots, but they were acquitted. The Trump administration has emboldened the GOP to employ every dirty trick imaginable to get and hold onto political power. Former Attorney General Eric Holder is campaigning for Kemp's opponent for Governor, Stacy Abrams. The most recent poll shows the race to be a dead heat.

In the previously mentioned Waller County Texas saga, a Democrat Congressional candidate named Mike Siegel was arrested at the county courthouse when he tried to deliver a letter protesting the suppression of the student voters' rights. Before ordering the arrest, the judged asked what political party he belonged to. When he said, "Democrat," that was enough to

Book Two (09/2018-11/2019)

get him put in *cuffs*. Siegel was a guest on *The Rachel Maddow Show* tonight and told the story of his ordeal, and how the Texas Secretary-of-State has straightened things out in favor of him and the students of Prairie View College. They have some pretty partisan judges in Texas.

In our continuing southern border crisis, there are still one hundred and thirty-six children and teens incarcerated with little being done to reunite them with their parents. One of the most heart-wrenching stories involves a five-year-old girl who was coerced into signing (scrawling) her name on a legal document which waived her rights. She was finally reunited with her mother four months later, thanks to public outcry about the gross injustice of this case.

The issue has faded from the headlines, but the tent city to house the ever-increasing number of unaccompanied children who cross our border seeking sanctuary, has grown immensely since the "zero tolerance policy" has supposedly been rescinded. There are an estimated thirty-eight hundred beds now in that community. There is a growing outcry for the resignation of Stephen Miller, the architect of this heinous policy. Trump is said to be "considering a new policy."

Journalist Jamal Khashoggi wore an Apple watch that recorded his murder and transmitted the recording to a remote devise, where it is now proof of who his killers were. Trump is still hedging about how to react to the growing clamor over the Saudis' murder of Khashoggi in Turkey, pretending that the proof doesn't exist. He is trying desperately to avoid alienating an ally, both of the US and of him personally. He relies heavily on Saudi capital, to the extent that they virtually *own* him.

The GOP is cutting its expected losses in the coming midterm by shifting financial backing to those few races where the Republican candidate still has a chance.

The Enemy Within: A Chronicle of the Trump Administration

A federal judge has ordered the release to the Mueller team of a document considered to be the "roadmap" that laid out the procedure for impeachment in the Watergate case against Nixon. This would be a useful attachment to Mueller's report when he submits it to Congress.

Trump succumbed to pressure again and issued a strong threat of punishment to Saudi Arabia for the Khashoggi murder, but still doesn't say what or when that would take place.

There is a new Cold War developing because of the tariffs and statements made by Donald Trump aimed at the Chinese, contrary to his professed friendship with the Chinese leader Xi.

Oct. 15-21

As we begin the second half of the month, it seems like every day reveals another way in which the Republicans, on every level of our government, are trying to steal another election. They are using every trick at their disposal, bordering on Gestapo tactics, to keep minorities from voting. Today's list of topics leads off with the latest news on that sorry story.

Adding to the aforementioned crimes against Georgia's voters, is the revelation that about ten percent of the absentee ballots cast in that state lately have been disqualified and discarded. But equaling the Georgia scandal is the story out of North Dakota, where Democrat Senator Heidi Heitkamp, who squeaked out a one percent win in her last Senate contest, thanks to heavy support from that state's many Native American voters, is now in the fight of her life for reelection. Her problem is magnified by the Republican-controlled state legislature, which has just passed a new law requiring every voter to have a valid residential address. That is a big problem for the Native Americans who live on a reservation where their only address is a postal box number. The US Supreme Court has (alarmingly) upheld that law. Tribal leaders are now

Book Two (09/2018-11/2019)

working furiously on a plan to produce a local reservation map that will delineate addresses for the occupants.

Then we have the small-scale incidents, like when Georgia's Republican Senator, David Perdue, was approached and questioned by a student with a cell phone. When Perdue noticed that the lad was using his phone to video the confrontation, he snatched the phone out of the student's hand and proceeded to walk away with it. He later said that he thought the boy wanted to take a selfie with him. Really?

The Saudi government has now admitted that Jamal Khashoggi was indeed killed in their consulate in Turkey, but they have come up with two alternative cover stories that defy believability. First, they offer that he was *accidentally* killed during an over-exuberant interrogation. Then they said it was the work of "rogue killers." The fact that the Turks know that one of the cleaning crew, who were apparently the "interrogation" team, had a bone saw as part of his equipment, is pretty damning evidence.

Trump seems to be accepting these lame stories, so he has made himself part of a cover-up of a crime no one else in the world is buying. This president seems to have no trouble accepting denials from all sorts of monsters, as long as they "strongly deny it." He points out that he is trying to avoid jeopardizing large arms contracts with Boeing, Lockheed and Raytheon that would cost jobs, but the Saudis are too locked in to American products to switch to other sources at this point. It is now up to the US Congress to do something about this atrocity.

Vanity Fair reports that Michael Cohen, without benefit of any kind of plea agreement, has spent over fifty hours in talks with several prosecutors, including Robert Mueller. This has to be Trump's worst nightmare.

The Enemy Within: A Chronicle of the Trump Administration

Senator Elizabeth Warren decided to take Trump up on his offer to contribute a million dollars to a charity of her choice if she would take a DNA test to back up her claim of Native American descent. She has taken a test and it showed that she does indeed have a three or four generation ancestor who was an American Indian. Trump, of course, will never honor the deal. He says the only way he will do so is if he administers the test himself.

In a lengthy *60 Minutes* interview with host Leslie Stahl, Trump managed to make a complete fool of himself again, on many issues. Here are a few of his most laughable ones. When he was asked if he believed in climate change, he replied, "Yes, but don't worry about it—it will change back." When asked why he mocked Dr. Ford during a recent rally, he denied that what he said was mocking, only stating facts. Then he added that "it doesn't matter—we won." When asked about "loving" Kim Jong Un, he doubled down on his affection for him and Putin.

The students who helped found the "March For Our Lives " movement, Emma Gonzales and Ramon Contreras, have been touring the country mobilizing young people to get to the polls this November 6 and vote for Democrats. If anyone can motivate these first time voters, these two can.

Several of the fifteen "suspects" involved in the murder of Jamal Khashoggi have been found and proven to have close ties to the security team of Saudi Crown Prince, Mohammed bin Salmon (referred to as MBS). *The New York Times* has identified nine out of the fifteen members of the hit squad and one of them is a buddy of MBS. Another, the one wielding a bone saw, is a forensic expert. In the midst of all the furor over this heinous crime, Secretary-of-State Pompeo has arrived in Riyadh to meet with the Crown Prince and discuss the situation, all smiles, like everything is just fine. This is a regime that already has a record of killing tens-of-thousands of people in Yemen.

Meanwhile, Trump is comparing this case to the Kavanaugh debate, stating that in both cases there was an assumption of guilt before proof and in the Kavanaugh case he was proven to be innocent, which of course is just another lie. He also told an even more blatant lie by saying that he "has no financial interests in Saudi Arabia." He must have forgotten that he very recently delineated and boasted of *many* financial benefits that he has received from them.

Brian Kemp now has three law suits filed against him by Georgia Civil Rights Groups, because of his long-running and still current voter suppression. One of those suits is from Gwinnett County over the abnormal number of disqualifications of absentee ballots. They also have a record of over 670,000 voter registrations, Georgia-wide, being cancelled in 2017 alone. In Georgia's early voting, *more than triple* the votes have already been cast for the upcoming midterm, than were cast in 2014's midterm.

Trump continued to expose his disgusting attitude toward women by calling Stormy Daniels "Horseface" as he crowed about a court's decision in his favor over the non-disclosure agreement (which will be appealed).

Trump reacted to the news about Cohen's talks with prosecutors by labeling Cohen a liar. The tapes will show who the liar is.

The cover-up of the Khashoggi murder is starting to look a lot like the assassination of JFK in its blatancy. It again leads off today's news items.

Our CIA Director-turned-Secretary-of-State, Mike Pompeo, has returned from his visit to Saudi Arabia. He has nothing to say in response to questions about what the King and Crown Prince had to offer about the killing of the *Washington Post* journalist. Trump has clamped down on information-sharing about the case with the US Congress. He has asked Turkey for a copy of the audio tape that they have of the killing. No response yet. Former CIA Director Brennen says that he is perplexed by the brazenness of the crime, when it could have been carried out with much better secrecy.

The Washington post published their slain journalist's final article. Here is an excerpt: "Arab governments have been given free rein to continue silencing the media at an increasing rate. The Arab world is facing its own version of the iron curtain." This is the kind of journalism that got him killed. It is also the kind of dissent that is causing Trump to declare our press as "the enemy of the people," an attitude enthusiastically adopted by his fellow despots, like Mohammed bin Salmon.
The Washington Post says, "The Trump administration and the Saudi family are searching for a mutually agreeable explanation for the death of journalist Jamal Khashoggi--one that will avoid implicating Crown Prince Salmon, who is among the President's closest allies, according to analysts and officials in multiple countries."

The United Arab Emirates (UAE) offered the Trump campaign huge financial help in 2016 and it was eagerly accepted, even though it was illegal to do so. These gifts involved George Nader and Eliot Broider, who are under investigation by Mueller.
Their main contact with Saudi Arabia was through a Saudi General named Ahmed al-Assivi, the Deputy Chief of Saudi Intelligence, who is now being set up to be the fall-guy (the "rogue killer") for the Khashoggi murder, *and for* the alleged financial collusion. Trump has repeatedly claimed that he has no financial dealings with the Saudis, but in the recent past he has also bragged about why he liked the Saudis, because they

pay him "hundreds of millions of dollars" for the use of his various properties.

In North Dakota, a coalition of Native American Civil Rights organizations is fighting back against the unfair resident requirements placed on reservation dwellers. They have presented a plan to Secretary-of-State Kemp that should solve the problem. But will he accept it?

A busload of black senior voters was about to drive off for the polls to vote early, when they were stopped and forced to leave the bus by state officials—no reason given. This is under investigation. In one county in Georgia the line to cast an early ballot was so long it took three hours to reach the booth.

The demographics are changing quickly in the state of Georgia, and soon the blacks will be in the majority, which is why the Republicans are using desperation measures to minimize their voting power.

Senator Blumenthal, on Chris Hayes' *All In* TV show revealed that he and other Senators are preparing a suit against Trump for emoluments violations. We keep hearing about things like this, but it seems to be going nowhere.

When Secretary-of-State Pompeo was repeatedly asked by reporters if Jamal Khashoggi was dead, he could not answer as he turned and walked away. Trump, on the other hand, has now admitted that basic fact, but will go no further on the issue that has been consuming the civilized world for the past few days.
He cannot even *fake* a show of empathy for the horrific death and dismemberment of an American resident.

In Georgia, early and absentee ballots are routinely being rejected by human reviewers, if they feel that the signature on

The Enemy Within: A Chronicle of the Trump Administration

the ballot does not appear, in their opinion, to match the one he/she has on file.

As the midterm election looms, the Republicans are not campaigning on their record; no wall, no repeal of Obamacare, a tax cut that has done very little for the lower 98% of Americans, ramming through of a very unpopular Supreme Court Justice, a disastrous immigration policy, and rampant corruption throughout his cabinet appointments, not to mention his own record on that score. They are not even dwelling on the one positive they could point to, the economy (although it is really only an extension of Obama's). Instead, they are campaigning against the Democrats' alleged "mob tactics." The only "mobs" are the ones the GOP, especially Trump himself, have generated and inspired by their extreme disregard or disdain for huge blocks of the electorate (woman, minorities, students, seniors etc.). To make matters even worse for this tactic, the very unpopular Newt Gingrich has joined the chorus.

The latest corruption target (swamp creature) is Interior Secretary Ryan Zinke. He has continuously spent taxpayer money for personal flights and other extravagances. He is now, finally, being investigated by that department's "watchdog" on ethics. He needs to join former HHS Secretary Tom Price in exile.

A new bombshell expose has broken regarding the crumbling FBI headquarters building in DC, which happens to sit across the street from one of Trump's most valuable hotels. The FBI building is in such bad shape that it has to be either completely renovated or moved to a new building. Plans were well under way to move it when Trump realized that a new *hotel* was going to replace it on that spot, where it would compete with his money-making property.

This decision is under the control of the head of the General Services Administration, a woman named Emily Murphy. She recently decided to change the plan and to renovate the existing building instead of moving, greatly benefitting the President, who denies having anything to do with her decision. Murphy also denied any contact with Trump, when questioned at a Senate hearing. However, there is a photo, shown by Rachel Maddow tonight, which plainly shows Ms. Murphy sitting in on a meeting with Trump in the oval office on January 24, 2018. Emails have been found that specify exactly what was discussed in that meeting and that prove Murphy lied to the Senate. The Congressional Oversight Committee has called for an investigation. This episode could be an impeachable offense, on its own.

There has been a flurry of activity of late by the Mueller team, much of it involving Paul Manafort, who has met with Mueller nine times since his guilty plea. Meanwhile, the Republicans are calling for Mueller to resign and Rod Rosenstein is still defending him.

We had an unusually heavy Friday Trump-news day today. The closer we get to the midterm election, the heavier (and more important) it gets. The following is still on Friday.

General Ahmed al-Assivi, the patsy whom the Saudi Regime is pinning Khashoggi's murder on, has been fired! That's right, not arrested and charged—fired. They are trying to sell the world on the ridiculous story that his death was the result of a quarrel that escalated out of control. So this man started a fight with a group of fifteen men who were trying to extradite him, one of which was packing a bone saw. And then they would not even admit he was dead for a few days. And Trump is accepting this bullshit story, calling it credible and "a great first step." The story is an insult to the intelligence of any sane person.

Senator Swalwell says that the US should have the FBI's legal attaché in Turkey look into the matter, and should stop all arms sales to the Saudis.

The Enemy Within: A Chronicle of the Trump Administration

Meanwhile, Trump held another pep-rally, this one in Montana, where the Republican Congressional candidate recently bodied-slammed a reporter to the floor because he was vexed by the questions being asked. Trump's support for him included heaps of praise for the way he took care of that pesky member of his arch-enemy, the press. So he not only endorses the *candidate,* he endorses violence against dissenting media coverage, including murder apparently.

Latino voters, as well as blacks, are systematically being suppressed from voting, especially in southern states with a high Latino population growth. In one example, Dodge City, Kansas moved their only voting place well beyond the city limits, making it much more difficult for low-income voters to reach.

Robert Mueller and his team of investigators are going after *current* efforts (by both Russia and China) to meddle in the *upcoming elections*, as well as the one that started their probe. It is apparent that the Russians are spending more and more money on their interference-campaign.

A Russian woman named Elena Khusyaynova has been charged by the DOJ for midterm election interference, using propaganda bots (robot-generated internet messages), designed to divide US voters and to taint Mueller's image as an honest and impartial investigator. Trump denies it is happening.

The Houston Chronicle, one of Texas' largest newspapers, has endorsed Beto O'Rourke for Senator over Ted Cruz, via a blistering editorial pointing out Cruz's flaws and calling O'Rourke "most impressive". Let's hope it helps because Beto has slipped back a bit lately.

Early voting in many states, including Georgia, has tripled over 2014's rate in these first few days. Democrats generally benefit by a high voter turnout.

Book Two (09/2018-11/2019)

In Florida, one local issue of major concern is the increasing Red Tide and Green Algae caused by rampant pollution coming from a few local industries. The problem has been exacerbated by Trump's *repeal* of several regulations that were put in place by previous administrations. This issue alone may be enough to turn the state from a reddish purple to blue.

The President of Turkey says he will tell the world, as early as tomorrow, what happened in the red-hot murder case that occurred in his country. This should be interesting. Jared Kushner decided this would be a good time to joke about the deceptiveness of middle-easterners, and included the denizens of Washington D.C. in his jibe as well.

The Washington Post reports that Mueller is closing in on Roger Stone (who is so fanatically right-wing that he has a huge tattoo of Nixon on his back) and his connections and correspondence with WikiLeaks during the Trump campaign. He is considered to be the connection with the Russians in the quid pro quo conspiracy. Stone, like Michael Cohen before him, has proclaimed, "I will never roll on the President," which would indicate that he has something he could "roll" about.

A new Republican dirty trick is to promote propaganda that encourages far-left voters to cast their ballot for fringe candidates that support their extreme liberal views, rather than the main-stream Democratic candidate, thus effectively throwing their vote away.

The New York Times reports that the GOP is working to reinstitute that disastrous and inhumane "no-tolerance" child-separation policy at the southern border, as the caravan of fleeing immigrants makes its way closer to the US. This is designed to scare those freedom-seekers from coming to our country, and to appeal to the racist base.

The Enemy Within: A Chronicle of the Trump Administration

Oct. 22-28

Long-time hawk-turned-dove, John Bolton has visited Moscow and told the Russians (and the world) that he does not believe that Russian interference, if it existed, had any effect on the 2016 election of Donald Trump. He says that China has interfered much more than Russia has. This is equivalent to inviting the Russians to "go right ahead with your current meddling." Bolton has become the latest in a long line of Trump's lapdogs.

Trump is now promising a ten percent cut in taxes for the middle class to be passed right after the election. Another promise that he has no intention of keeping. The next tax cut will again benefit the top one or two percent, *if* it gets passed, which is highly doubtful after the Democrats retake control of the House.

Democrat candidate for governor of Florida, Andrew Gillum, now has a twelve point lead on his Republican opponent, Ron DeSantis. But Abrams and Kemp are still in a dead heat in Georgia. Abrams needs a bunch of those withheld and disqualified ballots.

The lines for early voting in Georgia and elsewhere are breaking records, as enthusiasm reaches an all-time high. New generic polls show that the Democrats have a nine point lead, with female voters preferring the Dems by *twenty-five points*.

Despite the Republicans best efforts to repeal Obamacare throughout the better part of Trump's first year in office, the plan is still very much alive and is more popular than ever, and health care is the number one issue among voters this year.

The Republican candidates keep lying about how determined they are to retain insurance that covers pre-existing conditions, after they voted over seventy times to do just the opposite. Trump recently passed a law that allows insurance companies to deny such coverage. They are counting on voters having short memories or not paying attention.

The Reagan-era arms control agreement with the Russians is due for extension, and the Russians are urging the US, through National Security Advisor John Bolton, to stick with the pact. But Bolton seems to be against it for some reason—so his hawkishness is still very much alive in the form an impending new arms race. This is *insane!*

The President of Turkey issued a very disappointing statement on the murder of Khashoggi in his country, in which the only thing of substance was his question; "Where is the body?" Good question, but hardly the tale of facts he promised. Trump condemns both the killing and the cover-up as "badly conceived", but follows it with "the King strongly denies it." Always willing to believe "strong denials" from anyone that supports him or his party.

In a debate in the race for governor of Georgia, Kemp denies any voter fraud or suppression, in spite of a mountain of convincing evidence, along with his admitted concern about voter turnout size.

Trump, at his latest pep-rally, proudly referred to himself as a "nationalist." He seems to equate "nationalism" with patriotism. Most people consider the word to be a shorter way of saying, "white nationalism", one of the major aspects of Nazism. Even if *he* doesn't think of it that way, many of his followers do, and will assume he is of like mind. They have plenty of reasons to think so.

President Trump's belligerent rhetoric, which has encouraged foreign despots like the Saudi King and/or Crown Prince to eliminate a thorn in their side, has also had an effect on his fellow Americans.

The Enemy Within: A Chronicle of the Trump Administration

Today, at least ten explosive devices were delivered to various prominent and outspoken opponents of Donald Trump, including: the Obamas, the Clintons, former Intelligence Director John Brennen, liberal Democrat financial supporter George Soros, former AG Erik Holder and Representative Maxine Waters. Fortunately, the devices were poorly constructed pipe bombs and no one was hurt because they were detected in time. A huge manhunt is underway to track down the sender. This incident shows that the brainwashed Trump supporters have reached an alarming point a paranoid mania.

Trump has tweeted that Republicans will support health care, including pre-existing conditions, and the Democrats won't, but the record since Trump took office screams just the opposite. The lies get more blatant and ridiculous every day.

In Georgia, a judge has blocked the practice of discarding ballots willy-nilly. The ballot hoop-la has probably stimulated the voter turnout because *four times* the usual number of early votes have already been cast and we still have almost two weeks to go.

Trump labels the Saudi murder cover-up "the worst in history" (I know one that was worse, but that's another topic). The visas of the killers have been revoked, and some of them have now been jailed.

Trump has been repeatedly warned from day one that his IPhone is not secure and he should be using the secure phone they issued him. But he has refused to give up his phone that he loves to tweet with, which allows the Russians, Chinese, or anyone with the knowhow, to listen in to all of his conversations. This practice is at least as bad as the server problem for which Trump wants to lock up Hillary. White House officials are concerned enough about this breach to talk to *The New York Times* about it, which is the only reason we now learn of it.

Book Two (09/2018-11/2019)

The Republicans are now running on a campaign of fear, not even mentioning their highly vaunted tax cut or the economy.

A new poll that shows the Democrats with a twenty-five point lead with women voters, while the Republicans have a fourteen point lead with men. Trump has only himself to blame for this disparity.

Additional explosive devices are still being turned up, all targeting prominent Trump critics. The authorities have traced the sender to Florida, from whence the packages were mailed, and they seem to be closing in on the would-be mass assassin. Trump is trying to lay blame on the media, particularly CNN, for the pipe bomb scare. He implies, by the use of quotes around the word "bomb" in his tweet, that it is just another hoax. He cannot even *fake* any concern about the welfare of the targets, the latest of whom include Joe Biden and Robert De Niro. Biden addressed a large gathering and had this to say about the threat: "My hope is that this recent spate of pipe bombs being mailed will make everyone wake up and realize that we have to put this country back together again. This division, this hatred, this ugliness, has to end. Words matter."

Especially the words of the President of the United States. Brian Williams, on his MSNBC program *The Eleventh Hour*, played brief excerpts of former presidents Carter, Reagan, Clinton, George W. Bush and Obama, speaking to the nation after major tragic events. There is *no comparison* between the empathy and eloquence of these leaders, from both parties, and the words we continue to hear from the imposter who is playing president today.

In regard to Trump's unsecured IPhone use, he says that he won't use the one issued to him by his Intelligence people because it is "slow and buggy." His reluctance to give his

The Enemy Within: A Chronicle of the Trump Administration

favorite phone up has been a concern of several members of the White House staff for months, to no avail.

Now that someone leaked the problem, they are trying to downplay it by saying that he doesn't learn, or remember, *anything* of importance anyway, so there is little chance of his giving away anything significant to those who are listening in. But other officials in the cabinet say he has already leaked some secret data. Yet, he never fails to bring up Clinton's emails at his rallies.

In the previously-mentioned Dodge City voter polling fiasco, the single voting place that was moved to a location a mile or so outside the city, was not only *inconvenient* for many voters, it also had the *old* address listed on a mailer sent out to remind people to vote. When this created a furor, it was corrected. Nice try, Republican city officials.

In Arizona, the fight for the Senate seat being vacated by the retiring Jeff Flake is between two women. The Republican candidate, Martha McSally, tries to avoid talking about health care, the number one issue for most voters, because she has repeatedly voted against the Affordable Care Act. This makes it hard to believe her now as she promises to maintain coverage for pre-existing conditions, one of the main issues Republicans had with Obamacare.

More and more farmers are admitting that they have been hurt financially by the Trump tariffs. A clear case of "buyer's remorse."

Trump is now talking about closing the southern border completely as the big caravan of refugees draws closer. He is filling his racist cult followers with all sorts of lies about who is part of this group and who is sponsoring it, and they just eat it up.

Book Two (09/2018-11/2019

NBC News is reporting on a new concern of the Mueller investigation. An associate of Roger Stone named Jarome Corsi, an extreme right-wing conspiracy-theorist, may have had advance knowledge that the emails of Clinton's campaign chairman had been stolen and given to WikiLeaks. Mueller's team has reviewed messages between members of the Trump team in which Stone and Corsi seem to take credit for the release of those emails. In one message, Corsi claims to be working on getting a "blanket pardon" for Julian Assange, founder of WikiLeaks, and says, "Something big is about to go down."

When Newt Gingrich was asked by a TV interviewer what would happen if Trump were to be subpoenaed for his tax returns, he replied, "Well, we'll see if the Kavanaugh fight was worth it." This is an unabashed admission of just why Kavanaugh was selected from that lengthy list of potential justices.

The big news of the day is that the MAGA bomber, as he has come to be labeled, due to the abundance of Trump propaganda decorating his van, has been identified and arrested. He is a Florida resident named Cesar Sayoc, and he has a far-from-clean record. He has attended several Trump rallies where he heard our president encourage violence against the news media and Trump's other critics on several occasions. He considers himself to be "a soldier in Trump's army." He is now known to have sent out at least fourteen packaged IEDs which, because he is not a very good bomb maker, did not kill anyone.

Trump reacted to the news of his arrest by highly praising the FBI, the agency he has spent the last two years undermining. Then he reverted back to his attack on the mainline media for "treating him so unfairly and dishonestly." His rhetoric continues to be more divisive and inflammatory than we have ever heard before from a US president. He is totally incapable of behaving like a normal human being, never mind, a president.

A white-nationalist/neo-Nazi group from California named *The Rise Above Movement,* led by a man named Robert Rundo, has been fomenting riots at political gatherings, including Charlottesville, and for months has been beating up anyone who is anti-Trump. He and seven other members of this group have been arrested.

An east coast version of this type of group calling themselves *The Proud Boys* has also seen several arrests recently. A cache of arms was also found in Oregon belonging to yet another such group. All of them see themselves as soldiers in an army for Trump. But they have been infiltrated by under-cover law-enforcement agents, and basically broken up. Our law-enforcement agencies and our president are on a collision course that is both disturbing and dangerous. It feels like we are on a potential road toward civil war. The fate of our country depends on the results of the upcoming midterm election.

When Trump was asked by a reporter if he will now tone down his rhetoric in view of the pipe-bomb scare, he replied, "I *have*, but I could also tone it up." He *hasn't*, and he probably will tone it up.

It is obvious, and has been since day one, that Donald Trump has no desire to be the President of the whole country. He only wants to satisfy his racist and under-educated base, which he hopes to use to maintain his power and continue to enrich himself and his family, in flagrant disregard for the Constitution he swore to protect and defend.

Geraldo Rivera has fostered and supported the extreme right's conspiracy-theory that the MAGA-bomber story is all a hoax perpetrated by the left to disparage the right. According to TV interviews with Trump supporters, and reading comments

Book Two (09/2018-11/2019)

by them on Face Book, this idiotic idea is being eagerly swallowed by the cult. They gladly grab hold of this straw without even Googling the suspect's background, or watching the news about him and his recent life and activities.

Ex-Republican Steve Schmidt appeared on MSNBC's *The Eleventh Hour* tonight and offered the following observation on this mind-set: "Anybody who doesn't see the clear connection between the atmosphere, and what occurred here, has suspended disbelief, or is complicit and dishonest, or is simply so brainwashed that they've stopped being able to think for themselves." I believe that his third option is the most likely among those three options. Since Sayoc's arrest, Rivera has retracted his cockamamie theory and admitted that the suspect is a right-wing nut.

In Dodge City, the ACLU filed suit to force the city's officials to relent and keep both old and new voter locations open for this coming election, which would solve the confusion they created with their erroneous mailer's location. Early voting around the nation continues to double or triple the numbers recorded in 2014's midterm. Enthusiasm among Latino voters has risen from a level of 47% at this year's beginning, to 71% now. The entire population is obviously more involved in this election than ever before, which is probably the sole benefit gained from the disaster of the current administration.

Barack Obama has been delivering impassioned anti-Trump, anti-GOP speeches at huge rallies, in which he emphasizes the importance of getting off the couch and getting to the polls on November 6, or before.

The fact-checkers have been keeping a record of Trump's lies and misrepresentations almost from the beginning of this nightmare. He continues to set new records for weekly totals of brazen, provable lies. Lately, he has been talking more, which means he has been lying more.

The Enemy Within: A Chronicle of the Trump Administration

The level of violence continues unabated. On top of the attempted mass murder of prominent Democrats, we had another assault-rifle attack (that notorious AR-15 again). This time it was on a Jewish synagogue in Pittsburg.

Eleven people were killed and several others were wounded, including four police officers. The shooter barricaded himself inside the building before eventually surrendering. He is a forty-six-year-old man named Robert Bowers, who was wounded in the exchange of gunfire. He is facing twenty-nine felony charges while in the hospital for his non-life-threatening wound. He has no previous criminal record. This was the deadliest attack on Jews in American history. The victims were elderly people who were public service volunteers.

The pipe-bomber, Cesar Sayoc, will be prosecuted in New York instead of his home state of Florida, because that is where the first bomb package was sent. A combination of fingerprints and social media entries led to his identity.

There has been non-stop discussion this weekend as to what extent President Trump is responsible for both the MAGA bomber and the synagogue shooter. His utter failure to speak out forcefully in condemnation of their acts, along with his repeated bragging that he is a "nationalist", virtually screams approval of this sort of violence against his (and his cult's) enemies. This country has been put on trial in the eyes of the world, and the verdict will be delivered this November 6.

The level of violence with a political motivation in our country will almost certainly be escalated for the foreseeable future. We must all be alert and on guard. It's really getting crazy out there.

The issue of the first-amendment right to free speech is now under reexamination. We have long known that it does not extend to the right to do things like yell, FIRE, in a crowded theater, so *should* people have the right to openly display images of people's faces with a bullseye target superimposed on them? Or other threats of that nature? Should that not trigger at least a strong surveillance of people who openly foster hate and violence?

Trump has stepped up his attacks on the main-stream media—demanding that they stop their "unfair and dishonest fake news".
In essence, he is forbidding them to report on the very things that he himself says.

There is a famous quote, used in the old comic strip, Pogo, which says, "We have met the enemy and he is us." It is very appropriate to what we are seeing in our current president. How much longer must we endure him? How much longer can we afford to?

MSNBC's Morning Joe program, hosted by former Republican journalist and commentator Joe Scarborough, had two other prominent Republicans on as guests. Rick Wilson and Charles Sykes joined Joe in denouncing over the air, in the strongest terms possible, the damage that has been and is still being done to the Republican Party by Donald Trump. More and more conservatives are speaking out, but the sense of disgust and dismay has yet to make much headway among the Republican members of our Senate, in whose hands the fate of our country will ultimately be determined.

The Enemy Within: A Chronicle of the Trump Administration

Book Two (09/2018-11/2019)

November, 2018

Oct. 29-Nov. 4

A little month-merge to keep the weeks going from Monday to Sunday.

Donald Trump keeps blaming the press for the rise in violence aimed at his critics and at Jews and other minorities, while his hateful rhetoric gets hotter by the day. He is sending 5200 troops to the border to join the National Guard members already there, which combines for a larger force than we currently have in Syria and Afghanistan put together. This army has no legal ability to do anything more than perform service and maintenance duties because of the Posse Comitatus Act. He speaks to his devoted base as though he is sending them down there to defend against that "army of invaders" consisting of families who are fleeing for their lives.

Trump plans to visit Pittsburg to show his support for the people affected by the synagogue massacre, but the mayor has asked that he postpone that trip until they have had a chance to bury their dead. Typically, he does not appear to be intending to heed that request.

Trump's complete lack of empathy prevents him from being able to even *consider* cancelling any of his political and ego-boosting rallies in respect for the dead and mourning. He told his adoring crowd at his latest rally that he almost cancelled it because he got caught in the rain and wind, so he was "having a bad hair day." In that same speech, he referred to himself as "the greatest conservative of all time." He has no clue how egomaniacal that sounds to anyone other his brainwashed cult followers.

The Enemy Within: A Chronicle of the Trump Administration

In the wake of the synagogue massacre, Republican Congressman from Iowa, Steve King, is seeing calls from his fellow Representatives for his *expulsion,* because of his openly expressed white-nationalist views.

Trump's latest demonstration of his abysmal ignorance of our Constitution is a declared intention to change the law which gives American citizenship to any child born in the United States, including to migrant mothers. His first "inaccuracy" was when he claimed that we are the only nation that does so. His second, is thinking that he can bypass the Congress by using an executive order to change the Constitution. Even Speaker Paul Ryan has openly called this claim "false."

Trump phoned the newly-elected extreme right-wing president of Brazil to congratulate him. He joins the ranks of Trump's several authoritarian buddies around the world. The rise of the far-right across the globe has been very scary, and it started soon after trump's election.

As expected, Trump defied the request that he postpone his visit to Pittsburg for a week, and once again went where he wasn't wanted. No one greeted him at the airport, and his motorcade was met by a crowd of protesters blocking a street it was using, forcing them to reroute.

Iowa Congressman Steve King, after being condemned by his fellow Republicans for his white-nationalist views, is now in a dead heat with his Democrat opponent in a race he won in the *last* election by *23 points.*

In 2004, George W. Bush signed an anti-Semitic review act to uncover and fight against acts of anti-Semitism in this country. Since then, there have been a succession of three people who held the office of US Special Envoy for monitoring and combatting this type of persecution. The third one left at the end of the Obama administration, and it has not been refilled under Trump. Secretary-of-State Pompeo was recently asked about this post by a reporter, and he said he would do something about that. So far, what he has done about it is…nothing.

Donald Trump, explained his hesitancy in reacting to the Saudi's murder of Khashoggi, as his unwillingness to risk losing his big arms deal with them, because its loss would cost the US over a million jobs. A thorough examination of that claim proves that it is exaggerated by a huge multiple that is difficult to pin down, but the actual loss is an extremely small fraction of his claim.

The FBI is now investigating a newly uncovered plot to tarnish the image of Special Prosecutor Robert Mueller. It involves a phony watchdog company and several women who have been paid to accuse him of improper sexual advances. The scheme is going to land a few people in jail before long.

Oct. 31 (Happy Halloween!) And so we wrap up what I firmly believe will be the last month of the Trump administration's relatively free ride, before he receives the double-barreled blow of the midterm election followed by the Mueller report. Here is how his very bad month ended.

In this last week before the vital midterm election, Trump and the GOP candidates are ramping up the lying about who is best suited to protect our health care, especially pre-existing conditions.
Do they really believe that people are going to forget their all-out effort to repeal the Affordable Care Act, their number one priority when Trump took office? It is quite obvious that they are running scared,—*very* scared.

Kanye West has now completely reversed himself from his embrace and gushing praise of Trump when he visited the Oval

Office a few weeks ago, and is now disowning the president. GOP candidates across the country are seeing their siblings and relatives *endorse their opponents.*

Secretary-of-State Pompeo has finally spoken out against Saudi Arabia's barbaric war and starvation of the neighboring country of Yemen; something we have yet to see our president do.

The fight to solve the polling place debacle in Dodge City is now being led by a high school senior who just turned eighteen. He is being inspired and aided by MSNBC's Rachel Maddow, who has visited the city and blown completely out of the water the city officials' excuse for moving the one polling location far outside the city limits.

It is ironic that Democrats lost control of the House back in the Obama midterm because of the unpopularity of Obamacare, and now the Republicans are scrambling to embrace the features of that plan because it has become more popular than either political party.

The Pentagon says that they have no intention, despite what the President says, of sending troops to the southern border where they would have no legal standing to do much of anything.

In what may be the most significant event yet in the Mueller probe, the sealed document referred to as the "roadmap" for the Nixon/Watergate prosecution, has been released and is being examined in detail by journalists, as well as Mueller and his team. It contains the full testimony and evidence presented and evaluated by the Grand Jury in that case.

It could, and might well be, the model for Mueller to use when he presents his findings to the House Judiciary Committee, where, if it follows the path set by Watergate, it will then be presented to the Senate for their verdict on removal of the President. Or, used as an inducement to force resignation (again).

AS we actually begin the month of November, Trump is now talking about sending 15,000 troops to the Mexican border, instead of the 5200 he planned to send Monday. This would cost the country approximately $50 million, according to budget estimates. This military intelligence assessment was not authorized to be released, but it was leaked anyway by someone who believed the public needed to know about this scam. Civilian vigilante groups have been taking it upon themselves to make armed patrols along the border, knowing that neither the National Guard nor the Army would have the authority to use force on civilian refugees. But they are a big headache rather than a help for the real border patrol personnel.

Trump made an unprecedented political speech from the White House podium, in which he made one of the most outrageous statements yet. He actually instructed his troops to shoot at anyone who crosses into the US and so much as throws a rock. This response would be a capital crime for anyone who obeys that order. He followed that insanity up with the equally outrageous *lie* that "the Democrats are going to destroy our health care system and you're not going to have any health care."

In the Dodge City polling place dispute, a judge *unbelievably ruled against* the ACLU's law suit to get the original polling building reopened, even though it is *not* blocked by construction as claimed. In North Dakota, Native Americans are making some slow progress in creating new residence ID's. An attempt to get the new law repealed was *denied* by the federal judge in that case. Trump's success in stacking the courts with conservative judges is working for the Republicans.

The Enemy Within: A Chronicle of the Trump Administration

Trump continues to refer to the approaching caravan as "an invasion." The GOP is now airing a wildly inaccurate and inflammatory video which depicts "rampant Democrat-sponsored violence." Scare tactics at its worst.

While the Republican candidates are trying desperately to convince voters that they will protect coverage of pre-existing conditions, a coalition of twenty Republican-led states are suing, claiming that Obamacare is unconstitutional. A ruling on that case is imminent.

The synagogue shooter, Robert Bowers, has pled guilty, necessitating a trial in which he will get to espouse his hate filled motivation to the world. He wants to be a martyr to his cause of white supremacy.

The New York Times has reported that Steve Bannon's and Roger Stone's emails indicate that they knew about and were discussing information three days before WikiLeaks published Clinton's stolen emails. This knowledge adds greatly to Mueller's case against Stone and the rest of the Trump campaign. Look for a deluge of indictments to pour forth shortly after the midterms are decided.

Oprah Winfrey stumped today for Georgia's gubernatorial candidate Stacy Abrams, with a masterful speech worthy of a presidential candidate, although she still denies that she has any such intention.

The following very important races are in an extremely close tie with only five days remaining:
Georgia Gov. ...Abrams (D) v. Kemp (R)—46.9 to 46.7;
Florida Sen. ...Nelson (D) v. Scott (R)—46 to 46;
Missouri Sen. ...McCaskill (D) v. Hawley—45 to 45;
Arizona Sen. ...Sinema (D) v. McSally (R)—46 to 46;
Wisconsin Gov. ...Evers (D) v. Walker (R)—47-47

Book Two (09/2018-11/2019)

And there are many more, just as close. It's going to be an interesting, nail-biting night into Wednesday morning for a lot of people.

In this last week before the most important midterm election ever, the country seems to be holding its breath and speculating continuously about what to expect by midnight Tuesday night. Here are the highlights.

A judge has ruled that thousands of ballots being held or disqualified are valid and must be counted. Early voting in Georgia has more than doubled what it was in 2014. It shows a fourteen point gender gap, women over men. The ladies are *pissed!* The rest of the world is marveling over why we make it so difficult for people to cast a ballot.

The white supremacist Iowa Representative, Steve King, was invited to be a guest on Lawrence O'Donnell's *Eleventh Hour* show tonight, but he declined the opportunity to espouse his racist philosophy. Couldn't take the heat of a head-to-head conversation with a man like O'Donnell.

Larry Kudlow, Director of the National Economic Council, has opined that "…the minimum wage is a terrible idea." Now there's a champion of the middle class!

Michael Cohen, while he was Trump's personal attorney, insisted that Trump did not have a racist bone in his body. Now, he is telling *Vanity Fair* that over the years he heard Trump make *many* racist remarks, such as "black people are too stupid to vote for me."

Trump and Obama made nearly simultaneous rally speeches with vastly diffrent tones, ideas and views of the world. The contrast could not be starker.

The Enemy Within: A Chronicle of the Trump Administration

In his last ditch effort to avert disaster at the polls on Tuesday, Trump continues his rhetoric of fear and hate, combined with lying about who will provide the best health care for the country, instead of trying to capitalize on the good economy and the good new job numbers. He continues constantly to be his own worst enemy. Here are a few observations this weekend as we head into that crucial midterm.

It has become clear that states that passed new voter ID laws shortly before the 2016 election helped Trump beat out Clinton in close races like Wisconsin. A total of twenty-three states had new restrictions, which are still affecting this midterm as well as 2016.

These two elections have highlighted the fact that the suppression of minority voters has been going on ever since LBJ signed the Voting Rights Act back in 1965. Gerrymandering has been one of the most effective devices used by the Republicans to tilt the playing field. Kris Koback, who is running for Governor in Kansas, is one of the main architects of the suppression tactics.

Since the synagogue massacre, there has been a rash of attacks on Jews across the country, proving once again that violence breeds violence.

Nov. 5-11

In this final day before the nation makes one of the biggest decisions in its history, we have the following observations.

At his latest rally, Trump once again displayed his complete ignorance when he made this astounding statement: "Until now, no one knew what the midterms were." He meant, no one in the Trump family, of course. He transfers his own flaws onto everyone else.

Hero Chesley Sullenberger, who miraculously landed US Air Flight 1549 on the Hudson River when it was disabled and crashing, was a guest on Lawrence O'Donnell's *The Last Word* tonight. He said that for the first time in his life he is voting Democrat across the board in this election, because of Donald Trump.

The increase in new voters in this election has never been as high, thanks to the magnitude of controversy surrounding our current administration.

The Washington Post's Trump-lie counter has him currently at a total of 6,420 lies in 644 days, which is an average of five lies per day. Trump loves to brag about records. Here's one that he won't bring up.

In Florida, Nelson has moved into a slight lead in the Senate race, while Gillum and DeSantis remain deadlocked.

In the final pre-election generic poll, the Democrats hold a seven point lead over the Republicans. The question remains, how will that lead be distributed among the candidates?

An even bigger question is, will the polls be accurate?

And here we are at election day, and the polls were pretty accurate this time, and we have a mixed bag of good news and bad news. The good news is that although the "blue wave" was smaller than expected, it was big enough to return control of the House to the Democrats by a margin of over twenty seats when the smoke of some still undecided races clears. The bad news is that the Republicans actually *gained* two seats in the Senate. Heitkamp lost to Cramer in North Dakota, McCaskill lost to Hawley in Missouri, Donnelly lost to Braun in Indiana, and Scott beat Nelson in Florida, although it is so close that Nelson has not conceded and will wait until all the absentee and provisional ballots have been counted. Cruz retained his seat in Texas, edging out O'Rourke. A handful of races, including the

Georgia Governor race, are still undecided. These victories inspired Trump to declare "a tremendous success", in spite of the disaster of losing the House by a sizable margin.

But the most important thing that Trump has to be concerned with now is the impending Mueller report, which surely will not be long in coming, now that the election is no longer inhibiting him. Get ready for the axe to fall, Donald. And that report will not be hidden by this Congress.

With Democrats back in control of the House, three things become an instant certainty: Nancy Pelosi will resume her role as Speaker, the Trump agenda will hit a brick wall, and the Congressional investigations into the President's actions, both during the campaign and since he was elected, will be resumed in earnest.

Today (Nov. 7) was the second major historical day in a row. Things are really coming to a head now. The blockbuster of the day was the firing of AG Jeff Sessions by the now panicked president. His "resignation" was requested by Trump, which is tantamount to being fired. This is heading us into what can easily evolve into a Constitutional Crisis. What makes this move much worse is the fact that Trump bypassed Rod Rosenstein and replaced Sessions with a Trump loyalist/lackey named Matthew Whitaker, Sessions' Chief-of-Staff, who has written an op-ed and spoken on *Fox News* that he believes that Mueller has overstepped his bounds in his Russia probe. Whitaker has also defended Trump Jr. for his Trump Tower meeting with the Russian lawyer, one of the linchpins of the conspiracy case. He now has the power to severely limit Mueller, if not fire him. Given his known views, he should do what Sessions did and recuse himself from anything to do with the Mueller investigation. Trump's appointment of Whitaker over Rosenstein will be interpreted as another case of obstruction.

Book Two (09/2018-11/2019)

There are many groups around the country who have been preparing for this day and have planned for a huge number of protests across our nation to take place at 5:00 PM tomorrow. If Whitaker doesn't recuse himself it will create a crisis of ethics which will blow sky-high. California Senator Swalwell of the Judiciary Committee says that they will call for Whitaker's recusal, *and* to see Trump's tax returns.

The Democrat-controlled House can now invite Mueller to testify about any interference by Whitaker. They can also accept his report, as it stands, complete or not, if Mueller is removed.

Senator Lindsey Graham has said in the past that if Trump ever fired Sessions "it would be the end of the Trump presidency." It sure looks like we are heading in that direction.

Senator Blumenthal says that they have "a plan B" to protect Mueller and his probe. He also feels that Mueller is on the verge of issuing several indictments.

The Mueller report is going to blow the cover off Trump's crimes, no matter what happens, thanks to the Democrat control of the House. The only really big question is going to be, what will the Republican-controlled Senate do about it?

Trump held his longest press conference yet at the White House, where he extolled his "great victory" yesterday, seeming to ignore his loss of the House. He must have felt it though, because his speech was rambling and incoherent. At one point he called off the names of several Republican House candidates who lost "because they failed to embrace Trump's help." When correspondent Jim Acosta asked him questions that he didn't like, he told one of his female aides to relieve him of his microphone. When Acosta fended her off as she tried to wrest the mic out of his hands, Trump had Acosta removed from the room and revoked his press pass. His war on the free press is really getting out of control. The atmosphere in this White

The Enemy Within: A Chronicle of the Trump Administration

House has become one of political warfare. It is getting scarily dangerous.

Rachel Maddow tonight ran down a long list of Republican candidates running in red districts who lost, even though Trump supported them, or maybe, *because* Trump supported them. On the other hand, two Republican Congressmen who have been indicted and may be facing prison time, were reelected.

The Democrats did have some good news on the Senate battle: Scott Walker, Dean Heller and Kris Koback all lost their seats, offsetting the Republicans' gain a bit.

Senator Chris Coons spoke on TV and said that Trump has crossed a red line in appointing Whitaker, and is calling for bi-partisan steps to curtail the new acting AG. He says that Trump and his loyalists have adopted a "gangster-mentality."

The Blue Wave is turning out to be as big as expected after all. The biggest since the backlash to the Watergate scandal leading to Nixon's resignation. There are several House contests and a couple of Governor races that have yet to be decided, which were thought to be lost to the Republicans, But late returns have closed the gap considerably, which could turn things around completely, or at least force a recount. The Florida Governorship may go to Gillum after all, and the Senate seat is being hotly fought over, with Scott demanding an investigation into voter fraud in two Florida counties.

Eleven House seats are still undecided, with the Democrats already owning a thirty seat gain. The lead in the Arizona Senate race has already shifted to the Democrat, Kirsten Sinema, with the remaining votes likely to be heavily Democrat. The Georgia Governor race is still not being conceded by Abrams, as she is making gains in that count also. An openly gay Native American woman named Sharice Davids has beaten a four-term incumbent in a Kansas House contest--by *nine*

Book Two (09/2018-11/2019)

points. The cautionary tale for the Democrats going forward is that they must learn to relate better with *rural* America.

The most important aspect of the Democrats' win in the House is that they now control the Judiciary Committee and other committees that could have an impact on the ongoing check on the President. They will now be recalling several witnesses who gave dubious testimony in their previous hearing before the Republican controlled committee. The previous sham investigation will be reopened in earnest. The White House and other entities have been reminded by the House Judiciary that they *must* preserve all relevant documents and evidence related to the Russia probe and its offshoots. Hiding or destroying any of this is a federal crime.

The planned protests took place as scheduled across this nation, as people carrying banners and signs denouncing Trump's appointment of Matt Whitaker to be the acting AG, and thus the overseer of the Mueller investigation. They made it loud and clear that the country wants Mueller protected to finish what he and his team of prosecutors have started.

Today, it was unfortunately also made clear that the acting AG has the power to stop any move made by the Special Counsel that the AG deems inappropriate to the scope of his mandate. *The New York Times* printed an article written by constitutional experts Neal K. Katyal and George T. Conway (Kelly Anne Conway's husband), calling Whitaker's appointment unconstitutional. It is also *illegal,* because it was done for a corrupt purpose (to protect himself from prosecution), namely, obstruction of justice. This adds to a growing list of nearly a dozen charges of obstruction that Mueller can, and probably will, level against Trump when he issues his report. The firing of Sessions itself could be considered a separate case of obstruction, *or* considered as part of the Whitaker appointment charge.

The Enemy Within: A Chronicle of the Trump Administration

It is interesting to note that Whitaker's previous job before coming to the Justice Department was promoting the products of a company that, six months ago, had to pay a large fine for defrauding the public, and the company was closed down because of it. Many legal experts are describing Whitaker's appointment as "a coup", and "an assault of the rule of law." They believe that Whitaker will get himself in serious legal trouble if he goes after Mueller. This includes Andrew Napolitano, who voiced that opinion on *Fox News*, of all places.

Donald Trump Jr. says that he expects to be indicted soon. Maybe he has a contact who has tipped him off, or maybe it is just his guilty conscience showing. Several pundits have expressed that they expect a rash of indictments to precede, or come along with, Mueller's report.

In the razor thin Florida Senate race there is a legal battle raging, resulting from Governor Rick Scott's accusation of voter fraud in Broward County, aimed at election manager Brenda Snipes. A crowd of protesters gathered in her building shouting "lock her up".

No evidence of fraud has been presented and it is very doubtful that any will be found, but that doesn't seem to matter to these desperate people. Snipes was appointed to her post by Jeb Bush, so she is not the liberal plant they seem to think she is. The governor race between Gillum and DeSantis is nearly as close. There will almost certainly be a recount in both cases.

In the 2016 presidential election the Democrat got about three million more votes than the Republican, in Clinton's losing battle. In this midterm they got *six* millions more votes.

Our new Acting Attorney General, Matthew Whitaker, is very much involved as a target in the FBI's investigation into his former employer, the Florida company named *World Patent Marketing*. The company is accused of bilking several million dollars from thousands of consumers. Whitaker was served a

Book Two (09/2018-11/2019)

subpoena for company documents, but he ignored it. He is now in the position to oversee the investigation into a case involving himself—a clear conflict of interest. He will be under intense scrutiny by his own agency for this reason, as well as for his prejudice against the Mueller probe that he now supervises. His every action and utterance will be monitored. If he is not extremely careful, he could end up like John Mitchel, who was sentenced to two and a half years in prison for his role in protecting Nixon over Watergate.

Professor of Law Lawrence Tribe spoke on MSNBC tonight and declared that Matt Whitaker has *no constitutional basis* to hold his new post, which must be confirmed by the Senate. Everything he does at this point has no legal bearing and could just be ignored. He is obviously being used as Donald Trump's Roy Cohn, the infamous protector of Joe McCarthy. In fact, Trump has several times been heard on TV asking, "Where is my Roy Cohn?" Trump has repeatedly stated in the past few days that he does not know Whitaker, in spite of a previous video of him praising Whitaker as "a great guy." And *The New York Times* says that Trump first noticed Whitaker in the summer of 2017, and liked his comments about the Russia probe. He had Don McGahn interview him about joining the Trump team that July.

A new *Wall Street Journal* article puts a lot more meat on the bones of the story of Trump's conspiracy with Michael Cohen to pay the hush money to Stormy Daniels and Karen McDougle for the express purpose of avoiding a negative impact on his presidential campaign, which is the crime that Cohen pled guilty to. They point out that if he were not the President he would already have been indicted for this felony. This is a clear case for impeachment, but it is in danger of being blocked by the new Acting AG, if he is brash enough to take the tremendous heat that he would incur.

Trump landed in Paris for the commemoration of the one hundredth anniversary of the end of WWI, where he once again attacked the press and insulted three black female reporters. He is planning to meet with Putin while in France, although we would not know that if Putin had not told us about it. Apparently, Trump was hoping it would be a secret. The question is, WHY?

Trump's visit to France to take part in the ceremonies honoring the veterans on this significant hundredth anniversary of what use to be known as Armistice Day, turned out to be yet another embarrassment for our nation in the eyes of the rest of the free world. He opted out of the first ceremony with the cowardly excuse that it was raining. For this, he incurred the criticism and disgust of just about everyone. This slight adds insult to the injury he has already caused by not once, in two years in office, visiting our troops overseas, including the middle-east counties like Afghanistan. This is the same man, who as a candidate sold himself as the champion of the military.

With 99.97% of the votes counted in the Broward County Florida Senate race, a recount is assured and an overhaul of how the votes are counted down there seems to be in the cards. The race for Governor also is headed for a recount.

Michelle Obama has released a new book in which she takes Donald Trump to task on a variety of issues, especially his "birtherism" campaign.

Nov. 12-18

Trump has returned from overseas where he once again humiliated himself and his country by insulting our allies and slighting our heroic dead veterans. Then he did not even make what could have been a walking trip to Arlington National Cemetery to pay homage to those who are interred there. Polling of the current military shows that his approval and disapproval ratings are now dead-even at forty-three percent. As

Book Two (09/2018-11/2019)

another huge and very destructive forest fire rages in California, killing hundreds, Trump's only comments on the subject are to level blame on the California management of forestry. This is the new normal for a US president these days.

The Florida recounts began by machine on Sunday and the trend points to the probable necessity of a *hand* recount in both the Senate and Governor races. The gap continues to shrink the Republican leads. Gillum has retracted his concession in view of the late vote counts in his favor.

In Broward County the ballot format placed the Senate candidate choices in an obscure and awkward corner where many voters could have overlooked that element of the election entirely.

A federal judge has rejected current Governor Scott's attempt to seize and take control of the voting machines. In Arizona, Kirsten Sinema has pulled out a late win in her Senate race over her Republican opponent. This is the seat vacated by retiring Senator Jeff Flake. In Georgia, Abrams is still hoping to close the vote gap enough to prompt a recount there as well. Meanwhile, Trump is still maintaining claims of broad, massive voter fraud without a scintilla of evidence to back up that claim.

The New York Times reports that North Korea now has sixteen new missile sites since Trump's visit, which he claimed solved the threat from that rogue nation. What a fiasco that so-called summit meeting was!

The Washington Post reports that Trump is preparing to remove Kirstjen Nielsen from her post as Secretary of Homeland Security. They have not been on the same page very much since her appointment.

Roger Stone's associate, Jerome Corsi, says he expects to be indicted in the near future in what he calls a "perjury trap," for lying about communication with WikiLeaks. Corsi has a history of lying, including writing a book titled, *Where's the Birth Certificate?*, which helped promote Trump's first big lie in his campaign.

Axios has reported that the new Democrat-controlled House is "loading a subpoena cannon" with over eighty-five Trump-related targets, including his tax returns, and impeachment charges.

The midterm election proceeds, a full week after Election Day. A federal judge has ruled that the deadline for completing the Florida recounts will be extended. In deep red Mississippi, there will be a runoff election in the Senate race between Democrat Mike Espy and Republican Cindy Hyde-Smith, who is currently leading by only .5%. There are still several House contests that are undecided. The Democrats could end up with a gain of about thirty-eight seats.

Maryland's Attorney General, Brian Frosh, has filed a lawsuit challenging the appointment of Matt Whitaker to the US Acting AG post by Trump, calling it unlawful. He has asked that his suit be expedited for the good of the country. Former Senior DOJ official Max Axelrod was a guest on *The Rachel Maddow Show* tonight and agreed that this appointment is unlawful, and is the first such appointment in US history that did not have Senate confirmation. He questions whether Whitaker will follow the judgement of the Ethics Committee. Congressman Adam Schiff also weighed in with a forceful statement warning Whitaker as follows: "Heed this warning: The new Democrat majority will protect the Special Counsel and the integrity of the Justice Department. If Whitaker fails to recuse himself—all indications are that he plans not to—and seeks to obstruct the investigation, serves as a back channel to the President or his legal team, or interferes in *any way*, he will be called to answer. His actions will be exposed."

Book Two (09/2018-11/2019)

Trump's legal team is finishing up their written replies to Mueller's written questions on Russia collusion. This may be the last thing Mueller is waiting for before issuing his report.

The Trump administration continues to fall apart on a daily basis. In addition to the imminent firing of Nielsen, mentioned in yesterday's list of items, we have the following positions in serious jeopardy: Trey Glenn, the EPA Administrator for the Southern Region (who was the worst possible choice for the job Trump gave him), has been indicted for corruption charges while he worked as Alabama State Environmental Administrator; Interior Secretary Ryan Zinke has been referred to the DOJ for potential prosecution for corruption; multiple White House sources have reported that First Lady Melania Trump has demanded the removal of Deputy National Security Advisor Mira Ricardel because she has been interfering with the First Lady's plan for a trip to Africa. This is an unprecedented usurping of power from a First Lady.

The same White House sources have described Trump as having "retreated into a cocoon of bitterness and resentment." He has done virtually no work since the midterm election and his mental state continues to deteriorate on a daily basis. When the impending round of new indictments hits, it may produce a twenty-fifth amendment situation.

Three more House seat races were decided today (the 14th), in the Democrat's favor, with three million more votes yet to be counted in California alone. The Republican side of the house is now made up of ninety percent men, while the Democrat side contains thirty-eight percent men. This is the result of Trump's blatant and obvious misogyny. In North Dakota, the man who sponsored the bill to require specific Post Office addresses for the American Indians on a huge reservation in that state, and thereby blocked many from voting, was defeated in his bid for reelection to that state's legislation. That's *Karma* for you! In

The Enemy Within: A Chronicle of the Trump Administration

New Jersey, the Republican who led the fight to repeal Obamacare, also lost his seat in the House.

Trump is so flustered by these results that he can't refrain from spewing his nonsense about massive voter fraud, claiming that people are using disguises to vote multiple times. He again raised the issue of the need for voter ID, "you know--like you need to buy cereal at the grocery store." He apparently has never voted or gone grocery shopping. What does he think voter registration is for? Does he not know that every voter has to check in, if not with ID, at least with an address which is matched to the voter rolls and checked off? That's what the hoopla in North Dakota was all about.

Multiple lawsuits are ongoing in Florida over both the Senate and the gubernatorial races, as the deadline for completing the machine recount looms tomorrow. Echoing his president, Scott continues to rant about voter fraud. Roger Stone has been one of the driving forces behind the scores of protesters interfering with the recount process.

Apparently, Melania has succeeded in getting Mira Ricardel canned from her job as Deputy National Security Advisor, although Ricardel has yet to make her exit. *Vanity Fair* says that this is "a whole new level of insanity."

Rick Gates is *still* cooperating with the Mueller investigation, so he has not yet had his sentence established.

General Mattis says that the troops Trump has sent to the southern border are doing absolutely nothing, but are serving as "a confidence builder for the normal border patrol." For this, the federal government is spending about $220 million.

The DOJ's Office of Legal Counsel has decided that the appointment of Matt Whitaker as Acting Attorney General presents no legal problem. They seem to be alone in that assessment.

Book Two (09/2018-11/2019)

Retiring Republican Senator Jeff Flake has filed a bill to protect Robert Mueller from any interference in his investigation, and vows that the GOP will not be getting his vote on any of the upcoming judge confirmations until they put his bill to a vote.

The latest polls on Trump's reelection chances show the following breakdown: All voters: For=37%...Against=51%; Republicans: For=76%...Against=16%; Independents: For=31%...Against=59%.

This is a big incentive for Senate Republicans to vote to expel, when the President is impeached. Their chances in 2020 could only get better with his replacement, whoever that might be (Pence is not a lock).

Today, Nov. 15, was the biggest and most significant Trump news day since the midterm election. In increasing level of importance...

The official Democrat gain of seats in the House stands at thirty-seven with six races still undecided. New England Representatives are now 100% Democrat, and so are Orange County California's, long considered a conservative bastion. In addition to the huge gains in the US House of Representatives, the Democrats also flipped about 300 seats in *state* legislatures.

Trump's attacks on the press have even extended to his favorite program, *Fox News* and *Fox and Friends,* including his most ardent supporter and sycophant, Sean Hannity, for being "soft" and "dumb." He not only alienates this country's allies, he alienates his own supporters.

The Trump administration has leveled sanctions on seventeen Saudis for the Khashoggi killing, but it does not include the main culprit, the Crown Prince.

The Enemy Within: A Chronicle of the Trump Administration

Trump has extended his violence-inciting rhetoric to include Antifa, the anti-fascist group that was involved in the Charlottesville riot. In doing so, he could not sound more like a fascist himself.

Senator Lindsey Graham has met with our new Acting Attorney General, Matt Whitaker, and was then asked by a reporter what his feelings were on Whitaker's appointment. He replied, "As to the Mueller investigation, I'm confident that it is not in jeopardy. There is no reason to fire him. I asked him, 'Do you have any reason to fire Mueller?' He said he has no reason to believe anything is being done wrong with the Mueller investigation." Whitaker still needs to go, as he has stated that he has no intention of recusing himself. Trump's tweets today show how panicked he is, and how much information Whitaker has already provided to the principal target of that investigation, Trump himself. Here is a sample of those tweets: "The Inner workings of the Mueller investigation are a total mess. They have found no collusion and have gone absolutely nuts. They are screaming and shouting at people, horribly threatening them to come up with the answers they want. They are a disgrace to our Nation…"

Donald Trump Junior's friends are reporting that he is getting really nervous about the prospect of being indicted by Mueller. White House sources say that Trump "…is preparing for the worst."

The *Washington Post* has reported that WikiLeaks CEO Julian Assange has been charged with sealed offenses, probably related to releasing classified information to the Russians.

Trump's legal team is still delaying submission of their answers to Mueller's questions on collusion. They have had those questions for months. What is the problem?

Book Two (09/2018-11/2019

In an interview with a daily news publication, *The Daily Caller*, Trump was asked the following question: "Could you tell us where your thinking is currently on the attorney general position? I know you're happy with Matthew Whitaker, do you have any names? Chris Christie?" Here is his answer: "Matthew Whitaker is a much respected man. He's—and he's very importantly, he's respected within the DOJ. I knew him only as he pertained, you know, as he was with Jeff Sessions. And, you know, look, as far as I'm concerned this is an investigation that should have never been brought. It should have never been had. It's something that should have never been brought. It's an illegal investigation. And you know, it's very interesting because when you talk about not Senate confirmed, well Mueller's not Senate confirmed."

This rambling, nearly incoherent statement is tantamount to an admission that Whitaker was appointed because he was on record as being against that investigation. It was an admission every bit as damning as when he told Lester Holt that he fired Comey because of the Russia probe. Meanwhile, Whitaker says he has no intention of recusing himself.

Tonight, Rachel Maddow told us about a mysterious case that Mueller has filed in the D.C. Appeals Court, which is second only to the US Supreme Court in power and prestige. The briefs for this case are sealed, the hearings are closed to the public and the case has been given top priority. One of the appeals court judges for this case is a man named Greg Katsas, who worked in the White House under Don McGahn early in the Trump administration. He advised Trump on matters pertaining to the Mueller probe. Because of this, he has recused himself from the case described above, which is a red flag that the case involves that investigation. This is another sign that something big is about to go down.

At the same time, a status report that was due today on the state of Paul Manafort's level of cooperation, which will determine his sentence, has been granted a ten-day delay because the prosecution convinced the judge that they would have additional important information by that time. Another signal of a big shoe about to drop. Buckle up, everyone. Things they are about to start popping!

CNN sued the Trump administration for revoking journalist Jim Acosta's press pass to the White House. In a very quick decision the judge ruled in Acosta's favor, because of "lack of due process." His pass will be restored forthwith. The judge did not address the issue of first amendments rights.

In Georgia, Stacy Abrams reluctantly conceded that Kemp will become the next Governor, but gave a strongly worded speech about the way in which he won--because of his vote suppression tactics, which leaves his victory forever tainted.

Trump lied his tongue off today when he answered a reporter's question about the status of his answers to Mueller's written questions on collusion. He claimed, in no uncertain terms, that he answered Mueller's "easy questions" by himself with no help from his legal team. He might as well have tried to sell them the Brooklyn Bridge. He also revealed that he "hears that the Mueller investigation is coming to an end." Gee, I wonder where he got *that* information.

Tonight Rachel Maddow reviewed for us how extraordinarily weak Matt Whitaker's resume is for his new position as Acting Attorney General. She also described some of the scam products he was involved in promoting for *World Patent Marketing*, which bilked so many people out of so much money. Whitaker threatened consumers with legal action if they complained too loudly about these scams. As a result, he is now being investigated by the very agency that he (temporarily) leads, as well as being sued by several entities challenging his legality.

Book Two (09/2018-11/2019)

The CIA has publicly concluded that the murder of journalist Jamal Khashoggi was *ordered* by the Saudi Crown Prince, Mohammed bin Salman. In spite of this assessment, the Trump administration is seriously considering extraditing a Turkish Cleric and critic of the Turkish government, named Fethullah Gulen, who is a Green Card holder living in the US, back to Turkey, where he will almost certainly be tortured and executed for his opposition to the regime.

Trump's motivation for this proposed death sentence is to placate the Turkish government, which is now strongly at odds with the Saudis because of the killing of Khashoggi on their turf. Trump hopes to thus gain favor with the Saudis whom he relies upon greatly for financial favors. It is a close call as to who owns the biggest piece of President Trump—Russia or Saudi Arabia.

Kellyanne Conway's husband George is being quoted by White House insiders as referring to the Trump White House as, "a shithole in a dumpster fire." I wonder what the pillow talk is like in *that* household.

In Florida, the manual recounts finished on schedule and both Democrat candidates, Nelson for Senate and Gillum for Governor, have conceded defeat. Florida, lately considered a purple state, has turned more reddish. Some consolation for the Republican Party that just got *shellacked*, to use Obama's word for it, in the overall assessment of the midterm election.

Trump went to California to view the devastation caused by the biggest, hottest forest fire on record, which utterly destroyed the town of Paradise (Trump kept referring to it as "Pleasure" until corrected), making it a Hell on Earth. But instead of words of condolence and compassion, he criticized the "forest management" for not properly raking the forest floor like Denmark does. He said he has not changed his opinion on climate change, in spite of the fact that we just came through the hottest summer in the recorded history of the planet.

Republican Senator and Trump lackey, Lindsey Graham, of all people, has drafted a bill to protect Robert Mueller from being fired, but he says he is still being blocked by Senate leader Mitch McConnell.

In an interview on *Fox News* with Chris Wallace, Trump ridiculed retired Admiral William McRaven, the Seal Commander who conducted the operation that brought down Osama bin Laden. He sneered that the Admiral was a Clinton supporter and that bin Laden should have been killed a lot sooner. When he was asked, "How do you make decisions? Do you second-guess yourself?" he responded, "I don't think about it." This is, unfortunately, one of the very few true statements he has made in the past two years. The lack of thinking about any of his decisions is one of the many reasons he is uniquely unqualified for the office of president.

Multiple sources are claiming that Mueller will hand down dozens of sealed indictments in the D.C. court, many of them related to the Russia investigation, including Trump family members.

Nov. 19-25

Polls show that Trump's popularity and approval rating among the military has slipped considerably lately, due to his rash of snubs, criticism and outright insults toward the military in general and individual leaders in particular. The number who disapprove now stands even with the number who approve.

In Mississippi, there will be a runoff election on November 27, to decide the race for a US Senate seat. A debate is scheduled between the candidates, Democrat Mike Espy and Republican Cindy Hyde-Smith. Hyde-Smith has been embroiled in controversy lately for inappropriate remarks that she has tried unsuccessfully to explain.

Book Two (09/2018-11/2019)

Because of Republican-produced gerrymandering, the states of Wisconsin, Michigan, Pennsylvania and North Carolina have elected a plurality of Republican *State* legislators in spite of decisively losing the popular vote in the state overall.

In that previously mentioned interview with *Fox News'* Chris Wallace, Trump, in addition to his other off-the-wall comments, claimed that "he did not know about Matt Whitaker's comments about the Mueller investigation"—another blatant, bald-faced LIE!

Remember when Donald Trump, the candidate, ranted and raved about Hillary Clinton's improper use of her private email account to conduct state business—the reason for those "lock her up" chants. Well, we have just learned that daughter Ivanka has been doing the same thing, for quite a while, until she was "instructed about the rules" by White House staff. She claims ignorance that it was wrong. Did she pay no attention to one of her Dad's major issues during the campaign? Is this ignorance, carelessness or arrogance?

Sixteen Representatives have signed a letter in opposition to Nancy Pelosi being reinstalled as Speaker. She has an uphill battle.

Trump's "busy schedule" today consists of two commitments: checking out the arrival of the White House Christmas tree; lunch with VP Pence. Tomorrow, only one thing on his schedule so far—presentation of the National Thanksgiving turkey. Ironically, it is a **good** thing that he does so little actual work as president.

Trump still insists on siding with the Saudis and against our intelligence agencies on the issue of placing the blame where it belongs in the Khashoggi case. His gift of a free pass to that regime greatly diminishes our standing in the eyes of the rest of the free world. It benefits only Trump and his son-in-law Jared Kushner. His excuse, that he wants to protect billions of dollars and thousands of jobs that the Saudi arms deals produce, is grossly exaggerated if not outright false. Even more harmful, is what he is doing to the confidence level within our CIA and other agencies and, to an unknown extent, the confidence of the American people in those agencies.

Trump has now submitted his answers on collusion to Mueller. He still needs to answer questions on obstruction, preferably in person, before this investigation can satisfactorily be completed. There seems to be no prospect at this point that any such meeting will take place, unless Mueller subpoenas him, which is getting less and less likely.

The current communications that are now almost certainly taking place via a back channel between Trump and Matt Whitaker mirror exactly what Nixon was doing with the head of the Criminal Division of the Justice Department, Henry Peterson, during the Watergate investigation, which became a huge legal problem for both of them. Former General Counsel for the DOJ, Jim Baker, has written a lengthy memo about this violation of the separation-of-powers via improper communication, which he calls a "roadmap" to how this sticky issue should be handled.

Jerry Nadler, who will be the new House Judiciary Committee Chairman, vows that one of their first acts this January will be to subpoena Whitaker. They will be sure to ask him about *The Washington Post*'s recent article revealing that Whitaker was paid large sums of money between 2014 and 2017 by a conservative non-profit organization named *The Foundation for Accountability*. Paid for what? If not curtailed, you can expect that Whitaker will not only continue to serve as Trump's spy and Mueller-blocker, but will also begin an investigation into Trump's number one enemy, Hillary Clinton.

Book Two (09/2018-11/2019)

The New York Times has reported a new blockbuster story that adds still more evidence of obstruction by the President. According to former Trump attorney Don McGahn, Trump tried to get him to pressure the DOJ to not only open investigations into both Comey and Clinton, which is an impeachable offence in itself, he wanted them immediately *prosecuted* in conjunction with those proposed investigations. McGahn painstakingly explained to Trump that they do not have the power to do that sort of thing, and saved a memo about the discussion for posterity, which you can be sure is now in Robert Muller's hands. It has long been obvious that Trump knows little if anything about our justice system or the separation of powers within our system of government.

Out of a combination of unprecedented ignorance of US law and political norms, together with autocratic power-hunger, this president is a very dangerous loose cannon. He is not only an enemy of the nation he purports to lead, he is again and again his *own* worst enemy.

The Democrats' vote gap in the midterm election was almost nine million over the Republican candidates, making it the biggest margin in history, including the midterm right after Nixon resigned over Watergate. *The New York Times* reports that Trump is losing his grip on his own supporters to some degree.

Each day now we are learning more about the very dubious record and character of newly appointed (Acting) AG Matt Whitaker.

Trump today publicly thanked Saudi Arabia for lowering oil prices. But only nine percent of our oil comes from that nation. Meanwhile, he continues to dismiss the murder of Jamal Khashoggi, which is a part of his consistent alignment with autocrats around the world. He thus gives a green light to any of them to commit murder, even against citizens of other countries, at their will.

Rudy Giuliani has surfaced again to tell NBC that if Mueller subpoenaed Trump for questions on obstruction, "I doubt he would comply."

The other day Trump criticized the ninth circuit court in California, and one "Obama judge" in particular, for their several rulings against the President since he took office. Today, Supreme Court Chief Justice John Roberts responded with the following tweet: "We do not have Obama judges, Bush judges or Clinton judges. What we have is an extraordinary group of dedicated judges doing their level best to do equal right to those appearing before them. That independent judiciary is something we should all be thankful for."

This was a very rare and striking statement from a Chief Justice, showing how serious he considers Trump's despotic attitude toward what is supposed to be a separate and equal branch of our government. Trump immediately responded with another lengthy, aggressive response. If and when a Trump-related issue reaches the Supreme Court, the President may have an ally in Kavanaugh, but he has given the *most* influential justice plenty of reason not to side with him, including his obvious undemocratic tactics and seeking of personal power. Roberts' views could be the decisive factor in the final stage of the case against Trump. He sure does like to shoot himself in foot—or wherever.

Nov. 22 (Happy Thanksgiving!)

In addition to being Thanksgiving, this is also the fifty-fifth anniversary of the assassination of President John F. Kennedy. It was hardly mentioned this year. As I do every year, I pondered the question of whether the American public will ever be given the truth about his murder. I doubt it will happen in what is left of *my* lifetime.

Book Two (09/2018-11/2019)

I wonder how many families, gathered around their Thanksgiving dinner, felt that they had to walk on eggshells to avoid any mention of the potentially explosive subject of our very divisive and controversial president. Probably pretty close to all of them.

At a news conference in Palm Beach, Florida, Trump answered quite a few more questions than usual. He once again denied that the CIA had "concluded" that Khashoggi was murdered on the order of the Saudi Prince. A "very high degree of confidence" is not good enough to get him to side against his most lucrative friends, so he uses semantics as a shield.

Trump doubled down on criticism of the ninth circuit in California. He is furious over their repeated rebuffs on major issues like the Muslim ban, separating parents and children at the border, and blocking asylum seekers.
He says he will close that border completely, and will even go as far as shutting down the government if he has to, "in order to make us safe from the invasion of immigrants." He has even authorized the use of lethal force by our troops, who are still there, wishing they were home for the holiday instead of camping out with their buddies, doing next to nothing.

With very little happening on the Trump front on this Black Friday it is a good time to look back and summarize where we stand as far as the status of the Trump administration and the condition of our nation are concerned.

First, where are we on the case of Russian interference and the Trump campaign's collaboration with it? Here are the major facts so far.

Twenty-five Russians have been indicted for hacking into election-related data bases for the purpose of influencing the

The Enemy Within: A Chronicle of the Trump Administration

election in Trump's favor. They have fled back to Russia and are beyond our reach.

At least five campaign members have been indicted, pled guilty and are cooperating with prosecutors for crimes related to conspiring with the Russians, and several more *expect* to be very soon.

Multiple meetings were held between Trump people and Russians, and at least one of those (the June Trump Tower meeting) is known to be for the purpose of gaining compromising data on Clinton.

In an effort to cover up their participation in the above conspiracy, Trump has committed the following actions which could be considered obstruction of justice.

Jan. 27, 2017......Trump asks Comey to "let Flynn go."

May 9, 2017......Trump fires Comey because of "the Russia thing."

May 12, 2017 ....Trump admits to Lester Holt that he fired Comey because of Russia.

June 2017 ......Trump tells Don McGahn to fire Mueller (McGahn refuses).

Aug. 26, 2017....Trump screams at Mitch McConnell for not "protecting him."

May 2018 ....Trump launches attack on the FBI and DOJ in general.

May 29, 2018 ....Trump pressures AG Sessions to fire Mueller (Sessions refuses).

May, June 2018...Trump hints at pardons for potential "flippers."

Aug. 1, 2018......Trump tweets that AG Sessions *should* put a halt *right now* to the Mueller investigation.

Nov. 7, 2018......Trump fires AG Sessions and installs Sessions' Chief of Staff Matt Whitaker as Acting AG.

Along with the above described *major crimes* perpetrated by Trump and his allies, we have the seriously deleterious effects that Trump has had on this country since taking office, as follows.

Racists, Neo-Nazis, despots and conspiracy nuts have been emboldened.

The free press and freedom of speech are under constant attack.

The separation of powers in our government has been weakened or ignored.

Efforts to combat climate change have been seriously restricted. A new federal report on the catastrophic effects of climate change was released today and was virtually ignored by Trump and the right wing media. Trump's only comment was, "I don't believe it."

Our allies around the world no longer trust or depend on us.

Our status as leader of the free world has virtually disappeared.

The Supreme Court has been shifted drastically to the Right.

North Korea is still a nuclear threat in spite of Trump's delusional statements to the contrary.

The country is more divided than at any time since the Civil War.

Most of our president's time has been spent on vacation or on the golf course, opposite of what he promised his supporters in the campaign.

We have now entered the final stage of the Mueller investigation, which means that we have probably entered the final few months of the Trump presidency. Expect the fur to fly, and soon.

In Mississippi, the upcoming runoff for Senator between Democrat Mike Espy and Republican Cindy Hyde-Smith this coming Tuesday has devolved into a war of words about racism.

The Enemy Within: A Chronicle of the Trump Administration

Several major companies in that state have criticized Hyde-Smith and endorsed Espy, largely because of her embarrassment to her state. Unfortunately, many Mississippians are not embarrassed, but are in complete agreement with her racist views. This Tuesday will finally end the seemingly endless midterm of 2018, and it will be very telling as to whether Mississippi has evolved as much as Alabama showed that *it* has when it defeated Roy Moore.

A New York state judge has denied a request to dismiss the case against Donald Trump, his family and the Trump Foundation for using it for their personal slush fund.

Jerome Corsi continues to be the current pressure point for Robert Mueller. It remains to be seen how much he will cooperate with the Mueller probe in exchange for a reduced sentence for his role as a partner with Roger Stone for collusion with Russians during the campaign.

Trump is trying to defuse the new scandal over his daughter Ivanka's improper email use by saying it is quite different from what Clinton did with her personal server. This is the classic case of a difference without a distinction, magnified by the fact that she should have known better.

The "invading" immigrant caravan has finally reached the US border on Sunday. *Fox News* describes it as "a mob containing some bad characters." Trump has stated that they will not be allowed to cross over the border until the court approves asylum for each individual. Mexico is preparing to hold them there while the legal mess is being addressed. The question is, for how long?

Legal scholar and Trump defender Alan Dershowitz was interviewed on TV this weekend and one of his most interesting observations was when he said, "The Mueller report, when it comes out, will be devastating to the President." It sounds like he knows something and is not just making an assumption. What is puzzling about him is that he still thinks that impeachment is not the way to go with this very destructive and dangerous President. How can we afford to wait another two years?

Nov. 26-30

We lead off the week with a new bombshell in the news. It could be major!

The ten-day extension granted by the judge in the Manafort case, for the prosecution to complete their assessment of Manafort's cooperation level, expired today and we now know the reason for that extension request. Shockingly, Manafort breached his plea agreement by lying repeatedly on a variety of subjects, according to Mueller's team of prosecutors. That means he can be given the full sentence for the crimes for which he pled guilty, plus additional time for the new charge of perjury. The only explanation, other than Manafort losing his mind, is that he expects a pardon from the President. If Trump does that, he will put the frosting on the already very large cake of obstruction that he has presented the Mueller team. Manafort denies lying, and wants to proceed with sentencing as if he intends to appeal it. What makes this decision so insane for him is the fact that, even if Trump pardons him for the crimes adjudicated in this D.C. federal court, Paul still faces serious charges of a similar nature in Virginia and New York state courts, where Trump has no pardon power. He will still spend several years behind bars.

George Papadopoulus began serving his two week sentence today.

The Democrats won yet another House seat today, this one in the red state of Utah, bringing their net gain to thirty-nine seats with still one more undecided race to go, in California.

The Enemy Within: A Chronicle of the Trump Administration

As immigrants who have walked several hundred miles to flee for their lives tried to enter the United States to seek asylum, they were *teargassed,* including women and children. A lot of it was caught on tape and will be seen around the world. Another huge black eye for our country, thanks to our clueless President. Of course his racist base will love it.

Russia has escalated tensions in Ukraine, by blocking the strait into the Sea of Azof, which borders both countries, and ramming Ukrainian ships. Trump's response was, "I'm not happy about it." It will be interesting to see what he says to Putin at the upcoming G20 meeting in Argentina this week.

The latest poll shows Trump's *disapproval* rating at its highest point so far, at a historic *sixty* percent.

A British newspaper, *The Guardian,* has come out with the astonishing story that Paul Manafort not only lied to the prosecutors during his period of "cooperation" with the Mueller team, he also held at least three secret meetings with WikiLeaks CEO Julian Assange around the time he was being appointed as the chairman of the Trump campaign for President. The source for this story is unknown, but we know that Mueller has emails between Roger Stone, Jarome Corsi and Assange that confirm communications between the Trump team and WikiLeaks about the emails stolen from Clinton's campaign chairman, John Podesta, and how they could use those emails against Clinton. This is the link between the Russian hacker side of the conspiracy and the Trump side, which belies Trump's continuous claims of "no collusion." This development will prompt Mueller to reveal to the judge what his case is against Manafort, which will give us a snapshot of some of what he will have in his report.

If that is not bad enough news for Trump, we also have a report from the *New York Times* that Manafort kept the Trump legal team in the loop as to what he was being asked about, and what he was telling them at every step along the way. This means that Manafort's "flip" was phony and that he was really serving as a spy for Trump.

This has to be the most blatant case of obstruction, by both Manafort and Trump, that we have seen yet, and no matter what becomes of the Mueller probe, Congressman Adam Shiff assures us that the House will be launching a full investigation of their own into this unprecedented violation. The weird thing about the *Times* story is that the source was Rudy Giuliani, of all people.

Jarome Corsi is being charged with lying to Robert Mueller's team on several subjects, exposed through evidence found on exposed emails to Roger Stone, but he rejected the offer of a plea deal. He was given a draft of three documents (that were passed on to the White House) which spelled out what Mueller has for evidence of lying about communicating with WikiLeaks. This was to give him the option of pleading and cooperating if he wished to. These documents are now public and are another snapshot into what Mueller has.

General Motors has announced the closing of a plant in Michigan and three others across the nation, contrary to the promise Trump made to his supporters during the campaign, and in spite of Trump's huge tax cut which saved the company tons of money.

Hines-Smith easily won reelection over Mike Espy in the Mississippi runoff for Senate. Racism still reigns supreme in that reddest of all the states. In the last still undecided House race, in California, the Democrat has moved ahead. When that one finally ends, the Democrats will have gained a total of *forty* House seats. It really was a tsunami, at least in the House of Representatives.

The Enemy Within: A Chronicle of the Trump Administration

And it keeps getting worse for our besieged President. On her show tonight Rachel Maddow again showed us the amazing parallels between the Watergate prosecution and the current Mueller Russia investigation. The charges, evidence and probable outcome are a mirror image of each other, especially in the area of obstruction, except that in Trump's case the evidence for that crime is much more open, public and egregious.

For example, today Trump answered a reporter's question about a pardon for Manafort with the following statement: "I have not taken it off the table." This statement alone provides a case for obstruction *and bribery.* Rachel's guest, Benjamin Wittes, Editor-in-Chief of *Lawfare*, ticked off several episodes which mirror the charges that went into the articles of impeachment against Nixon. No one in the Nixon administration ever dared to mention the word "pardon" because they knew how toxic it was.

With the new revelation yesterday about Manafort's double dealing involving passing information about his talks with the Mueller team on to the White House, the lawyer on both his team (Kevin Downing) and the President's team may be in deep trouble. No joint-defense privilege exists here because of Manafort's plea agreement.

The number of immigrant children who are being held in that tent city/detention center in Texas, has now swelled to more than twenty-three hundred and is continuing to grow. In addition to the problems of little schooling opportunity, poor health-care, and almost non-existent legal representation, they are being supervised by a staff that has inadequate or no security clearance.

Senate Republicans have again blocked Jeff Flake's bill to protect Mueller, but fifteen state Attorneys General have filed a suit to install a legitimate US AG, which *should* be Rod Rosenstein.

Book Two (09/2018-11/2019

Trump restricted CIA Director Gina Haspel from attending an Intelligence meeting to discuss the Jamal Khashoggi murder. He knew she had the goods on MBS and he did not want to hear it.

Today, fourteen Republican Senators voted against Trump's wishes on a bill pertaining to continuing our support for Saudi Arabia's war on Yemen. They are all angry over Trump's attitude in favor of the Crown Prince in spite of the overwhelming evidence that he had Khashoggi killed.

Nancy Pelosi easily won the vote for the House Speakership—two hundred and three to thirty-two

Donald Trump says he always speaks "from his gut" which he says he believes more than he does most people's brain. He just issued a statement about climate change which is a good example of his "speaking from his gut". Here is the verbatim text of that statement. "One of the problems that a lot of people like myself – we have very high levels of intelligence but we're not necessarily such believers. You look at our air and our water, and it's right now at a *record clean*. But when you look at China and you look at parts of Asia and when you look at South America, and when you look at many other places around the world, including Russia, including – just many other places – the air is incredibly dirty. And when you're talking about an atmosphere, oceans are very small. And it blows over it and it sails over. I mean, we take thousands of tons of garbage off our beaches all the time that comes over from Asia. It just flows right down from the Pacific, it flows, and we say where does this come from? And it takes many people to start off with. Number two, if you go back and you look at articles, they talked about global freezing, they talked about at some point the planets could have freeze to death, then it's going to die of heat exhaustion. There is movement in the atmosphere, there's no question, as to whether or not it's man-made and whether or not the effects that you're talking about are there, I don't see it – not nearly like it is. Do we want clean water? Absolutely. Do we want clean air to breath? Absolutely. You can take a match like this and light a tree trunk when that thing is laying there for more than 14 or 15 months, and it's a massive problem in California."

And that Dear Reader, is an exact reproduction of how it was worded. But it is *far* from the most incoherent batch of idiocy that this self-proclaimed "very intelligent" man has ever blessed us with.

Another day, another bombshell report. The long-awaited shoe named Michael Cohen has finally dropped on President Trump. After scores of hours in conference with the Mueller team, he has agreed to plead guilty to one count of lying to the prosecution about Trump's Moscow Tower project.

This, it turns out, was to be financed by the VTB Bank, one of the largest in Russia and one which was under US sanction. This deal was being negotiated for months, up to and after Trump became the Republican nominee for president. This was in direct contradiction with Trump's oft-repeated claims that he had no business dealings with Russia. Cohen's complete cooperation with Mueller shows no sign of being a false promise and will be far more damaging to Trump than Manafort would have been, even if Paul had been the real deal. He has already exposed Trump's numerous contacts with high-ranking Russians close to Putin, if not with Putin himself. Former US Solicitor General Neil Katyal says that this development is enough, by itself, to begin impeachment proceedings, and this is only the beginning of what Cohen has to offer the prosecution.

One of the most serious impacts of this revelation is the degree to which our President has been compromised by Russia through his illegal activities. This explains his continuous obsequiousness to Putin from the very beginning. Prominent lawyers are now saying that they believe this date will be known in history as the beginning of the end of the Trump presidency. *I believe that the Comey firing was the beginning of the end, and today's date is the start of the final countdown.* Now, Trump has switched from lying about dealings with Moscow to saying that it was during the campaign when "I could do anything I wanted to." Maybe he intends to plead, "Innocent by reason of insanity."

In relation to the above, Buzzfeed News reports that Felix Sater, a former mobster and real-estate developer, was involved with Trump in the Tower negotiations and Trump offered Putin a fifty million dollar penthouse apartment in that tower as an enticement. He confirms that Cohen was deeply involved with this deal from January to June of 2016, during the height of the campaign, working with "individual one" (i.e. Donald Trump).

Trump has arrived in Argentina for the G20 meeting, but he has canceled that planned meeting with Putin. Too awkward at this time I guess. It seems that every time Trump takes one of his trips abroad, all hell breaks loose and not in his favor.

Today closes out a very bad week and a very bad month for our besieged president. There were no new bombs dropped on him today but the news was still pretty bad.

The main topic of discussion continues to be the startling degree to which Trump is compromised by Russia's apparent blackmail ammo that Putin has hanging over his head in relation to his obsession with getting his long-coveted Trump Tower in Moscow, and the crimes he committed to achieve that goal. The Russians are famous for their technique of acquiring what they call "kompromat" on the people they plan to use in some way to their advantage. This strategy was extensively discussed in the Steele dossier, almost two years ago. This coming Tuesday, Mike Flynn's case will become much clearer as he is sentenced, and the judge will delineate the charges against him and the crimes described in some detail, including his communications with Russians about those sanctions they were eager to see relaxed.

Flynn's Deputy National Security Adviser, Kathleen (KT) McFarland, has also been charged with the same "false statement" charge, which she later retracted. It is no coincidence that those Moscow Tower negotiations came to a screeching halt on June 19, 2016, the day that the fact the DNC's server had been hacked by Russia became public. The other aspect of this plot is that Felix Sater and Michael Cohen worked together to expedite the plan to exchange a Moscow Tower for relaxing those sanctions, with a fifty million dollar penthouse suite thrown in as frosting on the cake. In doing so, they worked with one of Putin's chief aides, Dmitri Peskov. They are both in serious hot water *over that action alone*, along with several others.

Robert Mueller has not only obviously changed President Trump from a "subject" to a "target" of his probe, he is also focusing on Donald Trump Jr. and Ivanka for their role in the illegal activity of the Trump Organization and Trump Foundation, and for participating in the quid pro quo of the Moscow Tower deal.

At the G20 meeting, Putin and MBS were all broad smiles as they warmly greeted each other, with the knowledge that they both have the US President by the short hairs.

That midterm is still not quite over. In North Carolina, the House seat race in the ninth district, which was called for the Republican candidate by a mere handful of votes, has not been certified because of voter fraud with the mail-in ballots. There may be a redo of that election. In Montana, Democrat Jon Tester was reelected in spite of a series of four rallies by Trump to support the Republican challenger, and in spite of the fact that Trump had won that state over Clinton by a healthy margin in 2016.

Book Two (09/2018-11/2019)

Conservative editorial writers have started preparing their readers for some upcoming very bad developments surrounding their unorthodox but beloved President.

Ex-President George Herbert Walker Bush passed away today at the age of ninety-four. He was one of the last of the old-guard of moderate, rational, experienced and ethical Republicans, and one of the two, along with John McCain to whom this book is dedicated. He will be missed.

The Enemy Within: A Chronicle of the Trump Administration

Book Two (09/2018-11/2019)

December, 2018

Dec. 1-2

This weekend, as we start the last month of 2018, Roger Stone appeared several times on TV trying to explain his inconsistent communications, during the Presidential campaign, about the WikiLeaks dump of emails to hurt Clinton. The more he talks about it, the more confused he seems and the guiltier he appears. He knows that Mueller is closing in on him and he is panicking, knowing his emails can hang him.

The Associated Press reports that James Comey will testify before the House Intelligence Committee on this coming Friday. It will not be a public hearing, as Comey would like, but at least they will release a full transcript of it afterward. It should be both interesting and revealing.

Trump and China's leader, President Xi, met for two hours in Argentina about the trade/tariff problem. Trump came away claiming that they made a *huge* deal that will greatly benefit both countries. As usual, he was either very confused about what they agreed to, or he was just plain lying again. The Chinese don't know what he is talking about, and the US officials who were attending the meeting say that the most that was agreed upon was a ninety day truce and hold on tariffs, while they continue to negotiate. In other words, they are right back where they started before Trump began his dangerous tariff war.

Today, the Mueller report will begin to be revealed, to some extent, and at least a large portion of the country's voting public, who have not been paying as close attention as they should, could be in for a big dose of reality. Meanwhile, Trump continues to shoot himself in the head every time he opens his mouth.

The Enemy Within: A Chronicle of the Trump Administration

Our panicked President is desperately lashing out at Robert Mueller as the Special Prosecutor prepares a new major development, according to people close to his office. Trump obviously is very apprehensive about what Cohen is telling the Mueller team.

He has stated in public to reporters that Cohen and his wife should both be jailed, which is the crime of witness-tampering by our president.

As far as the loss of Manafort's cooperation is concerned, Mueller has Gates' and Flynn's information on the same subjects, so he doesn't really need Manafort. Trump's latest public crime was a tweet in which he revealed that Manafort made the following self-incriminating statement: "I will never testify against Trump." This is a blatant attempt to pressure and influence the witnesses in an ongoing investigation—an impeachable crime, one of the articles used against Nixon in Watergate.

A filing has just been released pertaining to Michael Cohen's plea agreement which will detail his level of cooperation with the Mueller probe. When it becomes public, in the near future, it will go a long way toward revealing what Mueller has on the President. There will be a similar release tomorrow, as mentioned last week, pertaining to Mike Flynn's case, and another one this coming Friday as to Cohen. *Yahoo News* reports that a memo is coming out about the Manafort case, which will be released to the public. They also say that they believe that Mueller is preparing for "the end game" in the Russia investigation.

Tonight, Rachel Maddow told us about a Miami Harald report about Labor Secretary Alex Acosta's very questionable deal he gave to serial child-molester Julian Epstein a decade ago when Acosta was a Miami prosecutor. He worked with a political consultant named McCrea Dowling, who was running a ballot stealing scheme for years in that county. Epstein served a mere thirteen months in a "country-club" prison in West Palm Beach. He deserved many years behind bars. He was also given a "no-prosecution" agreement. Acosta in being sued by several of Acosta's victims, who will shortly get their day in court. Acosta is likely to be the next of the swamp creatures to leave the Trump cabinet. Another example of Trump's "best people".

The outgoing Wisconsin Republicans are doing their best to strip the incoming Democratic Governor of as much power as they can in the few days they have left, especially in the area of voter's rights, which they know is what cost them the Governor race.

Late this evening the sentencing memo for Michael Flynn was released to the public, and in spite of numerous redactions was quite educational as to where the Mueller investigation stands at this point. Mueller is recommending to the judge that, because of Flynn's "substantial cooperation", he should receive little or no jail time. The memo lists *nineteen* separate interviews with Flynn in which he provided very useful information about three investigations, including one "criminal" probe. The redacted areas themselves are a sign that the subjects related to those blacked out areas are still under investigation. One has to wonder if this will do any good if Whitaker receives an *un-redacted* version that he can pass on to Trump. The amount of redactions are an indication that Robert Mueller has a high degree of confidence that he is not about to be reined-in any time soon by Whitaker. They work in the same organization, so he should know.

The recommendation for a light sentence for Flynn should serve as an encouragement to others who are under the gun, to follow his example rather than do what Paul Manafort did. Trump should have taken Obama's advice, during their transition meeting, not to hire Flynn for *anything* because he was toxic. One question *not* answered by this release is, why did Flynn feel that he had to lie for this President? Several people close to Trump, and Trump himself, should be very concerned.

Some Republican Senators, especially Lindsey Graham, say that after talking with our Intelligence Officials they are convinced that the Saudi Crown Prince is definitely guilty of having Khashoggi killed, and should be condemned by all decent countries, including the USA. Perhaps they have started breaking away from Trump.

Bill Priestap, who is the current Assistant Director of the bureau's counter-intelligence division, announced that he will be leaving the post shortly, making him the *eighth* high-ranking person to leave the FBI since Trump took office.

When he was promoted to his current post, he was leading the original investigation into Russian interference in the 2016 election before the appointment of the Special Prosecutor. An intriguing development.

The Dow plunged almost eight hundred points on the news that Trump's announcement about a "huge trade deal" with China was just blowing smoke.

The main event today was the state funeral for the forty-first President of the United States, George Herbert Walker Bush. It was an impressive but solemn affair, attended not only by President Bush, but by all the living ex-presidents and their wives. The eulogies were very touching and sprinkled with considerable humor. They were also laced with quite a bit of not-so-subtle comparisons being diplomatically drawn by the speakers, between the character and accomplishments of the *deceased* leader, and the *current* one. Trump might have been wishing he had been banned from this event like he was from John McCain's. He looked very uncomfortable sitting in the first seat on an aisle, with his wife to his left, followed by Barack and Michelle Obama, Bill and Hillary Clinton and Jimmy and Rosalynn Carter. He may well have been pondering what his own future funeral would look and sound like, given the way his presidency is going.

It was a bit unusual, to hear a one-term president who was soundly beaten in his re-election bid by newcomer Bill Clinton, (for two very strong reasons) so roundly and effusively being lauded for his character and shining example of what a president should be. After voting for him the first time, I and a large segment of the country turned on him because of: A. breaking his promise of "no new taxes", which adversely affected the economy, and; B. ending the Gulf War to push Saddam Hussain out of Kuwait and depose him, by prematurely withdrawing US forces.

This left Saddam in power and left it to his son to go in and finish the job. But these were mistakes in judgement of the type all presidents are prone to make in the most difficult job in the world. They were political misjudgments, not character flaws that demean us as a nation in the eyes of the world.

Maria Butina, the Russian agent who is now in jail in the US, and the one who, at a press conference during the campaign, asked Donald Trump how he felt about the sanctions on Russia that Obama had imposed, and where Trump answered, "I don't think we need sanctions," is now negotiating a plea deal with the prosecution. This could be another huge headache for Trump.

Donald Jr. and Kushner are in severe jeopardy from Butina and the other cooperators as well. Roger Stone and Rudy Giuliani both said that "we don't know that Flynn has testified against the President." They are whistling past the graveyard. Why would Mueller recommend a light sentence for Flynn if he did not deliver the goods? And Flynn is far from the last axe to fall. We still have the Manafort sentencing memo coming out this Friday, but Cohen will be the heaviest blow of all.

Six Senators (three Republicans and three Democrats) have introduced a bill condemning the Saudi Crown Prince for the murder of Khashoggi, contradicting Trump, General Mattis and Secretary Pompeo, who are still trying to cast doubt on MBS's guilt.

In North Carolina's ninth district, the Mark Harris campaign officials were served subpoenas for their role in the plot to collect and falsify hundreds of absentee ballots. They worked with a consulting company that hired dozens of people to go to the homes of voters who had requested one, and collected them from those unsuspecting voters who thought these people were just saving them some time and a postage stamp. These ballots then turned into votes for Harris. This scheme had also been used in the primary and in fact had been going on for years. It looks more and more like that election will have to be redone.

The Washington Post reports that the Saudi Arabian government paid Donald Trump $270,000 for 500 rooms at one of his towers, after the election. This is *another* in-plain-sight violation of the Constitution's emoluments clause. What other foreign powers are paying our President for favors, we might reasonably ask?

Three days ago a story broke about voter fraud in the ninth district of North Carolina. We can now report that a criminal investigation has been opened in the case. Democrat House candidate Dan McCready has retracted his concession that he made on election eve when he seemed to have lost to Republican Mark Harris by a little over nine hundred votes. McCrea Dowling, that political hack that the Harris campaign hired to use his tried-and-true ballot-stealing scheme to help Harris win his House seat, had--back in the 2016 race for Governor of the state-- launched a suit against the Democrats for voter fraud, *while he was in the midst of employing the same ballot-stealing tactic that he repeated in the recent midterm.* During that trial, he is on record "confessing" to what he does to gather absentee ballots as a matter of course, like there is nothing wrong with it. Apparently, this district of North

Book Two (09/2018-11/2019)

Carolina has been a cesspool of political corruption for decades. McCrea was a guest on Rachel Maddow's show tonight and called on Harris to end his silence on this fiasco. A decision to redo the election for this seat has not yet been made, but it is heading that way.

The *New York Times* reports that for some time now, Donald Trump has been employing an undocumented alien as a maid at his home in Bedminster, New Jersey, the location of one of Trumps' favorite golf clubs. Trump claims that he was not aware of it. This is the second such case that has been exposed in this location.

As a result of Trump's trade war with China, the trade deficit that the US is now facing is at an all-time high. Because of his policies, a recession is predicted by economic experts to hit the US before the 2020 election.

Democrat Senator Richard Blumenthal has filed a lawsuit against the President for violations of the emoluments clause--a case he and others have been planning since October. Also, attorneys from Washington, D.C. and Maryland issued subpoenas to *thirteen* Trump business entities on Tuesday, December 4.

Democrat Senator Amy Klobuchar, of the Senate Judiciary Committee, said on Rachel's show tonight that they are asking the Justice Department where things stand in regard to Matt Whitaker's conflicts of interest vis-à-vis the Mueller investigation. So far, they have seen no response. She also said that the Acosta/Epstein scandal should be thoroughly investigated. This woman is considered to be a probable presidential candidate in 2020.

In an interview with *Atlantic* magazine, Rudy Giuliani said, in answer to a question about Trump's written answers to

Mueller's questions on collusion, "Answering those questions was a nightmare. It took him about three weeks to do what would normally take two days." He also claimed that they have abandoned any plan to submit a rebuttal report to the anticipated Mueller report. But there are conflicting statements on that score. We will have to wait and see. Any rebuttal will almost certainly only add to the mountain of guilt.

Trump's lawyers have resumed talks with the Mueller team. What about? Maybe just to follow up and clarify his answers.

The man now under consideration for US Attorney General is a former AG under George H. W. Bush named William Barr, who is being described as a more qualified version of Matt Whitaker. He has spoken out negatively about the Mueller probe almost as much as Whitaker has. With his background he will probably be confirmed by the Senate with little problem.

Tomorrow's two memo releases should be even more explosive than Flynn's on Tuesday, especially the one regarding Michael Cohen. Stay tuned. It's getting more interesting by the day.

Trump has ramped up his very ill-advised and downright insane Tweet attacks on Mueller and his whole "illegal" probe. He continues to sound guilty and terrified.

On this sixty-seventh anniversary of the Japanese attack on Pearl Harbor, a few "bombs" landed on Donald Trump and company. Another very bad week for our increasingly panicked president.

Three separate legal memorandums were filed today pertaining to the Trump administration. Two involved Michael Cohen--one from the southern district of New York state, and one from the Mueller team of prosecutors. The third spelled out the ways in which Paul Manafort violated his agreement of cooperation with the Mueller team as part of his guilty plea. All were quite damaging to the President, but the Cohen filing was the most devastating. One of the most interesting takeaways was the introduction, in the New York memo, of a new synonym for the word "collusion" or "conspiracy". Many of the communications revealed in these memos between the Russians and members of the Trump campaign involved the word "synergy" as they described the plans about exchanging relaxing sanctions for help in getting Trump elected. If any evidence was needed to make the connection between the two parties involved in the Russian-Trump conspiracy to steal the election (and it was not even needed) this memo certainly provided it.

The further confirmation of Trump's direction of Cohen in the hush-money payments was the frosting on the cake of the case for treasonous conspiracy. The New York memo goes so far as saying, "Individual 1 (i.e. Trump) has *committed felonies*."

But the most important revelation was the number of provable communications between the Trump team and multiple Russians from 2015 through early 2018. There is more than enough now, even without the redacted information, to convict Trump of several crimes if he were not the POTUS, and certainly enough to proceed with a bill of impeachment early in January. And that is without even getting into the question of the many episodes of obstruction of justice.

All this comes in spite of the fact the Cohen's level of cooperation so far has been much less than expected. This could change after his sentence is announced, especially the one from the New York court, where the prosecutors have recommended a very stiff penalty. Mueller has been relatively quiet about Cohen in comparison with New York. He may feel he is getting more out of Cohen than they have. It is interesting that the New York memo is forty pages long and blistering, calling for years in prison, while Mueller's memo is a mere seven pages which indicate that Cohen provided *useful information* about contacts (seven meetings) with the Russians and others in the Trump team, particularly about the Trump Tower Moscow project. These two memos sound like were referring to two different men.

It seems clear that the Mueller report will address at least three crimes committed by the President: A. Campaign finance law violations (hush-money); B. Conspiracy with Russia to sway the election result; C. Obstruction of justice. I believe there will be several more added to this list, such as tax fraud, bank fraud and emoluments violations. In the face of all this damaging evidence, Trump tweets, "Totally clears the President. Thank you." Totally *delusional*—again.

The only remaining question about the impeachment of this president is: will at least twenty Republicans have the incentive or the courage to stand up and do what is right for the sake of the country (and maybe save their own career in the process)?

In the D. C. (Mueller) memo pertaining to Paul Manafort, they listed five areas in which he lied to the prosecutors. Here is that list:
A. interactions with Konstantin Kilimnik (Russian Ambassador); B. Kilimnik's participation in obstruction; C. wire transfer to a firm working for Manafort; D. info about another DOJ investigation (Mueller's?); E. contact with administration officials. But in spite of his lies, he apparently did provide some useful data to Mueller. The sixteen page memo on Manafort listed, as part of his plea violations, an actual meeting with Ambassador Kilimnik.

Former Secretary of State Rex Tillerson was interviewed by Bob Schieffer on *Face the Nation*. Tillerson was forthright in his description of how frustrating it was to try to control and guide the President. Afterward, Trump responded to Rex's comments by saying, "He is dump as a rock and lazy as hell." Always the counter-puncher!

Chief-of-staff John Kelly has been called to answer questions by Robert Mueller. This news comes as Trump announces that Kelly will be leaving has post at the White House at the end of this month/year. It will be very interesting to hear what Kelly has to say after he is free of that unenviable job. Remember, this is a man who called Trump an idiot *while* he was working for him.

According to *The New York Times,* the Saudis have been cultivating Jared Kushner for years. He is now their strongest advocate and defender in the Khashoggi case. He and Prince MBS talk by phone frequently. Kushner's indictment seems to be imminent, along with several others.

Soon-to-be ex-Speaker Paul Ryan and other Republicans are questioning the late results of California House races that all went to the Democrats, implying some sort of voter fraud--all the while saying absolutely nothing about the *proven* fraud that has been uncovered in North Carolina and North Dakota.

Jerry Nadler, the soon-to-be Chairman of the House Judiciary Committee, was on CNN Sunday and said that they plan to investigate whether Donald Trump's offenses rise to the level of impeachment.
Most of the other Democrats interviewed talked in terms of *when,* not *whether,* impeachment will happen. Nadler also expressed his opinion that a sitting president *is* indictable, and that Trump will face charges, if not while president, then after he leaves the office.

Florida's Republican Senator, Marco Rubio, was also on CNN speaking out strongly against letting MBS skate on the Khashoggi murder. He also spoke out against the election officials in North Carolina's ninth district and Harris's backers who paid for corrupt vote stealing. He may be a minority of one among Florida politicians.

James Comey, whose firing by Trump led to the appointment of Special Prosecutor Robert Mueller, was brought in to testify again to the House Judiciary Committee in a closed session, and his testimony took up 253 pages of text. You can bet that he had plenty to say about the status of Mueller's probe, especially as it pertains to Trump. My problem with Comey is that in one sentence he says that every American should use every breath to oust Trump from office, and in the next sentence he favors voting him out rather than impeaching him. Why does he advocate giving this dangerous president two more years to continue his ruinous policies and decisions?

This Saturday evening I sat and watched about fifteen minutes of *Watter's World,* with host Jerry Watters, on *Fox.* He and his three cohorts were discussing the merits of the Mueller investigation in terms that made my stomach churn. Their gross misrepresentations of who Mueller is, and what he has for evidence, which we *know* about, were mind-blowing. It left me puzzled—are they really that blind/stupid, or are they really that corrupt/dishonest? Either way, it will be interesting to see what they have to say after the axe falls on their favorite president.

On Sunday I watched a rerun of a March episode of *Law and Order SVU,* which I had somehow missed when it was first shown. The special victim in this story was a ten-year-old girl from Guatemala who had been ripped away from her mother after they crossed our southern border.

The girl was then sent off to New York City while the mother was held in a Texas detention center waiting for her asylum petition to be adjudicated. In an effort to bring attention to the unfairness of this inhumane "no tolerance" policy that was concocted by Trump aide Stephen Miller and backed by AG Sessions and Trump, SVU's star Olivia Benson arrested the federal agent who had taken the girl and brought her to New York. She charged him with kidnapping. After a complicated legal battle, and getting herself in hot water over this action, Olivia was able to use her contacts and persistence to get the girl and her mother reunited. The scene at the end of the program was heart-wrenching, as they released the girl from the huge cage full of scores of other kids, who watched longingly as one of them was rejoined with her mother.

With all the other turmoil going on surrounding this hideous administration, this ongoing shameful catastrophe has been eclipsed and, for most of us, put out of our minds. As I watched, I was thinking that Trump should be forced to watch this episode, even though it would probably have little, if any, impact on his so-called heart.

Dec. 10-16

Trump's planned replacement for departing John Kelly *was* Nick Ayers, the Chief-of-Staff for Vice President Pence. But Ayers threw him a big curveball and told the President that he intended to return to civilian life next year. Trump found this very humiliating and he is pissed! He is also having a very tough time finding a plan B, that he was not prepared for.

The man Trump wants to appoint as US Attorney General, William Barr, was previously asked by Trump to be his defense attorney, but Barr was not interested in the job. He was aiming a little higher I guess, and it looks like he is going to get it. It is interesting to note that Barr formerly worked with Robert Mueller at the Department of Justice.

Trump now has yet another flipping witness that will be very dangerous to him. Maria Butina has pled guilty and agreed to "cooperate fully" with federal prosecutors. She is the *one* Russian that we have in custody. More information has now been revealed about her interactions with the NRA and its negotiations with the Russians during the 2016 campaign. One startling fact is that the NRA contributed $30 million to the Trump campaign at a time when they were relatively cash-poor. This was *triple* the amount that they provided to the Romney campaign in 2012. They were also conducting illegal coordination with the Trump campaign, tied to their efforts to support a gun-rights group in Russia, led by Russian politician Aleksandr Torshin. The FBI was investigating this issue, including Butina, which led to her arrest. Torshin has suddenly "retired." Butina's boyfriend, Paul Erickson, is now a target of the FBI for his involvement as a foreign agent.

Talk of impeachment is now rampant on all TV news channels. Most of it centers on the crime of campaign finance violations in the form of the hush money payments. But it is now pretty obvious that this felony is the *least serious* of the crimes that Mueller will accuse him of when he delivers his report. Here's what I predict we will see, in the order of most to least serious: A. Conspiracy/treason with Russia in trading the reduction of sanctions for help in getting elected; B. Obstruction of justice to cover up the conspiracy; C. Witness tampering; D. Tax and bank fraud; E. Money laundering; F. Campaign finance violations; G. emoluments violations.

In Comey's recent Congressional testimony, he equated the Trump campaign's plot with Russia to effect the election and undermine our democracy, to previous acts of treason in our history. The *Daily Beast* believes that Cohen's sentencing memo shows that between the cooperation of Flynn, Manafort, Gates, Cohen, and now, Butina, Mueller has the proof of Trump's "collusion". The *Washington Post* reports that Russians interacted with at least fourteen members of the Trump team during both the campaign and the transition period. The *New York Times* says that the Southern District of New York could subpoena Trump's testimony while he is in office. Legal expert Lawrence Tribe opines that Trump can indeed be indicted regardless of any pardon by VP Pence.

Book Two (09/2018-11/2019)

Even if prosecutors decide to wait until the President is out of office to indict, he will be very tempted to follow Nixon's lead and resign in exchange for clemency.

Forty-four former Senators have presented a letter to the current Senators calling upon them to defend our Democracy as the Mueller probe closes in. This may have the biggest impact of all on those Republican holdouts.

Trump's latest juvenile tweet rants included the alternate-reality claim that the latest memo revelations "contain no smocking (sic) gun." An amazing conclusion to draw in the face of all the damaging data in these memos. After all the ridicule he has generated by his misspellings and grammar, you would think that he would do a little proofreading—but not this narcissist.

President Trump and Vice President Pence held a public and televised conference with Democrats Nancy Pelosi and Chuck Schumer today to discuss the upcoming budget crisis and try to prevent a shutdown of the government on December 21, which would put millions of government employees out of work just before Christmas. It was a huge mistake on Trump's part to make it so public because it was an optics disaster. First of all, Pence sat there throughout the meeting like a robot, never saying a single word. But he still came off much better than Trump, who was the usual petulant childish clown, as he kept repeating his lies about the border wall and threatening to close our government down if he did not get the funding ($5 billion) toward building it.

The contrast between his two opponents' demeanor and comments, and Trump's, was all too obvious to anyone on either side of the issue. They politely tried to point out the fallacy of his statements on how much of the wall was already built (zero) and how effective it has been (crossings have been reducing gradually for years). He heard none of it, while he

The Enemy Within: A Chronicle of the Trump Administration

clambered on in his own delusional version of reality. Several times he repeated that "I am proud to shut down the government over the wall," (if he doesn't get his way).

Afterward, Nancy observed that "The wall is like a manhood thing with him." Later in the day, Leon Panetta, whose former posts included the Director of the Office of Budget Management, said that "this meeting's performance was a classic example of how *not* to govern a country."

Questions that have long puzzled reporters, and anyone closely following the Trump/Russia developments, include the following: (A) Why did the Trump administration wait eighteen days after Sally Yates gave her testimony to Congress, which included a warning about Michael Flynn's illegal involvement with Russians, both before and during the Trump campaign, before Trump finally fired him?; (B) Why did Trump ask Comey and Dan Coats to go easy on Flynn because "he's a good guy"? (C) Why did Flynn feel it was necessary to lie to the FBI about talking to the Russians about sanctions, which *could* have been a perfectly normal discussion of policy? All the lies indicate that the discussions were of an inappropriate if not illegal nature, such as a quid pro quo deal with Russia. Tonight, Rachel Maddow gave us some insight into the answers of those questions.

One year ago the *New York Times* exposed emails that prove that Mike Flynn communicated about his contacts with Russians and the subjects of those contacts, with several other members of the Trump team. This included his own son, as well as Reince Priebus, Steve Bannon, Sean Spicer and M. C. McFarland, all of whom also lied about those contacts. They knew that the contacts were devastatingly improper.

Flynn was sentenced to one year of probation, one year of community service and a modest fine. This extremely light sentence indicates how satisfied Mueller and the judge were with his level of cooperation.

Book Two (09/2018-11/2019)

Former Senator from Connecticut Chris Dodd was one of the drafters of yesterday's memo to the current senators, about Trump's failure to protect our democracy. He was a guest on Brian William's news show, *The Eleventh Hour,* to discuss how that letter came about. He said, "We are very worried about the potential emoluments issue." Why did it take two years before someone became concerned about what has been going on since day one of this administration?

Michael Cohen was today sentenced to three years in a New Jersey prison, which was light, considering how severe the New York sentencing memo was worded. Tonight, Rachel Maddow was able to show us large chunks of Cohen's address to the court before he was sentenced. He expressed a sincere sense of shame and regret for his actions and said that he acted out a sense of "blind loyalty"-- meaning, of course, to Donald Trump. In spite of the assistance Cohen provided to the New York prosecutors, the judge felt that Cohen was holding something back, so sentence was immediately pronounced when he was finished addressing the judge.

To the three years of incarceration, which will begin on March 3, 2019, he received a year of supervised probation and a $50,000 fine. Lanny Davis, Cohen's former lawyer, was a guest on Maddow's show tonight and said that Cohen wants to tell America everything he knows about Trump's and his family's participation in all sorts of crimes, and will do so as soon as Mueller issues his report and the opportunity presents itself. The many audio recordings that the raids on his home and offices produced weeks ago will provide much corroboration to what Cohen has given them verbally on the "core issue" of collusion, so Trump's labelling him as a proven liar will not have the desired effect.

The New York State Attorney General is pursuing the investigation into the Trump family for their potentially illegal real estate holdings, the June Trump Tower meeting with the

Russian lawyer and emolument violations. The Trump Organization and its CFO, Allen Weisselberg, and the entire Trump family are in legal jeopardy with Robert Mueller for the same crimes. The organization repaid Michael Cohen much more than the $130,000 that he paid Stormy Daniels in hush money, to try to ensure that the truth would not come out. We should expect indictments to be issued for *all* concerned.

To make matters even worse for the Trump family, the New York prosecutors have granted immunity to *American Media Incorporated*, and its founder, David Pecker, in exchange for their cooperation and full disclosure of everything, including dirt that Pecker has been keeping in his safe for years. More corroboration for Cohen.

Legal scholars have offered that there may be an exception made to the untested "rule" that a sitting president cannot be indicted. That exception would be the case where his crimes helped get him elected to the office which now protects him. There is also the danger that the statute of limitations could run out before that accused president left office, thus allowing him (or her) to escape justice. This problem needs to be resolved by clear-cut legislation so this dilemma never crops up again.

Senator Orrin Hatch, Republican from Utah, when asked by reporters to comment on the latest Trump legal problems said, "I don't care, he's doing a good job as president." That's how low the Republican Party has sunk under Donald Trump.

The Saudi war on Yemen has been killing and starving men, women and children by the millions for years, *with our help*. Our government continues to support the Saudis with arms shipments, simply because they help us resist the Iranians. Trump has the additional incentive of his very lucrative personal deals with them. Congress is now, *finally*, preparing to pass legislation to halt our financial aid.

Book Two (09/2018-11/2019)

The above mentioned Yemen-war bill was passed by the Senate today by a vote of 56 to 41, in spite of the complication of being attached to a controversial farm bill. The problem is that Trump will almost certainly veto it.

NBC News reports that there is now proof that Donald Trump was in the room with Cohen and David Pecker when hush-money payments and the purpose for them were discussed. Trump is now trying to dodge the problem by claiming that "Cohen should have stopped me because he's the lawyer."

He is apparently going to plead ignorance of the law, as his best (only) defense. But that does not hold up in view of all his attempts to hide the facts.

Marina Butina has now pled guilty to being an agent of a foreign government and conspiring with the Trump campaign for that government, and has agreed to fully cooperate with federal prosecutors. The Russian link with the campaign confirmed by a Russian. She may be deported back to Russia at some point when this is all over, but she'd better avoid that at all costs if she values her life. Her boyfriend, Paul Erikson, is mentioned as a co-conspirator, working with Russian, Alex Torshin, to establish a very private back-channel between Republicans and Moscow.

Trump's inauguration Committee took in 107 million dollars, *double* that of any previous such affair. No accounting has been made as to what happened to the huge amount of *unspent* money, as Rachel Maddow has been pointing out for months. Federal prosecutors are now (finally) seeking answers to the questions about it, such as who contributed, how much, and where did the money go? Ivanka Trump has been implicated because she played a major role in the planning and oversight of the committee that raised and controlled the funds. This included negotiating the price for the use of Trump properties during the days surrounding the "gala event."

The Enemy Within: A Chronicle of the Trump Administration

Insiders at the White House say that Jared Kushner is a leading candidate for Trump's new Chief-of-Staff. Trump knows he wouldn't have to hear very many "no's" from *this* pick.

A seven-year-old migrant girl died of dehydration and exhaustion while in custody in a Texas detainment camp. This will require investigation.

We should all prepare for the possibility of a president named Nancy Pelosi, because there is a good chance that VP Pence will not escape indictment in this mess before it is over.

Julian Castro, Obama's HUD Secretary, is the first Democrat to declare his intention to run for president in 2020. There will be a *lot* of others.

Trump's Director of the Office of Management and Budget (OMB), Mick Mulvaney, has been selected to replace John Kelly as his Chief-of-Staff, but Mulvaney insisted that it be in an "acting" capacity so he could exit whenever he felt the need. Smart! Trump was frustrated and desperate to find someone to fill that role, because he was getting embarrassed by all the turn-downs for the position. Nobody wanted the useless and thankless job. I wonder if Trump was aware that, in the final stage of the Presidential campaign, Mulvaney referred to Trump as "a terrible human being."

A Trump super-PAC has spurred yet another investigation, for improper campaign donations from foreign entities. The *Washington Post* report read as follows: "The inquiry focuses on whether people from Middle Eastern nations – including Qatar, Saudi Arabia and the United Arab Emirates – used straw donors to disguise their donations…" This project was *also* under the direction of Ivanka Trump.

Book Two (09/2018-11/2019)

Michael Cohen was interviewed by George Stephanopoulos on *Good Morning America* today. He spoke very forthrightly and openly in spelling out how Donald Trump directed the hush-money payments for the express purpose of protecting his presidential campaign, and he was fully aware that it was wrong. He said in effect, "Trump's accusations that I am lying won't hold up because Mueller has more than ample corroboration." He is referring, not only to Cohen's taped conversations, but to all the testimony from other "flippers."

A former KGB Russian spy name Jack Barsky, now residing in the US, was a guest on Bryan Williams *Eleventh Hour* tonight and expressed how Putin viewed the Trump presidential campaign team. They were considered to be "inviting and easy targets for compromising." No kidding?

Trump is trying to equate his hush-money payments to the case of the John Edwards scandal in 2012, for which he paid a political price, but not a legal one, but there is *very little* comparison to be made between the two cases. Rudy Giuliani says Trump's crimes are not "big", and therefore not grounds for impeachment. Rudy, do you really think Mueller and team, or the rest of the country are going to buy that assessment?

A federal judge in Texas today declared the Affordable Care Act (Obamacare) *unconstitutional,* on the basis of the removal of the mandate requiring coverage. It will remain in place pending appeal. This is another huge black eye for the Republican Party that repeatedly, in the lead-up to the midterm election, promised to maintain pre-existing conditions protection. Any bets on how far that judge's ruling will fly?

Secretary of the Interior Ryan Zinke will be the next swamp creature to be drained from the Trump swamp of corruption. He will be leaving at the end of the month, under a cloud of *fifteen* inquiries into *ethics* violations. He also leaves facing a *criminal*

The Enemy Within: A Chronicle of the Trump Administration

investigation. He is the *thirty-sixth* Trump administration member to leave this collection of "the best people."

The father of the migrant seven-year-old girl who died under US care (mentioned above), says he has no issues with how his daughter was treated by the border patrol personnel. Something smells fishy here. Was he bought off? We know one thing for certain--the Trump policies have forced refugees to take desperate and dangerous measures to get into our country.

Wisconsin outgoing Governor Scott Walker succeeded in getting his bill passed that will restrict the powers of the incoming Democratic governor and restrict voters' rights. Florida and Michigan are trying to do the same type of thing. All of them are ignoring the will of the people who voted against them.

As he celebrated the Texas judge's ruling against Obamacare, Trump proclaimed, "We are going to get very good health care." Legal scholars are saying, "...the ruling is insane."

Now that the Senate has voted to end support for the Saudi-Yemen war, the pressure is mounting for Trump to end arms shipments and press the Saudis.

Trump's anxiety over Cohen's testimony against him prompted his latest Tweet on the subject to include the labeling of Cohen as "a rat." This is the type of Mob-speak that James Comey described several months ago in his book and in his testimony to Congress.

Dec. 17-23

As we begin the last week before Christmas, there is very little Christmas cheer in our White House. Here are a few of their major concerns.

Book Two (09/2018-11/2019)

There is now a total of *thirty-seven* investigations into Donald Trump's various enterprises, and more to come in the near future as the Democrats take control of the House of Representatives.

The FBI has released a key memo, known as a 302 form, pertaining to the Mike Flynn sentencing. Although redacted, it is revealing about the charges against him that go way beyond his lying. In addition to his contacts with Russian Ambassador Kislyac about sanctions, he was also being *bribed* to the tune of a half million dollars for his help in trying to extradite Turkish government dissident M. F. Gulen, now residing in Pennsylvania, whom the Turkish president has been trying to get his hands on for years. Flynn completely changed his attitude about Gulen to accept this bribe.

Two of Flynn's contacts and co-conspirators in this deal have been indicted. The one who is still in the United States has been arrested. He is a former member of the Trump transition team named B. R. Kian. Trump is still considering handing over Gulen to the Turks. Flynn is scheduled to be sentenced tomorrow. Trump, Pence, attorney Don McGahn and Reince Priebus *all* knew that Flynn was under FBI investigation during the transition period, as they were warned about him by Obama, and he was *never-the-less* given the post of National Security Advisor. We *still* don't know why Flynn et al lied so repetitively about these subjects.

There is proof that Russian troll groups made thousands of robo-calls for the purpose of suppressing the black vote by feeding false information. These are the same groups that helped Trump get elected and have also been attacking Robert Mueller in their efforts to protect him and protect their investment, using fake social media accounts. The GOP, aided by Russia, has made black voter suppression their number one priority for years. It was successful in the 2016 election, but not so much this year. Well-known media commentator Malcolm

The Enemy Within: A Chronicle of the Trump Administration

Nance says that "the Russians now *own* the minds of fully one third of the American population."

The local director of the segment of Homeland Security in charge of the custody of those thousands of children incarcerated in the Texas camps says that 1300 children have sponsors lined up to take custody of them as soon as the necessary paperwork is completed. But it is being held up by the Trump administration, part of the policy of cruelty to dissuade migrants.

There is a *new* wrinkle in the border policy. All migrants who cross the border are now being numbered, using black marker on their arm. What's that about?

After James Comey finished his latest round of testimony before Congress, he spoke to reporters and made some interesting comments, including that Trump has "a complete disregard for the rule of law" and that the Republicans "…have a shameful lack of concern about it."

Tennessee Senator Lamar Alexander says he will not seek reelection. Maybe he will start a trend similar to the one that we saw in the House. This frees them to be a voice of opposition against Trump that is sadly lacking among Senators so far.

There *is* talk in the Senate about the possibility of a primary to select alternatives to Trump for 2020, *if* he is still president then.

The sentencing hearing for Flynn did not go as planned at all. After reading over the un-redacted version of the prosecution memo, the judge decided that the charges against the man were too egregious to warrant the light sentence recommendation made as a reward for his cooperation. He told Flynn that he had "sold out his country" in the deal with the Turkish government to extradite Gulen, the cleric dissident. He gave him the option of going ahead with sentencing today,

Book Two (09/2018-11/2019)

which would involve some prison time, or take a ninety day delay in which he could continue cooperating and perhaps persuade the judge (no promises) to be more lenient. Flynn took the delay.

The most significant thing that came out of this hearing was the grilling that the judge gave him at the outset. The questions he asked and the answers Flynn gave, left no doubt whatsoever that the BS theory Trump and his supporters like *Fox News* were trying to sell, that Flynn was the victim of a perjury trap, was *utter nonsense*.

The first of at least a half-dozen hammer-blows that are going to rain down on Trump and family, landed on them today as the investigation into the Trump Foundation (that phony charity that was really a big Trump piggy bank) broke wide open. The judge in the case called it "a criminal enterprise." The foundation was forced to close and liquidate their few assets. This criminal enterprise is out-of-business and Trump, his three adult children and their Chief Financial Officer David Weisselberg, are in serious legal trouble. So begins the first of the thirty-seven cases ginning up against the President. He is in for a very rough few months.

If we needed any further proof of how dangerous our current president is for the safety of our country and the world, he provided it today.

With the pressure getting unbearable, Trump decided he needed another distraction, so without consulting anyone on his cabinet or anyone at the Pentagon, he announced that the United States was about to withdraw all its forces from Syria, declaring they were no longer needed there because "ISIS has been defeated." No details have been provided and everyone concerned is perplexed and alarmed by this action. Reporters who asked White House staff about it were referred to the Pentagon, while the Pentagon referred them back to the White House.

The Enemy Within: A Chronicle of the Trump Administration

It appears that our leader has gone completely off the rails and is just winging it. This decision came shortly after Trump hung up from a phone call with Turkish President Erdogan, during which he apparently discussed the subject. It also comes right after the Flynn court hearing where Flynn's dirty deal with Turkey was a main topic. While NATO nations are alarmed, the Syrian dictator, the Turkish dictator, Iran, Iraq, and Russia are *delighted* by this news. It leaves our allies, the Kurds, "twisting in the wind", says outgoing Senator Claire McCaskill. This could be Trump's most devastating mistake so far. Even his supporters in Congress won't like this crazy move, made without consultation with *anyone.*

Robert Mueller is asking the House Intel Committee for the transcripts of Roger Stone's testimony before them. This is another indication that he is preparing to charge Stone. He may get those transcripts tomorrow but, if not, he will certainly get them after the Democrats take control in January and Adam Schiff heads that committee.

Because of an accidental release of a memo on the Maria Butina case, we learn that she has been subpoenaed to testify before the D. C. Grand Jury shortly. She has requested that her gag order be removed. The prosecutors are balking at that request because they say it might interfere with an "imminent" criminal litigation. Hmmm.

A sealed document in the Cohen case was placed in a "vault". It must be a *hot* one.

By a bi-partisan vote, the Senate passed a budget bill, which includes *a fraction* of Trump's requested $5 billion for border security, which would keep the government open for a few more weeks. But will Trump sign it?

Book Two (09/2018-11/2019)

The last General, and last voice of reason that might keep some semblance of control over our severely erratic commander-in-chief, has turned in his resignation to Trump in an act of protest over his policies. The announced pullout of Syria was the last straw for "Mad Dog" James Mattis, whose resignation letter made history with its terseness and lack of even a salutary signoff. He is also the first Secretary of Defense to *ever* voluntarily resign. This leaves Secretary of State Pompeo as the only "adult in the room" and he is pretty much of a yes-man to Trump, a very dangerous situation. Mattis will not be leaving until February so Trump has a little time to find a replacement, but that will be a very difficult task under the circumstances, and the person he ultimately chooses will almost certainly be another yes-man.

The Trump government becomes more of an empty shell every day. We have a ship-of-state that in plowing along with no one at the helm.

All national defense experts are saying that "our national security is in serious danger." Putin held a rare press conference in which he expressed his glee over the Syria pullout, then added, "…what about Afghanistan?"

After agreeing to go along with the compromise budget bill, containing one and half billion for border security rather than five billion for a wall, Trump heard from his favorite right wing commentators like Rush Limbaugh and Ann Coulter, and abruptly changed his mind. He now says he will *not* sign to keep the government open, and blames the Democrats for it, after he so firmly declared in his recent pow-wow with Schumer and Pelosi, that he "would be proud to own it." He has painted himself into a corner that will involve his complete humiliation to get himself, and the country, out of his self-inflicted mess.

Trump has suddenly dropped the sanction on Russia's VTB Bank and its main backer, Oleg Deripaska, who was so

The Enemy Within: A Chronicle of the Trump Administration

intimately linked to Paul Manafort and his business dealings with Russia, including the Trump Tower-Moscow deal.

In the face of the Judiciary's Ethics Committee ruling that Matt Whitaker needs to recuse himself from all things related to the Mueller investigation, Whitaker refuses to do so, declaring himself "cleared" of any conflict of interest in the case. Actually, he may be less dangerous to Mueller than William Barr, Trump's choice for an official AG, whose views on the Mueller probe seem even *more* prejudiced than Whitaker's. He has stated that the President can fire anyone he wants, including James Comey, for whatever reason.

The House re-voted on the budget bill and included the five billion that Trump wants, knowing full well that the Senate lacks the votes to pass it and send it on to Trump to sign. The Dow dropped another five hundred points on this development, to its lowest point in fourteen months. Trump has been in "bunker mode" in recent weeks as personal crises continue to mount, according to twenty-seven current and former White House officials. His mental state continues to become more and more a serious concern.

Chuck Schumer has labeled this "the most chaotic week of the most chaotic administration in our history." With a government shutdown imminent at midnight tonight, the House members have adjourned until tomorrow noon and the Senate has gone home for Christmas, all because Trump takes his marching orders from *Fox News* and other extreme right commentators. It is interesting and ironic that Republican Jeb Bush predicted this standoff and its effect back in July of 2016. Trump's new Chief-of-Staff, Mick Mulvaney, is on record saying, "…building a border wall is absurd and childish." How long do you think he will last in this White House? In the face of the shutdown, Congress calls an emergency meeting to discuss the problem of the *labeling of ingredients in cheese*, which they say will affect small businesses.

Book Two (09/2018-11/2019)

Even more than the shutdown, the subject of the repercussions of our pullout from Syria is being discussed today. No one likes the idea of handing an easy victory to dictator Bashar al-Assad. This is seen as the biggest "balance-of-power" blunder in many years.

With the impending departure of James Mattis, the biggest White House concern seems to be, who will control our uncontrollable president? This is now a national emergency, and the staff all know it. Gordon Humphry, the former Republican senator from New Hampshire, says it is time to start considering the twenty-fifth amendment solution.

Trump has repeatedly lashed out at Whitaker about his lack of action in regard to all the bad news about his (Trump's) legal problems that are stacking up by the day. Of course, there is only one thing that Whitaker *could* do, and that is to interfere with the Mueller probe. This would be fatal for both Whitaker and Trump at this stage, and Whitaker knows it. Merely pressuring him on it is adding to the long list of obstruction evidence. But Trump even expects Whitaker to help him with the Southern District of New York prosecutors, over which he has no influence.

The judge in the Maria Butina case granted her request and lifted the gag order. Maybe we are about to hear more interesting information from her.

The numbers being written on the arms of migrants, we have been told, is for the purpose of sequencing them for their turn at processing through the asylum court, while they are waiting on the Mexico side of the border. Finally, a bit of organization in the system, distasteful though it may be.

The Enemy Within: A Chronicle of the Trump Administration

The Supreme Court voted to block Trump's ban on asylum seekers at the border by a five to four decision, with Chief-Justice Roberts voting with the liberals.

The Dow plunged another five hundred points today, in response to the impending shutdown. It is now at its lowest point in a decade. So much for Trump's one and only positive "achievement."

As the nation goes into its third partial shutdown of this administration (essential services remain open) the Senate goes home until after Christmas, while the country is waiting for the leaders to try to thrash out some kind of compromise agreement. Trump has conceded that he would settle for a steel slat fence that he could call a wall, but the issue is the five billion dollar price tag he is still looking for. As the weekend went into Sunday, it looked like this shutdown will last at least into the New Year, until the Democrats take over the House on the third of January. They are offering a compromise of 2.6 billion dollars for border security in general, no wall or steel slat fence, but Trump shows no sign of being in a compromising mood.

CNN had a curious bottom-of-the-screen banner running on one of their news shows Sunday. It read: "Right wing personalities pulling Trump's strings?" Why would they end that with a questions mark? There is no question about it.

Trump finally came to understand that Mattis' resignation letter was a diplomatically-worded rebuke of the President and his policies. He reacted by having Secretary-of-State Pompeo inform the Defense Secretary that he must leave this month, not in February as offered. Trump has already designated his replacement. It will be Mattis' Deputy Secretary, Patrick Shanahan, whose experience for this position is questionable at best.

There are reports that Mueller may issue at least an interim report by mid-February. Congressman Adam Schiff assures us that they will make sure that the bulk of that report, with security redactions where necessary, will be released to the public. That will be a historic day like no other.

Dec. 24-31 Merry Christmas!

The state of our president's mind was once again on full display on the day before the Christmas Holiday, when he could not resist putting out the following pitiful tweet: "I am all alone (poor me) in the White House waiting for the Democrats to come back and make a deal on desperately needed Border Security." Needless to say, this ill-advised attempt at soliciting sympathy produced more mockery than any other reaction. He is suffering from an isolation that he brought upon himself, as one by one, his cabinet and his aides melt away, either of their own volition or because he fires them, and even his wife is spending the holiday at Mar a Lago without him because he is stuck trying to salvage a financial problem that he himself has created.

The news channels spent most of their air time over these two days reviewing what has happened over the past year in Trump-land. They reminded us of several events and policies which may have faded from many minds because of the volume of unprecedented things that have deluged us over that period of time.

These events included: (A) the disgraceful way our government neglected the devastation that befell the people of Puerto Rico who were hit by one of the worst hurricanes in their history; (B) the inhumane policy of child-parent separation that they used as a deterrent against migrants at our southern border, which still holds over six hundred kids incarcerated in a tent city in Texas, wondering what happened to the parents who have been deported to their homeland and now are "whereabouts unknown"; (C) the extreme corruption of many of his appointees that led to their eventual departure in disgrace; (D) the massive amount of taxpayer money he spends on his frequent golfing trips, the ones he swore during the campaign

The Enemy Within: A Chronicle of the Trump Administration

that he would never take as our president; (E) the continuous and voluminous emoluments violations. These are a few of the most obvious and serious problems which are *not* under the scope of his *most* serious problem--the Mueller investigation.

The other subject that got a lot of attention is what we can expect from the new Congress when the Democrats take control of the House of Representatives in a couple of weeks. Among the most important will be: renewed investigation by the House Judiciary Committee into several areas, including collusion with Russia; more intensive oversight into ongoing investigations, including recalling witnesses and subpoenaing documents, such as Trump's tax returns; restoring, or at least attempting to restore, several of the regulations to protect the environment that Trump has removed or blocked.

The partial government shutdown continues with no compromise in sight, while Trump goes on TV to lie that he just signed a contract to build one hundred and fifteen miles of the wall, something he has no power to do even if he had the funds allocated for it. He doesn't have any idea how to extricate himself from this hole he has dug himself into by listening to his right-wing wackos.

A second young child, an eight-year-old boy from Guatemala, has died in United States custody at our southern border. This has prompted the government to change its policy to include medical checkups of all immigrants in our custody.

The Dow dropped another 650 points on Monday, still in a freefall.

Rachel Maddow reviewed some of the most amazing upsets by women of color over entrenched Republicans in deep red states like Kansas as part of a blue wave that took place in the recent midterm election—results that dramatically showed to what depths the Republican party has sunk and the price it has paid for continuing to support a president who makes Richard Nixon look like a choir boy.

It was a very busy and quite crazy day-after-Christmas today, starting with another disastrous visit abroad by our totally clueless and increasingly desperate president.

Trump closed out his second year as president by making his first trip to visit our troops overseas. He went to Iraq and met with a contingent at an airbase, which included a secret Seal Team, which he managed to expose during his remarks. Instead of just praising and thanking them for all they do for our country, he used them as a captive audience who had to listen while he treated it like it was a campaign rally and attacked his political enemies, those unpatriotic Democrats who are opposing his border wall. This is another violation of the tradition that politics stop at our borders and shores.

He also defended his rash, seat-of-the-pants decision to withdraw from Syria, by announcing that "we are no longer the suckers of the world." No, what we are now are the patsies who are in full retreat from any dictator who curries his favor, like the Turkish president whom he talked to the day he announced that withdrawal decision.
Then he crowed about giving them their first pay raise in years, which he said was a ten percent increase. Two lies here: this was *not* their first raise in years, and it was not even close to ten percent.

To add insult to injury, Trump did not even meet the Iraqi president while he was visiting that man's country. It is not that there is no one left to advise him against making all these faux pas, it is that he doesn't listen to *anyone's* advice.

Trump's "bone spur" excuse for avoiding military service has always been suspect, but we now have confirmation from relatives of the doctor (now dead) who traded a phony diagnosis of spurs for free rent at a Trump property. Our president sure likes to make use of improper quid pro quos.

For several months there has been speculation about a *very* secret D. C. grand jury subpoena for documentary information from an unnamed foreign company, which has refused to comply with that subpoena. After several sealed-off court appearances about it, where the subpoena was upheld, the case has been referred to the Supreme Court, who is now considering whether to weigh in on the case. What makes it look like it has something to with the Mueller investigation is the fact that one of the federal judges involved in the decision in favor of the validity of the subpoena, was given his judgeship by Trump, so he recused himself from this case. This one is getting interesting. Thank goodness that Ruth Bader Ginsberg has recovered from her lung surgery and is back on the Supreme Court bench. Her record of never missing a vote during her time as a Justice is still intact. Bravo, Ruth!

ICE has transported and released hundreds of immigrants at a bus station in El Paso, Texas, apparently with no help or guidance as to where to go and what to do from that point in their US adventure.

Former National Security Advisor, Susan Rice, has issued the following statement to the *New York Times:* "In abandoning the role of responsible Commander-in-Chief, *Mr.* Trump today does more to undermine American national security than any foreign adversary."

Vladimir Putin has announced that Russia has now added a new missile which flies at several times the speed of sound, making it impossible to stop. No comment from Trump.

We are now in the fifth day of the partial government shutdown—all because Trump made a ridiculous and

Book Two (09/2018-11/2019)

impossible promise to his supporters during the Presidential campaign, and they still expect him to fulfill that promise, refusing to accept reality.

The Dow suddenly reversed its downward trend and zoomed up over a thousand points today—the largest one-day ever. It's a roller-coaster!

Over the Christmas break, Trump had someone take several photos of him, sitting at his Oval Office desk doing phony work, including signing a fake bill that one of the photos revealed was nothing but a blank sheet of paper. He must think that everyone is as dumb as he is.

The partial shutdown continues into its sixth day, with Trump not giving an inch and the Republicans still trying to sell the fantasy that somehow, someday, Mexico is going to pay for the border wall that is never going to be built. It will be very interesting to see how this standoff ends and how Trump will try to spin what will be a humiliating defeat for him and his cult followers.

Four different intelligence sources claim that Robert Mueller has electronic evidence that Michael Cohen was in Prague, Czech Republic, as reported in the Steele Dossier, during August-September of 2016, in spite of Cohen's repeated denials. The reason this is an issue is because he is alleged to have met with Russians at that time and place to discuss Trump's election campaign and the Trump Tower Moscow proposal. This would seem to be a crack in Cohen's cooperation with the Mueller team.

Chris Hayes' *All In* show tonight focused on the fact that the Trump administration has had a serious, continuing staffing problem from day one, and it keeps getting worse. At present, there are 126 vacant positions, many of them *never* filled.

The Enemy Within: A Chronicle of the Trump Administration

Now it has reached the point where no reputable and qualified people want to be associated with this chaotic White House. They know it would forever be a stain on their resume. Several of the "filled" positions, such as his Chief-of-Staff and his Attorney General, are in the "acting" category. Many people now see Donald Trump as the "acting" president.

In spite of all his problems, Trump's approval holds at the historically low but steady 39%, about where it has been for months. It is disheartening to see how his base refuses to admit reality. They are like programmed robots.

For the eleventh consecutive year, Barack Obama was voted "the world's most admired man." And his wife Michelle was voted "most admired woman." I'm sure our president is not handling that news very well.

In that North Carolina ninth district House seat election fraud case, discussed in the December 5 entry of this chronicle, the investigation into Harris' ballot confiscation scheme is still ongoing and the race is still not settled. A do-over of this election looks to be inevitable.

The year ended with not much new happening in Trump world—just a lot of reflection as we looked back on one of the most interesting, bizarre, frustrating and dangerous years in this country's history. The first three of these adjectives are pretty obvious, but some of you may ask why I included "dangerous." The reason is quite simply because I feel certain that every one of this country's adversaries must see how vulnerable we are right now, when we are essentially without *any* rational leadership at the controls of our government. Who is there to guide our impulsive, inexperienced, reactionary president, if Russia, China, Iran, or some rogue group like ISIS decides to test our will? And would he listen, even if there were someone available?

Book Two (09/2018-11/2019)

Trump has gotten so desperate over the shutdown standoff which he has created, and for which he has publically claimed ownership, that he is threatening to completely close the southern border. He has no idea how harmful this action would be to our economy, which depends a great deal on the flow of materials between the US and Mexico. He is a man who has attached a vice to his (pick a body-part of your choice) and keeps tightening it until someone forces him to stop.

Trump is now trying to blame the Democrats for the death of those two migrant children at the southern border. He has never accepted the blame for anything and never will. He is literally incapable of it.

Secretary Nielsen visited the borders of Texas and Arizona and came back to admit that the system is "clearly overwhelmed." How do you think that happened, Kirsten?

The year's end meant the last day on the Trump team for Generals Kelly and Mattis, and with their departure the sanity level at the White House drops precipitously.

The anti-Trump news media, which these days is almost all of it, devoted much of their year's wrap-up by revisiting the many ways in which Trump has harmed his own image by foolish and ignorant actions. But perhaps the biggest blow to that image was the *Times'* expose that he was far from the self-made billionaire he likes to present himself to be.

He was born with the proverbial silver spoon, and was financed by his father by the hundreds of millions of dollars before he ever began to succeed on his own, and that "success" was tainted by several bankruptcies and even more by conning and fraud scandals. Mitt Romney tried to tell everyone who Trump was during the campaign for the presidency, when he publicly labeled Trump "a conman."

The Enemy Within: A Chronicle of the Trump Administration

President Trump summarized his own appraisal of how his first two years in office have gone, by making the following classic-Trump statement: "I will tell you, there has never been an administration, and I'm very proud of this, an administration that has done more than the Trump administration, in the first two years in office." Well, he is right in *one* way to interpret that statement. He is responsible for more lies, more corruption, more harm to our ecology, more alienation of our allies, more enabling of our adversaries, more divisiveness, more support of racism, more weakening of our standing on the world stage, and last but by no means least, more *criminality*, than any president in the history of this great nation.

Book Two (09/2018-11/2019)

January, 2019

Jan. 1-6 -- Happy New Year!

We begin the New Year with the shutdown going into its eleventh day, with no end in sight. That topic leads off today's list of newsworthy items.

Trump is beginning to sound like he wants to negotiate, but he doesn't seem to be ready to budge an inch on his demand for a solid wall. He has invited eight leaders of Congress to the White House for a meeting tomorrow to discuss the issue, but at this point, it seems that Pelosi and the Democrats, who are about to take control of the House this Thursday, hold all the cards. You can bet that this one won't be open to the cameras and the public, like that last humiliating meeting. A large part of the problem is in the definition of the type of wall they are talking about. Even Trump himself is inconsistent in what he will accept, and people like Rudy Giuliani and Lindsey Graham aren't helping matters with their talk about a metaphor for "border security." They are trying to give Trump some "wiggle room" to help him out of the box he has put himself in, but he keeps managing to open his mouth and put himself right back into that box, by insisting upon something as close to concrete as he can get.

Mitt Romney, who is about to become a new Senator from Arizona, has come out strongly against the President, in an article published in the *Washington Post*. In it Mitt says; "I will act as I would with any president, in or out of my party. I will support policies that I believe are in the best interest of the country and my state, and *oppose* those that are not. I do not intend to comment on every tweet or fault. But I *will* speak out against significant statements or actions that are divisive, racist, sexist, anti-immigrant, dishonest or destructive to democratic institutions." It sounds like we *may* have a new voice of reason among the GOP lackeys.

Retired General Stanley McChrystal, in an interview on TV last Sunday, strongly criticized Trump's plan to withdraw from Syria. He also labeled him "immoral and a liar".
Trump's response, via tweet of course, was to say that "the general is known for his big, dump mouth. Hillary lover." The alleged adult's version of, "I know I am but what are you?"

Some disturbing videos have been discovered which show migrant children in a border detention camp, being physically abused by their so-called caretakers. That camp has been closed and an investigation has been launched.

Chief Justice John Roberts has weighed-in on that above-described mystery subpoena of a foreign company which has refused to comply. Although four Appeals Court judges have ruled in Mueller's favor, Roberts issued a "stay" on the case and gave the Special Counsel a week to provide his argument for continuing to press the subpoena. Even if Roberts decides to back him up, it is difficult to see how they can persuade the country involved to comply. I hope we eventually find out what country and what company.

An American citizen named Paul Whalen has been "detained" by the Russians in Moscow and accused of espionage. Whalen was there to attend a friend's wedding. This could be a bargaining chip that the Russians plan to use to get their hands on Maria Butina.

Massachusetts Senator Elizabeth Warren plans to visit Iowa this coming weekend as a first step in testing the waters for her probable presidential run next year. She has the qualifications. The question is, would she be too divisive, with her reputation of being too far left?

Book Two (09/2018-11/2019)

On his last day as a President who has the advantage of control of both branches of Congress, Trump held a cabinet meeting which was a frightening look at just how unhinged he has become over the prospects of his future. Item one is only a brief snapshot of that alarming picture.

The most bizarre cabinet meeting ever held at the White House began with Acting Attorney General Matt Whitaker, praising Trump and thanking him for his devotion to his job for remaining, alone, in the White House over both recent holidays.
This was a totally obsequious ass-kissing which was both unprecedented and laughable. Many of the others at the table must have been wishing they had brought barf-bags. Trump then proceeded to go on a ninety-minute, rambling, incoherent and largely inaccurate speech on the Soviet Union's invasion of Afghanistan so many years ago, as though that war had something to do with, or teach us, about our involvement there today. He probably could have made a good point if he had any of his facts straight. But he left his captive audience wondering to themselves—what the Hell? One of the many crazy statements made by this delusional man was—"I think I would have made a very good general." This, from a repeated draft dodger.

Later in the day, Trump held his meeting with the eight Congressional leaders to negotiate about the shutdown. It went nowhere. Neither side is giving an inch on the wall question.

Today saw the actual departure (as opposed to notification thereof) of Ex-Chief-of-Staff John Kelly, ex-Interior Secretary Ryan Zinke, ex-Secretary-of-Defense James Mattis, and ex-UN Ambassador Nikki Haley whose replacement is an inexperienced neophyte named Heather Nauert.

The prosecutors in the Maria Butina case are arguing for a continuation of her gag-order, because without it she could affect an on-going investigation. We can expect an offer from Russia to swap her for Paul Whelan.

The Supreme Court has already received what it was seeking in the way of briefs from both sides of the subpoena dispute in that mysterious case against "company A" from "country B". They must now decide if they want to proceed to render a decision or defer to the lower court's decision. The secrecy applied to this case is unprecedented at this level, and it no doubt relates to the Mueller probe. Stay tuned!

We have learned a few things about Paul Whalen--that American arrested by Russia for alleged spying. He is an ex-marine who was dishonorably discharged for "bad conduct" and "attempted larceny."
 He is also a fervent Trump supporter, which makes him even more of a tempting swap offer. His background excludes him from any possible role as an intelligence asset, so the charge against him is completely drummed up.

Senator Elizabeth Warren was interviewed on *The Rachel Maddow Show* tonight. She left no doubt that she is running for president next year, and I believe she will be a force to be reckoned with. At this point, I see only two serious contenders—Joe Biden and Beto O'Rourke.

Here are my predictions for the year 2019: (A) The Mueller report will be a huge bombshell hitting the President, his family and the GOP in general; (B) Several people close to Trump will be indicted, and *he* will be named as an unindicted co-conspirator; (C) The Republicans, in order to salvage their party's image, will begin to repudiate Trumpism; (D) Donald Trump will leave office before Labor Day, either by resigning or being impeached by the House and convicted by the Senate.

Book Two (09/2018-11/2019)

On this first day of our new House of Representatives with the Democrats in the majority for the first time since Trump was elected, we had a lot of interesting action.

Nancy Pelosi is now the Speaker of the House; Adam Schiff is the Chairperson of the House Intelligence Committee; Jerry Nadler is the Chairperson of the House Judiciary Committee (he believes that a sitting president *can* be indicted); Maxine Waters is the Chairperson of the Finance Committee. They will *all* be very uncomfortable pains in the President's backside.

The new House immediately passed two bills to reopen the government (for two spans of time) and passed them on to the Senate, where Mitch McConnell will probably not even put them to a vote unless Trump gives him the nod.

Representative from California, Brad Sherman, reintroduced his bill of impeachment that he first filed in 2017. His charge is obstruction of justice in the firing of James Comey.

Tonight, Rachel Maddow pointed out that Trump's recent deranged defense of Russia's invasion of Afghanistan at yesterday's bizarre cabinet meeting, was the third time he has made up something of this nature to curry favor with Putin. The first was a commentary about the aggressiveness of little Montenegro. The second was a fairy tale about Poland being about to attack Belarus. This is Putin's puppet at work.

MSNBC's Brian Williams, on his show *The Eleventh Hour* showed us a collage of TV snips in which Trump bragged about how he "knows more about (pick any subject) than anyone, believe me." He actually believes that he is an expert in all things. This is extreme delusion to the point of insanity.

Here is an interesting new stat to ponder.
Female House Members
1989   16 Democrats 13 Republicans

The Enemy Within: A Chronicle of the Trump Administration

Now   89 Democrats 13 Republicans

With the shutdown going into its fourteenth day, here is where things stand.

After a two hour meeting to try to resolve the budget standoff, the Democrats came out of it saying that "it was rather contentious." They seemed quite pessimistic about the lack of progress. Then Trump gave us his assessment of how it went, and it was even worse. He went into another of his incomprehensible rants in which he bragged about the latest job numbers (incorrectly of course), gave us more lying gibberish about border security, and admitted that he had told Pelosi and company that "the shutdown might drag on for months or even years." This statement is amazingly stupid on two levels. One, because there is no way in Hell the Congress or the country would stand for this to go on much longer than it already has. Two, because even if he could achieve that dubious goal, it would only add to his unpopularity and speed his exit. Another meeting is planned for tomorrow. Let's hope it goes better.

Tonight, Rachel Maddow enlightened us about Maine's outgoing Governor Paul Lepage, who was beaten in the midterm election by Democrat Janet Mills. His final action on his way out was to pardon a white man who was convicted of drug dealing. This is shortly after he threw the book at a black man for a far less serious crime. Racial profiling in action. He has also blocked health-care coverage for his constituents. Reversing this action was the first thing Mills did on taking office.

On their first day in control of the House, the Democrats proposed a resolution labeled HR-1, which will do the following: institute nation-wide automatic voter registration; put an end to biased gerrymandering; allow two weeks of early voting nation-wide; return voting rights to ex-felons after their sentences have been served; provide funding for all states to use paper ballots if only for backup; make election days into a federal holiday; force candidates for president or vice-president to release ten years of their tax returns. This will be tough to get passed by this Senate or signed by this president, but maybe someday soon.

Trump's use of undocumented aliens at his Bedminster Golf Club is now under investigation.

There is a great deal of talk about impeachment. Not *whether* to go for it but when. We will almost certainly get only one shot at the goal of using that means of removing our worst nightmare, so we better have all our ducks lined up before making that move. This means waiting for Mueller's report and the next batch of indictments, no matter how long it takes, and no one believes that it will be much longer now.

The D.C. federal judge has granted a six month extension to the Mueller investigation. This means that any report issued during February, as expected, will be an interim report, not a final one.

Our borderline-illiterate president now wants to refer to his shutdown as a "strike", which has just the opposite meaning of a shutdown. He actually declared that the impacted federal employees "are his biggest fans." If they were before, they are a lot less so now, Mr. President. Why don't you ask them yourself?

If Trump is indicted and the case goes to the Supreme Court to see if what has never been tested before is constitutional, the two Justices who were given their seat on that bench by Trump need to recuse themselves because of an obvious conflict of interest. If they do, the vote will almost surely be in favor of indictment.

Trump is now talking about getting his wall built by declaring a "state of emergency" and using the military and its budget to get it done. This could turn into a constitutional mess and get him into even more trouble than he is already in.

National Security Advisor John Bolton is attempting to steer Trump away from his precipitous plan to withdraw all our troops from Syria. He took it upon himself to announce that we will *not* be pulling out any troops until the Turkish government guarantees that they will not attack the Kurds after we are gone. That will probably earn him an departure from this administration.

Jan. 7-13

As we enter the seventeenth day of the Trump shutdown, the President is still having all kinds of problems explaining exactly how he would spend the 5.6 billion dollars he is demanding from Congress for border security, which still *must* be a "wall" in his mind and in his speech, but the *type* of wall keeps fluctuating. He is labeling the immigrant problem an emergency because he claims that, "So far in the past year, about 4,000 terrorists have been stopped at the southern border." The truth is that the accurate figure of such apprehensions is SIX! Far more are stopped at airports, but even *there* the number does not approach 4,000. He continues to tell bald-faced lies that are instantly *proven* to be lies. Only a madman would keep doing that after being constantly exposed. He is still being controlled both by Putin and by *Fox and Friends*. No new meetings have been planned to resume negotiations to put an end to the shutdown, and Trump is now planning to give an address to the nation on all TV channels to push his "national emergency" scheme. The Democrats are planning an immediate response to what Trump has to say.

His plan to use the military budget and manpower to build his wall is unconstitutional and will not happen, but he either doesn't realize that fact, or doesn't care as long as he looks strong to his brainwashed base.

Book Two (09/2018-11/2019)

Eight hundred thousand federal employees are not getting paid during this shutdown, including those deemed "essential" and are forced to keep working without pay if they want to keep their jobs. These people are now feeling the effect of the shutdown and the grumbling has begun, even among his followers. Erosion of his base is inevitable as he keeps trying to keep an impossible promise that never should have been made. So far, five Republican Senators have joined the Democrats in calling for an end to the impasse.

Senator Swalwell says that his committee plans to call Acting AG Whitaker to testify before them. There will surely be questions about his attitude and his plan in regard to Robert Mueller and his team of prosecutors.

It is on record that Trump and Putin talk by phone frequently. The transcripts of these calls are recorded and can be subpoenaed by Congress. We may eventually come to find out just how much influence the Russian leader has over our president.

Tonight Rachel Maddow informed us about an interesting legal case currently underway which involves Vladimir Putin's former cook, a man named Yevgeny Prigozhin. This man is also the financier of the Russian "troll farm" which was so instrumental in using social media to influence the result of the 2016 presidential election of Donald Trump. He and his company were targets of one of Mueller's flurries of indictments a few months ago, and since they are out of Mueller's reach, you would expect them to just sit back and thumb their collective nose, but instead Prigozhin has responded by pleading not guilty and hiring American lawyers who are using the "discovery procedure" to request decades of information that goes way beyond the parameters of this particular case.

The Enemy Within: A Chronicle of the Trump Administration

They obviously hope to obtain useful information about what Mueller has developed during his broad probe, which would help them toward preparing their defense or the defense of the Trump team, and even challenge the whole Mueller investigation.

Prigozhin's lawyer has recently been severely reprimanded for filing unprofessional and inappropriate briefs, especially pertaining to the discovery request. An interesting sidelight to this case is that Prigozhin used a very lucrative kick-back scheme to enrich not only himself but also an oligarch named Leonid Teyf, who is now in a North Carolina jail for a murder-for-hire plot.

Here is a short, incomplete list of the serious problems Trump is wrestling with, and will be for quite a while. (a) The government shutdown, (b) The embarrassing wall-promise failure, (c) The loss of control of the House of Representatives, (d) The many investigations into his words and actions, *not* involving the Mueller probe, (e) The coming legal assault from the Special Counsel investigating his conspiracy with the Russians.

The consensus from reporters and voters in Iowa is that Elizabeth Warren is making an outstanding impression with her early campaign style and content, sending "chills" among her audiences.

Trump held his first Oval Office Address to the nation tonight, an occasion normally used only for the most significant announcements. This one was heralded as a vital pronouncement about the shutdown and border security issues in which the country has been embroiled for eighteen days now. In one of the few occasions where he used a teleprompter, and stuck to it, he spoke for ten minutes and said nothing new, making no declaration of a "national emergency" as previously threatened, and no proposals for a way to get himself and the country out of the crazy box he has put us all in. Nothing but a monotone, boring recitation of his usual refrain of how we are in a crisis at the southern border and we need to build a barrier to resolve it.

There were the usual gross exaggerations and falsehoods, which were immediately repudiated by Speaker Pelosi and Senate Democrat leader Schumer, who demolished Trump's argument with ease.

It was obvious that neither the President nor his two opponents wanted to be taking part in this strange and unnecessary charade. They pointed out that the only "crisis" at the border is a humanitarian one caused by the inhumane policies the administration has instituted.

By this coming weekend we will have achieved the longest government shutdown in our history with no apparent progress toward a resolution. To add insult to injury, Trump sent out two messages to his base—one before the speech and one afterward—asking them to contribute to a fund to build the wall, but the money was shown to be actually targeted to the fund for his reelection campaign. This is a case of outright fraud, as well as a case of desperation. It seems to be the one and only reason for the speech.

At least three Republican Senators are ready to vote with the Democrats on the bills to solve the budget issue and re-open the government. Only one more is needed to make it a majority and put the pressure on McConnell to put it to a vote.

It has long been known that Michael Cohen worked with Felix Sater, during the transition period and early in the Trump presidency, to get the sanctions dropped on Russia, and in particular the VTB Bank. The primary motive for this effort was because they and Trump were trying to get financing from that bank for the Trump Tower-Moscow project. Now, thanks to an unintentional revelation by a Paul Manafort document that was not sufficiently redacted, we learn that Mr. Manafort was equally involved in those efforts and lied about it during his "cooperation" with Mueller, part of the reason he is now serving time. It also reveals that he shared a ton of data with Russian intelligence agent Konstantin Kilimnik, which included polling data from the Presidential campaign to be used to target the right people in the Russian social media propaganda program. Kilimnik then passed that data on to Oleg Deripaska, a GPU agent who is one of the main links between the Trump campaign and Russia, links that constitute a conspiracy to affect the election.

Natalia Veselnitskaya, the Russian lawyer who attended the notorious June 2017 Trump Tower meeting, was indicted by Mueller, back on December 12, 2018, for lying and providing false information about a money-laundering scheme in which she was involved. The indictment was kept under seal until now.

Congress is challenging Trump's lifting of the sanctions on Oleg Deripaska and his company. They want a meeting between Treasury Secretary Steve Mnuchin and "all interested members."

The Supreme Court has declined to rule on the issue of the subpoena battle involving that mysterious "company A from country B," meaning that the lower court's decision stands and Mueller wins. Now, how to enforce compliance, and *who are they anyway*.

The New York Times published a lengthy article today expanding upon yesterday's big revelation about Manafort's clear "collusion" with the Russians by passing confidential polling data to use in helping to get Trump elected, in exchange for not imposing the sanctions levied upon them by President Obama as a punishment for invading Ukraine. This a "smoking gun" as far as Manafort, Trump's campaign manager, is concerned. Now it is only a question of, how much did Trump know about it and when?

Trump met with Pelosi and Schumer again today, for about one minute. Trump walked in and asked if they were going to give him his wall. Pelosi said, no, and Trump said, bye-bye, and walked out.

NBC reports that Rob Rosenstein intends to stay on his job as Attorney General until Robert Mueller files his report, which he expects to be in early March at the latest. After that, William Barr, if confirmed by the Senate, will be able to block any public release of that report. But public demand will almost certainly force that report to be leaked by someone.

The Washington Post reports that the White House is preparing an aggressive defense against the expected onslaught of prosecutions, and has hired *seventeen* new lawyers to help in defending the President in all of those cases. This shapes up to be a huge battle between two branches of our government. Nixon tried this same tactic and failed.

The Senate has scheduled a hearing to be held on January 15 on the nomination of William Barr for Attorney General. Barr has refused to meet with any Democrat Senators until after the hearing, which is not the usual procedure for these issues. Those Democrats have several significant concerns about Barr because of his obvious attitudes about important issues, such as the Mueller probe. For what it's worth, *Washington Post* says that leading Senators have "promised" that, if confirmed, Barr will not stop the Mueller probe.

Four Senators (that number seems to keep fluctuating) and eight Representatives have deserted the GOP ranks on votes to end the shutdown. Leader Mitch McConnell has been strangely silent on the issue.

The Enemy Within: A Chronicle of the Trump Administration

The Mark Harris election fraud case is still being investigated, so he is still unable to assume his ill-gotten seat in Congress.

The big story of the day is that Michael Cohen has a February 7 date to testify *publicly* before the House Oversight Committee in what could be almost as devastating to the Trump administration as the release of the Mueller report will be when it comes out.

Trump went to Texas to visit the southern border and see for himself the "crisis" he has been raving about, with no particular objective stated, and with no further attempts to resolve the shutdown, which is now being felt nationwide and causing growing protests and shrinking support for him. McConnell is still standing in the way of any vote on the bills that would end the shutdown, and his excuse, that Trump would not sign it, is invalid because with his leadership he could secure enough votes to override Trump's veto. He is now even *more* responsible for the mess than Trump.

Several Democrat committee leaders held a confidential meeting with Treasury Secretary Mnuchin on the subject of those sanctions on the Russian companies and oligarchs, particularly Oleg Deripaska. After the meeting, Speaker Pelosi said it was the worst and most useless briefing she has ever participated in. Apparently, Mnuchin was not at all forthcoming in answering their questions.

Democrat Senator Mark Warner, ranking member on the Intelligence Committee, appeared on *The Rachel Maddow Show* tonight and objected strenuously to William Barr's nomination for Attorney General, because of his obvious prejudice against Robert Mueller, and the fact that Barr was the driving force behind the blanket pardon of those involved in the Iran-Contra scandal at the end of the Reagan presidency. It sounds like that confirmation hearing is going be wild.

The New York Times reports that Mueller is looking into at least a dozen Ukrainians who came to D. C. for the inauguration of President Trump, to propose a "peace plan", but it was actually to discuss how to remove those pesky sanctions. Here is an excerpt of their article. "The investigations are playing out against growing indications that some of the Ukrainians who came to Washington for the inaugural, or their allies, were promoting grand bargains, or "peace plans" that are aligned with Russia's interests, including the lifting of sanctions."

Former Solicitor General Neil Katyal states that the Mueller report will definitely be made open to the public. He also believes that if Trump declares a national emergency to try to get his wall, it will be grounds for impeachment. As if we needed any more grounds than has already been provided.

Justice Greenberg has missed several votes since her lung operation. She is recovering at home and studying the issues before the court, but unable to be present. This is raising concern about the possibility of losing another justice for Trump to replace. On the bright side, her doctor says that he is not concerned—she is progressing nicely. Hang in there, Ruth.

We have now set a new record for the longest shutdown is US history (22 days), with still no end in sight and no ongoing or planned negotiations. Senator Lindsey Graham is not helping matters by tweeting, "Mr. President, declare a national emergency, NOW. Build a wall, NOW." But the Republicans on the whole are feeling trapped in a box of their president's own making, and almost every day one or two more are jumping ship.

The Enemy Within: A Chronicle of the Trump Administration

A breaking *New York Times* story is getting even more attention by the news media than the shutdown. Up until now, we have thought that the Mueller investigation was the offshoot of the FBI's probe into the discovery that the Russians had interfered with the 2016 election. But before that even became an issue, the FBI was looking into Trump's words and actions during his campaign and during his early weeks as president. Here is a sample of the article they just published, starting with this eye-catching headline: "FBI Opened Inquiry into Whether Trump Was Secretly Working on Behalf of Russia". The story included the following sentences: "The inquiry carried explosive implications. Counterintelligence investigators had to consider whether the President's own actions constituted a possible threat to national security." "Agents also sought to determine whether Mr. Trump was knowingly working for Russia or had unwittingly fallen under Moscow's influence", and if his actions constituted "working on behalf of Russia against American interests." This means that before a Special Prosecutor was assigned to investigate the ties between Russia's interference and the possible collusion by the Trump campaign in those efforts, the FBI was already looking into his actions that bordered upon treason. I say "bordered upon" only because the technical definition of treason requires that a state of war exist when the aid to the enemy is provided. While we are not in a state of war, we have been serious adversaries on the brink of war on several occasions since World War Two. Since becoming president, Trump has had only praise for Putin and sided with him against his own intelligence agencies on every issue. His meetings with Putin have been held in secret and he has never elaborated on what they discussed. He still uses his own, private and unsecured cell phone with which he could be talking with Putin on a daily basis with no accountability.

The White House's response to the *Times* story was "This is absurd."

Book Two (09/2018-11/2019

Presidential historian Jon Meacham says that the two most important people in our country today are Robert Mueller and Supreme Court swing vote, Chief Justice, John Roberts.

In an important follow-up to the bombshell *New York Times* story about the early FBI investigation into the suspicion that Trump was wittingly or unwittingly acting as an agent for Russia, *Washington Post* reports that all of Trump's meetings with Putin have been secretive to the point of his actual confiscation of the stenographer's and the interpreter's notes. It is not known if he has destroyed these notes, but we need to get the answer to that question. If they still exist, they should be subpoenaed, and if he destroyed them he should be charged with the crime of destroying government records.

Trump is always bragging about records being set under his administration. In spite of what he told Pelosi and Schumer about being "proud to own the shutdown", I doubt he will do much crowing about the fact that he is now responsible for the longest shutdown in US history, and is making no effort to end it. All the polls show that a large majority of the country blame him and the Republicans, not the Democrats, for the mess that is financially impacting millions of Americans more and more each day that it goes on.

A third major topic of the day is the question; what justifies the declaration of a national emergency? And what are the limits of presidential power when one is declared? Very few people, if any, believe that the immigration problem justifies such an action, which is probably why Trump has been hesitating about taking this action that he has been chomping at the bit to take.

I find it a bit amusing to listen to so many TV pundits discussing which of the several potential Democrat presidential candidates would have the best chance to beat Trump in 2020.

The Enemy Within: A Chronicle of the Trump Administration

They all talk as though it were a given that he would still be president by then. Naïve, or just cautious?

Jan. 14-20

The House Democrats are looking at the possibility of subpoenaing the interpreter who was present at the secretive Helsinki meeting between Trump and Putin.

Rachel Maddow's guest tonight was former Chief of the DOJ's Counter-intelligence and Export-control Section, David Laufman. Mr. Laufman said, "It is a painfully anguishing thing to acknowledge that the President of the United States is a clear and present danger to the national security of the United States." He was referring, of course, to the latest revelations about Putin's obvious influence over Trump's actions and policies, especially his attitudes toward NATO and our allies in general.

Rachel Maddow also reviewed for us the highlights of the confirmation hearings for the Attorney General nominee Bill Saxbe, back in the Watergate saga, in which Saxbe was profoundly grilled by the Senators about his attitudes and intentions. She used this case as an example of what we should expect from our current Senate tomorrow when they hold their hearing with William Barr. It will be done openly and televised so it will be very interesting to see how it goes.

Barr's prepared opening contains the following statement in regard to the Mueller investigation: "The country needs a credible resolution of these issues. If confirmed, I will not permit partisan politics, personal interests, or any other improper considerations to interfere with this or any other investigation." Great news, if he means it!

The Daily Beast reports that Mueller is investigating Kevin Nunes' and Mike Flynn's actions during the first year of the Trump presidency. Nunes may be seeking immunity into return for his cooperation. Another flipper?

Book Two (09/2018-11/2019)

There is a vote scheduled tomorrow on the lifting of sanctions on Oleg Deripaska, which were originally approved in an almost unanimous vote. This was discussed the other day with Secretary Mnuchin with no satisfaction on either side.

Steve King, the white-supremacist Republican Representative from Iowa, has been removed from all committees as a "scolding" for his latest racist remarks. He finally became too much for even his Republican cohorts to stomach. They still continue to be silent about *Trump's* racism, however.

At his opening confirmation hearing today AG nominee Bill Barr voiced *most* of the right things pertaining to the Mueller investigation, but hedged as to how much of Mueller's report he would allow to be made public. This could become a big problem at some point, because the American public will not tolerate any form of a cover-up of the findings of Trump's criminality. He also hedged on the question of his recusal as to Mueller and his probe, even if it is requested by the DOJ's ethics committee. The most encouraging thing about this development is that former head of the DEA and several other important posts, Chuck Rosenberg, one of the most reasonable and knowledgeable people frequently seen on TV, was satisfied with Barr's answers about his attitude and intentions in regard to Mr. Mueller.

The New York Times' latest Trump story reminded us that Trump has, on several occasions, talked about withdrawing from NATO, and he is now raising that issue once again. This would be the biggest gift that Vladimir Putin could possibly be given, and would be the frosting on the cake of the case that Trump is what amounts to an agent of the Russians.

The Senate voted to continue those sanctions on Oleg Deripaska and company, 57-42, with eleven Republicans voting along with the Democrats. But there is still another, broader vote to come on the subject which will require sixty votes to pass. Chuck Schumer says that he feels the latest evidence of Trump's bootlicking for Putin is beginning to change GOP minds.

Trump may have destroyed *his* notes and transcripts of his secret meetings with Putin, but you can bet that Vladimir has not, and now he has another thing to hold over Trump's head.

Great Britain's government is in at least as much trouble as ours because the vote on Brexit did not go Theresa May's way, and she is now facing the probability of a vote of "no confidence" tomorrow, which is their form of impeachment. The two greatest bulwarks against Russian imperialism are in a historic state of vulnerability.

The second, broader vote by the Senate, to maintain the sanctions against Oleg Deripaska and company, failed to pass by 57 to 42, short of the 60 needed in this case, so Trump and Putin win another one of their joint prizes. Chuck Schumer says that the Democrats will challenge that decision.

AG nominee Barr wrote a three hundred page memo a while ago, describing his record and his opinions on important questions of law, which he used as a job application for this post. It is filled with inaccurate statements about various laws, which were challenged by the Senators. It also exposed his belief in some old disproven conspiracy theories related to the Clintons.

As we dealt with the twenty-fifth day of the Government shutdown, Alexandra Ocasio-Cortez went through the Senate chamber loudly asking, "Where's Mitch (McConnell)? The Senate leader is AWOL at a time when the country is in crisis. This is not a good time to be taking a plane trip within this country, as the air-traffic controllers, who have a very stressful job under the best of circumstances, have the additional stress of working without pay. Some of the other people in this position are the Secret Service Agents who have to protect the President and his family. I wonder how much effort they are anxious to put into *that* job these days.

Four Americans were among those killed by a bomb placed by ISIS in a market area in Syria. This occurred almost simultaneously with the claims by both Trump and Pence that "ISIS has been defeated", as justification for Trump's plan to withdraw our troops. A mirror image of Bush's "Mission Accomplished" faux pas.

Trump's state-of-the-union address was scheduled for January 29, but it turns out that the President must wait to be invited by the Speaker-of-the-House to come into the Congressional chamber for that purpose. Speaker Pelosi has told him to hold off on that visit until the shutdown is over, because they don't have the money to adequately protect him.

The New York Times reports that Trump told them that "we are getting crushed on the shutdown." That's right, you are. Time to do something.

Rudy Giuliani, on CNN, claims. "I never said there was no collusion by those close to the President. Just not by *him*." Trump is not the only one who is dumb enough to tell an instantly disproven lie.

Here we go with yet another major bombshell revelation in the Trump corruption saga. One of the most devastating stories so far in the Trump saga was just uncovered by *Buzzfeed News*, who revealed that Cohen has testified that he was *directed to lie* about the Trump Tower-Moscow project "by Donald Trump", and he has the documentation to prove it. This is straight-out collusion *and* suborning perjury. It is every bit as much of a

The Enemy Within: A Chronicle of the Trump Administration

smoking gun as Trump's directive to pay off the ladies he had affairs with and lie about it. The story also implicated the Trump children who were in on the project from the beginning. This report is yet to be corroborated by other news media, but *Buzzfeed* is staking its reputation on it. Cohen is certain to be grilled about this when he testifies to them on February 7.

Vanity Fair reports that Michael Cohen has documentation that he paid an Information Technology company to rig a CNBC poll to favor Trump during the Presidential campaign (the ploy failed). This constitutes a campaign contribution which must be reported. Failure to do so is a crime.

As a retaliation move for Pelosi's snub, Trump suggested that Pelosi take a commercial flight to Afghanistan without realizing that this would violate the law against this kind of flight for those who are in the line of succession for president during a crisis period, like the shutdown. Once again, he has no clue about the rules of the government he is supposed to be leading.

The Senate vote to maintain sanctions against Deripaska and company may have failed but it is encouraging to note that the bill passed the House by the overwhelming vote of 366 to 53, with 136 Republicans voting in favor. Too bad it was in a losing cause.

Bill Barr went through his second day of confirmation grilling today and left several senators still unsatisfied with some of his answers. There seems to be little doubt that he will be confirmed with this group of Trump lackeys.

The Washington Post reminds us that Trump has consistently restricted financial aid to Puerto Rico, which goes along with his crazy boast about the loss of "only six lives as a result of the hurricane." The official final count exceeded three thousand, but he has never attempted to correct his error. He has shown

Book Two (09/2018-11/2019)

zero regard for the American citizens who inhabit this tiny island "surrounded by lots and lots of water."

The big news of the day, and practically the *only* Trump news of the day, was a very unusual statement from Robert Mueller's office that disputed some of the *Buzzfeed* story that had the whole country buzzing yesterday. Here is the significant part of that statement: "*Buzzfeed*'s description of *specific* statements to the Special Counsel's Office and characterization of documents and testimony obtained by this office, regarding Michael Cohen's Congressional testimony *are not accurate*" (emphasis by author).

Notice that the statement does *not* spell out what part or parts of the *Buzzfeed* story they dispute, and certainly does not dispute the major revelation that Trump "directed" Cohen to lie about the Trump Tower Moscow project. Mueller seems to be disputing some of the details about the alleged documentation that supports that main point. The story prompted what has been characterized as "a feeding frenzy" among the news media and an increase in the calls for impeachment *now,* without waiting for Mueller's report.

Everyone is guessing why Mueller would put a damper on the story, but the most reasonable guess, in my opinion, is that he is trying to discourage a premature rush into any filing of bills of impeachment before he has a chance to present his full case to the Congress. As I said earlier in this book, we will only get one shot at this and we better make it count with ALL our ducks lined up, and I'm sure Mueller feels the same way. The editor of *Buzzfeed* is asking the Special Counsel's Office for elaboration of what the objection is, but they are unlikely to get an answer. Unfortunately, the criticism of the story has given the Trump team ammunition to cast doubt on the whole story and raise the "fake news" cry again. His supporters will eat that right up. Chuck Rosenberg, one of the most savvy law enforcement voices frequently heard these days, says that there is no question about that kernel point, that Trump directed the lie.

Another major point to this Moscow tower issue is the fact that Trump has repeatedly stated that he had zero business deals going on or planned with the Russians, a lie told over and over, whether he directed Cohen to lie or not.

The only other item worth mentioning today is Trump's statement that he will make a major announcement pertaining to the shutdown, tomorrow at 3:00 pm. Capitulation of some sort, maybe?

Trump's big shutdown announcement turned out to be just another of his attempts to distract the nation for a few minutes away from our constant agony over the mess both he and the entire country are now finding ourselves in because of his complete incompetence.

His proposal was a feeble attempt to resurrect a form of the old DACA for WALL agreement that was proposed months ago. It was dead-on-arrival. Pelosi labeled it "a non-starter."

Let's review what developed just in the week just ended. Here is a list of the latest revelations, any *one* of which would have been devastating to any previous administration.

Monday—Former Chief of the DOJ's Counter-intelligence and Export-control Section, David Laufman, characterized Trump's actions in regard to Russia and Putin, "a clear and present danger to the national security of the United States."

Tuesday—Trump again talked about withdrawing our country from NATO, which would essentially destroy the only thing discouraging Russia's imperialist ambitions.

Wednesday—Rudy Giuliani, Trump's chief mouthpiece, admitted that there was collusion among those close to Trump.

Thursday—Two huge stories: the *Buzzfeed* story about Trump instructing Cohen to lie to Congress; the *Vanity Fair*

Book Two (09/2018-11/2019)

story about Cohen paying a company to rig a poll in favor of Trump during the campaign.

Jan. 21-27

We start the new week with Rudy Giuliani and the Trump Tower-Moscow issue dominating the airwaves.

In his usual disastrous attempt to defend the President, Giuliani keeps making statements from which he then has to back-peddle and explain, which ends up only making him and Trump look worse. His version of when and what was said between Trump and Cohen, on the subject of that very significant Trump Tower Moscow plan and negotiations, changes from hour to hour, ever since the *Buzzfeed* story broke. But in the midst of all the crazy contradictions is his admission that Trump was working on that goal right up to the day of the election, *and* that he talked with Cohen about his Congressional testimony, without coercing him to lie, of course, so the chat was "a perfectly normal thing for him to do."

Buzzfeed continues to stand by their story. It is important to remember in all this smoke, that what Michael Cohen was sent to jail for was lying about the timing of the start and end of those Trump Tower Moscow negotiations with Russia. That subject was obviously worth lying about in his (and Trump's) eyes, which is a strong indication of consciousness of guilt.

Senate leader McConnell is preparing to present a new bill to the Senate in a feeble attempt to end the shutdown, which apparently is the same offer that Trump suggested in his big address the other night, and which has no chance of being accepted by the Democrats or getting sixty votes in the Senate. Perhaps the plan is to lose first, then capitulate in some way. But Pelosi still insists; "Open the government first and then we can talk."

The Enemy Within: A Chronicle of the Trump Administration

Several Democrat Congressmen are calling for the transcripts of the testimonies given during the earlier investigations to be released to the public to the extent possible without compromising national security or ongoing investigations. That goes as well to the upcoming testimony of Cohen on February 7.

As evidence is being shown that Trump has had several images of himself photo-shopped to make him look thinner and his fingers look longer, George Mills of the *Washington Post* writes, "He is an almost inexplicably sad specimen. It must be misery to awaken to another day of being Donald Trump...His childlike ignorance--preserved by a lifetime of single-minded self-promotion--concerning governance--and economic guarantees, that whenever he must interact with experienced and accomplished people, he is as bewildered as a kindergartner on String Theory."

Trump's first half of his term ends today with the lie-counters showing us a grand total of eight thousand, one hundred and fifty-eight misstatements of fact.

Senator Kamala Harris has added her name to that of Senator Elizabeth Warren, Senator Kirsten Gillibrand and Representative Tulsi Gabbard as those who are running to become the Democrat nominee for president next year.

Today was Martin Luther King Day, and our president said nothing to commemorate it.

As we reach day thirty-two of the longest government shutdown in US history, the financial misery grows for an increasingly large segment of our work force, including vital services that are now in a dangerously weakened condition. It is only a matter of time before we suffer a major catastrophe of some sort as a direct result of Trump's stubborn insistence on a wall which never had a chance of being built, for several reasons that have little to do with the political debate.

An old emergency plan that was created to help us operate through the bird flu crisis a few years ago has been resurrected as a potential means of alleviating the current situation. Let us hope saner heads will prevail before we need to use it. So far, Trump and McConnell on the right, and Pelosi and Schumer on the left, are at an impasse and are not even talking to each other. McConnell has re-emerged from hiding and is preparing to present two bills to be voted on by his Senate; Trump's proposed solution that he voiced once again the other night, and Pelosi's proposed solution which offers funds for increased border security, but no wall. Mitch knows that neither of these bills have much, if any, chance of passing, and he is making no effort to use his position as their leader to persuade Congress of the need to get this mess resolved.

Former Democrat Senate leader, Harry Reid, had this to say about Senator McConnell: "I believe that Mitch McConnell has ruined the Senate. I do not believe the Senate, for the next generation or two, will be the Senate I was there for. It's gone. The old Senate is gone." Congressional historian Norm Ornstein says, "Mitch McConnell is the weakest Senate leader in history. He is completely under the control of Donald Trump. A tragic thing for the country."

Both *The New York Times* and *Politico* have reported that Trump is "apoplectic" over Rudy Giuliani's latest statements which have contradicted the lies that Trump has been consistently telling for months. Rudy even talked about "going through all the tapes." *That* would be interesting!

The new House Judiciary Committee, led by Democrat Congressman Jerry Nadler, has released a list of questions that they plan to ask our "acting" AG Whitaker. They are all

The Enemy Within: A Chronicle of the Trump Administration

pointedly relevant to the Mueller investigation and to the one being conducted by the Southern District of New York. Mr. Whitaker will face these the day after Michael Cohen testifies to them on February 7.

The House voted today to bar this country from withdrawing from the NATO alliance. The vote was 357 to 22, with 149 Republicans included in that 357. Even the GOP knows how insane that move would be.

Michael Cohen is now saying that he needs to postpone his testimony to Congress because his family is being threatened by both Donald Trump and Rudy Giuliani. Some of Trump's tweets have had that flavor, encouraging law enforcement to go after Cohen's father-in-law for example, but Cohen seems to be implying that the threats have been more direct. If that is true, and he has any kind of proof, like a recorded phone call, Trump gave the prosecution more ammunition on which to indict him. This sounds like a clear case of witness intimidation. Here is the wording of the relevant law on that subject. "Whoever knowingly uses intimidation, threatens, or attempts to do so, with intent to Influence, delay, or prevent the testimony of any person,.."

Representative Elijah Cummings, who heads the Oversight Committee, says that comments from Trump and Giuliani are "mob tactics, and Cohen *will* be testifying, even if he has to be subpoenaed.

House Speaker Pelosi tells Trump, "There will be no state-of-the-union speech until the government is re-opened." Trump responded by saying, "She's afraid of the truth." Then he found out, via a note from Nancy, that he has no power to enter the Congressional chambers to deliver this speech unless a resolution is passed by both chambers specifying that an invitation can be extended.

Book Two (09/2018-11/2019)

This is a humiliating defeat that he was not prepared for, because he still doesn't grasp that the three branches of government are independent (or at least, supposed to be). Somebody please tell that to Acting AG Whittaker.

On Friday Paul Manafort has a court date to discuss his breach of the cooperation agreement on which he signed off, which will determine the length of his sentence.

People are now beginning to be evicted from their homes for failure to pay their rent, as a direct result of this insane shutdown. And Trump's response to their plight is the modern equivalent of Marie Antoinette's famous dismissive line, "Let them eat cake." His typical amount of empathy.

Presidential candidate for President, Senator Kamala Harris, was a guest on Rachel Maddow's show tonight. She pointed out that Trump's shutdown has greatly affected our national security, the very thing that Trump stresses as the essential need for his border wall. He does not grasp the priorities of the nation or the people who live in it.

Both of those bills to end the shutdown, mentioned a couple of days ago, failed to pass the Senate, as expected. The Democrats' bill came the closest with a vote that only missed be three, with six Republicans voting for it. So what now?

Commerce Secretary Wilbur Ross say's "I can't understand why people might need to go to food banks. They should go to the grocery stores, landlords etc. and work something out." He has no more clue how the world works than Trump has.

Mild-mannered, quiet and unassuming Senator Michael Bennett publicly and loudly ripped into Senator Ted Cruz over his insensitive remarks about the shutdown's effects on our population. Bennett's performance was called "a *Mr. Smith goes to Washington* moment." The *Washington Post* reports that the Republican Senators are clashing with each other over the shutdown. Senator Ron Johnson told McConnell. "This is all your fault!" They are truly cracking.

We just learned that two career FBI Security Specialists began conducting a background check on Jared Kushner shortly after he became part of the Trump administration, and it raised some concerns. They rejected his application for a top secret security clearance but their supervisor, Carl Kline, overrode that rejection. When Kushner applied for the level of security clearance *above* Top Secret, the CIA got involved and conducted a harsher background check. They asked how he even had the Top Secret clearance. Congress is now investigating how he, John Bolton, Michael Flynn and his son, K. T. McFarland and others received even the Top Secret level of clearance. Apparently, Kline overrode rejections at least thirty times.

Trump's suspicious relationship with Germany's Deutsche Bank has come under renewed and intense scrutiny as that bank becomes exposed to money laundering schemes to the tune of billions of dollars involving Russia. Intelligence Committee Chairman Adam Schiff and Banking Committee Chairwoman Maxine Waters plan a joint investigation into this bank and its ties to Donald Trump and Jared Kushner.

Michael Cohen has been subpoenaed to appear before the Senate Intelligence Committee.

What was supposed to be a big story on this day in Trump world (that Paul Manafort would finally be sentenced for his perjury crimes) turned out to be a dud after he got all dressed up in his best suit instead of his orange jump-suit for the occasion. The judge informed him that he was not yet ready to make a ruling on that question, and postponed it. But it would have been greatly overshadowed in any case by two huge new developments in a pretty close time frame.

The first of the two blockbusters was the pre-dawn raid and arrest of long time Trump associate/advisor Roger Stone—an event that Stone has been expecting for some time now. He was indicted and charged with seven counts, most of them related to his links to the WikiLeaks stolen emails affair and its connection to the Russians.

His indictment implicates Steve Bannon, among others in the Trump orbit, for "directing" (there's that word again) Stone to communicate with Julian Assange, head of WikiLeaks, for conspiratorial purposes involving Russian attempts to get Trump elected.

In the raid that resulted in Stone's arrest, his home was searched for additional evidence. One of the lies Stone is being charged with is his identification of the person whom he employed to make the final connection to Assange. He said it was a radio show host named Randy Credico, but it was actually conspiracy-theorist Jarome Corsi, whom we have heard about on several previous occasions, and who has already been charged for lying by the Mueller team. Paul Manafort is on record as saying that "Roger Stone is so connected to Donald Trump that it is hard to decide what comes from Roger and what comes from Donald." And so, we have another link in the chain that leads directly to Trump. The big question coming out of this development is, will Stone or Corsi be the next one to flip and testify against Trump?

The second blockbuster landed an hour or so later, when Trump decided that this would be an opportune time to announce that he was ready to, at least temporarily, end the shutdown (for three weeks) during which he expects both sides to meet and come to a satisfactory agreement, meaning he still thinks it will include money for his useless wall. There will be a

The Enemy Within: A Chronicle of the Trump Administration

Conference Committee established to thrash this out, during which they will discuss money for enhanced border security (without a wall), solving the humanitarian crisis involving separated children and parents, and DACA.

Ann Coulter, who along with Rush Limbaugh, scuttled the original agreement that would have *prevented* the shutdown, now labels Trump "the biggest wimp in US history." She personifies the meaning of the word "extremist."

Representative from California Eric Swalwell of the House Intel Committee says that they plan to release to Mueller the transcripts of the testimony of *all* the witnesses who appeared before that previous sham of an investigation that was controlled by the Republicans.

Only a couple of interesting comments pertaining to the Trump saga worth reporting this weekend.

Trump had a very bad week between feeling the need to concede on the shutdown standoff, and seeing his close advisor and confidant Roger Stone arrested. So he went on a tweet rampage again, first trying to say that reopening the government was not a concession, then going on to attack all his enemies including the "fake news" channels and all his accusing "liars", and finally blasting out an all caps "WITCH HUNT". Well, so far six important witches have been exposed.

Stone, who in the past has sworn that he would never turn on Trump, now says that "cooperation is not off the table. Cohen said the same thing before he finally decided that he and his family had to come first.

The most pressing question of the year continues to be, why are so many people in the Trump camp lying so consistently about things that should not be a big deal? What are they all hiding?

Book Two (09/2018-11/2019

February, 2019

Jan. 28-Feb. 3

A very busy start to the week—thirteen newsworthy Trump-related items.

February will be a very busy and very significant month, with several court appearances and/or sentences scheduled to take place, plus the Senate confirmation hearing on William Barr for Attorney General.

A new bill was introduced by the Senate Intel Committee, backed by both Democrat Senator Blumenthal and Republican Senator Grassley, which would make it a law that *all* Special Prosecutors' reports will be made available to the public, probably triggered by the prospect of Barr becoming the new Attorney General.

Senator Blumenthal also is pushing for several witnesses to be re-interviewed by Congress, including Donald Trump Jr.

Acting AG Whitaker says that "the Mueller report is close to being completed." He certainly is in a position to know.

Former CIA chief John Brennon had this to say about Trump and his attitude toward his own intelligence agencies: "Your cabal of unprincipled, unethical, dishonest and sycophantic cronies is being methodically brought to justice. We all know where this trail leads. If your utter incompetence is not enough to run you out of office, your obvious political corruption surely will."

Book Two (09/2018-11/2019)

Former Starbucks CEO Howard Schultz is exploring a possible independent run for president, which could be another spoiler candidacy.

The big Trump tax cut that was supposed to "trickle down" to the middle class has proven to be a complete failure for everyone except the super-rich, just as Trump intended it.

Michael Cohen has agreed to testify to Congress, but in a closed session rather than in public. A date of February 8 has been set.

Paul Manafort's court date for the Southern District of New York has been indefinitely postponed, because of ongoing related investigations.

The Trump organization has fired twelve undocumented maintenance staff at his golf club at Westchester New York, after they had been working there for several years.

The shutdown cost this country $11 million. And we may see it resumed in a couple of weeks.

Senator Kamala Harris attracted twenty thousand people to her first campaign rally in Oakland CA, her home state. A great start!

A new poll on the country's view of how this administration is doing, shows the following results: Heading in the right direction—28%; On the wrong track—63%

A collective meeting of all the heads of our various intelligence agencies was held today, in which every one of Trump's opinions and actions on a wide variety of important subjects were strongly disputed, namely: North Korea, Iran, ISIS, cyber security threats, the secret meetings between Trump and Putin, and Russia's interference in our past and future elections. According to the *New York Times* and *Financial News,* a *new* secret meeting was revealed, taking place during the G20 meeting last November—the one when he supposedly *cancelled* a planned meeting with Putin, but actually held one that we are just hearing about.

Congresswomen Jackie Speier reveals that Treasury Secretary Mnuchin personally benefited greatly by the Senate's refusal to reinstate those sanctions against Deripaska and his companies, which constitutes a clear conflict of interest. This issue is certain to be revisited.

Tonight, Rachel Maddow told us about a man named Andrew Miller, who worked closely with Roger Stone in those communications with WikiLeaks in the scheme to use the emails stolen by Russia to influence the 2016 election. Miller was subpoenaed to testify to the D.C. grand jury, but has not honored the subpoena. He was planning to use this case to challenge the legitimacy of the Mueller probe. This is the same grand jury that indicted Roger Stone, and would normally have been disbanded after his arrest, but has not been, because they still have some unfinished business—and probably not just involving Stone or Miller. Best bet? Donald Trump Jr. who seems to have lied to all three of the committees to whom he gave testimony.

The Republicans have been dragging their feet in appointing their members to various congressional committees. This is hamstringing the intelligence committees who cannot release the transcripts of those who have testified to the prosecutors until they have both parties represented.

Michael Gerson, a former speechwriter for George W. Bush, has written an op-ed for *The Washington Post* in which he states that "Donald Trump is a fraud," the same label that Mitt Romney gave him during the campaign. Gerson says that the

Book Two (09/2018-11/2019)

final proof of this is his utter defeat by Nancy Pelosi over the wall funding issue. But that's not proof he's a fraud—it's proof he is an inferior negotiator.

New Congresswoman from Georgia, Lucy McBath, whose son was killed by a white man for driving with his radio playing music too loudly, has filed a bill on the general topic of gun safety. She should carry some weight in that area.

Donald Trump and his National Security Advisor, John Bolton, are talking about possible military action against Venezuela, because of their new dictatorial regime. Trump has also announced sanctions on that country. Funny, I thought he loved dictators.

Our intelligence agencies are again warning that Russia is preparing to launch another interference campaign on the next election, but Trump is not listening.

Roger Stone has pled guilty and claims he has no intention of turning states evidence. That's what they all say, until they face reality.

There is growing bipartisan opposition to another shutdown when we reach February 15 and the reprieve runs out. Trump tweets that if the Democrats are not preparing a plan that includes funding for a wall, they are wasting their time. He still seems unaware that the Senate can override his veto and the winds are definitely heading in that direction. Any declaration of an emergency as a last gasp measure will cause an immediate challenge in court. In the meantime, he is trying to use eminent domain to seize a patch of land on the border that includes a small catholic church. That church is fighting him every inch of the way. This would be the first of scores of cases of such private property that would have to be seized in order for any worthwhile fence to be constructed, and then it would not do what he thinks it will.

The Republicans have finally named their members of the House Judiciary Committee, which frees up the Democrats to release those vital transcripts to the prosecution teams, which in turn will produce more indictments for lying to Congress.

As previously reported, the Russian company that was subpoenaed by Mueller in relation to the election interference, contested that subpoena in order to get "discovery info" with which they could get a good idea of what Mueller has for evidence. The judge in that case has just rejected their filing for "incorrect wording." Stay tuned.

One of Trump's big promises during the campaign was that he would bring back thousands of jobs, many of which would come from a new mammoth plant being built here in the US by a Chinese firm named Foxconn. That whole plan has fallen flat. There goes another promise.

The Democrats' bill to make Election Day a national holiday, in order to give more voters the opportunity to get to the polls, is being ridiculed by Mitch McConnell as "a power grab." That's right Mitch, it is allowing more people to take advantage of the "power" to vote, which you are well aware is not a good thing for your party.

Howard Schultz's entry into the race for president in 2020 is being roundly questioned and criticized as a very dangerous move that could result in four more years of Trumpism. There is very little chance that Trump will even be in the race then, but after 2016, anything is possible.

Trump had his usual childish response to the very critical comments made by his Intelligence Chiefs yesterday. Here is what he had to say to close out his customary tweet rant: "They

Book Two (09/2018-11/2019)

are wrong!--Perhaps Intelligence should go back to school." This is an unprecedented insult to his whole self-appointed intelligence community. Senator Schumer sent a letter to DNI Dan Coats asking him and the other directors to please educate Donald Trump on foreign policies and the facts related to them.

The problem is that he *cannot be educated.* Many have tried and many have failed, e.g. Generals Kelly, Mattis, and McMaster. He really believes that he knows more than anyone on any subject.

The way you can be sure that someone is of below average intelligence, is when they say things such as, "I'm like a very smart person. I have very good brain. I have the best words." Smart people do not have to tell you how smart they are. It is quickly obvious, and so is the reverse. If only ignorance were his only drawback.

Robert Mueller's indictment against the Russian operatives whom he charged with hacking into our data bases to subvert the election of 2016, contained the following passage: "The Russian co-conspirators communicated with US personnel about the release of stolen documents, which included a person who is in regular contact with senior members of the campaign of Donald Trump." This is a final, decisive link between the Russian and the Trump sides of the conspiracy to steal the election.

The judge in the Roger Stone case granted Mueller's request for more time to examine the mountain of documentary evidence taken from Stone's home when they arrested him. She has until October if she needs it before she starts his trial.

Trump met with DNI Coats today and came out of it saying that the media mischaracterized the comments made in Wednesday's joint meeting where all the intelligence chiefs were very critical of the President. Once again, he is just plain WRONG in this assertion.

The Enemy Within: A Chronicle of the Trump Administration

Trump made the outrageously inaccurate statement that he is losing a ton of money being president. Not only is he raking in all those illegal emoluments from his hotel towers and golf clubs, he saves millions as a direct result of his big tax cut for him and his rich friends, on top of his not insignificant salary that he promised he would not collect, but has.

Trump says he is giving up on negotiations with Pelosi and Schumer. It is a waste of time, so he will proceed with a different tactic. Maybe, the declaration of emergency? If so, he will again be rebuffed by his intelligence and threat-assessment people who never had the southern border on their list of threats.

The NRA is now trying to distance themselves from that shady business trip involving Maria Butina and the Russian "gun rights group." It's not looking good.

Senate leaders have obtained information on Donald Trump Junior's phone records, which will include that interesting call to a blocked number he made during the infamous Trump Tower meeting in June of 2016.

We start the new month with our country continuing to from bad to worse on a daily basis. It was bad enough that our president withdrew our country from the climate-change treaty, and the Iran treaty, and has been threatening to withdraw from NATO, which would essentially *destroy* that bulwark against Russian aggression. He is now about to scuttle the INF (Intermediate-range Nuclear Forces) treaty with Russia, which has been in effect since it was signed by Ronald Reagan and Mikhail Gorbachev. He thinks he can show us how tough he is being with Russia by taking us back into a nuclear arms race, which will be another huge gift to Putin.

Book Two (09/2018-11/2019)

Trump has repeatedly proclaimed that "we have built a lot of the wall" and "we have a lot of money to build it." Both claims are *false!* He says Pelosi's opposition is harming our country and that many Democrats want the wall to be built. He continues to be totally delusional on this and many other subjects.

Roger Stone has been shooting his mouth off so much since his arrest that the judge has threatened to impose a gag-order on him is he continues. This is the same no-nonsense judge who presides over the Manafort case. Stone's trial is not scheduled until late summer, maybe even October.

Trump claims that Rod Rosenstein, now once again the D*eputy* AG, has told him that he is not a target, or even a subject, of the Mueller probe. If you believe this one, bought any bridges lately?

The Democrats are preparing to force the release of Donald Trump's tax returns, along with several other investigatory moves. It will be interesting to see how much he struggles to resist this pressure that he has not had to face for his first two years in office.

When a *New York Times* reporter asked Trump about his Trump Tower Moscow project, Trump downplayed it as an "exploratory" inquiry with no real progress having been made, so he technically has no real "business" with Russia. There was certainly a lot of communication on the subject for it to be considered "no business." And again, why all the lies?

Trump's denials of any witness tampering on the part of himself or any of his associates shows his ignorance about what constitutes the meaning of that crime.

The Enemy Within: A Chronicle of the Trump Administration

Trump is now trying to paint himself as a defender of a free press in his latest interview with the *Times*. This from the man whose favorite war cry is "FAKE NEWS," and the one who constantly criticizes and insults reporters.

With so much going on these days, it is easy to forget about the fact that there are still hundreds of children in what amounts to concentration camps at our southern border, who are still waiting to be reunited with their parents. And the number continues to grow on a daily basis. But the worst aspect of all this misery is that our government is not even *trying* to remedy this awful situation. They have given up, citing a lack of funds and a lack of any kind of plan for tracking people.

The strange and disturbing dispute this past week between Trump and his Intelligence Directors, has provoked a frank and informative assessment by a writer for the *Washington Press*, of Trump's most serious problem facing him, and more importantly, our nation's security. Their story goes as follows.

"Pity the poor intelligence officials tasked with briefing our special-needs president with the information he requires to make crucial decisions concerning America's national security. They go out of their way to dumb things down to a level where they think President Trump might be able to comprehend the information that they are trying to get across. They employ *pretty pictures and diagrams as visual aids* so he might be able to absorb information in a manner that doesn't require big words. They call him Mr. President repeatedly to attract his attention like a cat's caretaker might use a laser pointer to get a feline's full attention."

Let the seriousness of *that* sink in.

Feb. 4-10

Trump's intelligence officials are still trying to convey and warn about his lack of knowledge or interest in foreign affairs, calling it "willful ignorance." Here is a sample of what they are telling the press. "Senior intelligence officials are breaking two

Book Two (09/2018-11/2019)

years of silence to warn that the President is endangering American security with what they say is a 'stubborn disregard' for their assessments. After a briefing in preparation for a meeting with British Prime Minister Theresa May, for example, the subject turned to the British Indian Ocean Territory of Diego Garcia. The island is home to an important airbase and a U.S. Naval Support Facility that are central to America's ability to project power, including in the war in Afghanistan. Officials familiar with the briefing say, the President asked two questions: "Are the people nice, and are the beaches good?" Unlike stupidity, ignorance can be corrected, if the subject wants to correct it. Unfortunately, our president doesn't even believe he has that problem—never has and never will.

Someone in the White House leaked a very informative story to *Axios* over the weekend. Trump is spending at east sixty percent of his time in the White House with what he labels "executive time," meaning, watching TV (mostly Fox News), calling friends, and just plain relaxing. He still does not read the daily briefing reports. In other words, it is another area in which he is doing the exact opposite of what he promised he would do all throughout his campaign.

The judge in the Southern District of New York has issued a subpoena to Trump's inauguration committee for all documentation pertaining to the inaugural fund (money collected, from whom, how spent, what is left and where is it?). The whole thing looks a lot like influence peddling, as well as misuse of funds. Everyone connected to that affair is in very hot water.

Trump's latest venture into fantasyland is his proclamation that "I can't be impeached because I'm doing the best job of any president in history." This is the very definition of the insanity called megalomania or, clinically, pathological narcissism.

The Enemy Within: A Chronicle of the Trump Administration

Paul Manafort had another day in court today where Mueller's team spent four hours laying out the lies that he told which nullifies their plea agreement and should strongly impact his sentence. The judge will define his fate sometime in March.

For the past several days there has been an uproar about the Democrat Governor of Virginia, Ralph Northam, who apparently had his picture taken for his medical school yearbook in 1984, where he was either the man in blackface or the one net to him in KKK garb, he's not sure which at this point. It was just exposed and the racism of it has prompted calls for his resignation. He has resisted those calls up to now, but the pressure in mounting. I have not mentioned this topic before because it did not seem to fit the subject of this book, but in one way it actually does. You see, those calls for him to resign are coming primarily from the members of his own party, which stands out in contrast with the way the Republicans sat in silence for years as people like Steve King and his ilk spouted their racist hate. It shows who has the moral high ground.

Several Republicans are now warning Trump against his threat to declare a national emergency. It will be interesting to see if he refers to that possibility in his state-of-the-union speech tomorrow night. That speech is a must-see, not only to count how many false statements he comes up with and what his general tone and thrust is, but what Stacy Abrams has to say about it in her rebuttal a few minutes later.

The only topic of the day is the President's seventy-five minute State-of-the-Union speech last night, which for the first hour or so was the most reasonable-sounding and well-delivered one that he ever gave. Someone must have tidied up the wording of what he wanted to say, and convinced him to stick to the teleprompter for a change. Whoever that was, kudos! Not an easy thing to do. But it was too good to last, and sure enough, he finally got around to saying the things he really wanted to say. He justified his withdrawal from Syria with the misrepresentation that ISIS has been squeezed into a tiny fraction of the territory where they had been in control, equating that with a complete elimination of the threat. He implied that if the Democrats wanted any real governance from him they should back off their plans to investigate him.

But the biggest bomb was when he officially announced his withdrawal from the INF treaty with Russia. His gifts to his puppet-master seems to have no bounds.

I was very disappointed in Stacy Abrams' rebuttal address, which was obviously prepared completely in advance rather than a "response" to what Trump said. She gave a good presentation of the Democrat platform and hopes for the future, but I expected her to point out where Trump was wrong in *his* address. She left that job to the fact-checkers and journalists on the cable news shows.

House Intelligence Committee Chairman Adam Schiff announced today that, in spite of Trump's not-so-implied threat last night, his committee is opening a multi-faceted investigation which will explore the following subjects: (a) Russian government operations to influence the US political process; (b) any links or coordination between Russia and Trump associates; (c) whether any foreign actor holds leverage over or has sought to compromise Donald Trump; (d) whether Trump or associates have been vulnerable to foreign pressure or sought to influence US policy for foreign interests; (e) whether any foreign or domestic actors solicited to impede investigations.

This should be enough to give Trump a queasy feeling in his big belly. Trump's response was to label Schiff a "political hack" who is "bent on presidential harassment."

It is looking like the Mueller probe may not be the biggest threat to the President. It is somewhat limited to the constraint of topics which have some link to the Russian interference in the 2016 election. There are several other investigations that are on other topics and are completely unrestrained like the one mentioned above.

For the first time in eight years the House is addressing the problem of gun violence. They are also going after that chaotic fiasco at the southern border where kids in the thousands haven't seen their parents for months.

Maria Butina's boyfriend, Paul Erickson, has been charged in North Dakota, with eleven counts of money-laundering and wire fraud. He has been released on bond—for now.

In his SOTU speech, Trump promised that he would not allow this country to slip into Socialism. Either he doesn't understand that we are already pretty much at that point, with our programs of Social Security, Medicare, Medicaid and several other government programs that make it possible for the lower and middle classes to survive with dignity; or he is well aware of that fact and wants to roll back such vital programs. God help us, and God help *him* if he tries to do that.

On December 12 we learned about a plea agreement that AMI and it's CEO David Pecker made with the Mueller team to cooperate in the case in which Michael Cohen is also embroiled, regarding both the hush money payments to Trump's "girlfriends", and some pay-for-influence deals with the Saudis. That deal was contingent upon AMI not committing any crimes in the meantime or for years into the future. Now we learn that one of Trump's and Pecker's biggest adversaries, *Washington Post* owner (and richest man in the world) Jeff Bezos, was being blackmailed by Pecker and company. He was threatening to expose very personal and damaging information, including nude photos they obtained through stolen emails, if Bezos didn't stop publishing negative articles about them, Trump, and the Saudis' Crown Prince, about the Khashoggi murder. Bezos decided he had had enough, and turned the tables by exposing

Book Two (09/2018-11/2019)

the stuff himself and filing suit for their politically motivated blackmail/extortion. This will nullify AMI's plea agreement and add another crime to the list for which they will be prosecuted. Trump is intimately involved in this whole case as the "individual one" referred to in the charges against Cohen and AMI.

Robert Mueller's latest revealed (though heavily redacted) documents in the Manafort case show that he is focusing on Manafort's correspondence with Ukrainian Konstantin Kilimnik. What was their motive and why were they lying?

The Republicans are trying to tie the lack of a border wall with the prevalence of gun violence in the US. They are desperate for any sort of justification for the wall at this point, ignoring the fact that the majority of Americans do not want such a wall. Acting AG Matt Whitaker will testify before the Senate's Judiciary Committee tomorrow to answer questions on a wide variety of subjects—most importantly, where he stands on the Mueller investigation.

It was a typically busy day for a Friday, with several very serious Trump-related threads to try to wrap our head around.

Matt Whitaker's hearing before the House Judiciary Committee today was nothing short of a national disgrace. The acting chief law-enforcement personage in the country gave us a clear image of why his appointment was for strictly political reasons, and his qualifications for the position, or lack thereof, had absolutely no bearing on his selection by our equally unqualified president. His attitude and non-answers were contentious, rude, crass, disrespectful and evasive from the beginning. The questioners did a very good job of at least trying to pin him down, and made him look really bad as he tried his best to play to his primary audience, Donald Trump. The pressure on him was so heavy that he drank several bottles of water during his hours in the hot seat.

When he was grilled about the "zero-tolerance" policy at the border, especially the lack of tracking of parents so that they could reunited with their children, he was stymied and dismissive. As to his interaction with the Mueller probe, he claims that he has not and will not interfere in any way, but the Senators repeatedly warned him that he had better stick to that policy.

In any case, we only have another week to sweat it out with him before his assignment expires and William Barr becomes the new AG, assuming the Senate confirms him. Even though Barr's past attitude toward the Special Counsel's power and scope have also been pretty scary, he appears to be an improvement over what we have now, and he will almost certainly be confirmed.

The AMI vs. Jeff Bezos case described yesterday has another aspect beside the crime of blackmail. That relationship that AMI has had with the Saudis, along with the Trump team, especially Jared Kushner, could turn out to be even *more* damaging to Trump and company. David Pecker seems to be very nervous about this Saudi aspect. It may prove to involve something even bigger than a blackmail charge. It has been exposed that this type of blackmail is standard operating procedure for this media company, according to sources from *within* that organization. They also have an inexplicable history of publishing very complimentary articles, and even a glossy booklet, praising the Saudi Crown prince and his policies.

Virginia Governor Ralph Northam has still not resigned, and his Lt. Governor, Justin Fairfax, is now *also* embroiled in an equally serious scandal involving charges of sexual assault by two women. He too has been called upon to resign or face impeachment by the Democrat lawmakers. It looks like Virginia won't be turning blue any time soon.

Book Two (09/2018-11/2019)

Maria Butina who has a plea agreement with her prosecutors, was scheduled for sentencing today, but both the defense and the prosecution asked for a postponement because they are not finished yet with her testimony. She apparently has a lot to tell them. The judge agreed to delay it until February 26. Michael Cohen's sentencing was also postponed until February 28. It sounds like something big is about to take place before the end of this month.

Those recently fired illegal immigrants that Trump finally decided needed to depart his Bedminster golf club are only the latest in a long list in a continuous pipeline that ran from a small town in Costa Rica directly to Trump properties. One of them told a reporter, "...my entire town practically lived there (Bedminster)."

The Trump re-election campaign fund has spent nearly $100,000 of the donors' money to pay Kushner's legal fees. That *can't* be legal!

Former Trump bodyguard, Keith Schiller, has been summoned to answer questions by Robert Mueller *and* Congress about payments of $15 thousand per month, for no apparent reason.

Roger Stone's lawyers are objecting to the fact that his case has been linked to the case of the Russian email hackers, *which Stone himself admitted to* when it was first exposed. Stone has been complaining about the "Gestapo tactics" of the police when they came to arrest him, but a video of that operation shows nothing of the sort. It was a textbook operation.

Subpoenas issued by the Southern District of New York suggest the possibility that they involve a RICO (Racket Influenced and Corrupt Organization act) charge against the Trump organization.

The Enemy Within: A Chronicle of the Trump Administration

In spite of the above, and other black clouds gathering, Ivanka Trump says she has "zero concern" about any of the probes going on around her whole family. Either oblivious or stupid.

It was a relatively uneventful weekend in the Trump saga. The most important comes first in my short list.

The end of our temporary reprieve in the shutdown fiasco looms ahead this coming Friday, and negotiations seem to be at a standstill at this point. Trump's Chief-of-Staff, Mick Mulvaney, says that a national emergency may be declared, which would end up in a court battle. A compromise that includes a few sections of a new barrier being added to what already exists, where they are deemed rational, with a couple of billion dollars being allocated for those and other more technical security measures at the ports of entry, would be a reasonable solution. Let's see if both adversaries can be that reasonable.

Alexandra Ocasio Cortez is pushing a program named "The Green New Deal" which would do a lot to combat Trump's very environmentally harmful policies on the all-important problem of climate-change.

Massachusetts Senator Elizabeth Warren and Minnesota Senator Amy Klobuchar announced their candidacy for president this weekend, adding to the growing list of Democrats, including five women, who want their shot at unseating Trump, who probably won't even be President in 2020 if there is any justice in this country.

This weekend seems to be a good point to speculate about what may be in the works this month, according to several previously mentioned indicators. So far, we have seen the indictment and arrest of Trump's National Security Advisor,

Michael Flynn, his election campaign manager, Paul Manafort, and Manafort's chief aide, Rick Gates, all of whom have pled guilty and are cooperating with the Special Prosecutor. We have also seen the indictment of the Chief Financial Officer of Trump's company, Allen Weisselberg, and Trump's personal attorney and fixer, Michael Cohen, who have been charged and are cooperating with Mueller. More recently we have seen the indictment and arrest of Trump's long-time supporter and advisor, Roger Stone, who has not yet flipped but it is probably only a matter of time. The only people above them to go after now, short of the President himself, are members of his family. Ivanka seems to have had little to do with the Russian conspiracy (her financial crimes will be prosecuted by the Attorney General of New York), but the odds are very high that the next indictments will go to Donald Trump Jr. and Jared Kushner. They will either come just before or simultaneous with the presentation of at least the first installment of Mueller's report to the US Attorney General, William Barr. That could well be the February surprise.

Feb. 11-17

Trump held another pep rally today, this one in El Paso, Texas—the city where he recently tried to sell his lie that crime has been greatly reduced there because they built a wall separating it from Mexico. The fact that the El Paso crime rate was impressively low *before* their wall was built was immediately pointed out, but that did not deter him from repeating his con-job at the rally. It was a strange choice of venue for Trump, because he lost to Clinton in that city by 69 to 26 percent in 2016.

At the same time, only a couple of miles away, Beto O'Rourke held his own rally to a much larger crowd than Trump's (but of course Trump lied to his crowd about it) where he described how vulnerable Trump has become because of his lies and anti-American policies. He related stories of the heroism in both world wars by illegal Mexican immigrants who died for their new country.

The brother of Jeff Bezos' mistress, a man named Michael Sanchez, is now known to be the source of that damaging personal data given to the Enquirer for the purpose of helping Donald Trump, whom he supported. He was a friend of Roger Stone and others in the Trump camp. He obviously did not expect his action to backfire as it did against the media giant.

One of Trump's recent tweets exposes the real reason he is so adamant about his wall. He is not really concerned about keeping down the crime rate. Here is his real purpose: "Gallop poll: 'Open borders will potentially attract 42 million Latin Americans.' This would be a disaster for the US. We need the wall now!" In other words, "You know we can't let all those brown people into our country to further pollute the gene pool." This is the *definition* of racism.

The previously mentioned revelation coming out of Manafort's hearing transcript, which ties him to Kilimnik for the quid-pro-quo deal of "we relax sanctions etc. while you help Trump get elected," now appears that it might have been a deliberate signal of where Mueller is going and how much he has as evidence. A warning of things to come?

Senator Klobuchar held her first rally in her home state of Minnesota in a snowstorm, which drew an impressive crowd in spite of the weather. Some of them arrived there on skies. Then this evening she was a guest on the *Rachel Maddow Show*, where she was quite impressive. She is in her third term as a Senator, winning big each time, and is well liked, even by her Republican cohorts, because she has a centrist reputation. Her only drawback so far seems to be her tough attitude toward her staff. They always seem to come up with something negative when the candidate is a woman.

Book Two (09/2018-11/2019)

A bipartisan deal has been struck by both the House and the Senate to pass a budget that includes less than $2 billion for a small section of fence and enhanced technical security measures. The main bone of contention in their negotiations was not over the wall, but over the number of detention beds to fund for those immigrants being held while their case is being heard, and the number and type of ICE raids on those who have been here for years. Trump won't like this deal at all, but he may feel compelled to accept it after he lost so much support over the last shutdown. His friends on *Fox* certainly won't want him to take it. The ball is squarely in the President's court now.

It looks and sounds like Trump is ready and willing to grudgingly sign off on the agreement that will avoid another shutdown. At his rally yesterday he lied to his crowd of sheep again, by telling them that the construction on the wall was already underway and the new bill ensures that it will continue. His new slogan is Finish the Wall. The crowd ate it up, but his ultra-right media puppet-string pullers are not happy at all. Trump is probably wishing he had never created this Frankenstein monster of an issue during his election campaign, but he also realizes that he would not have won without that hypnotically racist goal.

Mitch McConnell supports this agreement and expects Trump will sign it. Trump tries to save face with the following tweet: "I want to thank all Republicans for the work you have done in dealing with the Radical Left on Border Security. Not an easy task, but the Wall is being built and will be a great achievement and contributor toward life and safety within our country!" As predicted, accepting defeat and calling it a win.

The next major bone of contention will be the newly proposed Green New Deal, proposed by Alexandra Ocasio-Cortez, which is being strongly backed by progressives, but strongly condemned by conservatives for being too restrictive on certain businesses. It will come down to how many people want to try to save the planet for our children. This battle will continue long after Trump is out of office.

The Republican-controlled Senate Intel Committee has come out, even before their sham investigation is over, with the very premature and misleading statement that they "have found no *direct* evidence that there was any collusion with Russia by the Trump campaign." There are *two* types of evidence that are admissible in court. The other is *circumstantial,* such as when you hear a shot in the next room and you run in to find a person standing staring at a body with a gun in his hand. You did not see him shoot but the conclusion is obvious. If they want *direct* evidence they will probably get their fill of it when Mueller issues his report.

One of Trump's super-donors, billionaire and coal magnate Bob Murphy, is about to be rewarded for contributing $300,000 to the Trump inauguration fund *after* the inauguration was long over. Trump is *pressuring* the Tennessee Valley Authority to continue using Murphy's company's obsolete coal plant instead of updating their equipment as planned. He did so via this tweet: "Coal is an important part of our electricity generation mix and *@TVAnews* should give serious consideration to all factors before voting to close viable power plants, like Paradise #3 in Kentucky!" This is classic quid-pro-quo corruption at the highest level.

The recently-revealed August 2, 2016 meeting between Manafort, Gates and Kilimnik, which was held in the Grand Havana Room at 666 6th Ave. in New York, owned by the Kushner family, has become a strong focal point of the Mueller probe. The topic of the so-called "Peace Plan" involving the Ukraine-Russia conflict, and the sanctions that were imposed by the Obama administration because of it, is one of the main linchpins of the conspiracy charge. Manafort is due back, after a couple of postponements, in court tomorrow.

Book Two (09/2018-11/2019)

Former Senator Heidi Heitkamp, on the *Rachel Maddow Show* tonight, said that she has no regrets about voting against Brett Kavanaugh for the Supreme Court, even though it cost her re-election to her Senate seat. If only there were more politicians who put country ahead of self-promotion.

Presidential candidate Senator Cory Booker also appeared on Rachel's show and gave us a look into his ideas. He said he plans to vote against the confirmation of Bill Barr for AG because he feels he has many of the views of former AG Sessions. Let's hope not, but I fear he is probably right. Booker says that if he gets the nomination he will most likely select a woman for his running mate.

At a filmed meeting today Trump was upbeat enough to be in a celebratory mood. He even suggested that our country should give serious thought to having a parade, with fireworks, on our next Independence Day. In addition to never having done any grocery shopping, he has been hiding in a cave every July 4th all of his life, I guess.

Paul Manafort had his very important day in court today, and it did not go well for him. The judge listed three topics that he deliberately lied about, for which she is nullifying his plea deal and rejecting any recommendations for clemency. He will now probably get a sentence that will consume the rest of his life. That sentence will be handed down on March 13 in the D.C. court.

The third of the three topics about which he lied, knowing that he was gambling with his fate by doing so, was that August 12, 2016 meeting with Russian intelligence agent Konstantin Kilimnik, where he not only discussed sanctions but also handed over polling data that could be, and was, used by the Russians to influence the 2016 election. The only rational reason, says Representative Adam Schiff, for lying about this subject, in his position, would be to try to maintain some degree of grace with the President and leave the door open for a pardon.

Adam Schiff also declared that his Intel Committee will use every power at their disposal to ensure that the Mueller report will be presented both to Congress and to the public.

Tonight, Rachel Maddow gave us an interesting summation of how, in every case involving Trump's prosecuted allies and staff—Flynn, Manafort, Cohen, and several others—they have lost on every step along the way through the courts. Mueller has yet to lose one, in his huge and lengthy investigation.

The House Judiciary Committee has accused Matt Whitaker of lying during his recent hearing, and they have summoned him back to clear up his testimony. If he doesn't do it voluntarily, they *will* subpoena him.

At the end of August, Manafort-linked lobbyist Samuel Patten, pled guilty to making illegal contributions to the Trump inauguration committee, and for failing to register as a foreign lobbyist for the Ukrainians. He has now had his sentencing date set for April 12.

During his campaign Trump promised to greatly reduce, if not eliminate, the national debt, which he criticized Obama for increasing. But in his two years in office *he* has increased it by 2.1 trillion dollars, to a record total of $22 trillion, and economists predict that, with the current tax rates, it will keep on increasing at that pace.

The House Judiciary Committee has proposed a resolution called the Bipartisan Background Check Act, which is the first major gun-violence legislation since 1993. Let's hope it passes both chambers.

Book Two (09/2018-11/2019)

Insiders have revealed that Trump has installed a new $50k system for practicing his golf swing inside the White House, so even when he can't get away to one of his properties to play, he can spend some of his voluminous "executive time" with his new toy, while telling everyone that he works longer and harder than any president before him.

Many people are discovering that their tax refunds are smaller this year as a result of Trump's big tax cut that primarily benefitted the super-rich. Trickle-down economics has failed once again, just as predicted.

The controversy over the Green New Deal sounds a lot like the one over Obamacare. They both need some tweaking on an item by item basis, but the goal is essential.

Trump talks about "finding the funds" to continue adding sections of fence to his "concrete wall," the one he now describes as so high that trying to climb over it would be like scaling Mount Everest (another of his patented narcissistic lying exaggerations). It will be interesting, and a bit nerve-wracking, to see where he intends to grab the money, which will probably be hotly contested by both sides of the political aisle.

Trump signed the budget bill today (Valentine's Day) and then declared a national emergency, against the advice of practically everyone, in a last ditch effort to acquire the funds to keep adding to his wall. It will be declared unconstitutional almost before the ink dries. He has absolutely no basis for claiming an emergency. The bill passed the Republican-controlled Senate by a vote of 83 to 16, with a few Democrats voting against it because it conceded too much money, in their opinion. This left Trump no choice but to sign it or see his veto overridden. He ended up with less wall money than was in the agreement that he had in his hand before he let Ann Coulter talk him out of it.

The Enemy Within: A Chronicle of the Trump Administration

The Republican Senators' attitudes now may be foretelling how they will vote on the impeachment issue when they have to face it. They are driven by self-preservation and that goal is no longer leaning toward supporting this president. Sarah Sanders delivered her usual lying spin on Trump's humiliating defeat on the wall quest, with a statement that included the following: "The President is once again delivering on his promise to build a wall, protect the border, and secure our great country."

William Barr was confirmed today by the Senate and is now, for better or worse, our new Attorney General.

Former Acting FBI Director Andrew McCabe is out with a new book titled, *The Threat*, in which he goes into considerable detail about the danger that Trump's mental state has caused and is causing to the USA. He tells about several occasions when they discussed the possibility of invoking the Twenty-Fifth Amendment to have him removed from office and replaced by Pence, but they would need the backing of Pence and that was very unlikely, so they refrained.

Trump just had his annual physical exam and once again was pronounced to be in excellent shape, not only now but well into the future, which is a very risky foretelling of how well his health will hold up considering his eating habits and job pressure.

Trump made a short but unusually crazy speech outside the White House today to explain his totally unjustified border emergency. He included the incredibly stupid (even for him) declaration that "I didn't have to do it, I just wanted to speed things up." Nothing like shooting down your action before most people can even absorb the magnitude of the *problem* with your action. It isn't an emergency if "you didn't have to do it", Mr. President; and it isn't an emergency when the rate of flow of illegals over the border is at its lowest point since the early

Book Two (09/2018-11/2019)

1970's; and it isn't an emergency when the Americans along the border do not see a problem.

Have I mentioned before that he is his own worst enemy? Ironically, this is his most redeeming character trait, because it means he will provide that much more reason to impeach him. You know you have a problem when one of your staunchest backers, Ann Coulter, says this about you: "No one thought, oh, look, he was governor of the biggest state in the union! He used to run the CIA! He was Reagan's Vice President, you know, he was FDR's. No, it was *one thing*. The promise he made every single day at every single speech. So forget the fact that he's digging his own grave. This is, just look, the only national emergency is that our president is an idiot." Well said, Ann.

Parroting the exact words of his other friends on *Fox News*, Trump explained that his directive will no doubt be rejected by the 9th circuit court in California, after which he will bypass the appeals court and bring it directly to the Supreme Court where he expects it will be found to be constitutional, because he now has a four to three majority of conservatives there, thanks to his two appointments. But Chief Justice Roberts may not be the ally Trump assumes him to be.

In addition to his undermining of his own case for an emergency, Trump's unusually degree of incoherence and rambling gave several cabinet and law-enforcement officials deep concern about his deteriorating mental state. For example, retired General McCaffrey said, "listening to Trump's talk today was very disturbing and worrisome because of both its content and its incoherence."

Andrew McCabe's new book reveals that when the Intel Committee Directors told Trump about North Korea firing a new ICBM, he said he does not believe it because Putin told him otherwise. No puppet?

The Enemy Within: A Chronicle of the Trump Administration

Roger Stone's indictment shows that he was linked to those GRU officers who hacked the emails, through his communications with WikiLeaks and Guccifer 2.0, the hacker's tag name. The two main personal links on the Russian side were Konstantin Kilimnik and Natalie Veselnitskaya, paired with Americans Paul Manafort and Donald Trump Jr., the *core* of the conspiracy to elect Trump.

The Probation Office and Robert Mueller have both recommended to the Virginia court that Manafort be sentenced to between nineteen and a half years and twenty-four and a half years in prison, plus a fine of $50 thousand to $24 million. Additional time and fines will eventually come from the Southern District of New York. Manafort is obviously hoping for a Trump pardon, but Trump should know that such a pardon would be seen as another powerful case of obstruction.

The House Judiciary Committee will be putting together the same evidence and case as Robert Mueller, according to Chairman Adam Schiff, so firing or squelching Mueller won't help Trump much at all.

William Weld has announced that he will be running as an alternative candidate for the Republican Party in the 2020 election. He says the Republicans in Congress are "suffering from 'Stockholm Syndrome'."

The House Intel Committee has opened an investigation into whether Trump has been compromised by a foreign power, namely Russia, and has become an agent of that country.

Trump specified where he intends to appropriate funds to "continue" building his wall. The sources are: (A) $1.3 billion from Congress; (B) $600 million from the Treasury Department's Drug Forfeiture Fund; (C) $2.5 billion from the Department of Defense Counter Drug Activation; (D) $3.6

Book Two (09/2018-11/2019)

billion from the Defense Military Construction Project. The legal counter-measures are underway.

Vice President Pence attended the annual Security Conference today. This one was in Munich, Germany. When he opened his remarks by sending greetings from the President of the United States, Donald Trump, he paused for the expected applause, only to be greeted by an embarrassing silence. So much for Trump's claim that he has "restored the respect of the world for our great nation."

Feb. 18-24

McCabe's book *The Threat* has stirred up more of a flurry of reaction and concern than most of the other Trump exposure books that have been produced in the past couple of years. It is bound to have an impact on the general public's image of this president, who is already holding on by his fingertips. There are alarming conversations among upper echelon FBI personnel, about the appearance that Trump was an agent of the Russians and that was what actually triggered, along with the firing of Comey, the appointment of Special Counsel Robert Mueller. McCabe smartly preserved the notes, memos, and investigation structure of this topic, in case Trump stepped in to stop them at some point in the future. So far, sixteen states have filed law suits against Trump's emergency declaration. Congress is preparing a resolution to stop it, which Mitch McConnell will have no choice but to bring up.

When Mueller subpoenaed Deutche Bank early in his probe, and crossed Trump's "red line" of his finances, the President was so angry he tried repeatedly to get someone to fire the Special Counsel. Now, the House Intel Committee has started to follow that same path of "follow the money." There will be no presidential interference with *that* probe.

The Enemy Within: A Chronicle of the Trump Administration

Roger Stone made the very stupid mistake of posting on Instagram a photo of the judge in his case, showing a pair of crosshairs next to her face. When he came to his senses, he removed it and issued a written apology, but this probably won't help his case very much. This is the same judge that is presiding over Manafort's case and the one involving the GRU hackers. She is not someone you want to piss off.

This is President's Day, and crowds of people across the country observed it by protesting against their president's emergency action.

Four candidates for the Democrat nomination for president toured the country this weekend, *all of them* drawing huge crowds.

The investigation into the North Carolina voter-ballot fraud case, which benefitted Mark Harris, has produced substantial evidence of criminal behavior. Now the election committee has to decide if it is warranted to have a new election. A decision is due tomorrow. Harris could be in deep trouble. In addition to ballot collection and filling in, there is also evidence of witness tampering.

Rod Rosenstein will be leaving the DOJ in March. It will be interesting to see who replaces him as Barr's Deputy.

Japanese Prime Minister Abe has written a letter to the Nobel Peace Prize Committee nominating Donald Trump for the prize. He confesses that he did so at Trump's request. Narcissist-in-Chief, meet your latest loyal Suck-up.

Well, the whirlwind of Trump saga news keeps swirling more furiously by the day. One of Trump's favorite targets in his ongoing war against freedom of the press, the "failing *New York Times*", has now published a multi-page article covering a couple of very important--one could say--"explosive",

Book Two (09/2018-11/2019)

revelations that will further add to the growing case of obstruction against the criminal who we have leading our country. This heads today's list of items.

Four NYT journalists collaborated to write the following story. One week into Trump's presidency, Sally Yates, the Deputy Attorney General under Obama, testified to Congress that they had conclusive evidence that Trump's National Security Advisor, Michael Flynn, was compromised by the Russians, and subject to being blackmailed. That warning to Congress and to the White House went unaddressed for an unexplainable *eighteen days,* before Flynn was "fired" by Trump. Now, it is revealed that Trump told his spokesman, Sean Spicer, to *say* that he had fired Flynn, when Flynn actually left without being asked. Trump lied to make it look like he finally acted on the warning.

The *Times* story also told, thanks to whistleblowers, about Flynn's lengthy effort to promote a deal to transfer nuclear energy technology to Saudi Arabia, who has no need for peaceful nuclear power. That technology can easily be used, not just to generate electricity, but to create nuclear bombs.

Another major topic in that Times story involves Trump's two-year effort to control, or even squelch, the investigations that were obviously headed toward targeting him. House Judiciary Committee chairman, Jerry Nadler, has sent a letter to Matt Whitaker asking him to come back and explain his apparent false statements about President Trump's communication with him on the subject of the investigations that are underway; and if he applied any pressure to get a Trump loyalist named Geoffrey Berman assigned to oversee the New York case against Cohen. Whitaker is on record as saying his role as AG was "to jump on a grenade for Trump." To this, Trump responds with his usual defense: "Fake News!" *Politico* reports that the Manhattan court may ignore the DOJ policy of not indicting a sitting president, and just go ahead and test that unwritten rule.

In the North Carolina vote fraud case, that Republican candidate for Congress, Mark Harris, who won the seat by less than a thousand votes, communicated with McCrae Dowless, the man who hired the firm that executed the fraudulent vote-handling scheme. Redo of the election may be imminent.

In the Georgia version of voter fraud, involving the Governor's race which Stacy Adams narrowly lost, she is still fighting the highly mismanaged election, not for herself, but for future candidates.

Roger Stone will appear back in court Thursday to explain his threatening Instagram photo of the judge. He will be lucky is he is not remanded immediately to jail.

Trump is back to promoting his superfluous "Space Force" plan, which is an even bigger fantasy than his border wall. Just another attempt to distract.

The replacement that Trump has chosen to replace the departing Rosenstein is Jeffrey Rosen. He is currently in the Department of Transportation and has the usual zero experience in anything related to the DOJ, just like all of Trump's appointments. On tonight's Lawrence O'Donnell show, Andrew McCabe described how tough a job Rosen is stepping into. Lots of luck, Jeffrey.

Bernie Sanders announced his entry (once again) into the Presidential race. He is facing a very different set of circumstances this time around. I predict—zero chance of getting the nomination.

McCabe's new book, *The Threat,* was reviewed, vetted and approved by several high-ranking officials of the FBI before it was published. Among the many shocking things the book reveals is the fact that Trump has expressed a serious desire to use military force, essentially start a war, with Venezuela, for the purpose of confiscating their ample oil deposits. If you only read one book about the problems with the Trump administration (beside this one) you should read McCabe's, *The Theat*. Between him and James Comey, what becomes very clear is; what we have sitting in the Oval Office today is the most powerful and dangerous mob boss in our history—just this side of a full-out dictator, which is what he fervently wants to become.

Several in-the-know sources are saying the Mueller report is going to be presented before this month is over—only one week to go. It could happen a day or two before or after Cohen's testimony to Congress on the 27th. I am still expecting it to be accompanied by at least three indictments. I will be surprised if this report is Mueller's final say on the subject. McCabe is expressing confidence that it will be at least partially shared with the general public. It looks as though, because of the timing, its release may have been at the command of new AG Barr. Between Mueller and Cohen, Trump may be in for a devastating end to the month.

McCabe, on tonight's MSNBC program, *All In,* described his first meeting with Trump in the Oval Office right after Comey was fired and McCabe was made acting FBI Director. Trump went on a rambling monologue about why he fired Comey and how everyone at the FBI was so happy to see him go (completely untrue). It had the feeling, McCabe said, of a loyalty test.

Politico reports that there is already underway a concerted campaign, via social media, to undermine the Democrat candidates for president, similar to what they did in 2016.

The Enemy Within: A Chronicle of the Trump Administration

The FBI has arrested a neo-Nazi, white-supremacist who was planning on executing a mass murder of white people, concentrating on Democratic candidates and MSNBC hosts. He had a huge cache of weapons, including assault rifles, in his home, and writings in which he expressed the desire to wipe out the whole human race. He was a former Coastguardsman and ardent Trump supporter.

Roger Stone faced the judge today and was sternly reprimanded and officially gagged, but was not remanded to jail, so he got lucky.

Michael Cohen is scheduled to appear before *three* Congressional Committees in three days this coming week, the last of the three, in open court. Roger Stone's sentencing date is scheduled for March 8.

The North Carolina election board has voted to redo the midterm election for the contest for Representative to Congress, between Republican Mark Harris and Democrat Dan McCready, due to proven ballot fraud in November. I'll predict that Harris's less-than-a-thousand vote edge will disappear.

Trump's Labor Secretary, Alex Acosta, has been charged by a federal judge for giving a secret, non-prosecution agreement to a serial child-molester. His resignation is imminent.

Nancy Pelosi has sent a letter to Congress stating that Donald Trump's "emergency" declaration is unconstitutional and must be stopped.

In 1973, during the Watergate scandal, there was a question raised as to whether Vice-President Spiro Agnew could be indicted for the several crimes for which they believed him to be guilty. The Attorney General at the time, Robert Dixon, concluded that Agnew *could* be, but that the President could not, because of the vital importance of his position. That "policy" has remained the standard ever since, but there is nothing in the Constitution which backs it up, nor has it been made into law. Leon Jaworski, the Special Prosecutor at that time, did not agree with that finding, but before he could test it, Nixon resigned. It is time to reconsider testing it.

The Mueller report is said by several sources to be on its way any day now. But we have heard that story before. I won't hold my breath, but I'll be crossing my fingers.

The Prosecutors in the southern district of New York (SDNY) say they have prepared a whole set of charges, different from those that Mueller will bring (to avoid the double-jeopardy problem), that they will level against Manafort, even if Trump pardons him for the federal crimes. Cohen has been providing a wealth of dirt on Trump's financial dealings and his business organization that involved Manafort.

Cohen will almost certainly provide that same sort of information to the Congressional committees he will meet with next week, which will be devastating to the President, and of course he has already given it to Mueller.

Several right-wing nuts, acting as Trump spokesmen, have been ranting about the *probability* of a second Civil War if Trump is impeached. An actual war is probably not likely, but a rash of domestic terrorism attacks certainly can be expected, because that is how crazy those kooks have become, with Trump's incitement.

In North Carolina, in addition to a do-over election for that disputed House seat, there will be criminal charges filed against all those who had a hand in the ballot fraud.

Director of National intelligence, Dan Coats, said that they expect "foreign actors" to use even more sophisticated tactics to interfere with the *next e*lection. Of course, Trump is still pretending not to believe any of it, all the while privately cheering Putin on.

The Daily Beast has asked all the declared presidential candidates if they would sign a pledge not to use stolen data in their campaign. The only one who refused was Donald Trump.

A source in the Mueller team says that the report will *not* be released this coming week. That person did not rule out that it would be out shortly.

Over this weekend there was non-stop discussion about when we could expect the Mueller report to be released, how much of it the public, or even Congress, would be able to see of it, and what impact it will have on the President and the nation. The impact will not depend so much on what Mueller's conclusions are, but on what evidence he is able to provide that back up those conclusions. That evidence must cover at least the two most serious of his many crimes: the conspiracy with Russia to influence the election in his favor; the several attempts to obstruct the investigation into that conspiracy.

Adam Schiff, Chairman of the House Intelligence Committee, vows that the report will be made public, except for sensitive material related to national security, even if they have to subpoena documents and Robert Mueller himself. They are putting pressure on AG Barr to be as transparent as possible.

Trump is preparing for his second summit meeting with North Korean leader Kim Jong Un. They will meet in Hanoi, Vietnam this coming week. He may be able to see how little Kim has done toward denuclearization, and he will no doubt praise him for it.

Trump has chosen his new Ambassador to the UN. She is Kelly Craft, who is ambivalent about climate change, and has

Book Two (09/2018-11/2019)

the usual amount of experience we see in Trump's post assignments—none.

Mueller's sentencing memo in the Manafort case finally came out on Saturday. It was twenty-five pages of summary, plus eight hundred pages of appendices. There was no recommendation for clemency, but just the reverse.

The Enemy Within: A Chronicle of the Trump Administration

Book Two (09/2018-11/2019)

March, 2019

Feb. 25-March 3

The House resolution against Trump's emergency declaration, that they started preparing last week, is now ready to be presented for a vote tomorrow, and already has the support of at least two Republican Senators. Former Director of 3former intelligence officials have signed a memo to Congress stating that Trump's "emergency" does not in fact exist.

When Trump last met with Kim Jong Un he agreed to cease joint military exercises with South Korea, as part of his deal for Kim's denuclearization. This, Trump has said, was done at the advice of Vladimir Putin. There has been no sign of any such action on Kim's part. Now, there is broad concern among our military about what else Trump will give Kim, without getting anything in return. The House Intel Committee has raised the alarm about the rise of authoritarianism around the world, as Trump heads to conduct what he sees as another "lovefest" with the murderous dictator of North Korea.

Paul Manafort's lawyers have filed a lengthy brief detailing why they believe that their client should be given leniency in his sentencing, due on March 13. They claim there are only "minor crimes" listed, not anything serious like collusion with Russia. Do they think that passing reams of polling data to Kilimnik isn't collusion?

Maria Butina will appear in court tomorrow for a status hearing on her case of spying etc. She has been cooperating with prosecutors and may get off with nothing more than deportation to Russia, but she may find that she is "persona-non-grata" at home.

The Wall Street Journal reports that the House Judiciary Committee has evidence that Trump *has* discussed with

The Enemy Within: A Chronicle of the Trump Administration

Whitaker the prospect of putting Geoffrey Berman, a Trump supporter, in control of the New York case against Cohen. If true, they have a perjury case against Whitaker.

A former Trump campaign staffer named Alva Johnson has filed a lawsuit against Trump for forcibly kissing her during his 2016 campaign. She is also suing for unequal pay due to her race and gender. She is a former avid supporter of the President, but is now completely disillusioned about him. She is the seventeenth woman to make such a charge.

More and more Republicans are showing their complete denial of man-made climate change, something that stems in large part by their dependence upon major donors like coal magnates.

On Rachel Maddow's show tonight, Brennan said that he expects Mueller's report to come out in March and will be accompanied by more indictments, including Trump family members.

As Trump was ridiculing people who wear glasses, a new poll came out that shows that the number of Americans who say they "would never vote for Trump" has reached 57%!

Today begins three straight days of testimony by Trump's former personal lawyer and fixer, Michael Cohen, who will soon be spending a few years behind bars at a federal penitentiary. The man who has often said he would take a bullet for Donald Trump and would never turn on him, reached the point in his life and situation where he felt he had no choice but to tell the real story of working with the biggest conman this country has ever seen. His first hearing was a closed session before the Senate Intelligence Committee, and it took a good ten hours. We have no way of knowing what was asked and what he answered, but Senator Warner commented afterward that it confirmed his suspicion that he was involved in the most significant period of his life. *That* is certainly food for thought.

Cohen began his opening statement by apologizing to the committee for lying to them the previous time that he testified. He realizes that if he is caught lying at any point this week he will be in even more trouble, involving a longer jail sentence than he is already facing.

Cohen says that his testimony tomorrow, in public, will be backed up by documentation, including checks for hush-money payments and other crimes, which were signed by Trump. Tonight, Rachel Maddow described this week as "The end of the beginning." I believe that it is more like the end of the third quarter—maybe even the equivalent of the two-minute-warning of a football game.

Republican Congressman from Florida, Matt Gaetz, tweeted the following threat, trying to intimidate Cohen the day before he begins spilling his guts: "Hey Michael, do your wife and father-in-law know about your girlfriends? Maybe tonight would be a good time for that chat. I wonder if she'll remain faithful when you're in prison. She's about to learn a lot…" Intimidation of a witness is a federal crime! Here is the statute: "Whoever corruptly, or by threats or force, or by any threatening letter or communication, influences, obstructs, or impedes or endeavors to influence, obstruct or impede the due and proper administration of the law under which any pending proceeding is being had, shall be fined under this title, and imprisoned not more than 5 years." So, who do we call?

Trump has arrived in Hanoi for his meeting with Kim Jong Un. He will surely be distracted by worrying about what Cohen is saying to Congress and to the entire country, and will have little time to watch it.

The Enemy Within: A Chronicle of the Trump Administration

Trump's latest accuser, Alva Johnson, was a guest on Chris Hayes' show *All In,* tonight. She described in detail her encounter with Trump in a campaign RV while she was working for him. He did exactly what he bragged about being able to do on the Access Hollywood tape, minus the crotch grabbing part. She says she has no intention of giving up her fight for justice in her law suit.

The House voted to block Trump's emergency declaration by a vote of 245-182, with 13 Republicans voting with them. Trump is sure to veto it if it gets though the Senate, and it looks like it might. The question is, will there be enough Republican desertions to override the veto?

The House also subpoenaed the administration for documents pertaining to the child-separation/kidnapping policy still haunting our southern border.

One of the officials who oversaw that border policy was grilled for hours by the House Judiciary Committee today. He had no satisfactory answers to their questions, and is being asked to return.

Maria Butina's lawyers say that they are not yet ready to deport her because she is not through with her cooperation with the prosecutors.

In the do-over of the North Carolina House seat election, Mark Harris has withdrawn and will not be on the new ballot. The voting will be deferred until October to give the Republicans time to select a new candidate.

Rachel Maddow offers the possibility that Mueller may accompany his report with an envelope of sealed indictments that could be used as a lever to pry a resignation out of the President. Makes a lot of sense. On the other hand, former

Book Two (09/2018-11/2019)

Attorney General Eric Holder is of the opinion that a sitting president *can be indicted*. Let's find out!!!

BOOM! We have just heard a figurative double-barreled 12-guage shotgun going directly into the President's mid-section. Michael Cohen's lengthy testimony to the House Oversight Committee today was riveting, revealing and devastating to the entire Trump organization.

Ranking Republican Congressman from Ohio, James Jordan, did his best to try to postpone, or at least delay this hearing on the grounds that they had not had ample time to review the documentation that Cohen submitted to go along with his testimony. It didn't work. This is the same Congressman who ignored the complaints about the athletic coach at Ohio State that had abused dozens of young men over a course of years. Throughout the hearing, the Republicans made no attempt to defend Trump or offer contradictory evidence to dispute any of Cohen's allegations, which were extremely damaging. The best they could do was continuously discredit and disparage Cohen as a proven liar, which he readily admits to and is about to go to prison for. The point that they studiously avoided is that Cohen's lies were at the behest of, and for the purpose of covering up the crimes of the President.

Cohen spoke about at least five different areas of criminality that Trump was involved with if not responsible for, and he indicated that there were *more* crimes that he has been talking about with the prosecutors of the southern district of New York, and could not discuss with Congress at this point. Those areas that he *did* discuss included: (1) At least *eleven* checks written by and signed by Trump, Trump Jr. and CEO David Weisselberg for the payment of the hush money to the women that Trump wanted to hide his affairs with; (2) A conspiracy with two of his lawyers, *after* he was in office, to cover up his illegal activities; (3) Tax and bank fraud crimes which explain why he is so unwilling to release his tax returns. He greatly feared any release would trigger an audit like the one he repeatedly lied about by saying he was already under an audit, but was not; (4) His lies about knowing that WikiLeaks was about to expose the stolen emails. This is shaping up to be considered a major RICO case against the entire Trump organization.

Alan Weisselberg and/or Donald Trump Jr. may be the next to be summoned to testify to this committee. Lawrence O'Donnell's evaluation of today's event is that it was "the smoking gun" in the case leading to Trump's impeachment, with those checks being exhibit A. I believe several more of those will follow before this saga is over.

Democrat Congressman Gerry Connolly, on O'Donnell's *Last Word* show tonight, said that the most important thing that came out of today's hearing was that "We had confirmation that the Trump Organization, headed by Mr. Trump, is by any other name, a criminal enterprise."

Cohen, through his testimony today, became the new "John Dean", who put the icing on the cake of the Watergate case against Nixon.

Nearly as important as was the Cohen testimony to the state of our nation, we had the shameful and desperate attacks by several of the Republican members of the committee, as they exposed their blatant partisanship to try to protect their leader at any cost to their own image. I wonder how they are going to explain their performance to their children and grandchildren in the future when history paints this administration and the Republican Party as the most corrupt in our history.

Meanwhile, Trump is in Hanoi, trying to bargain with his second favorite dictator, next to Putin of course, while being distracted by what is going on at home.

On *Morning Joe,* with former Republican Joe Scarborough this morning, Joe described watching, with a group of some of his Republican friends, the disgraceful performance of the Republican Congressmen yesterday. Several of them said, after watching the hearing for several hours, that they were ready to join Joe in the "former Republican" category.

Trump left the summit meeting with Kim a couple of hours early, admitting that things did not go as planned, and sometimes "you just have to walk away." What a huge waste of time, money and prestige. I guess you better resume those joint military exercises with the South Koreans, Mr. President.

In addition to coming away empty-handed, Trump also added insult to injury on the subject of the prisoner that Trump managed to get released from a North Korean prison on his first summit meeting. Otto Warmbier was in very bad shape when he arrived back home in a coma, from which did not recover before he died less than a week after his return. There were signs of torture and malnutrition. Trump says he discussed this case with Kim during their second meeting, and Kim assured him that he was profoundly sorry for what happened, but did not know about the man's bad treatment until after he learned about it from US sources. Of course, Trump was quick to admit that he took Kim at his word, as he does Putin's denial of election interference. He believes dictators over obvious facts and his own intelligence agencies—in every case.

Republican Congressman from Florida, Matt Gaetz, managed to join the Oversight Committee yesterday for Michael Cohen's hearing, even though he is not a member of that committee. He played a part in the Republican assault on Cohen, and had sent that threatening tweet to Cohen a day or so earlier, trying to intimidate him in advance of his testimony—a clear case of witness tampering, for which he apologized (under pressure). His actions earned him the praise of the President when he landed back in the US.

The Enemy Within: A Chronicle of the Trump Administration

Much of yesterday's testimony dwelled on falsified evaluations of the worth of several of Trump's big, expensive properties; grossly *inflating* their worth to banks to help obtain huge loans, and *deflating* their worth on his tax statements. Cohen produced years of documentary evidence to back up his story of long-term cheating in these areas. In one such case he evaluated a property at between five and ten million dollars on his tax return, but evaluated it at over two hundred million dollars to get a loan from Deutche Bank to buy the Buffalo Bills football team, when the real value was about $50 million.

Cohen's lawyer, Lanny Davis, was a guest on the *Rachel Maddow Show* tonight, where he described his client's closed testimony to the House Judiciary Committee *today* as more explosive than at yesterday' open session. He calls it "a game changer." It dwelled mainly on lies and obstruction. Paul Manafort is facing a lengthy prison sentence for doing this same sort of thing. House Financial Committee Chairwoman Maxine Waters says that Deutche Bank has finally started to cooperate with them and has begun handing over financial records that her committee has subpoenaed.

Congresswoman Rashida Tlaib, Democrat from Michigan, was a guest on Chris Hayes' *All In* show tonight. She discussed a subject that has long been ignored--Trump's blatant disregard for and violation of the emoluments clause of our Constitution, by failing to divest himself of any of his profitable properties. She is pushing hard on this issue now. She also had a lot to say about the GOP's offensive use, by Congressman Mark Meadows from North Carolina, of a black female, Lynne Patton, who was chosen by Trump to be head of Housing and Urban Development. She was used as a prop, standing behind Meadows, representing "proof" that Trump is not the racist that Cohen labeled him.

We are at a point now where it is difficult to know who should pursue which of Trump's several crimes. There are four

Book Two (09/2018-11/2019)

very powerful and determined sets of investigators coming at the President at the same time: The Special Counsel, Robert Mueller; the Southern District of New York's lawyers; The Attorney General of New York State; and at least three committees of the House of Representatives. It is hard to say which of these present the greatest danger to Donald Trump and family. One thing is certain, his pardon power will do him very little good.

Cohen ended his marathon week of testimony by appearing today in front of the House Intel Committee, headed by Adam Schiff, who said after this hearing was over that they ran out of time to cover all the bases, so Cohen will return to continue his testimony on March 6. In the meantime, they will be talking to former Russian mobster and long-time business associate of Donald Trump, Felix Sater, and could also be calling on members of the Trump family soon.

There is a renewed uproar today about the previously reported attempt to get a Top Secret security clearance for Jarod Kushner, after it had been denied by the CIA because of problems with his background check. Trump told John Kelly to grant it to Kushner but Kelly refused—one reason why he was fired. Trump is still denying this story.

Conservative Republican Bill Kristol wrote the following about his former political party: "Conservatives have spent over half a century disproving the claim that we are the stupid party. Now, under Trump, conservatism is embracing, indeed reveling in...stupidity. At the same time, *New York Times* reporter Peter Wehner writes, "Republicans on the House Oversight Committee tried to destroy the credibility of Michael Cohen's testimony, not because they believe his testimony is false, but because they fear it is true. By now, Republicans must know, deep in their hearts, that Mr. Cohen' portrayal of Trump as a 'racist', a 'con man' and a 'cheat' is spot on. So it is the truth they fear, and it is the truth—the fundamental reality of the world as it actually is—that they feel compelled to destroy."

These two men are very concerned about how the GOP has adopted Trump's level of corruption and immorality, which is destroying the party.

It gets more and more amazing and disturbing that so many Republicans in Congress and so much of the general public can so stubbornly and irrationally cling to their allegiance to this president in the face of so many facts that they now have to confront about him and his crimes. It is like a case of mass hypnosis, beyond even the cult mentality.

March 4-10

Trump is trying to take some solace in the fact that Manafort's sentencing documents in the D.C. court, contained no reference to Russian collusion, which would indicate that Paul left that subject out of his cooperation agreement so as not to close off all hope of a Trump pardon.

The House Ways and Means Committee has filed a request for Trump's tax returns. They will not be alone in that quest. *Everyone* wants a crack at those returns after Cohen's testimony. Cohen said yesterday that he "is in constant contact with the SDNY prosecutors", conveying the "game changing" information his lawyer referred to. He is trying to change their negative opinion of how much he has been cooperating.

John Kelly and Don McGahn both wrote memos-to-file about Trump's over-riding of the CIA's denial of a top-secret clearance for Kushner. He can't lie his way out of this case of nepotism.

Since Cohen's testimony Wednesday, seen around the world, impeachment talk has increased considerably. Cooler heads are trying to tamp it down because it would be premature to proceed without the Mueller report to further support the case for removal of a president.

The increased pressure on the release of Trump's tax and business records, was helped considerably by the astute questions by freshman Congresswoman from the Bronx, Alexandria Ocasio-Cortez. Another stunning similarity to the case of Watergate/Nixon. Ms. Cortez has become the new favorite target of the right-wingers, not only for her skillful ability to get at the truth of a matter, but because she has suddenly become the darling of the Democrats, especially the more progressive segment. The Republicans have resorted to labeling her as a "socialist" for her views, and her sponsorship of the Green New Deal. They are throwing out all sorts of crazy scare theories about what she is trying to do to our country. She really has them riled up to the point of idiocy. She really got under their skin when she pointed out that Trump has a golf club in her neighborhood in the Bronx that was paid for by tax-payer money, which means he is profiting off a socialism-obtained property, the bad kind of socialism, as opposed to the good kind like Social Security Medicare, etc., etc.

Trump delivered his longest campaign-style speech ever at an address to the Conservative Political Action Committee (CPAC) on Saturday. He ranted and raved on a wide variety of topics, primarily his various enemies. He was particularly hard on James Comey, whom he called "a bad, bad cop." The Mueller investigation moved up a notch, from being a "witch hunt" to being "bullshit." According to the Trump-lie-counters, he told a total of 104 falsehoods during this speech. He also tried to sell the silly excuse that he was joking when he famously called for Russia to steal Clinton's emails during the campaign. The length, tone, profanity and incoherence of this diatribe showed just how panicked and desperate he has become, with the walls closing in on from all sides.

The Enemy Within: A Chronicle of the Trump Administration

There are now four Republicans, with the addition of Senator Rand Paul, who are planning to join the Democrats' resolution to block Trump's so-called emergency to build his wall. We will need about nine more to override Trump's veto.

The House Judiciary Committee has opened a very broad investigation into the world of Donald Trump. They have sent out letters to eighty-one individuals or entities, including the FBI, requesting documents related to any of the questionable activities of this president which relate to their charge of repeated abuse of power. It is clear that the committee is laying the groundwork for impeachment. The Republicans are crying that this a blatant case of overreach. It certainly could be considered a dragnet, but one that is justified by all the smoke that has been swirling around this White Houses for many months, and has recently been magnified greatly by the Cohen testimony. That list of 81 was augmented by a request for the notes from those secret meetings between Trump and Putin that the President has gone to great lengths to hide. Committee Chairman, Jerry Nadler, says that they have already begun to receive some of the requested documents, and promises to comply by several other letter receivers. Nadler may have just become as big a threat to the Trump presidency as Robert Mueller.

The latest case of presidential abuse of power is his attempt to block AT&T's acquisition of Time Warner (owner of CNN). A *New Yorker* investigative journalist reports that Trump pressured Gary Cohn, the former director of the National Economic Council, to get the DOJ to block the deal. Motive? Trump hates CNN, one of the main purveyors of "fake news."

Part of the "new information" that Cohen revealed at the closed session to Congress on Thursday involved discussion of a pardon between Trump's lawyers and Cohen's lawyers. This could be construed as another case of obstruction that could be added to the dozen or do other instances.

Book Two (09/2018-11/2019)

We now know that *Fox News* reporters knew about Trump's hush-money payments to Daniels before it became widely-spread news, but Rupert Murdock killed the story to protect Trump. Fox has long been nothing but the propaganda arm of the Trump administration

Sebastian Gorka, who was an adviser to Trump for a few weeks, then went to *Fox News* before he also left there, equally abruptly with no explanation, was one of the keynote speakers at that recent CPAC conference. He spouted the new party line which included ridiculing AOC for the sponsorship of the Green New Deal, which is somehow going to "take away your cows and your hamburgers and your trucks." What kind of drug are these people on?

Matt Whitaker has surprisingly left the DOJ, even though he had been offered a new position there after Barr replaced him as AG. He has agreed to return to Congress and testify further about Trump's desire to rid himself of the Mueller investigation. Could he be flipping?

Two more candidates have jumped into the Democrat race for presidential nominee: John Hickenlooper of Colorado and Jay Inslee of the state of Washington. Inslee is running primarily on the one issue of climate change and how to combat it to save our planet. Inslee was a guest tonight on Rachel Maddow's show, and was quite impressive. He has an excellent record of progress in his state and is serving his second term as Governor. Washington was the first state to vote to condemn Trump's Muslim ban.

Several anti-Trump commentators have expressed doubts about the wisdom of using impeachment to remove Trump from office, instead of waiting to vote him out. Why have the impeachment remedy in the Constitution if you are not going to use it in a case as loaded with corruption and criminality as this one? They were about to use it against Nixon before his resignation saved them the trouble—for crimes far less numerous than Trump's. They even used it against Clinton for *one* issue of sexual impropriety, about a hundredth as much as they have on Trump. As I have stated before, and will keep on stating—*we cannot afford twenty more months of this make-believe president trying and failing to lead our country in these dangerous times.*

A *New York Times* report says that the New York state insurance regulators are investigating the Trump Organization, as a result of Michael Cohen's testimony last week; testimony elicited by our new star Congresswoman, Alexandria Ocasio-Cortez. They have subpoenaed all relative documents. Trump needs an aide just to keep track of all the investigations and lawsuits.

One statistic that is easy to lose sight of in all the information coming out of Cohen's three days of testimony is that he showed copies of no less than *eleven* checks from the *Trump Trust*, which is nothing more than a "fig-leaf" account, made out to Cohen and signed by Trump, his son Donald Jr. of his CFO David Weisselberg to reimburse Michael for the hush money.

Part of Cohen's testimony dealt with meetings between his lawyers and Trump's lawyers, Jay Sekulow and Rudy Giuliani, on the subject of a pardon for Cohen. Cohen has said he has not been offered one and would not accept one. This statement has been met with some skepticism, of course.

Trump not only used his presidential power to ignore the intelligence community about the inadvisability of granting a top secret security clearance to his son-in-law, Jared Kushner, he did the same for his daughter Ivanka.

Book Two (09/2018-11/2019)

On Lawrence O'Donnell's *Last Word* show tonight, former DNI John Brennan said exactly what I have been predicting— that Mueller will combine the presentation of his report with several indictments, which will probably include a family member or two.

Another guest of O'Donnell was Cohen's lawyer, Lanny Davis, who expressed surprise and disappointment that his long-time friend, Senator Lindsey Graham has stooped so low as to continue to serve as a prop and mouthpiece for a president like Donald Trump. Especially since Graham used to refer to Trump as a "jackass", etc., etc.

Trump has refused to turn over to the House committees any of the documents they are demanding, still making the now disproven claim that he is under audit by the IRS. He may be subpoenaed for them.

Roger Stone is on the ragged edge of failing to comply with the judge's gag-order, and may end up in jail because of it. How stupidly arrogant can you get? His own lawyers drew up the terms of the gag-order.

Fox News' Trump mouthpiece, Sean Hannity, says he has started his own investigation into the Democrat candidates for presidential nominee. You can't accuse *Fox* of not being all-in when it comes to Trump. When Trump is removed via impeachment, or resigns, look for *Fox News* to foment an insurrection.

A Muslim Congresswoman's criticism of Israeli Prime Minister Netanyahu has been misconstrued, misrepresented and blown out of proportion by the Trump supporters for several days now as being anti-Semitic in nature. This is a shameless attempt to deflect from Trump's problems and biases against

Muslims. Unfortunately, it has had some success in causing some wrangling among the Democrats.

On Wednesday, Michael Cohen returned to resume his testimony before the House Intelligence Committee, accompanied by several suitcases full of documentation. Afterward, the members of that committee agreed that the time was well spent, as they learned a lot of new information from Trump's long-time attorney and fixer.

Federal prosecutors from New York, Virginia and the District of Columbia have issued subpoenas for information about the Trump inauguration fund. Trump was deeply involved with every aspect of this affair, including where the money came from and where it was spent.

Using Cohen's treasure trove of documentary information, the New York prosecutors are looking closely into Trump's financial reports involving his expensive properties.

The House's Homeland Security Committee put Homeland Security Secretary, Kirstjen Nielsen, under some serious questioning today about the continuing condition along our southern border in regard to the children still being detained there. She was visibly shaken by their questions and had great difficulty giving anything close to informative or rational answers, especially when it came to the question about the kids still being cooped up in "cages". She disputed the use of that word to describe the large metal containment pens that they are being housed in, trying to restrict the word "cage" to something small to house a pet dog or bird. Whether one refers to it as a cage, a pen, an enclosure or anything else of that nature, nothing changes the fact that it is way past time to put a stop to this barbaric policy—not to try to dodge the question.

Book Two (09/2018-11/2019)

That FBI building-renovation case reported a few weeks ago is now being investigated by the Democrat-controlled Congress, using their subpoena power.

The White House has refused to hand over any of the requested documents to the various committees which have requested them. *More* subpoenas will be issued.

There will be twelve primary debates held for the Democrat Candidates this year, and none of them will be hosted by *FOX News*.

One of the revelations coming out of Michael Cohen's three days of testimony last week, which was elaborated upon yesterday, is the fact that Cohen's lawyers, Jay Sekulow and Abbe Lowell, advised him on editing documents and emails, and coached him on what to lie about in regard to his crimes when he first testified to Congress weeks ago. He may have gotten them into some hot water by following their advice.

It has been shown that Donald Trump himself, as well as members of his family, was heavily involved with every aspect of the planning for his inauguration, including the financial aspects.

Trump's tariff and trade policies have greatly increased our budget deficit to $310 billion, an increase of 77%, rather than lowering it as he promised to do during his campaign for president.

Today Paul Manafort received his sentence from the judge in the Virginia court, and it was a huge shock. In spite of the recommendation of the prosecutors that he be given a sentence within the guidelines for his crimes, which specified a range of between nineteen and a half years and twenty-four years in prison, the judge sentenced him to a mere forty-seven months.

This outrageous slap-on-the-wrist has raised cries of some sort of payola being involved. Manafort did not even express any contrition or remorse for his numerous illegalities. He still faces two other sentences form courts in New York and D.C., but the judges in those cases have the discretion to make their terms run concurrently with his first sentence if they also want to go easy on him. That would be adding even further to the injustice.

Manafort's lawyers came out of this farce announcing (for Trump's sake) that there was no evidence of collusion with Russia found against Paul (angling for a pardon from Trump). This spurred a lot of discussion about who said what in the days leading up to this trial and sentence on the subject of a pardon, which leads to questions about those talks being further evidence of obstruction.

The House passed HR-1, the sweeping election-rights resolution that they have been working on since the midterm. Now it is up to the Republican-controlled Senate to see if they are on board with the idea of reducing the current road blocks that have been placed in the way of many voters in recent years.

There is continuous speculation about where in the White House the leaks are coming from, especially those pertaining to documents about the issuance of those controversial security clearances for Kushner, Ivanka and several others in the White House, which have found their way into the hands of the House Oversight Committee. Some of these memos expose Kushner's communications with the Saudi government, in which sensitive data were shared.

As a backlash to the furor caused by Congresswoman Ilhan Omar's controversial remarks about Israel, the House has voted to condemn all hate speech by members of Congress. It was supported overwhelmingly by the Democrats and by twenty-three Republicans. It also passed a "voting and ethics overhaul" bill.

Book Two (09/2018-11/2019)

Former *Fox News* executive Bill Shine, who has recently served as Trump's umpteenth communications director, has abruptly left the White House with no explanation, to go to work on Trump's reelection campaign. Who will be next on that chopping-block of a job?

Trump basked this weekend in the "fact" that the Manafort sentencing memo from the judge declared expressly that "there was no evidence of conclusion with the Russians." This was another of numerous falsehoods. There was no mention of any such evidence because that was *not* one of the crimes he was charged with in that case. This is strictly in the province of the Mueller probe. Let's wait and see what he has to say on that subject when he testifies.

Congresswoman Ilhan Omar continues to receive a lot of criticism, especially from Republicans, over her comments about Israel. The GOP is being very hypocritical (again) by their holier-than-thou comments, in view of their attitude toward Muslims and other groups they condemn as anti-America.

Democrat commentators are unified in their contention that the Mueller probe's verdict on "collusion" will have little effect on the question of impeaching Trump, because there is a multitude of other crimes that have nothing to do with collusion with Russia.

The latest polls show that the top issues with voters today are health care and climate change. Neither of them strong points for the Republicans.

Trump is due to release his new budget proposal on Monday, which is bound to be met with stiff resistance, especially if it seeks additional billions for his stupid wall.

Among Democrat candidates for president, Joe Biden (not yet announced) and Bernie Sanders are in a virtual tie for top spot among the voters as of today, far ahead of the rest of the field. But that is bound to change several times before all is said and done.

March 11-17

We have a pretty busy week coming up with a lot of court action taking place.

First up will be Manafort's date tomorrow, to be sentenced by the federal judge in D.C., where his maximum sentence could be ten years. He is not apt to get off as easy with this judge as he was in Virginia. She can make his term run consecutively of concurrently, which will make a huge difference to how many years Paul will spend behind bars. This is the court where he was convicted of eight felonies and pled guilty to ten more as part of his cooperation agreement, which he did not honor.

On Wednesday, Michael Flynn was back in court for a sentencing hearing, which may result in him *finally* getting sentenced. On Thursday, Roger Stone will appear before the judge to explain why his recently republished book should not be considered a violation of the gag order she imposed on him. Then on Friday, Rick Gates, who has been cooperating with the Mueller probe for many months, gets his turn when he files an updated status report that will affect his sentence. This is today's version of "All the President's Men."

The Trump administration's scandal de jour involves the Chinese owner of a massage parlor, operated out of Mar a Lago, named Cindy Yang. She has been selling access to the President to her Chinese government contacts and bigshots who would like Trump's ear. She has appeared in several photographs with Trump and family members.

Book Two (09/2018-11/2019)

Erik Prince, the former Blackwater Security founder, who has attended some of the meetings with foreign nationals under mysterious circumstances, has admitted that he was part of a Trump Tower meeting back in August of 2016, with contacts from Russia, which he subsequently lied to Congress about. More evidence of collusion?

In the uproar the Republicans have created about the "evils of socialism", AOC shed some light on their dark picture by how the Democrats favor *Democratic Socialism*, which places the emphasis on *Democracy*.

Trump's new budget proposal would take a huge sum out of Medicare to use for that wall of his. He promised his followers that he would never touch Medicare or Medicaid. Another promise he is trying hard to break.

It is now revealed that Paul Manafort's legal fees have been paid by a Trump Super-pack, concealed by a kick-back scheme and repeatedly lied about.

Mueller's team has been looking into the Trump team's dealings with a couple of former Soviet Union countries for real-estate projects. The architect for these places disappeared when a reporter from CNBC tried to contact him to ask questions about these projects.

Fox News is showing its blatant prejudice against Muslims as two of its star mouthpieces, Jeanine Pirro and Tucker Carlson, have not been bashful in their remarks using disgusting language when referring to Muslims and Muslim nations like Iraq. Their record proves that this is the way they have thought for many years, and they are very representative of the overall tenor of the garbage that *Fox* puts out on a daily basis. And this is what our president watches and listens to every day, to the exclusion of everyone else.

The Enemy Within: A Chronicle of the Trump Administration

Speaker Pelosi declares that "I am not for impeachment. He's just not worth it." The Constitution says that a president can be impeached and removed "for high crimes and misdemeanors." There is a wide range between a misdemeanor and a high crime. If the multitude of crimes already racked up by Trump, even before the Mueller report is presented, do not qualify for impeachment, then what the Hell does? And why is it in the Constitution if it is not going to be used in a case this flagrant?

The state of New York's new Attorney General, Letitia James, is shifting into high gear her investigation into Donald Trump's financial transactions over the last several years. This includes sending subpoenas to several banks, in particular, Deutche Bank, which has been the only one willing to grant loans to Trump lately.

Mike Flynn is asking the judge in his case for a ninety-day extension before he is sentenced. He is not likely to get it, because the Mueller team says that he is through with his cooperation with them. We will know tomorrow if he gets lucky.

Democrat freshman Representative Katie Porter is making herself another rising star in the image of Alexandria Ocasio-Cortez. She has shown that she too knows how to ask the pointed, important questions during her five-minute time allotments. She had the CEO of Wells Fargo squirming in his chair today about the way they do business with their loans to consumers.

When a second Boeing 737 airliner crashed recently, killing all passengers and crew, essentially every country on Earth except the US and Canada immediately grounded this model. Trump spoke on the phone with the CEO of Boeing, and he accepted the assurance of his golf buddie, that the plane was

Book Two (09/2018-11/2019)

safe, so he decided on that factor alone not to ground them. If one of those planes takes off from a US airport and crashes, those deaths will be on our president. It is relevant to note that Trump has yet to appoint an FAA Administrator for this country. The job has been filled by an "acting" administrator for over two years.

Senate leader Mitch McConnell's poll numbers in his home state of Kentucky are now at an all-time low for that position (33% favorable to 56% unfavorable). This means that he will probably follow Speaker Paul Ryan's example, and decline running for reelection in 2020. That event would be almost as welcome as seeing the departure of Donald Trump.

Manafort was sentenced today by the judge in D.C., and it was quite a different story from how he was treated in Virginia the other day. He was given 73 months, 30 of them to run concurrently (there's a big break), and 43 of them to run consecutively, which means added to the 47 he was given by Virginia. So he will be in prison for seven and a half years, minus time already served. The very touchy question of whether Trump will pardon him got immediately more complicated by the fact that as soon as the sentence was announced, the District Attorney in Manhattan indicted Manafort for sixteen similar but different felonies (avoiding double jeopardy). Several of these, Paul has already pled guilty to in his plea agreement with Mueller. These new charges can net him another twenty-five years in prison, and Trump has no pardon power on these state crimes. So knowing that a pardon would not help his campaign manager very much, if any, and would look very bad for Trump, he better think twice about issuing that pardon.

In spite of a strict admonition by the D.C. judge, not to push the mantra of "no collusion evidence," because it is a non-sequitur in view if the fact that Manafort was not being charged with the crime and the question played no part in her sentence, his lawyers left the courthouse and immediate began mouthing that very mantra. This was aimed of course for Trump's ears.

Manafort's sentence was doubly bad for Trump because several of his crimes were committed in collaboration with the Trump organization, so he becomes an unindicted co-conspirator yet again.

Matt Whitaker met today with Senators Nadler and Collins to answer questions about some of his previous testimony before Congress. Afterward, Nadler said that Whitaker did *not deny* several of the allegations of improper communications between Trump and various prosecutors, including phoning the District Attorney in the New York investigation. The obstruction never lets up.

The Mueller team is looking into email evidence that "pardon dangling" was common through a back channel set up by the White House.

The question is raised once again: Why did Manafort and several others lie about things like passing polling data to Russians, at the risk of being jailed on perjury charges, if not to hide the conspiracy with Russia to get Trump elected?

Oregon's Democrat Senator Jeff Merkley describes his visit to the child-jails in Texas, where he questioned three boys who told him that they were persuaded to "behave themselves" or they would never have a chance of being sponsored for release. Records show that the kids' average stay in their cage is *sixty-seven* days. This is the real border crisis!

On two big Senate votes today Trump took two humiliating defeats. The Senate passed the resolution to *block* his attempt at declaring a national emergency over his wall, by a vote of 59-41, with *twelve* Republicans joining *all* of the Democrats. They then *passed* the one to stop supporting the war in Yemen by 54-

Book Two (09/2018-11/2019)

46, with five more Republican defections than anticipated. Trump will veto both of them but it is no longer a sure bet that his veto cannot garner enough votes to override him. It seems that more and more of his faithful henchmen are growing a spine.

Congressman Lacy Clay (D) from Missouri, took Secretary of Commerce Wilbur Ross to task in no uncertain terms when he questioned Ross about trying to get a citizenship question added to the census form, and then lied to Congress about it. Clay told him he needed to resign. His comments were seconded by freshman Congresswoman Ayanna Pressley (D) from Massachusetts.

The House voted 420 to 0 to make the Mueller report, when it is turned over to the US Attorney General, open to the public. Unfortunately it is non-binding.

The *New York* Attorney General has charged the Trump Foundation, which is supposed to be a charitable organization, with several illegalities, and has ordered it to pay $8.4 million in restitution and fines.

A New York appellate court has ruled that a president *can* be sued in state court. A former Apprentice contestant is suing Trump for unwanted sexual groping.

The Republicans in Congress have released the full transcripts of the testimony of two former FBI employees. Lisa Page's and Peter Strzok's testimony about their attitudes and comments about candidate Donald Trump during his campaign caused such a stir that it cost them their jobs. Many weeks ago the GOP had released a few selected *snippets* of their comments, hoping to use them to show how biased they were and, therefore discredit the whole FBI investigation at its very beginning. When that did not have the desired effect, they decided that maybe the whole ball of wax would do the trick. Once again, the content of the transcripts did nothing but harm to their contention, as a reading of the complete transcripts showed how restrained the pair was in their *actions*, in spite of their critical *words*.

Two of Robert Mueller's top prosecuting investigators have just left his team to return to their normal FBI duties. One of them, Andrew Weismann, was the architect of the prosecution of Paul Manafort. He has been repeatedly attacked by the Trump lackeys at *Fox News*. This is seen as another indication that Mueller is beginning to wrap things up and is nearly ready to file his report.

Throughout both his campaign and his presidency, Donald Trump has consistently endorsed and praised "toughness" among his adoring supporters, even offering to pay the legal bill for anyone who was arrested for attacking a Trump critic. At another point he hinted that the second amendment people might have something to say about a President Clinton, if Hillary won. His hateful speech has already caused a significant rise in all sorts of attacks across the country over the past two years, with no expression of condemnation on his part.

But his crude and un-presidential tongue has now risen to a point where it becomes what amount to a call for an insurrection that could blossom into an all-out civil war. In an interview today at Breitbart, that furthest right of all right-wing rags, formerly led by our old friend, Steve Bannon, Trump made the following incendiary statement: "I can tell you I have the support of the police, the support of the military, the support of the Bikers for Trump—I have the tough people, but they don't *play* tough—until they go to a certain point, and then it would be very bad, very bad."

Michael Cohen testified the other day about how Trump has always employed the Mob's technique of using a form of code to relay his requests or desires to his underlings. This is a classic example of that type of code. His dictatorial fantasy comes through loud and clear.

Retired General Barry McCaffrey responded to Trump's latest threat against democracy by writing: "This Trump language is incredibly provocative and dangerous. This is an incitement to violence. Trump misreads law enforcement and the US Armed Forces. They are non-political and law based institutions. Swear to support the Constitution, not a person."

Are you listening Nancy Pelosi? **We cannot wait until January of 2021 to rid ourselves of this threat to our nation. Impeachment and removal must follow the release of the Mueller report, like a sentence follows a verdict.**

For two years, Donald Trump was able to call all the shots because he had the support of both houses of Congress. He seems to feel that he should have that power all the time. He envisions himself having the power of is idols, Vladimir and Kim, and wants it so bad he tries to acts as if he did. That has made him America's public enemy number one.

A couple of days ago a crazed gunman, with the apparent assistance of at least one cohort, entered first one and then a second mosque and shot to death a total of forty-nine people, including children. He was captured without having to be killed and a manifesto by him was found in which he proclaimed that he was a white-nationalist who was inspired by Donald Trump. Trump responded with expressions of sympathy and outrage but added that he "does not see white-nationalism as a threat." Every day Trump's madness spreads further into our society and will reach a point of no return if it isn't stopped soon (if it isn't already too late.)

Today Rick Gates' sentencing status was reviewed and his prosecutors asked for and were granted a sixty-day extension for further cooperation from Gates on the subject of the Trump inauguration scandal. This is his fifth postponement. He seems to be a fountain of information.

Trump has made a lot of very strange appointments to posts that his appointees are uniquely unqualified to hold. One of the worst was his appointment of Scott Lloyd, an anti-abortion activist, to the job of Refugee Settlement Director. Lloyd tried (but failed) to block the abortion of a seventeen-year-old immigrant rape victim after she had crossed our border. He has kept watch on all cases of pregnant women attempting to enter the US. He uses a spreadsheet containing all of their available data. The ACLU sued him and won their case. He said he would "refrain" but keeps right on tracking the pregnant women.

Trump says, "They hate the word 'invasion' but that's what it is." But the fact is that last year saw the fifth-smallest illegal crossings since 1973 (forty-six years).

As expected, Trump vetoed the anti-emergency bill just passed by the Senate. Now let's see if they have the guts to override.

The deadline for compliance with the House request for documents from 81 entities will come due this Monday. There have been many, but nowhere near total, responses to that request. Some subpoenas are likely to be issued, including to the White House.

Although Ivanka Trump was surprisingly not among the 81 listed, several of those who *were* on the list were specifically asked for documents related to her in several categories, including emoluments.

Trump is still repeatedly tweeting that the Mueller investigation and report have no legal status. Wishful thinking that only makes him look guiltier.

Book Two (09/2018-11/2019)

March 18-24

House Judiciary Committee Chairman Jerry Nadler announced that they will be investigating the rise of White Nationalism in the U.S., including in the military. *USA Today* reports that, "Human Rights leaders are concerned that the U. S. is exporting extremism on a global scale." Trump downplays the problem.

Nadler says he has received tens of thousands of documents in response to his committee's request from those eighty-one individuals and entities. They include thousands from, of all people, Steve Bannon. *None* from the White House, however.

The Deutche Bank officer with whom Trump dealt most often on his loan deals, which amounted to around a billion dollars, in spite of his several red flags, was a woman named Rosemary Vrablic. She is now under the scrutiny of both Mueller and the Southern District of New York. Were those loans a case of incredibly bad judgement on the bank's part, or done at the direction of Vladimir Putin?

It has just been revealed that the home of Eliot Broidy, who we previously learned was one of the three clients of Michael Cohen, along with Donald Trump and Sean Hannity of *Fox News,* and who was vice-chairman of the Trump inauguration fund-raising committee, was raided by the FBI back in July of 2018. This raid was prompted by the fact that they had evidence that he had ties to the Russians. He has been closely associated with Cohen, Rick Gates and George Nadir. They teamed up to create a back-channel to the Russians, the UAR and Qatar for the purposes of money-laundering, influence-peddling and conspiracy. That raid produced reams of incriminating data.

Kellyanne Conway's husband George says that the mental condition of President Trump is getting worse. Trump tweeted or re-tweeted fifty times over the weekend, attacking many of his most feared enemies. Some of his tweets contained further attacks on the deceased John McCain, whom Trump can't seem to let go. *The New York Times* says, referring to the GOP, "A party that continues to defend this president is simply beyond redemption." It may even be beyond restoration.

The warrant used for the raids on Michael Cohen's offices and home were issued because the FBI suspected him and investigated him as early as July, 2017, for nothing to do with Donald Trump. It was prompted by his payments to Russian oligarch Viktor Vekselberg, contrary to Trump's claims of a witch hunt aimed at him. This was revealed in spite of eighteen pages of redactions made to protect "ongoing investigations against others," involved with an illegal campaign contribution scheme.

A Trump transition team official named Bijan Kian, who was a business partner of Michael Flynn, has a trial coming up where he is being charged with being an agent of a foreign country. He is also a witness in the case against Flynn, which makes them opponents in their cases, each requesting documents from the other and being denied. His trial will be only the second one since the Mueller probe began, since all the others were convicted or pled guilty. Kian's trial brings out more data about that mysterious meeting in the Seychelles reported earlier that involved Erik Prince and a Russian official named Kirill Dmitriev, where they set up a back channel to the Kremlin.

Devin Nunes is suing *Twitter* for $250 million for allowing hurtful tweets toward him to be transmitted. What about Trump's tweets? What about the First Amendment?

Protests are growing around the country over the lack of action on climate change, which is a scientific fact still denied by Trump and many of his supporters. In fact, by the GOP in

Book Two (09/2018-11/2019)

general. They will not concede that our planet is in serious danger.

The Washington Post is petitioning the court to release unredacted filings in the Paul Manafort case, which they want by Thursday (tomorrow), but Mueller says he needs until April 1 to complete "something".

Rod Rosenstein is staying on at the DOJ a little longer to act as "a heat shield" for Mueller.

Trump held a very amiable meeting today with the dictatorial leader of Brazil. He really loves all the authoritarians!

Trump has blasted George Conway for his cracks about Trump's mental health, adding fuel to the fire that is the Conway marriage.

On the first day of Spring, the newly released court documents reveal that there is now evidence that Michael Flynn was among those who were in contact with the above mentioned Russian, Kirill Dmitriev. Inquiries about this subject gets a "no comment" from both sets of attorneys.

Mike Flynn, Hope Hicks, AMI and Cambridge Analytica are all cooperating with the Congress's request for documents, but still *nothing* from the White House. Trump is stonewalling. Subpoenas are imminent. Nixon tried this stonewall tactic and failed. So will Trump.

Trump has seemed obsessed with John McCain ever since he was the deciding vote which defeated Trump's attempt to destroy the Affordable Care Act. He has insulted him at every opportunity, and did it again this week, going as far as complaining that he was never thanked for approving McCain's funeral. This was in one of his fifty or so tweets today. The pressure is certainly getting to him.

Trump says he is considering imposing tariffs on foreign cars, a move which would harm our auto industry immeasurably. Republican reaction to the idea is negative.

Andrew Gillum, who narrowly lost his bid for Governor in Florida in the midterm election, has launched a voter registration drive in an attempt to turn Florida from purple to blue politically, and help defeat Trump in 2020 (if he is still president).

The Washington Post published an interesting fact about Trump's record with court cases so far in his term in office. Here is what they say: "Federal judges have ruled against the Trump administration at least *63 times* over the past two years, an extraordinary record of legal defeat that has stymied parts of the President's agenda on the environment, immigration and other matters."

Rumors and speculation are rampant as to the "imminent" submission and release of the Mueller report. Will it be the bombshell we are expecting? Will it summarize for us all the damning facts we already know about Trump's and his team's illegal actions, plus a lot we do not know? We can only hope.

Ivanka's and Jared's continued use of unsecured personal phones and emails, in spite of being warned against it, are now being investigated by Elijah Cummings, chairman of the House Oversight Committee. Cummings is demanding answers from the White House about why this is still being allowed, especially in view of Trump's uproar over Clinton's use of a personal server.

Jared Kushner and his brother both visited the Saudi Crown Prince early in Trump's term, without consulting our embassy about it--another serious breach of protocol. This prompted Cummings to demand documents related to these breaches be turned over to his committee by April 4.

On the 27th of this month, Felix Sater will testify before the House Intel Committee about the Trump Tower in Moscow deal. Sater was listed as a signatory on documents involved in that project.

It has been reported by the ACLU that ICE has tried repeatedly to deport natural citizens of this country "to their home country." This is moronic! The ACLU says that ICE routinely detains citizens by the hundreds and threatens them with deportation.

That Wisconsin power-grab by the out-going governor, Scott Walker, to try to limit the power of the newly elected Governor, Tom Evers, has been blocked in court, thanks to a suit by a coalition of advocacy groups.

Time has a cover and feature story on Alexandria Ocasio-Cortez and her rise to become the "lightning rod" and "firebrand" of the Democrat Party.

New Zealand is doing what the United States seems to be incapable of doing and is passing a ban on assault rifles in the wake of their recent mosque massacre. It is time for our government to stop kowtowing to the NRA!

AT LAST! On March 22 the long-awaited Mueller report has been submitted to Attorney General Barr. We know nothing about its contents as yet, but there is one very disturbing and, to me, incomprehensible surprise about it. There were NO indictments accompanying it, and none recommended. It is not surprising that the President was not indicted, because Mueller would not want to go against the existing guideline against indicting a sitting president, but no indictments against *at least* Donald Jr. and Jared Kushner requires a ton of explaining by the Special Counsel.

The AG says that he will give Congress the basics of the report by this weekend. How much will be exposed to the public is supposed to be up to him, but you can bet that Congress, led by Oversight Committee Chairman Jerry Nadler, will make sure that everything except national security concerns will come out, one way or another, even if they have to subpoena Mueller to report to congress. It is encouraging that Barr has said that he will consult with Mueller and Rosenstein about how much he should reveal.

We can all be relieved that Mueller was able to complete his work without interference from Barr, who says that he did not have to refuse any of the Special Counsel's requests, in spite of all of Trump's attempts to stop this investigation. Neal Katyal, former Solicitor General, says that "this is the end of the beginning, not the beginning of the end."

Trump should not be doing any victory dance over the lack of any indictments, in view of all the other authorities who are zeroing in on him.

This weekend will go down as one of the most significant in the history of the United States, and not for a *good* reason. Throughout Saturday and about two thirds of Sunday, speculation was non-stop about what and when we would learn the contents of the Mueller report. AG Barr tells us that he should be able to give a summation of the Mueller outline, which he is currently reading and analyzing. Meanwhile, Trump is being amazingly mum on the subject, as he holds his breath like the rest of America, but for a very different reason. The rest of us *should* be apprehensive about how much of the report we will be allowed to see. But after the news that there will be no

Book Two (09/2018-11/2019)

additional indictments from the Special Counsel, we are also very worried about what conclusions will come from the report.

At 3:30 Sunday afternoon there came a deafening THUD! This was Robert Mueller falling flat on his face and handing Donald Trump the biggest gift of his life and a huge boost to his re-election chances. AG Barr's brief letter to Congress informs us that Mueller found "insufficient evidence" that Trump was guilty of either conspiracy with the Russians, or obstruction of justice. On the obstruction question, Mueller specifically stated that the fact that they felt the evidence was *not conclusive,* did *not* mean that the report was an exoneration. He left it up to the AG to make that conclusion, and there is certainly no doubt about which way Barr will come down, given his bias.

This conclusion by Mueller is in direct contradiction to almost every legal expert, intelligence official (current and former) and constitutional scholar that have appeared numerous times on every news outlet in the country except Trump TV (*Fox News*). His conclusions were made to sound even more favorable to Trump by Barr's interpretation of what Mueller' summary actually said, leading Trump to joyfully proclaim that he "has been completely exonerated." His loyal followers will now be holding victory parties and dancing in the streets, oblivious to the fact that their master is hardly out of the legal woods. There is still the fact that the New York investigations into other crimes (hush-money payments and all sorts of tax and financial crimes) are still zeroing in on this president. This type of crime is what they used to bring down Al Capone.

The Democrat-controlled House of Representatives is intent on getting at the truth of several matters, starting with examining the full content of the Mueller report, to find out how he arrived at such a surprising conclusion.

The finding of "no collusion" is incomprehensible for many reasons, starting with the facts presented by this author in the "nutshell" account presented in the December 9, 2017 entry of this chronicle, plus additional meetings which were uncovered since then.

The conclusion of insufficient evidence on the *obstruction* case is even *more* mind-blowing. In the November 23 list of news items, I listed, by date, the publicly known instances of obstruction by Trump, which Mueller considers "insufficient". This list comes only from this author's own memory and notes. There are almost certainly many more instances available to Mueller. The President and his supporters are alleging that if there is no crime being charged, there was nothing to obstruct. But the other side of that coin is the question, if there was no collusion, why all the lying and attempts to thwart the investigation?

Everyone, including Trump and his team, should be determined to see the supporting evidence behind the shocking conclusions. If Trump and his hand-selected AG resist the efforts for complete transparency, this will be a clear signal that they are still trying to cover up the truth.

March 25-31

The new week begins with Trump continuing to proclaim that the release of the Mueller report completely exonerates him, in spite of the fact that one of the three partial sentences that his hand-picked AG decided to share with us specifically stated that on the obstruction question the evidence was insufficient, in Mueller's opinion, to charge him, but *did not exonerate him*. If he really believes that it *does* exonerate him then why is Barr showing reluctance to release the bulk of it to Congress?

Six House committee chairs are demanding to see the full report by April 2 (next Tuesday). The furor over the report can best be cleared up by Mueller himself testifying to Congress and explaining his conclusions, or lack thereof. The most mysterious question to everyone involved, including many

Book Two (09/2018-11/2019)

congressmen and political pundits, is; why did Mueller "punt" the issue of obstruction to the DOJ and/or Congress? Many people who know him well say that this is "not his style."

Barr had already concluded that there was not enough evidence of either obstruction or conspiracy, an opinion formed long before he received Mueller's report. He will stonewall any further release, in spite of his promise not to. He cannot and will not be allowed to cover this thing up. The handful of pages now known as "the Barr report" just won't satisfy anyone. Barr won't even tell us how many pages the report consists of. Mueller must have known that this would happen if he did not complete his job.

On Lawrence O'Donnell's *Last Word* show tonight, House Intel Committee member Eric Swalwell said that we need to hear from Mueller himself why he decided to pass the ball off to the DOJ and Congress.

Rachel Maddow has compiled a list of fifteen questions arising out of the Barr report, and reminded us that in Barr's previous memo, the one that was so instrumental in his being picked for the AG job by Trump, he expressed the opinion that a president "cannot obstruct justice," no matter what he says or does. She had the former Chief of the DOJ's Counterintelligence and Export Control, David Laufman, as a guest tonight. He is as mystified as the rest of us as to why Mueller was unwilling to draw conclusions based on the evidence he was able to produce, especially on obstruction.

Following Rachel, Lawrence had as his guest former *Assistant* Director of that same department of the DOJ, Frank Figliuzzi, who expressed the same bewilderment about Mueller's reticence, and speculated about his reasons.

In the Watergate/Nixon case of obstruction, a federal judge allowed a sixty-two page document containing grand jury data to be sent to Congress as a "roadmap" to be used in place of an

The Enemy Within: A Chronicle of the Trump Administration

indictment of Nixon. Something along that line needs to take place in Trump's case.

The co-authors of the book titled *Russian Roulette"* were guests of Chris Hayes' *All In* show tonight and discussed the many questions about the several contacts between the Trump team and the Russians during the Presidential campaign. They hope that somewhere in the Mueller report he discussed these questions. Particularly, why he felt the evidence for conspiracy did not rise to the level of a crime.

Trump and his minions at *Fox News* are now demanding an *apology* from the "liberal media" for all the "fake news" and "mean things" they have been saying for the past two years. Trump says, "No president should ever have to go through this type of harassment in the future." He wants to change the law! Outrageous but not at all surprising.

When considering whether or not the Trump team was or was not guilty of conspiracy with Russians, we need only consider these three known facts: One, the Russians have been proven guilty of interfering with the 2016 election in favor of Donald Trump. Mueller's report supports the findings of all our intelligence agencies on that question. Two, Trump immediately upon becoming president, relaxed the sanctions leveled against Russia for invading Ukraine. Three, there were several known meetings between the Trump campaign people and several Russians during the campaign, which they all lied about repeatedly. And then ask yourself, especially if you are still a Trump supporter, why would Putin go to such lengths to help Trump get elected? And why has Trump cozied up to Putin since taking office? Draw your own conclusions.

Feeling, erroneously, that he has been completely exonerated by the Mueller report, Trump is now focusing his attention on retaliation against his "enemies", the "liberal TV news media

Book Two (09/2018-11/2019)

and press." He is acting way too confident, and it is very apt to come back and bite him.

A DOJ official says that we will see the full report within weeks, not days as requested by Congress. With Barr's favorable interpretation of Mueller's report, why are they being so slow in releasing the details, and so sketchy about how much of it the Congress and public should see? Could it be that "the devil is in the details?"

Barr is getting a ton of criticism, including from former Attorney General Eric Holder, about the way he has inserted his interpretation of Mueller's comments about the evidence on the obstruction case.

Unable to take a few days to enjoy his biggest positive moment in many months before shooting himself in the foot again, Trump announced today that he is moving to get his Justice Department to act on a Texas court's determination that parts of the Affordable Care Act are unconstitutional, and therefore rule that the whole health care plan must be struck down--this without any Republican plan to replace it. This act will throw about twenty-one million people off their health insurance. He just can't stop being his own worst enemy.

That huge blue wave that gave the House back to Democratic control in such a convincing manner last November should have convinced him that this is not a winning position for him to take. Trump has repeatedly declared that the GOP "will become the party of health care," but he now wants to make it the party of NO health care.

After a year of the worst climate disasters in modern history prompted the Democrats to come up with a comprehensive plan to do something about the increasing danger of climate change, the Republicans think it is smart to ridicule the plan with juvenile jokes about it. That must go over big with the climate-change-denial crowd, but *sane* people take this issue seriously. We love our planet.

Trump has taken the unprecedented action of ordering a transfer of $1 billion from the Pentagon's Defense Fund to the Homeland Security Dept. to use to work on his wall/fence. Obeying that order is very likely to result in Congress changing the law to restrict the Pentagon from any such fund-shifting in the future.

The Supreme Court has rejected an appeal from the aforementioned mystery company belonging to the mystery country that is still being fined $50 thousand per day and still refusing to honor the subpoena they were served months ago by Mueller's team. It is not the company or country, but Mueller who is insisting on the secrecy about it. Maybe someday we will get an answer to that puzzle as well as the recently created ones.

When interviewed on TV today, James Comey, in response to being asked his view of Mueller's punt on the obstruction question, stated that "It doesn't make sense on the surface." Is he implying that there may be something *under* the surface (like in the report) that will make sense of it?

The Washington Post says that Adam Schiff of the House Intel Committee told them that "Undoubtedly, there *was* collusion."

According to a forthcoming book about her life, Barbara Bush, in her last days, no longer considered herself a Republican and kept "a countdown clock" on her bedside table for the day Trump left office.

Today, Trump tweeted that he was withdrawing sanctions from North Korea, which had not even been put in place yet. He continues to reward his second-favorite dictator (for whom he

Book Two (09/2018-11/2019)

has proclaimed his love) as the North Koreans continue to work on their nuclear missile program.

Vice President Pence made a speech in which he proudly announced that "we are going back to the moon." This statement has as much "truth" to it as Trump's brag that "ISIS has been defeated." NASA says the plan to go back to the moon is in the very early planning stage.

Our favorite freshman Congresswoman, AOC as she is now affectionately referred to, delivered a fiery and inspirational response to Republican Congressman Sean Duffy's attempt to paint the climate change issue as an "elitist false alarm," in a rambling Trump-like speech that made no sense. The Republicans should take note of the latest polls which show that 60% of likely voters in Colorado, 57% in North Carolina, and 57% in Maine, *support* the Green New Deal.

Education Secretary Betsy Devos plans to *eliminate* (not cut) funding for Special Olympics. She is getting a lot of well-deserved negative feedback on that idea, and refuses to answer any direct questions on the subject. She is an educational disaster!

In the oft-mentioned "mystery case", the judge was expected to dismiss the grand jury and release related documents, since Mueller has ended his investigation. But the prosecutors in that case said, "No, it is continuing robustly." The mystery remains alive.

In support of Trump's deranged rant against House Intelligence Committee Chairman Adam Schiff for the "crime" of being outspoken against his nefarious and unpatriotic actions, the Republicans on his committee, in their latest meeting, took Schiff to task and demanded his resignation. Schiff's response was classic, and will go down in history as one of the most

The Enemy Within: A Chronicle of the Trump Administration

memorable statements ever made by a politician. It is a little lengthy but well worth the time to read and ponder. Here it is:

"My colleagues may think it's ok that the Russians offered dirt on the Democratic candidate for president...that when that was offered to the son of the President, that son said that he would "love" the help of the Russians...that he took that meeting...that Paul Manafort also took that meeting...that the President's son-in-law also took that meeting...that they concealed it from the public...that when it was discovered a year later, they lied about that meeting...that the President is reported to have helped dictate that lie...that the campaign chairman of a presidential campaign would offer information about that campaign to a Russian oligarch...that that campaign chairman offered polling data to someone linked to Russian intelligence...that the President himself called on Russia to hack his opponent's emails...that later *that day,* the Russians attempted to hack a server affiliated with that campaign...that the President's son-in-law sought to establish a secret back channel of communications through a Russian diplomatic facility...that an associate of the President made direct contact with the GRU through Guccifer 2.0 and WikiLeaks...that the National Security Adviser Designate secretly conferred with the Russian Ambassador about undermining U.S. sanctions and lied about it to the FBI. You might say that's all okay, but *I don't think that it's okay.* I think it's immoral. I think it's unethical. I think it's unpatriotic. And yes, I think it's corrupt and evidence of collusion."

When the details of the Mueller report are released to Congress, and eventually to the public, there will be confirmation of every allegation made in Schiff's statement.

The full report has been revealed to be close to four hundred pages long, plus a multitude of appendices. Pelosi says that Barr's four page summary was "condescending, arrogant and not the right thing to do." In spite of the report's confirmation

Book Two (09/2018-11/2019)

that it was indeed the Russians who hacked the emails, Trump has yet to issue any statement that he is finally convinced of that fact.

The Washington Post published many details about Cohen's claim during his testimony--that Trump routinely exaggerated his financial holdings on official documents. Deutche Bank has finally begun to transmit the documents subpoenaed by New York prosecutors. A huge problem for Trump.

Trump claims that when (if) the court outlaws Obamacare, he will have a "beautiful new plan" ready to replace it. The GOP admits that no such plan is even on the drawing board, and they are very upset by Trump's stupid move.

Because of the intense backlash, Trump has reversed his decision to defund Special Olympics, embarrassing Betsy Devos. Sometimes, pressure works.

Trump held another one of his ego-rallies today, all pumped up over what he sees as complete exoneration by the Mueller report. He went off in his usual ranting manner against everyone on his enemies list, including the free press, Michel Obama and the whole Democratic Party. He bragged to his adoring crowd about how he is draining the swamp, while he has had more appointees resign because of corruption than any presidency in history, and he is still making very questionable appointments.

Chris Hayes' *All In* show tonight was completely devoted to a town hall meeting in which he interviewed Alexandria Ocasio-Cortez. She showed herself to be eloquent and knowledgeable on every topic that was brought up, but most importantly, on the issue of climate control. She emphasized that we need a mobilization on the scale of a world war in order to just *improve* our chances of saving this planet from becoming uninhabitable. Hayes played a collage of Trump and his puppets making fun of AOC and the Green New Deal she is co-sponsoring. Hayes asked her if she expected that much negative reaction. Her response was almost as brilliant as Schiff's response to his Republican "colleagues" yesterday. She said, "Yes. It is *next level*, but I didn't expect them to make *fools* of themselves." The audience roared its approval.

The House Oversight Committee has authority to, and will, subpoena the former White House Personal Security Director, Carl Kline, to testify about the security clearance policy which allowed Kushner, Flynn and about twenty-five others to be granted a Top Secret clearance after being denied by our intelligence agencies. They have also been authorized to subpoena Commerce Secretary Wilbur Ross and Attorney General William Barr.

House Judiciary Committee Chairman Jerry Nadler has asked Barr to work with him to get the grand jury material released to Congress. Barr seems determined not to comply. It is true that grand jury data is usually considered out of bounds, but his is a very special case. This issue may very well end up in court. The committee will expect to see it *all*, even if some may not be published for the public. Adam Schiff says that the AG has no authority or precedence to do or say anything about the Mueller report, other than turn it over to Congress, with no redactions other than those that are necessary to protect our national security.

Barr says that everyone is misinterpreting what he said in his summary, but his explanation sounds like doubletalk. His list of categories of redaction include the ridiculously broad and very shady—"…material infringing on the privacy or reputation of *peripheral* third parties." Is there any doubt about who would be included in the peripheral third party group? Trump has finally found his *Roy Cohn*.

The nutty conspiracy-theorists known as QANON (who believe that Clinton is the leader of the "Deep State" who molests or even *eats* children) are being encouraged and aroused by Trump's rhetoric that he consistently spews at each of his cult rallies. A large segment of our country has devolved into madness, while the GOP aids and abets the mad leader.

The Trump rally crowd now has a new female enemy to chant about. The new war cry is "AOC sucks!" They are all class, as usual, and she isn't even running for president (this time around). Give her ten years of experience in Congress (assuming two terms of the next Democratic president) and then watch her go.

Trump and Kellyanne are still living in their alternate universe with all their alternative facts, especially about the Mueller report. Joy Reed, on her *AM Joy* show, led a very interesting discussion about the two realities that our whole country is living with today. Real facts no longer matter to Trump's followers as they accept as fact whatever Trump says, in spite of all his provable lies.

Trump's policies at the southern border have caused severe overcrowding and underfunding as the detention centers are at the breaking point. Trump's solution is to completely close the border, which would produce a financial disaster.

Trump has ordered removal of the ban on drilling in the Arctic, but a federal judge has said NO, that is unlawful. He loses in court every time.

Joe Biden's prospects for getting the Presidential nomination has been set back considerably by an allegation by a female staffer that he inappropriately kissed her (on the back of the head). He is currently leading the field in the polls, but that was not likely to last, even before this new development. He is too old and too "establishment". New blood is what generates enthusiasm these days.

The Enemy Within: A Chronicle of the Trump Administration

While the USA is undergoing the chaos of the Trump administration, the UK is in even worse shape, as Prime Minister May's "Brexit" plan to withdraw from the European Union keeps failing to achieve a consensus in the British Parliament. So the two main bulwarks against Russian aggression are at their weakest point since the Soviet Union broke up.

Book Two (09/2018-11/2019)

April, 2019

April 1-7

For once, the beginning of the week coincides with the beginning of the month.

A White House whistleblower named Tricia Newbold, who is a non-partisan long time White House security advisor, is the one who informed authorities that as many as twenty-five people were granted security clearances against the ruling of the screening committees. This issue has reached fever level, partly because of all the lies that have been told by administration members, including the President, on the subject. One of the main points at issue is the fact that Trump, who *does* have the authority to grant clearances, failed to follow procedures that are in place for cases where there are questions about original objections.

Trump has been saying for weeks that he wants the Mueller Report released as fully as security will allow, but now he has reversed himself and is doing his best, along with his hand-picked AG to hide a lot of it. If Barr fails to release the report by tomorrow he will be subpoenaed by Congress. There are several large demonstrations being planned across the nation if Barr continues to try to cover it up.

The Chief D.C. Judge in the mystery case holds the same judicial position as that held by John Sirica, who ruled in the Watergate case that grand jury testimony and evidence *should* be handed over to Congress in special cases, a ruling that forced Nixon to resign. Barr's attempt to withhold that kind of information will be challenged, using this precedent, which is part of the "roadmap" for impeachment in these cases. She has already been asked to release the grand jury info that is not related to the still ongoing mystery case.

Preet Bharara, former US attorney for the Southern District of New York, and Eric Columbus, former Senior Counsel for the Department of Justice, were guests on Larry O'Donnell's *Last Word* tonight. They both concurred that Barr's comments, both written and oral, have been inappropriate. They pointed out that Jerry Nadler has the option to subpoena individuals (e.g. Don McGahn) as well as grand jury data.

Only 29% of the voting public, according to a new poll, think that the Mueller Report clears Donald Trump. This is smaller than the percent who support him, so some of them are not swallowing this particular lie.

Trump's new selection for the Federal Reserve Board is Stephen Moore, who has a checkered past and record, along with the usual amount of qualifications for the job that all Trump's picks have, which is *none*.

AOC reminded us today that Trump is still doing nothing to provide any assistance to Puerto Rico, and he is complaining that they are getting too much aid.

Senate Republicans were making no secret about the fact that they were rooting against Trump's effort to outlaw the Affordable Care Act, so he was pressured into backing off on that very unwise plan.

The latest entry into the Democratic presidential race is the mayor of South Bend Indiana, Pete Buttigieg. He is already catching on, and has raised $7 million so far in the few days since he declared. He was a guest of O'Donnell tonight and expressed these views: release the full report; pass a bill requiring that all future presidential candidates must submit ten years of their tax returns; repeal the tax cut for the rich and increase the size of the cut on the middle class; create a "wealth tax" on the super-rich.

Trump tried to explain why he is now objecting to the release of the full Mueller Report, in a lengthy, nonsensical rant in which he repeatedly and critically referred to the report's "oranges." About halfway between the dozen or so utterances of this word, he managed to clearly say the word he was trying to use, "origins". Many people have difficulty with their pronunciation of certain words—George W. Bush could not say "nuclear" correctly. But when you have demonstrated to the public and to yourself that you are having that problem with a word, you do not, if you have a functioning brain, keep using it over and over in the same speech. Add this to the pile of evidence he keeps providing us--that his mind is in a steady state of decline. A little later, he ended a statement on the subject of *normality* with the words, "I think I'm very normal."

Psychiatrists refer to this kind of statement as an example of "an unprovoked denial", which is what people use when they know they have an obvious deficiency of some kind and are trying to deny it to themselves as well as others. But even more important at the moment is the question; if he has nothing to hide, why is he suddenly reversing his stand on complete transparency?

Congress has sent a letter to AG Barr explaining the several reasons why they need to see the complete, unredacted report. Subpoenas are about to start flying in several directions, and you can expect that some fur will start flying as well.

Trump has ordered AG Barr to issue a warning to the Motion Picture Academy about the negative comments that actors and actresses frequently make about him and his administration during the Oscar awards show. Barr has complied with this order by issuing a threatening letter to the Academy demanding that they change the rules about movie releases, a clear attempt to quell free speech. The Academy will never knuckle under to this outrageous threat.

A Chinese woman named Li "Cindy" Yang tried and almost succeeded in entering Trump's Mar-la-go resort and golf club today, carrying on her person a thump drive containing computer malware. An alert desk clerk stopped her, after the secret service personnel on that cite had let her get that far. Time to re-examine security there!

The members of Robert Mueller's prosecution team are now expressing their deep frustration about the way that Attorney General William Barr has pronounced his own biased interpretation of their report. They have each prepared their own summation of their part in the overall probe, and feel that these should have played a role in Barr's description. They told the *New York Times* that they believe that the full report will be much more damaging to the President than the Barr report indicates. The question on everyone's mind is, where is Robert Mueller? Why doesn't he speak for himself instead of leaving it up to his employees to do it?
The word is that he is assisting Barr in deciding what needs to redacted from the report, so perhaps he is refraining from being antagonistic until that tricky and contentious job is done.
Former Solicitor General Neal Katyal was on Rachel Maddow's show tonight and expressed the view that what Trump and Barr are saying about the report and its release, is looking more and more like a cover-up.

Richard Neal, Chairman of the House Ways and Means Committee, is requesting ten years of Trump's tax returns from the IRS, and he wants them by this Wednesday. The IRS is obligated to comply with his request. Trump will be apoplectic.

Trump hates the towering wind turbines that sometimes operate close to his golf resorts, so he had some "interesting" remarks about them in a recent speech. They included gems like "I hear the noise from them causes cancer," and "they are graveyards for birds." Even his staunch supporter Chuck Grassley called these comments "idiotic."

Trump's porous security policy and blasé attitude about it was emphasized yesterday by the near miss at Mar-a-Lago by a Chinese woman. Trump's and his family's use of unsecured phones and emails are far more dangerous than Hillary Clinton's careless use of her personal server. He has become "the enemy within", and a clear and present danger to our country.

Democrat Lori Lightfoot, a black, gay female just won in a landslide (74-25%) to become the Mayor of Chicago, running against the long-time political machine of that city.

Those nation-wide protests mentioned in the April 1st entry took place today, since there has been no progress toward getting the full report released. Senator Richard Blumenthal, Democrat from Connecticut, spoke at one of the protest rallies, and made a clear case for release of the report. At another rally, House Judiciary Committee Chairman Jerry Nadler did much the same, and added that "we have ample reason to suspect his motives," referring to AG Barr's foot-dragging on this vital issue.

The Mueller team members, who have started speaking up about the short shrift their work has been given so far, say that they each prepared summaries of their section of the Mueller probe, which they prescreened for national security data, and they expected would be part of the revealed data to Congress and the public. They claim the evidence for obstruction is much more "acute" than Barr's summary indicated. The touchy question of grand jury material has an exception-precedent already established in the Nixon case.

The Enemy Within: A Chronicle of the Trump Administration

The Mueller team made the mistake of stamping every page of the report with the warning that it *might* contain sensitive material. Barr is apparently using that stamp as his excuse for holding things up as long as possible. Rachel Maddow, in discussing this excuse, calls it "absurd." It is also more evidence of cover-up. Other presidents have tried tactics like this and failed. So will Trump. A new poll shows that since the turn-over and summary of Mueller's report, Trump's approval rating has gone up only a tiny fraction of one percent.

Philip Lacovara, the attorney who won the battle over the Nixon tapes, was a guest tonight on the *Rachel Maddow Show*, where he characterized Barr's handling of the report issue as "clumsy," "puzzling," and "troublesome."

Adam Shiff says that he expects Robert Mueller to be required to testify before Congress. He also says that his Intel Committee is investigating Trump's inauguration, suspecting foreign influence played a role, which is a counter-intelligence concern. There are now *seven* open investigations into that inauguration.

Trump says that he plans to fight the release of his tax returns all the way to the Supreme Court if necessary. If he tries to coerce the IRS to withhold them he will be breaking the law—for so much as a phone call to the Agency. If he does make contact, the person so contacted *must* report it to the DOJ, or face the possibility of the same five year prison sentence that would face the caller. Trump should keep the Al Capone case in his mind. When a reporter asked Trump about what he intends to do about the request for six years of his returns, he said, "Speak to the Attorney General."

The other relevant law is the one that gives the House Ways and Means Committee the absolute right to demand tax returns from anyone, including the President, and that person *shall*

Book Two (09/2018-11/2019)

(must) comply. Treasury Secretary Steve Mnuchin says that he will consider any such request and will "protect" the individual. It looks like a huge court case is coming on this. In Nixon's similar tax case, he ended up having to pay nearly half a million dollars. If Michael Cohen's testimony was accurate, Trump will be lucky to get off with a fine much, much bigger than that.

In December, I described the outrageous case of Jeffrey Epstein's very lenient deal he got from prosecutor Alexander Acosta, now our Secretary of Labor. Epstein had been found guilty of running a teenage sex ring which ruined the lives of dozens of teenage girls.

Now Secretary Acosta wants to cut the budget of his department in a way that will have a huge negative impact on child protection capability. He was grilled today by House Democratic Caucus Chairperson Katherine Clark, and had a great deal of trouble coming up with anything resembling an answer to her questions. When Trump was asked about him today, he had nothing but praise for Acosta, adding the interesting tidbit that, "He is a guy who likes his women on the younger side." Birds of a feather!

The Republicans have persuaded Trump to back down on his second planned stupid move of the week. He has decided to at least postpone his closure of the southern border. Can it be that the GOP is starting to grow a spine?

Judge Beryl Howell, an appointee of President Obama, presides over the D.C. court whose grand jury heard the evidence pertaining to the questions of both Trump's alleged conspiracy with the Russians and his obstruction. She will be the one who makes the decision on whether or not an *exception* should be made to the standing law that grand jury material should not be made public, when the person involved is the President of the United States. The law seems to give her the

The Enemy Within: A Chronicle of the Trump Administration

discretion to make that kind of exception, but it is not cut and dried, so will no doubt be disputed.

Trump continues to be adamant in his refusal to release any of his tax returns. He must be hiding something pretty damning to welch on his promise to do so "when he was no longer under audit." That excuse never made sense to begin with, and even if it did *then*, it wouldn't now. He must have seen this problem coming because back in February of last year he appointed one of his supporters to the post of IRS Counsel, and prioritized his confirmation. He has now hired a new attorney to fight this tax battle with him. He is more desperate to hide this information than any other issue. The question looms—WHY? This new lawyer has written a letter to Treasury Secretary Mnuchin, asking him to withhold Trump's returns.

The IRS Commissioner is supposed to be the one to make those decisions, but the Treasury Secretary outranks him/her. Trump's new lawyer is an inexperienced neophyte, so the question is, is his letter a joke, or is it a crime, as explained in yesterday's post.

Twenty states, led by California's AG, are suing the President over his attempt to reallocate government funds to work on his southern border wall. Only Congress has the power to allocate funds, and the ignorant president is about to learn that. He went to the border in southern California to look over its section of the "wall"—a far cry from what he described to his followers that he would build—and praised it as though it was new and beautiful, which it was neither. There, he announced to the world that, "Our country is full! We can't take in any more people."

Cindy Yang's penetration of Mar-a-Lago has sparked an investigation into the level of security there. Since this is considered to be Trump's second White House, they need to address the risk level, pronto.

Book Two (09/2018-11/2019)

Pence is pushing Trump's sudden desire to launch another moon shot ASAP, almost as if they were not aware that we have been there and done that. Maybe he just wants to get the hell out of here before the shit really hits the fan. I think NASA is really more interested in getting us to Mars.

Democratic Congressman from Ohio, Tim Ryan, has announced his entry into the Presidential race. He was a guest on Lawrence O'Donnell's *Last Word* show tonight. He has a broad set of liberal ideas covering our entire economic system, including a "wealth tax" and "Medicare-for-all." He is a young, articulate prospect who may very well start to catch on, but he has a *lot* of competition.

The big news of the weekend was the resignation (forced?) of Homeland Security Secretary Kirstjen Nielsen. She and trump did not see eye to eye very much lately, so this move was fairly predictable. So, another of Trump's "best people" bites the dust. I would say. "Good riddance!" except that she is said to be the only one who was trying to prevent Trump from reinstating his policy of separating children from parents. Now, watch out!

AG Barr says that he is almost ready to turn the report over to Congress, perhaps this coming week. It should be a very big week, in several respects.

There was a lot of discussion about the huge field of Democratic candidates for president that we already have, and continues to grow. It is the biggest group in our history. Everyone wants a crack at the disaster we have in the White House today. The consensus among the sixty percent of voters who are not addicted to Trump's BS is that virtually *anyone* could beat the worst US president in history in 2020. But we cannot afford to get overconfident. Let that be *his* problem.

The Enemy Within: A Chronicle of the Trump Administration

Today I was checking out the latest Facebook posts, and I stumbled across a video of the final speech that Ronald Reagan made as president. It was very stirring in its portrayal of the way he saw what our country stands for. I will quote a short segment of that speech, made by the man the Republican Party considers one its greatest heroes (and so do I). Try to reconcile this view of who we are as a nation, with Donald's Trump's view of who we are, and ask yourself, how does the current Republican Party continue to stand behind Trump?

"Other countries may seek to compete with us, but in one area, as a beacon of freedom and opportunity, that draws the people of the world, no country on Earth comes close. This, I believe, is one of the most important sources of America's greatness."

April 8-14

With Nielsen out, Trump's policies toward immigration can be expected to get a lot tougher and less humane. Asylum seekers will feel the effects of this move immediately and severely. Trump's pick to replace Nielsen is the current Commissioner of U.S. Customs and Border Protection, Kevin McAleenan, who praised the tear-gassing of immigrants, including children, who got too close to the border a few weeks ago.

Trump then made Stephen Miller Head of the immigration part of Home Security. Trump's orders to border control agents, to deny entry to *anyone* for any reason are unlawful, and have forced those agents to turn to their superiors for advice, who are equally confused. He is also reinstating the child-separation policy, which was ruled unconstitutional months ago. Those kids who are still waiting to be reunited with their parents may not see them for at least two more years, and now he wants to start adding to this horrendous problem. Trump has gone completely off the rails in his frenzy to please his base of racists, knowing that they are his only source of approval and votes.

In addition to the departure of Secretary Nielsen, Trump fired the Chief of the Secret Service, Randolph Alles, and replaced him (in another "acting" capacity) with a long time Secret Service officer named James Murray. No reason for the change was given.

Trump's Chief-of-Staff Mulvaney says, "The Democrats will never see his tax returns. The law says otherwise. Brace for a pitched battle, all to protect the documents promised over and over that he would release. Years ago, it was ruled that the Chief of the IRS is the one who has the power to release tax returns that have been requested by Congress—not the Treasury Secretary. Mnuchin *cannot* interfere in Trump's behalf.

The Manafort-linked lobbyist, Sam Patten, mentioned in my February notes, has a sentencing date this Friday for his illegal activities involving the Trump inauguration. He has met nine times in his cooperation with prosecutors and they have been pleased enough with what he had to offer them that they are recommending leniency.

Today Trump announced a new, tougher stance against the Iranian Revolutionary Guard, who not too long ago he was in business with, to build a Tower in Azerbaijan. He now calls them a "terrorism group."

Representative Doug Collins has joined forces with Jerry Nadler in requesting Robert Mueller to testify before their Judiciary Committee.

There are two crucial issues being fought out between Trump, with the aid of its hand-picked Attorney General, and the U.S. Congress during this historic period in our history right now. The first one is over the release of the full Mueller Report, and the second is over the release of Trump's tax returns. The way in which these two issues are ultimately resolved will greatly impact our nation for decades to come.

The issue which carries the most weight and draws the most debate right now is the report. Attorney General William Barr was questioned for several hours today by the members of the House Appropriations Committee, and was unable or unwilling to provide much in the way of satisfactory answers to the members' questions. It became more and more obvious that he intends to drag his feet as long as possible on the issue of full release of an unredacted report, even to Congress. He will not even say whether or not Trump has seen any of the report.

The reasons he gives for being reluctant to release *grand jury* material are sketchy and evasive, and what he says about the Special Counsel being restricted in some ways as to his procedures, is just plain wrong, according to Neal Katyal, the man who helped write those guidelines. He is alarmed by Barr's obstruction tactics, which have earned the AG labels like "flunky", "toady", "fixer", etc.

Barr said that he saw no way that Congress could force the release of a full report, unless they got it from the Special Counsel himself. Sounds like a great idea! Let's do it? He says he does not plan to ask the court to clear release of grand jury material, even though previous AGs have done so. He did say that he would be ready to turn over his redacted version by the end of this week. House Judiciary Committee Chairman Jerry Nadler has vowed that once he sees the report from Barr, he will seek the courts OK to get this grand jury data that is so vital to understanding why the Special Counsel did not act on what he learned. To do so, he may have to open an impeachment proceeding as a reason for needing that data.

Barr said that Mueller had a voice in deciding what needed to be redacted. If so, then why is Mueller's team so frustrated about the way this problem is being addressed? Intel Committee

Book Two (09/2018-11/2019)

Chairman Adam Schiff says that he will demand to see even the information that involves a national security issue.

Barr also made the very telling statement that he believes there really was "spying on the Trump campaign going on." That issue was raised and addressed already, and put to bed.

As to the second of the two crucial issues, tomorrow (Wednesday) is the day that Congress expects to see six years of Trump's tax returns. IRS Commissioner Charles Rettig says that he and Treasury Secretary Mnuchin are "discussing" who should be the one to respond to the request. The law is clear that it should be Rettig, but Mnuchin—being the loyal Trump supporter—may not give in easily. Former IRS Commissioner Lawrence Summers was a guest of both Rachel and Lawrence tonight and he was adamant that since 1924 it has been the law that only the IRS Commissioner has the responsibility to respond to valid requests for returns.

On Rachel's show tonight she displayed and discussed the transcript of former General Counsel Jim Baker's testimony before Congress last year, in which he expressed the deep concern that he and his FBI colleagues had about the firing of James Comey, and the phony excuse Trump gave for the firing. They all considered it a clear case of obstruction.

On Chris Hayes *All In* show tonight he and his guests discussed Trump's record of lying and law-breaking, and commanding those beneath him to lie and break the law, including the guards along the southern border, all the while being aided by the acquiescence of the McConnell-led GOP Senate.

Trump was forced into the realization that his pick to replace Nielsen as Homeland Security Secretary did not follow the custom of following the chain-of-succession, so he told Nielsen to make her last official act before leaving, the firing of her Deputy. Heads are rolling right and left in the area of immigration, so that Trump has freer rein to take whatever racist action he needs to stem the flow of "all those criminals and rapists invading our country."

On Wednesday it was the Senate's turn to question AG Barr about the Mueller Report—specifically, about the level of redactions. He was no more forthcoming with them than he was with the House members yesterday. One of the other areas he was questioned about was his plan to gut the Affordable Care Act, which he admitted to leading. He pointed to the cost of the premiums and drugs, and once again claimed that Trump would immediately replace it with a much better and cheaper plan. Everyone in the world who pays any attention to the news at all knows that this is as big a lie as any of those that Trump has told. Of course, he is well aware that the Republican Party, much less Trump himself, has no such health care plan even on the drawing board. Every single question asked of him got a "Trumpian" answer.

Neal Katyal said that Barr is Trump's Attorney General, not America's. Speaker Pelosi remarked that Barr "is going off the rails." Professor Lawrence Tribe commented that AG Barr "has no shame," because of his attempt to resurrect the crazy "spying" story on the Trump campaign, that has been investigated and thoroughly debunked months ago. Katyal also says that "Barr makes Matt Whitaker look good. He has joined the tinfoil hat crowd, and totally distorts or disregards the rules." Adam Schiff calls Barr's testimony, "deeply disturbing."

Barr says he will release the redacted version of the report by the end of the week, but that gives him until Friday, before Congress goes on vacation until the twenty-ninth of this month.

Treasury Secretary Steve Mnuchin says he cannot meet today's deadline for the release of those long sought tax returns, with no justification offered, and with no right to be making that

Book Two (09/2018-11/2019)

decision in the first place. As explained in earlier daily entries, that decision is supposed to be the strict province of IRS Commissioner Rettig. When Rettig was questioned about this in front of the TV cameras, he looked very uncomfortable as he struggled to offer an explanation and failed.

Today was Kirstjen Nelsen's last day of work in the Trump administration, and she now has the daunting challenge of atoning for her contribution to the policy of separating children and parents at the southern border, and restoring her reputation.

The Wall Street Journal reports that the Southern District of New York has gathered a lot of information from White House insiders, pertaining to Trump's hush-money payments (as if we needed any more).

Trump claims that Obama was the one who began the policy of separating children at the border. Not quite a lie, but very misleading and misrepresented. Obama's policy only called for separating kids in extreme cases where the children needed to be protected. Trump has reached a new point of desperation to go to this extent.

Lawrence O'Donnell opines that Trump's last act before he leaves the presidency, whenever that might be, will be to pardon himself. First, that would amount to a confession to whatever he pardons himself for, and second, why would that even be allowed???

WikiLeaks founder Julian Assange was arrested today in London, and charged with "hacking" crimes related to the stealing of the Clinton emails, and for his conspiring with the Russians to broadcast the stolen data for the purpose of influencing the 2016 election. Trump, who about 400 times during his presidential campaign, declared how much he "loved WikiLeaks", now denies knowing anything about the company or Assange. He keeps believing he can lie about something that is immediately refutable and get away with it, and with his base he seems to right.

Pulitzer Prize winning journalist David Cay Johnson was a guest on O'Donnell's *Last Word* show tonight and said that Treasury Secretary Mnuchin is getting himself into serious legal jeopardy by inserting himself into the Trump tax return case. The law is very clear that *no one* can attempt to interfere with any request for tax information when it is made by Congress. He is flirting with a five year prison sentence and does not even seem to know it. Trump's Chief-of-Staff, John Mulvaney, may also have overstepped his bounds when he declared recently that, "The President will *never* turn over his tax returns."

Attorney General Barr's use of the word "spying" to refer to the legal "surveillance that was used during the Trump campaign as part of its investigation into the Russians, has come under so much backlash that he tried to walk it back today in a very awkward and embarrassing attempt to explain himself. He only succeeded in displaying how completely unqualified he is for his new job.

Former White House lawyer Gregory Craig has been indicted for his illegal communications with Ukraine and for lying about them.

Trump's older sister Maryanne resigned from her judgeship today as she was being investigated for her role, along with some of her siblings, in a tax fraud scheme which netted her millions of dollars, according to prosecutors. Her retirement from the bench mysteriously stopped her investigation. Some sort of deal made? Could this be one of Trump's reasons for being so dead set on hiding those returns?

Trump has nominated two men for chairs on the Federal Reserve Board, who are every bit as qualified as most of his

Book Two (09/2018-11/2019)

appointments have been—which is to say—zero! They are Herman Cain, a radio talk-show host/Tea Party activist, and Stephen Moore of the Heritage Foundation. Their confirmation will not go smoothly.

Recently, *Fox News* put out a poll which purported to show Donald Trump's approval rating had risen dramatically to 55% and crowed about how great he was doing, compared to the polls showed regularly by the "fake news channels." Today they had to confess that they "accidentally" used the *disapproval* percentage. So, who is purveyor of fake news?

Newcomer to the Presidential sweepstakes, Pete Buttigieg, has risen to third place, behind only Biden and Sanders in the latest Iowa and New Hampshire polls. Youth and knowledge are being considered over sexual orientation or length of service.

Barr says he has a redaction team working on the report (no word on who is on it) and it should be ready to turn over to Congress this coming week.

House Oversight Committee Chairman Elijah Cummings is subpoenaing a financial company named Mazars, for documents related to *any* of Trump's organizations. These would include memos about any concerns about any of those organizations. This could be as big and revealing as the effort to get his returns released.

Investigators are looking into why all of the donated money to Cindy Yang's massage parlor company that were made during the inauguration period have disappeared, and no records were kept.

Lobbyist Sam Patten received a very lenient sentence today because of his degree of cooperation with the prosecutors. No jail time, just three years' probation and a five thousand dollar fine. They gave no clue as to what kind of information he gave them, but it was probably related to Manafort's dealing with Konstantin Kilimnik of Russia.

Candidate Pete Buttigieg laid out an excellent picture of the state that our government is in today. He pictures it as made up, half by people who are grossly incompetent, and half by empty positions, some of which have been empty since day one of the Trump administration.

The Democrats have sent a strongly-worded letter to AG Barr, critical of the way in which he has consistently defended Trump (acting as his stooge, actually) and his improper use of the word "spy" in relation to legally-obtained surveillance.

Trump keeps threatening to punish Democrats for their stand on immigration, by unloading detained border immigrants on sanctuary cities—particularly in California. This plan is not only very misguided, it is not even feasible.

Trump tells the border patrol agents that he will pardon any of them who get into legal trouble by following his orders to stop the flow of migrants by any means necessary. This amounts to enabling criminal actions.

Democratic candidate Pete Buttigieg gave a JFK-like speech to a very large and enthusiastic crowd on Sunday, in which he covered just about every issue and topic of interest to today's voters, including getting rid of the outdated Electoral College. He may not be in third place very long.

April 15-21

Attorney General Barr says that his redacted version of the Mueller Report will be released to Congress this Thursday. It should be a very interesting day, first to see how much is and is

Book Two (09/2018-11/2019)

not redacted, and then to see what Jerry Nadler et al will do to force a much *fuller* version of it from this blatant cover-up.

Barr already had a reputation of being a Constitutional maverick because of his record in the W. Bush administration. His actions and words during the Trump saga have sunk him to a low that he will never be able to climb back from.

Rick Wilson, Republican political strategist, media consultant and author of the book titled, *Everything Trump Touches Dies,"* was a guest on an MSNBC show tonight. He discussed his dismay about the way Barr has transformed from strict conservative to Trump's puppet. The House leaders have written a lengthy memo to the DOJ requesting a briefing by Mueller and individual members of his team.

In the meantime, where are Trump's tax returns? Today, Congress delivered their subpoenas to several financial institutions, including Deutche Bank, for all Trump-related documents. Sarah Sanders says that Congress "is too stupid to understand Trump's tax forms." She gets crazier every day, and more desperate for ways to defend her boss, the indefensible criminal-in-chief.

The House Democrats are also seeking to question Stephen Miller about his immigration policies; in particular, his plan to punish sanctuary cities by dumping loads of new immigrants on them. He has long been dead set on ridding this nation of *all* immigrants, in whatever way possible. He has a clear case of white supremacy fever.

On Chris Hayes *All In* show tonight, he and several guests discussed the abominable level of hate rhetoric being spewed by Trump and his far right allies, as a backlash against freshman Congresswoman Ilhan Omar, one of the two Muslim women elected in the blue wave of last November. They are using her tendency to use poorly nuanced phrases when discussing the sad status of Muslim-western relations these days. They twist and misinterpret her comments in an obvious attempt to whip up anti-Muslim fervor, following Trump's lead that started on the first day of his presidential campaign.

Tonight, Rachel Maddow gave us a history lesson on the past record of duplicity by William Barr when he served as Attorney General under President George H. W. Bush. When Bush was attempting to drastically change the U.S. policy of non-interference in the affairs of other countries in his attempt to rid Panama and the free world of the dictatorship of Noriega, Barr served him in the very same way he is serving Trump today by using every means at his disposal to shield Trump from the dangers contained in the full Mueller Report. He is doing so at the expense of further tarnishing his image for the history books. We will find out tomorrow, when his redacted version is finally released, just how far he is willing to stick his neck out for his president.

Trump is very worried about what his closest former staff and cabinet members have told Mueller as part of their cooperation with that team, especially his former White House Counsel Don McGahn.

Trump has hired a new team of lawyers to help him stop the release of those explosive tax returns, but they have no power to block the subpoenas which have been presented. There is an increased Mob mentality and atmosphere in the White House these days, according to several Washington insiders.

Bernie Sanders spent an hour debating with *Fox News* hosts today, and Trump was not at all pleased with the way his friends handled this debate. The consensus is that Bernie was more than a match for them.

Trump has issued his second veto of his term. This one on Congress's attempt to stop America's support of the war in Yemen. So the slaughter will continue.

Book Two (09/2018-11/2019)

Trump now has an official challenger for the Republican presidential nomination next year. Bill Weld, from Massachusetts, is fairly well known and may very well be the coup de gras to Trump's re-election hopes. In every such case in recent history, where the incumbent was so challenged, he lost the re-election, or as in LBJ's case, resigned.

It is reported that the version of the Mueller Report that is being released tomorrow will be more lightly redacted than expected. It will contain a detailed look at the incidents of obstruction by the President. The House Judiciary Committee Chairman publicly read us a report he has written describing Barr's actions and words that have been inappropriately biased in favor of Trump, and disputing the idea that the AG intends to make a statement about the report just before delivering it.

A total of five House Committee chairs are outraged by Barr's plan to preface the report's release with more pro-Trump propaganda. He should let the report speak for himself, and Robert Mueller should accompany him for the presentation. The optics that Barr is creating for himself are destroying whatever reputation he once had. Only Congress, at this point, can decide if the obstruction evidence rises to the level of being impeachable. Nadler says that he expects to be issuing a subpoena soon for the full, unredacted version.

The White House staff is very nervous about their exposure of things they told Mueller's team; things that will infuriate the President.

A District of Columbia judge says that he wants to see the redacted version to deermine if it conforms to what he would expect to be released by a Freedom of Information Act suit. He is concerned about the level on transparency being allowed, as are we all. Barr has already discussed the report with Trump, which is another irregularity.

There will be *several* versions of this report, each with its own level of redaction, from heavy to none. Congress is confused about who is getting what version, since they have not been informed by the DOJ.

Trump is getting a little critical of some of the anchors at *Fox News,* for not being "faithful enough to him." He expects "his program" to be his loyal mouthpiece/propaganda machine. He was really upset when they had Sanders on the show recently and were shown up by him.

Republican Congressman Andy Barr publicly invited AOC to tour a Kentucky coal mine with him to see and hear what the miners thought about the Green New Deal. When Alexandria called his bluff and took him up on the offer, he danced his way out of it—invitation rescinded.

There have been a great many highly impactful days over the course of the Trump administration so far, but only a few of them have been truly historic in importance. In my mind, the ones that stand out as meeting that level are: May 9, 2017, when Trump fired FBI Director James Comey (because of "the Russia thing"); May 18, 2017, when the Special Counsel Robert Mueller was appointed to investigate everything related to Russian interference in the Presidential campaign; November 7, 2018, when Trump fired AG Jeff Sessions (because he didn't do enough to protect him); February 14, 2019, when the Senate confirmed William Barr as the new Attorney General (in spite of Barr's record of obvious bias toward presidents in general and Trump in particular).

Today, we can add April 20, 2019 to that list, when the Mueller Report, in spite of many redactions, was made available both to Congress and to the American people. Even a quick once over of this four hundred page document exposes AG

Book Two (09/2018-11/2019)

Barr's portrayal and interpretation of it as *completely at odds* with the report itself. We thought that the four-page summary that Barr gave of the report a couple of weeks ago was both unwarranted and blatantly biased to please Trump, but today he delivered a pre-release speech that not only reinforced that bias, but outdid it by a mile. He has now cemented his image for history as being nothing more than a hired gun to cover up as much as possible for his Mob boss.

Perhaps the *most* disgusting of all the things Barr said in what amounted to a Trump press conference, was the excuse he tried to provide for his boss for all those in-your-face episodes of obstruction. According to Barr, we must take into account the fact that the President was extremely frustrated and angered by the constant pressure being applied to him by the negative press, which inhibited his ability to do his job, and he reacted in self-defense, the way anyone might. This prompted Trump to start celebrating his "exoneration" yet again.

As to the report itself, there are already several noteworthy revelations to digest. We knew that Mueller explicitly stated in his report that, as to obstruction he was unable to make a definitive declaration as to whether the evidence reached the level of a crime. Because Mueller knew he could not indict a sitting president, he felt he could not directly accuse him either, so he is leaving it up to Congress to decide what to do with the evidence. We now know that he listed ten separate episodes of "attempts to obstruct", many of which were thwarted by refusal of his underlings to follow his orders.

Earlier in this book, I listed ten such episodes. It will be interesting to see if they are the same ten. Andrew McCabe, former FBI Director and author of *The Threat*, was a guest of Rachel Maddow tonight and calls the amount of obstruction evidence "an avalanche." As to collusion/conspiracy, McCabe believed that all that was missing was the "keystone" to tie the two parties (Russia and the Trump campaign) together firmly.

Did Mueller think they were going to be dumb enough to create a signed agreement of some sort?

Senators Amy Klobuchar and Kamala Harris both expressed the opinion that Mueller and Barr need to be brought before the Senate Judiciary Committee for intense questioning. Klobuchar said that AG Barr is acting as the President's lawyer instead of the county's top law-enforcement agent. She fears he might even interfere with the Southern District of New York's investigation. Harris says that he is acting like a Mob boss. They have scheduled him to appear before them sometime in May.

One of the most incriminating quotations so far exposed in the report is when Donald Trump himself, upon hearing from Attorney General Sessions that they have appointed a Special Prosecutor, exclaimed, "This is the end of my presidency. I'm fucked!" If that doesn't demonstrate a consciousness of guilt, what does?

The report contains *nothing* pertaining to Trump's or his organization's financial questions. Mueller is leaving that area strictly up to the New York prosecutors. He also specifies that all the evidence that he could not use against a sitting president will still be there when Trump in no longer the President, and he *could be prosecuted then*. So no matter what happens with the obstruction case, Mr. Trump is far from out of the legal woods.

Among the many individual events described in the ten major categories of obstruction, which Mueller laid out in his report, was the case of Corey Lewandowsky and his chat with Attorney General Jeff Sessions. The AG had recused himself of all matters relating to the investigation into Russian interference into the Presidential election, much to Trump's chagrin and anger.

Two days after Trump had directed Don McGahn to fire Mueller and was talked out of it by McGahn, Trump had

Book Two (09/2018-11/2019)

dictated a "suggestion" that he wanted Lewandowski to make to Sessions, which his campaign chairman wisely wrote down for posterity. In it, Lewandowsky was to relay Trump's urging for the AG to un-recuse himself and then redirect the FBI's probe to focus on future attempts to interfere and ignore the recently proven one. Lewandowsky repeatedly avoided carrying out the request, in spite of continuous pressure by Trump, and he locked up the note containing it, for possible future reference. A wise man indeed. Finally, Trump ordered him to fire Sessions, and that was also refused. Shortly thereafter, Lewandowsky was no longer working for the President.

The report details how this episode meets *all* the elements of the crime of obstruction of justice. It does the same for all of the other nine episodes. The details used to describe these episodes consume one hundred and twenty-eight pages of the report. The section ends by stating that charges could be brought against Trump as soon as he is no longer president, or could be used by Congress to impeach him.

Elizabeth Warren, on *The Rachel Maddow Show* tonight, became the first presidential candidate to call for Trump's impeachment as soon as they receive an unredacted copy of the report. She says it is incumbent upon Congress to do so, even knowing that the Republican-controlled Senate is unlikely to convict. "It is a matter of principle, not politics."

Immediately after her, Congressman Eric Swalwell echoed her opinion on this vital matter. He wants to hear from Mueller himself before proceeding. He also informed us that two hundred pages of the report are devoted to instances of collusion with the Russians, as opposed to the actual crime of conspiracy. They separate the two words, "collusion" as a lighter, less serious version of "conspiracy", sort of like the various levels of other felonies.

The Enemy Within: A Chronicle of the Trump Administration

Everything that the President says and does shows how concerned he is with what will be exposed, beginning with that comment mentioned in yesterday's entry that was uttered in the presence of several staffers when he was informed that a Special Counsel had been named. It is almost amusing, if it were not so disturbing, that when the report was initially described by Barr, Trump was euphoric and claimed his complete exoneration, but now he twitters that the whole report is "crazy bullshit."

The Mueller Report reveals that Trump's written answers that he agreed to offer instead of personally appearing before the Mueller team as requested, amounted to some version of "I don't remember", *thirty-seven times*.

On *Meet the Press* Saturday, Rudy Giuliani once again made a complete ass of himself when he responded to the host's question about Trump's willingness to accept "dirt" on Clinton from a foreign power. Rudy claimed, "There is nothing wrong with that. Any campaigner would have done that." He is supposed to be a lawyer. Did he not learn in law school that knowingly accepting stolen property is a crime? Also, accepting a campaign contribution, meaning *anything* of value from a foreign power is a campaign violation. It is difficult to say at this point who if the biggest Trump toady—Rudy or Bill Barr. Barr is certainly the most effective, via his position, than Giuliani.

The marital political divide between Kellyanne Conway and her husband George must have widened a bit this weekend when George published an op-ed article in the *Washington Post* expressing his opinion that Trump should definitely be impeached on the basis of the report, crime or not. He believes the evidence of obstruction is heavier than it was in Nixon's case, and he is right.

Since AG Barr's glowing summary of the report that he gave us on the day it was delivered, Trump's approval rating has dropped six points to a record low of thirty-seven percent. He is the only president in US history to have *never* reached a rating of fifty percent. He spent Saturday morning repeatedly tweeting his anger and frustration, then went down to Mar-a-Lago and faked being "the happiest he's ever been."

When Robert Mueller finally appears before one or more of the House Committees to answer their many questions about the report, the one I am most interested in hearing the answer to is this: "Mr. Mueller, if Donald Trump were not the President, would you feel that you had enough evidence to indict him on either the conspiracy charge or the obstruction charge?" If he answers that question affirmatively, or refuses to answer it negatively, choosing to decline to answer because of his devotion to standard DOJ policy, that should be enough for Congress to draw its own conclusion and proceed with the drawing up of a bill of impeachment. They must do their duty regardless of whether or not the Republicans in the Senate are willing to do theirs.

With all the attention focused on the report, it seems that the demand for the President's tax returns has been lost in the shuffle. Where do things stand, now that Treasury Secretary Mnuchin is continuing to ignore the law?

April 22-28

Trump is trying to sue Elijah Cummings and his House Oversight Committee for the "sin" of subpoenaing Trump's financial records from the Mazars Company. This suit has no legal standing and can only serve to slow things down a bit, while making the President look all the more like he is hiding something explosive. Mueller did not fully investigate Trump's taxes or finances, but is passing on any relevant data to

Congress and the SDNY to follow up, along with counter-intelligence data to the FBI.

Don McGahn has been subpoenaed by the House Judiciary Committee. They want to ask him about Trump's pressure on him to get Comey off his back, for starters.

A former secretary to Trump on his Organization staff named Barbara Res was a guest on Bryan Williams *Eleventh Hour* tonight. She described how often she and others on his staff would refuse or neglect to follow up on orders from Trump to do things they knew were at least unethical if not illegal. She observed that Trump has gotten a lot worse in that regard since becoming president. Mueller's report reveals at least *fifteen* instances where his aides did not heed orders they deemed too off-the-wall, damaging or illegal.

Rachel Maddow tonight delved into the mystery of DNI Dan Coats' complete reversal on a story he told several fellow members of the administration, that he had been repeatedly pressured by Trump to do something about "getting Comey off his back." When questioned by Mueller, Coats soft-peddled any such events. He needs to be asked about this.

Rachel also had the latest entry into the Presidential race, Representative from Massachusetts, Seth Boulton. Congressman Boulton says we should immediately begin the debate on Trump's impeachment, but not file any bill until we know all the facts. Sounds like a plan to me.

Near the beginning of the Mueller investigation, Donald Trump made the huge mistake of allowing the White House attorney, Don McGahn, to talk to the Mueller team without claiming executive privilege. As a result, McGahn has had more than one hundred and fifty conversations with Mueller and his team and has provided a ton of very damaging testimony against the President, according to the report. It seems that

Book Two (09/2018-11/2019)

Trump never really understood that the White House's lawyer works for the "office of the presidency", not for the individual holding that office.

What McGahn revealed about Trump's attempts to get him to pressure Comey to redirect the Russia investigation away from the President, is enough, by itself, to warrant impeachment. Now Trump is attempting to use the court to block the House's subpoena of McGahn to hear his testimony first-hand. Too late to declare executive privilege now, Mr. President. McGahn has become the modern-day John Dean. Bill Weld, who has become Trump's opposition in his own party's nomination, says that Trump is behaving exactly like Richard Nixon did during the Watergate subpoena process, which led to his resignation. House Oversight Committee Chairman Elijah Cummings says that Trump is trying to "negate democracy by subverting the Congress."

Secretary Mnuchin says that he will miss the deadline to surrender Trump's tax records, but will have them turned over on May 6. Sounds like a lot of doctoring going on there to me.

Our new Interior Secretary, David Bernhardt, is already under investigation for ethics charges by the Inspector General.

DNC Chairman Tom Perez warns all the Democratic candidates about the gross lack of cyber security that we now face because of this administrations complete lack of action to prevent a repeat of 2016.

Secretary of Commerce Wilbur Ross had agreed to the addition of the citizenship question to the new census form, which will result in many undocumented aliens avoiding turning in a form, thus reducing the population counts in many districts. This will greatly benefit the Republicans as it skews that way districts are drawn and represented. What's worse is that Chief Justice Roberts is ready to support this decision, calling it "critical to enforce the voting rights act", when in fact, it negatively impacts the rights of many voters.

The Saudis have been using multiple BOTS to promote their contention that the Mueller probe, which they label "Russiagate", was nothing more than a liberal hoax. Their Tweets and twitter accounts have been removed.

Trump simply cannot face the fact that Russian interference played a role in getting him elected because he feels, correctly, that it taints his presidency. So he will not lift a finger or allocate a dime to defend against it happening again in 2020.

Nancy Pelosi says that the GOP "should be ashamed of what the Mueller Report reveals—not ignoring it and defending Trump.

Trump has ordered his administration officials and aides to defy any and *all* subpoenas for their testimony or their documents. He wants a court battle in all these cases in order to run out the clock until the next election. Anyone who obeys that command is in serious danger of being held in contempt of court, so we shall see how many are willing to stick their neck out. In particular, Trump is desperate to stop McGahn from testifying.

Former Nixon attorney William Jaffress was a guest on Rachel Maddow's show tonight and said that Trump will get himself in even more trouble by so much as criticizing the subpoenas, and he cannot rely on the Supreme Court to bail him out—not in cases initiated by Congress.

Hillary Clinton published a big op-ed article in *The Washington Post* in which she expressed what should be done with the Mueller Report's revelations. She said Congress should hold bi-partisan public hearings to fill in the gaps left by the report. We also need a bi-partisan group to address the problem of the next Russian cyber threat. Here is a paragraph from that article. "The group that created our nation's founding document would already have judged Donald Trump unfit for office—and removed him—because he's repeatedly shown a dearth of the quality they considered paramount in a president: a willingness to put national interest above his own.

Rachel Maddow told us about a section in the Mueller Report involving a Russian who communicated with Michael Cohen and Donald Trump about "a tapes problem" that the Russians were holding over him as Kompromat. This took place well before the Steele dossier came out. So Trump knew about the existence of the pee-pee tape before McCabe told him of it.

Trump assumes, so he says, that Mueller has already looked at his tax returns and other financial data so why is everybody so hell-bent on getting their hands on them? It must be all fine. But Mueller's report does not cover that subject, so he is wrong on that score. We will still get them from the IRS and Mazars eventually.

Trump is desperately trying to contradict Don McGahn's testimony, as described in the Mueller Report; that the President tried to get McGahn to fire Mueller or redirect his investigation. He is planning to fight McGahn's subpoena all the way to the Supreme Court, which Trump mistakenly believes will shield him from an impeachment. His ignorance of the Constitution is amazing.

It is now known that Trump paid Kim Jong Un $2 million in what amounts to a ransom payment, to secure the release of their prisoner, Otto Warmbier. Trump is trying to pass this off as medical expense reimbursement, but that is laughable.

Fox News commentator, Judge Napolitano, has openly said on Trump's favorite TV channel that he believes that the

The Enemy Within: A Chronicle of the Trump Administration

President is guilty of several cases of obstruction. This is a man who is considered a friend of Trump, and whom Trump consulted about his choice for Supreme Court nominee.

Lawrence O'Donnell tonight pointed out that Donald Trump has never once, during his presidency, made any attempt whatever to win over anyone who was not already a supporter. He seems content to hold on to the base of around thirty-five to forty percent, which is nowhere near enough to win re-election.

Trump is renewing his threat to open an investigation into Hillary Clinton and has now tacked on several other of "angry Democrat" enemies that he feels need to be "exposed." Just another attempt to distract.

Joe Biden has finally made his official entry into the Presidential race. He brings the total of Democratic candidates to a nice round figure of twenty, which will probably never be equaled or topped. Hopefully, we will never again have a president whose performance inspires this level of incentive to have removed, which Trump has created.

While Trump tells (practically orders) Don McGahn to defy the subpoena for him to testify to the House Judiciary Committee, he simultaneously calls McGahn a liar for his statements about Trump's pressure to fire Mueller. Not a very smart way to handle a guy you are trying to influence.

The Mueller Report also provides lots of evidence of Trump, several times openly and publicly, "dangling" pardons to those he deemed a threat to him with their testimony.

The President addressed a gathering of the NRA today and ranted about the whole Department of Justice and the Democrats in the House trying to stage a coup to overthrow the government. He labeled them "traitors." If anyone is a traitor, Donald, it is you. He also tried once again to plead his case

Book Two (09/2018-11/2019

about his "very fine people" comments in response to the Charlottesville fiasco. He claims that "I answered perfectly." Obviously, he still does not understand the significance of his words—ever. He used the alleged admiration for General Robert E. Lee, and the protest against the moving of his statue, as the protestors' motivation for their "enthusiasm." Trump lavished praise on Lee and those who still idolize him, calling him one of the best loved American generals ever. This is the man who did his best to destroy us as a country, causing the death of millions on both sides of the conflict.

Elizabeth Drew, journalist, author and expert on the question of impeachment, published an article in *The New York Times* about the danger of *not* impeaching Trump. In it she stated the following: "The Democrats would also run enormous risks if they did *not* hold to account, a president who has clearly abused power and the Constitution, who has not honored the oath of office and who has had a wave of campaign and White House aides plead guilty or to a be convicted of crimes." I could not agree more.

Several knowledgeable people are now talking about how we are at a point where the future of how our government is to be structured, is at stake. It is right now heading toward an autocracy.

The twenty 2020 candidates are uniting under a pledge of unity against Donald Trump, no matter who manages to win the nomination.

Maria Butina was sentenced today after weeks of cooperation with the prosecution. She will serve eighteen months in prison, while the NRA, which she broke the law in an attempt to promote, is in a turmoil of leadership crisis between Executive VP Wayne Lapierre and President Oliver North. This organization is in hot water.

Former Deputy Attorney General, Sally Yates, who started the snowball rolling downhill toward Donald Trump back on May 8, 2017, when she testified before Congress about the problems involving Mike Flynn, commented about what the Mueller Report has to say about the evidence that Trump obstructed justice: "I've personally prosecuted obstruction cases on far, far less evidence than this. And yes, I believe that if he were not the President of the United States, he would likely be indicted on obstruction."

Book Two (09/2018-11/2019)

May, 2019

April 29-May 5

Trump continually speaks about the Mueller probe and its report as an attempted coup to overturn the government. He wants to turn the tables and start investigating Clinton, Obama and the whole Democrat Party. Talk about desperation! He and his children are trying to file suit with the Southern District of New York, against Deutche Bank, Mazars and Capital One to prevent their compliance with the subpoenas they have been served for release of Trump's financial documents.

The degree to which he is obstructing release of his finances and taxes shows the world that there is something devastating in there that he will do anything to hide.

Barr says that when he appears before the House Judiciary Committee he does not want to be questioned by any staff attorneys. Chairman Nadler says, "We decide how to conduct our hearings and meetings." There is plenty of precedent for allowing staff to ask questions, so Barr has a weak argument. Nadler also says that they will subpoena the AG if necessary. It should make for an interesting week. There is no decision yet on when Robert Mueller may be called in. That is the most important one to watch for.

Rod Rosenstein has submitted his resignation and will be leaving on May 7. In his letter he had a surprising amount of nice things to say about President Trump. I'm not sure if this shows class of lack of guts.

The latest poll shows that 55% of likely voters would definitely not vote for Trump, no matter who the opponent turns out to be. This is not likely to change for the better, the way things are going in Trump world now.

We learned today that Robert Mueller wrote a letter to William Barr stating his disapproval of the AG's interpretation of the report, and he did it in a tone that jarred the DOJ. So when Barr was asked during his recent questioning by Congress whether Mueller was in agreement with his summation, and answered, "I don't know," Barr was lying.

Mueller also stated in the letter that Barr should include the summaries of Mueller's staff members in the AG's remarks to the nation. Now Congress wants to see that letter.

Maxine Waters says that Barr and Trump are obstructing Congress at every turn. Several members of Congress are calling for Barr's resignation.

The Department of Justice has not yet set a date for Mueller to testify to Congress—more foot dragging.

New York State, led by new state AG Letitia James, is actively looking into all aspects of Trump's finances as they collect and analyze the documents they have subpoenaed from Trump's favorite financial institutions. She is one who has not been sued by the Trump family to stifle the subpoenas. AG James was a guest on *The Rachel Maddow Show* tonight and was quite impressive in her determination to get at the truth.

Senator Elizabeth Warren has now come out in favor of proceeding with impeachment hearings, after reading the Mueller Report and seeing how much evidence of obstruction it presents, even in the redacted version.

We start a new month with our political system and government getting crazier than ever. Today, we witnessed the most shameful and frightening performance from the man who is supposed to be the top law-enforcement official in the country, when he abandoned his allegiance to the general public to reinforce his complete devotion to one man—the President of the United States. His attempts to answer the questions from the

Book Two (09/2018-11/2019)

Senators on their Judiciary Committee would have been comical if the situation at hand were not so serious.

On at least seven occasions, he muttered, stumbled, hesitated and prevaricated as he tried desperately to walk a line between outright lying and saying something he knew Trump would not be pleased to hear. On more than one occasion he decided that lying was the safer choice. One of the most alarming things he said, which he is on record as saying *before*, is that if a person is falsely accused (as he believes is the case with the Mueller probe), attempts to block the investigation cannot be considered obstruction. That a man who is at the very top of the law-enforcement field does not realize that this is not only illogical in a fairness sense, it is just plain incorrect, thanks to the people who wrote our Constitution and the laws to enforce it. That he and Trump think like this shows how close we are to sliding out of democracy and into authoritarianism.

Hawaii's Senator Mazie Hirono publicly called Barr a liar in today's hearing and told him to resign. After being so embarrassed by the Senators, Barr is now definitely going to avoid another round with the House's interrogators tomorrow. He must know how bad he looks to the rational two-thirds of the country, and will have to be subpoenaed to get him in front of Nadler's committee.

Rachel Maddow had Hillary Clinton on as a guest tonight to discuss the situation. Clinton said that if Barr fails to show up tomorrow, he should be held in contempt of Congress, and if he defies a subpoena he should be impeached and removed. Calls for his resignation are growing more numerous and louder.

Rachel also filled in some gaps in what we already knew about correspondence between Barr and Mueller. It was more than the one letter that was mentioned yesterday. Mueller made it clear that he wanted the summaries of the report that were written by his individual prosecution team members included as part of the report, but Barr preferred to present only his own completely inaccurate summary. Of course, Trump tells the world what a "great job" Barr did, even though he admits he didn't watch much of it.

Kellyanne Conway again defied the Hatch Act and made illegal comments about presidential candidate Joe Biden when she spoke to reporters outside the White House. Another very pleasing performance in Trump's eyes, but could get her in some legal trouble.

As expected, Attorney General Barr was a no-show at today's House Judiciary hearing, so he can expect to be receiving a subpoena shortly from Chairman Nadler. In Barr's refusal, he referred to the use of staff lawyers to do some of the questioning as "unprecedented," which is just flat out wrong and he knows it. If he *doesn't* know it, it is another reason he should not be the Attorney General. Senator Kirsten Gillibrand joined the chorus of calls for Barr's resignation tonight on Chris Hayes' *All In* show, saying "Barr does not represent the American People."

One of the craziest comments Barr made in his Senate hearing was that since Mueller did not charge (indict) the President on either the conspiracy evidence or the obstruction evidence (adhering to the ridiculous DOJ guideline that a sitting president cannot be indicted), he should never have opened an investigation into him in the first place. In other words, the President is above the law, no matter what he does. This belief disqualifies him from having *any* role in our justice department!

Senator Amy Klobuchar sent a letter directly to Robert Mueller asking him if he had reviewed Trump's tax returns, since Barr would not answer that question. If so, she would like him to send her copies. There are indications that Mueller has been in contact with Nadler about arranging a date for his testimony. Trump will pull out all the stops to prevent this from happening, so Mueller may have to resign from the DOJ in order to set the record straight. If he does, he will become one of the biggest American heroes in our history.

The Republicans are starting to gang up on Mueller, knowing how dangerous he is to the Trump presidency. They are actually criticizing him for following DOJ policy and not issuing an indictment after spending all that time and money on his "witch hunt," a decision that they should be celebrating.

Lest we forget, with all this turmoil over the Mueller report, there are still many children in South Texas who have yet to be reunited with their parents, as a result of this administration's unforgivable failure to make and retain any records that would have allowed them to match kids and parents. They sent the parents back to their home country without getting addresses or means of communicating with them. These kids will end up being wards of the state and will be severely traumatized. Nice work Trump, Miller and Nielsen.

We now have our twenty-first Democratic candidate for president. He is Colorado Senator Michael Bennet, a relatively unknown quantity we will be learning about shortly I'm sure.

The big news of the day is an hour-long phone call Trump made to Vladimir Putin this morning. We heard about it, as is usually the case, from the Russians—not from Trump. When asked about it by reporters, Trump said they talked about a large variety of topics, including "the Russian hoax." But when pressed, he admitted that he did *not* bring up Russia's interference in the 2016 election or warn them against trying it again in 2020. He obviously is expecting and *hoping* for a repeat performance. He admitted that they *did* discuss the Venezuelan war issue, which Trump told National Security Advisor John Bolton and Secretary of State Mike Pompeo to speak against the Russians' interference in an effort to support the Venezuelan dictator Maduro. But when Putin denied any such interference in that call, Trump once again accepted his word. Still Putin's puppet.

The failure of AG Barr to arrear before the House Judiciary Committee yesterday has prompted more serious discussion of his possible impeachment, both for this episode of obstruction, and for lying in his Senate testimony about his knowledge of Mueller's disputing his interpretation of the report.

Treasury Secretary Steven Mnuchin has until Monday to release Trump's tax returns to Congress. He says he will "have a response" by then, but that is not the same as saying that he will actually produce the documents. All of Trump's delay tactics may hold things up a bit, but will fail in the long run.

Monday is also the deadline for Trump's banks to comply with the subpoenaed financial documents. They have submitted a lengthy list of the ones that are coming, once they get them all gathered up, and Trump's law suit against them has been settled.

Trump declares that Congress should not be looking at him any longer, because the Mueller probe is done, so that should be the end of it. Wishful thinking.

Presidential candidate Senator Kamala Harris was a guest on the Rachel Maddow show tonight, and was very outspoken and impressive about her assessment of the Barr vs. Mueller dispute. She anticipates decisive testimony by Mueller to bring the truth to the American People sometime in May.

Candidate Congressmen Eric Swalwell was on Lawrence O'Donnell's *Last Word* tonight. He stated that in his opinion, the greatest threat to American democracy today is that we have lost our friends and NATO partners, thanks to Donald Trump's attitudes and treatment of them.

Book Two (09/2018-11/2019)

New polls show that 82% of Democrats list climate change as their top issue in the next election. They also show that most of the well-known candidates running against Trump would beat him in 2020, with the exception of Elizabeth Warren who trails him by a single point, and who has climbed into third place behind Biden and Sanders, among Democrat voters.

It was a pretty quiet weekend. To me the most interesting (disgusting actually) event was when our Secretary of State Mike Pompeo, who had just been made to look silly by Trump in that phone call he made to Putin yesterday, made the absurd claim that "this administration has been tougher on Russia than any previous one." He was a guest on *Fox News* and attacked host Chris Wallace for asking him why Trump failed to raise the question of Russian interference in our election with Putin during their phone call. The next morning, former Republican Joe Scarborough on his *Morning Joe* program, called Pompeo "an absolute fool."

A new poll shows that 37% of Americans still believe that Trump is telling them the truth about the Russia issue. This is incomprehensibly insane at this point in the Trump record.

Trump now has reversed himself and says that Robert Mueller *should not* testify to Congress, "…because it is done."

The World Series winning Boston Red Sox have been invited to the White House to meet the President, as is the tradition. Several of the players and Manager Alex Cora, who is a native Puerto Rican, have declined, as is the trend among the professional athletes these days.

Michael Cohen begins his three-year jail sentence tomorrow in a cushy prison in New York.

The Enemy Within: A Chronicle of the Trump Administration

Future history books may consider this week to be one of the most significant in our nation's struggle for survival as a democracy against the tyrannical aspirations of our current president. We have three different vital issues coming to a head at the same time.

First, today is the deadline set by the House Judiciary Committee for AG Barr to hand over the unredacted version of the Mueller report, and he is showing no inclination to do so. Barr's lack of response will prompt Congress to hold him in contempt--that vote coming on Wednesday.

Second, Treasury Secretary Mnuchin is refusing to obey the law and release Trump's tax returns to the House Oversight Committee, which will result in a court fight he is doomed to lose unless the Supreme Court is now working for Donald Trump instead of the American People.

Third, tomorrow is the deadline for Don McGahn to hand over boxes full of documents covering thirty-six topics related to Trump's and McGahn's correspondence etc. to the House Judiciary Committee. McGahn was quoted over one hundred and fifty times in the Mueller report.

Mnuchin has stepped in it big time by refusing a direct order, backed up by clear-cut law. This action further supports the suspicion that Trump is desperately trying to cover up something very embarrassing, or even incriminating, about the contents of those returns. He is waging a losing battle on several fronts, including the records already being given to the SDNY by his various banks.

Over seven hundred former federal prosecutors have signed an open letter stating that the evidence for obstruction is so strong that if Trump were not president he would definitely be indicted on several counts.

The tax record flood gates have begun to open. Today, the *New York Times* ran a front page story revealing what their reporters were able to obtain about ten years of Trump's returns

Book Two (09/2018-11/2019)

spanning the period from 1985 to 1994. During this period, Trump somehow managed to avoid paying *any* taxes in all but one of those years. In fact, he *lost* over a billion dollars during that span, a rate of one hundred million per year. He was, in fact, his father Fred's charity case. This may be the reason he has fought so hard to hide his returns, but I have a hunch there is more to it than that, such as where did all that money come from in the first place, when business after business failed and he kept declaring bankruptcy? It's a good bet Putin and Russian oligarchs were a huge source, which would explain his need to stay buddy-buddy with Vladimir.

The squabble over Trump's returns highlights the fact that we need to investigate and revise how the IRS handles cases where it is necessary to see a person's returns as part of a criminal investigation. The privacy laws need to take a back seat in such cases.

Chris Hayes, on his show *All In* tonight, discussed how Trump uses Twitter as a tool to further his goal of authoritarianism. He makes it quite obvious that he is a Neo-Fascist wannabe.

Senate leader Mitch McConnell today made a despicable speech in which he tried to declare the Mueller investigation a "closed case", because he has now published his findings. Nothing could be further from the truth! Senator Chuck Schumer called him out on it, in no uncertain terms. He also reminded us that Mitch will not even bring a single bill initiated by Democrats up for a vote, continuing the obstructionism he began under Obama.

The House Judiciary Committee voted along party lines to hold AG Barr in "Contempt of Congress", for his refusal to turn over the unredacted Mueller report. That will now go before the entire house for a vote on passage of the resolution. This action

The Enemy Within: A Chronicle of the Trump Administration

was last taken in the 1930s, and never against an Attorney General. Congress has the right to pursue this down to a fine of $1000 or up to years of jail time, if the courts find in their favor.

Chairman Jerry Nadler says, "They are stonewalling. This is a lawless administration, defying all subpoenas." He wants both McGahn's and Mueller's testimony during this month, and adds, "We have never had a president who has ignored all subpoenas. If there is no collusion and no obstruction, what are they trying to hide?" Legal expert Neal Katyal says that Mueller could testify even after he resigns or is fired.

Donald Trump Jr. has been subpoenaed by, amazingly, the *Republicans* on the Senate Intelligence Committee, to reappear before them and clear up some of the things he told them earlier this year. He lied about how much he knew as to the Trump Tower Moscow project. He is fighting that subpoena. It looks like he has something big to hide.

Tonight, Rachel Maddow pointed out that there are several areas/topics that Mueller did not look into enough to include in his report. They include his taxes and other financial records, and that Moscow Tower deal. Among the questions he is likely to be asked when he testifies to the House is, Why not?

Meanwhile, Trump is fighting like crazy against everything related to that report, and is trying to claim "executive privilege" over the report. Here, the question is, why? Didn't he say it exonerated him!

On Lawrence O'Donnell's show tonight, he lambasted the gross hypocrisy of Republicans, especially Lindsey Graham and Mitch McConnell, for the one-eighty degree turnaround in their views of what is impeachable when it was Bill Clinton under fire, vs. what their view is now when it is Trump's turn under the gun.

Book Two (09/2018-11/2019

The Democrats are likely to remain divided over whether to impeach or not, for purely political reasons, knowing that impeachment can only be successful if the vast majority of the public is in favor of it. We are not there yet.

Trump's lawsuit, to delay Mazars' release of his financial records, has been fast-tracked by the court and it will be heard this coming Tuesday. It looks like several of his delay cases will be speeded up, so his new team of lawyers hired for this purpose may prove to be a waste of money, but then he probably has fixed it so we tax-payers are footing the bill.

Congressman Adam Schiff is proposing heavy fines on anyone who defies a subpoena, including Barr. Several of the judges on these issues are demanding a copy of the unredacted Mueller report.

Rachel had Schiff as a guest tonight and she asked him if opening impeachment proceedings would give the Democrats more ammunition to obtain the information, documents and testimony now being held so stubbornly by Trump and Barr. He said that all this obstructionism by them adds weight to the case for impeachment, and it may be the only way to overcome that obstructionism. He also said that his Intelligence Committee is focusing on the Trump-Russia conspiracy case because it is a "counter-intelligence problem."

The Republicans are falsely claiming that Jerry Nadler is demanding that AG Barr break the law by forcing the release of grand jury data. The truth is, Nadler is asking him to let the court decide if this warrants making an exception to that law.

Trump has said that when he asked Russia to find Clintons emails, he was joking. Now he is trying to pass off as a joke his response to a yahoo in his crowd of followers at a gathering in Florida today who yelled out ,"shoot them", in regard to immigrants trying to cross our border. Trump actually said,

The Enemy Within: A Chronicle of the Trump Administration

"…only in Texas can you do that." Yes, that is our President, folks, and he is no joke.

The Republican Party in several states, including Georgia, Ohio, Mississippi and Kentucky, are waging a renewed war against abortion and Roe v. Wade. Georgia's new law would charge with murder any woman who aborts after six weeks of pregnancy. Are they nuts in that state?

When the World Series champs, the Boston Red Sox, visited the White House today, minus their manager and several players, Trump took them on a tour that included the Lincoln bedroom. While there, Trump once again displayed his complete ignorance of US history (along with just about every other subject) by comparing the Sox losing a couple of games on their way through the playoffs, to Lincoln "losing the war." Aside from the fact that he should have said *"Lee* losing the war", the irrelevancy of the comparison is off the charts.

This is not your usual case of Trump being ignorant. This is a clear indication of the man's increasing metal problem. Have you read *The Dangerous Case of Donald Trump* yet?

Rachel Maddow's guest tonight was former General Counsel James Baker. He had a lot of interesting things to say about the Constitutional-Crisis-in-the-making facing us at this time. For one, he is quite concerned about the counter-intelligence aspect of the Mueller probe's subject and goal. Baker has seen very little about that in the report and hopes Mueller will fill in some gaps when he testifies to Congress, hopefully this month. Right now, that subject seems to be kept locked up in a "black box."

Baker has been a target of Trump's for years, as he is considered to be one of Trump's "angry Democrats." Baker says that DOJ employees will need to be willing to resign in order to tell the truth about this corrupt administration.

Several newspapers have reported and confirmed that Trump's new legal team has tried to get Don McGahn to put out

Book Two (09/2018-11/2019)

a statement that he did *not* consider the incident, of Trump's effort to get McGahn to fire Mueller, to be obstruction. Once again, McGahn refused to knuckle under to this desperate president. This action by his lawyers is yet another incident that could be construed as more obstruction.

Both IRS Chief Rettig and Treasury Secretary Mnuchin were subpoenaed today by the House Ways and Means Committee because of their unwillingness to turn over Trump's tax returns which were requested a couple of weeks ago. Congressman Adam Schiff says that they are about to start levying heavy fines on those who defy the subpoenas.

As to the *Times'* bombshell about Trump's incredible losses in business over that ten year period of their report, people are asking whether that indicates terrible business acumen or blatant tax fraud. The truth probably is that it is both.

Don McGahn is scheduled to testify to Congress on May 21st. If he fails to show up, he will be held in contempt of Congress.

It was a pretty quiet weekend, with Mother's Day taking up most of the news. The burning question lately is, Will Donald Trump Jr. submit to the Republicans' subpoena to come back to the Senate for a follow-up meeting? And what happens next if he defies that summons?

A lot of Republicans in Congress are speaking out against Burr's subpoena, as they continue to be died-in-the-wool sycophants for the President.

Trump told a reporter that it is perfectly reasonable and OK for him to pursue an investigation into Joe Biden's son Hunter for "conflict of interest" in regard to his business dealings with Ukraine. If there is something there that needs investigation it is

The Enemy Within: A Chronicle of the Trump Administration

up to the FBI or the CIA to handle it. The President is not supposed to tell them what to investigate—EVER!

On his MSNBC program, *Morning Joe,* Joe Scarborough informed us that Trump's tariff war with China is going to impose what will amount to a $200 billion tax increase on the American consumer in the form of increased prices. Chew on that, Trump fans!

May 13-19

The fight for the release of Trump's tax returns is being fought on two fronts simultaneously; the demand from the House Ways and Means Committee to the IRS/Treasury Department, and the subpoenas to his financial institutions—Deutche Bank, Capital One and Mazers. The Trump team is putting up stubborn resistance on both fronts, but the banks have started to comply and the Treasury Department, i.e. Steve Mnuchin, will eventually have to as well. The world is soon going to learn what Trump has tried so desperately to hide for so long, and it must be more than just what a bad businessman he has been, because that cat is already out of the bag.

Mnuchin asked the judge for a delay for his hearing because he is *so* busy, but the judge refused. In the meantime, the House Intel Committee is investigating Trump's Moscow tower deal, which they suspect is still a live project.

Attorney General Barr, aka Trump's number one personal lawyer, has assigned an attorney to look into the origins (Trump's "oranges") of the Mueller investigation and the people who initiated it—*again.*

Republican Senator and top Trump sycophant Lindsey Graham is advising Trump Jr. not to comply with the Senate's subpoena to re-testify before their Intelligence Committee, "because he has already done so for hours." That's bad advice, Donny boy, don't follow it or you will get into even more hot water.

Rudy Giuliani has decided to cancel plans for a trip to Ukraine where he would entice the Ukrainians to "meddle in the 2020 election on Trump's behalf." I guess the Democrats' exposure of his purpose dissuaded him.

One of the co-authors of *The Dangerous Case of Donald Trump,* Rick Reilly, was a guest on Lawrence O'Donnell's show last night and introduced his new book titled *The Commander in Cheat,* in which he exposes Trump's constant and longtime practice of blatantly and openly cheating at his favorite pastime, golf. But Reilly covers a lot more than Trump's golf cheating. Here is an excerpt from that book that O'Donnell read for us tonight: "He needs to be the best at everything. He can't stand not winning, not being the best. It had to have started very early in his development. To him, not being the best is like fingernails on the blackboard to you. He can't live with it. He exaggerates his golf scores and his handicap for the same reason he exaggerates everything. He has to. He exhibits all the traits of a narcissistic personality disorder. People with his disorder have no conscience about it. He has no sense of morality about things. He lacks empathy toward others. He is a very ill man."
Another confirmation of what most of us already suspected by the time his first one hundred days were up, if not before.

Rick Gates had his sentencing postponed for the sixth time today. Because he is *still* cooperating with the prosecution team.

Attorney General William Barr's initiation of an investigation into the Mueller probe's legality is being viewed as an attempt to intimidate the prosecutors in the FBI and the DOJ in general, making them hesitant to do anything that would incur the wrath of our dictator wannabe. Of course, it also serves as another deflection/ distraction from all of Trump's glaring legal and political problems.

The Enemy Within: A Chronicle of the Trump Administration

Trump's original team of lawyers, before the mass exodus began, may be in some legal trouble themselves. Michael Cohen's testimony to Congress opened up a big can of worms about the kind of advice the President was getting during those first few months. Congressman Adam Schiff is preparing to subpoena a few of them to get their testimony on record and see how it compares to Cohen's and to the actual events.

A federal D. C. judge has ruled that Trump's suits to block several subpoenas have no merit, and he was "astonished" by the arguments Trump's lawyers tried to make, that the Mueller probe was "an improper investigation." When the judge asked them if they also thought that the Watergate case was invalid, they responded, "Maybe. We would have to study it more closely." These toadies are actually trying to overturn or invalidate established law, all in an effort to kowtow to our dictatorial president.

Tomorrow is the deadline for the DOJ to turn the unredacted report over to Congress. Will they comply? Schiff says that his Intel Committee has received no information whatever from anyone on the subject of counter-intelligence since before FBI Director Comey was fired. All such data is currently being handled only by the FBI.

Trump Junior has agreed to reappear before the Senate, but only behind closed doors and with limits on time and subject. He has no power to call the shots, but the Republican Senators who subpoenaed him are caving on his conditions.

Massive financial fraud has now been exposed on the part of Wayne Lapierre and the NRA, involving many years of misusing dues money. The New York Attorney General is investigating.

The Justice Department did not turn over the unredacted Mueller report and its supporting evidence, as subpoenaed by

Congress. White House lawyers sent a twelve-page letter to Chairman Nadler in which they argued their case for the request being without foundation. Nadler calls their arguments "preposterous", and points out that in Nixon's case the third article of impeachment was his willful ignoring of subpoenas. Nadler says they are seriously considering charging "inherent contempt", a move not used since the 1930s, under Hoover.

This gives Congress the power to arrest and detain any government official who fails to comply with a subpoena. The letter to Nadler actually proclaims that *the president of the United States cannot be investigated.* In other words, Trump could actually shoot someone and not only would he *not lose any votes*, he would be held "above the law." This is too absurd, even for a first-year law student. They are leaving Congress no choice but to impeach.

Prominent Democrats are beginning to voice their concern over the inaction (so far) of the House to act. The pressure for filing a bill of impeachment is mounting daily. When Mueller has his day to speak to them and the American People; *that* should be the final straw.

A new state law, just passed in Alabama, bans almost all abortions, including those resulting from rape or incest. It would sentence doctors who perform them to *ninety-nine* years in prison. This is the most extreme such law among the several that are in the works in Republican-controlled states. The response is generally, "They have gone bonkers."

President Duterte of the Philippines is emulating Trump in his attacks on the press as "the enemy of the people." Dictators all over the world have been encouraged and emboldened, reinforcing each other in exerting their dictatorial powers as a result of the success that Trump seems to be having in our once democratic country. His influence is damaging far more than just the United States.

The Enemy Within: A Chronicle of the Trump Administration

Ted Cruz just elevated his level of craziness with a warning that we need a "Space Force" to protect us from space pirates. Please go back on your meds, Ted.

The Democratic presidential candidate list has now grown to a ridiculous number of twenty-three, with the recent addition of: Colorado Senator Michael Bennet, Colorado's Governor Steve Bullock, and New York City Mayor, Bill de Blasio. That first debate should be a hoot!

A new poll shows that both Biden and Sanders would beat Trump by a large margin. Even the relatively unknown candidates are running neck-and-neck with him before the debates even begin.

Today, a D.C. Judge ordered all the redactions pertaining to Michael Flynn removed from the Mueller report, which she wants to use when considering his case, and she wants that version to be released to the public by May 31. Another D.C. Judge has already received a completely unredacted version.

Also today, the judge in the Michel Flynn case released a document which spells out in detail what Flynn told the prosecutors about contacts between the Trump team and the Russians during the campaign, and about Trump's interactions with WikiLeaks. This document also contains the interesting tidbit that Flynn has turned over a voicemail recording in which Trump's then personal attorney called Flynn to discuss his pending plea deal in terms that could be construed as a warning. In other words, *obstruction via witness tampering*.

Meanwhile, Democrats in the House are reading aloud the Mueller report in a marathon filibuster-like performance aimed at getting out the truth.

Tomorrow is the deadline for Steve Mnuchin to produce Trump's tax returns. When he refuses, which he almost certainly will, what then?

Book Two (09/2018-11/2019)

Tonight, Rachel Maddow asked, "Where is Robert Mueller?" Very good question! One of the questions that Congress plans to ask him when he finally gets to appear, is this: "Did your office ever provide any assessment of the extent to which President Trump is acting—wittingly or unwittingly—to advance the interests of the Russian government: if so, has that assessment been provided in some form to Congress (and, if so, to which members)? If your office did *not* make that assessment, are you aware of the FBI or others in the government having produced such an assessment at any point, and do you know if that has been provided in some form to Congress?"

Trump refuses to sign on to a multi-nation pact condemning on-line terrorism or extremism, labeling it, anti-First Amendment. This from the man who attacks the free press at evert opportunity.

American farmers are suffering financially so much from Trump's trade war with China that he has decided to placate them by offering them a total of $15 million of our tax revenues to offset the damage he has done them. He has also given $62 million to two corrupt Brazilian brothers who own a large meat-processing business. Congresswoman Rosa DeLauro was a guest on O'Donnell's *Last Word* show tonight and provided us with the details of this outrageous bailout of a foreign entity.

We now have proof that two counties in Florida had their voting machines hacked during the 2016 election. No word yet as to what is being done about preventing any reoccurrence.

Chris Hayes, on *All In* tonight, said that the worst-case scenario that he envisioned for our country right after Trump was elected, is now well on its way to becoming reality. This scenario includes the topics of: trade war, Roe v. Wade overturn, war with Iran, etc. Now, Trump is talking about sending 120,000 troops if Iran misbehaves.

As expected, Treasury Secretary Mnuchin has refused to turn over Trump's tax returns to the House Ways and Means Committee. His reason is that he "finds it has no legislative purpose." The conflict between the Trump administration and Congress is "roiling to a boil." The Democrats *cannot* allow him to get away with this deliberate flaunting of clear law. It is time to invoke Inherent Contempt.

Trump's latest tweets against our law enforcement agencies actually accuse them of "treason." Not only does he continue to show his lack of understanding of what that word means, he is saying that reporting *any facts* that contain criticism of him is at least unpatriotic. He simply will not tolerate any criticism, but especially from the news media. At the same time, AG Barr says that he can see why Trump labels any investigation of him as a "witch hunt" or "hoax". He is out-Cohning Roy Cohn in his Mob-like defense of Trump. James Comey says that Barr should "stop sliming his own Justice Department." Court-fights over several aspects of Trump's and Barr's resistance are set to begin as early as this coming week.

Several Republican Federal Judgeship nominees have avoided answering the question: "Do you believe that Brown vs Board of Education was correctly decided?" In other words, "Do you believe in integration of schools? By hedging on an answer to this question they illustrate a desire to return to what they consider "the good old days of segregation." Senator Blumenthal says he was stunned by their nonresponse.

Republican Congressman from Michigan Justin Amash is the first of his party to agree that Trump's behavior is impeachable. He lists the following reasons for his stand against his president: 1. Attorney General Barr has deliberately misrepresented Mueller's report. 2. President Trump has engaged in

Book Two (09/2018-11/2019)

impeachable conduct. 3. Partisanship has eroded our system of checks and balances. 4. Few members of Congress have read the report.

One hundred Democratic Congressmen have signed a letter to the President warning him of the serious danger of a war with Iran, as a direct response to Trump's recent saber-rattling.

There were only a couple of topics worth commenting on related to the Trump saga this weekend.

The rhetoric from both Trump and the Iranians cooled for about one day before Trump enflamed it again with threats that were in a class with his "Fire and fury" statements to North Korea a year ago. He seems determined to distract us from his impeachment problem, even if he has to start a war to do it.

Democratic candidate Pete Buttigieg went on *Fox News' Town Hall* show this weekend and painted a very good comparison for everyone between what is *news* and what is *propaganda,* doing so in the *heart* of propaganda country. Joe Scarborough says that Pete "is the future of the Democratic Party."

May 20-26

Today's daily Trump news report I believe to be one of the ten or so most important days so far in the fight against the most corrupt administration in US history. Another in a long line of dams being broken in the quasi-legal wall, that the President has been trying to hide behind for over two years, has cracked and is about to engulf him in a quagmire of his own making, which I still believe will result in his removal from that office.

On Monday, we had the first in a lengthy series of upcoming court decisions that will decide the fate of the Trump presidency, and it did not go well for Mr. Trump. U.S. District

The Enemy Within: A Chronicle of the Trump Administration

Court Judge Amit Mehta ruled that Trump *cannot* order his accounting firm Mazars to ignore the subpoena that Congress has issued for Trump's financial records. In the 41-page opinion, the judge declared that: "It is simply not fathomable that a Constitution that grants Congress the power to remove a President for reasons including criminal behavior, would deny Congress the power to investigate him for unlawful conduct— past or present—even without formally opening an impeachment inquiry. This court is not prepared to roll back the tide of history."

This type of evaluation of Trump's efforts to cover-up his crimes will almost certainly be repeated over and over until they reach the Supreme Court. Then we shall see what that court is made of these days.

But even worse for Trump is the new revelation about Deutche Bank's cover-up of Suspicious-Activity-Reports (SARs) which employees of that bank generated as a result of spotting several instances of shady-looking (money-laundering) deals and transactions involving both Trump and Jared Kushner and the Russians, which took place during the years leading up to the 2016 election. These warnings were not only ignored by the bank's managers-- employees were silenced, and in one case, fired, for speaking out about this cover-up. Tonight, Rachel Maddow gave us the details of this story which was just reported by the *New York Times*. This story looks very bad, both for the bank and for the President. There has to be a pretty compelling reason why this bank was willing to make huge loans to Trump, when most other banks would not. Once again, his case is resembling the case against Al Capone as much as it is resembling the case against Richard Nixon.

Don McGahn says he will follow Trump's order that he not testify before Congress, even though he gave hours of testimony to Robert Mueller that was itemized to a large extent in his report. So he is going to defy the subpoena, breaking the law on the President's order—with no legal grounds for doing so

Book Two (09/2018-11/2019)

because executive privilege has already been waived-- another clear episode of obstruction.

This provides even more incentive and justification for beginning impeachment proceedings. For several decades, I considered the cover-up of the truth about the JFK assassination to be the greatest one in this country's history. That is no longer the case.

The GOP and Trump in particular have come down very hard on Republican Representative Justin Amash for adding his name to those calling for impeachment. They are trying to intimidate other Republicans who might be leaning toward following his lead. When asked how he felt about the backlash, Amash just shrugged it off because he expected no less. His action should have some effect on how Nancy Pelosi feels about this very controversial question that the Democrats are now wrestling with. She is still not ready, but she is right to wait until they hear from both McGahn and Mueller. McGahn should be told, "Testify as subpoenaed or go to jail."

Mueller should be very willing to testify, so why isn't he, even if has to resign to do it? He also should be forced if *not* willing. After hearing from those two people, go ahead with guns blazing, regardless of how the Republicans in the Senate are likely to act or not act. Let the blame and the shame fall on their heads for all of history.

The Trump Brand has suffered immensely from his presidency. The only Trump property that seems to be making any money these days is his hotel in D.C., just a block from the White House, where foreign dignitaries flock to have easy access to him—one of the many items in a long list of emoluments violations that have been taking place since day one. Even if his losses outweigh his gains from his office, those gains are still unconstitutional.

The Enemy Within: A Chronicle of the Trump Administration

A fifth migrant child has died while being held in a detention center on the southern border. This evil policy that is still going on in spite of all the negative reaction it has received from all over country and the world as a whole, is nothing short of second-degree murder on the part of the Trump administration!

The Washington Post has uncovered a memo issued some time ago by the IRS which completely negates Mnuchin's argument that the subpoena for Trump's returns "has no legislative purpose." The Treasury Secretary has no choice but to deliver them to the Ways and Means Committee immediately—no questions asked. The question remains—how do they force him to comply?

Now Hope Hicks and Annie Donaldson (Don McGahn's Chief of Staff) have also been subpoenaed. It will be interesting to see if *they* are going to knuckle under to Trump's "block" commands. He looks like he is in a state of complete panic about the way he is losing this war over his financial data. Richard Neal, Chairman of the House Ways and Means Committee, says that they have the law on their side. Jerry Nadler says that they will bring Don McGahn to court to enforce their subpoena for his testimony. Congressmen Lloyd Doggett, and Eric Swalwell say that they need to start imposing fines and making arrests for those who continue to defy the law. So DO IT, damn it!

The majority of the House Judiciary Committee are ready to start an impeachment inquiry, which is the prelude to writing the bill. Swalwell says that Trump has left them no choice but to take this drastic course of action, because of the lawlessness of this administration.

Both Steve Mnuchin and IRS Commissioner Chuck Rettig were hand-picked by Trump for their negative attitude about releasing returns. He also picked the Chief Counsel for the IRS, Michael Desmond for the same reason. He has systematically

Book Two (09/2018-11/2019)

built a wall of protection around himself, especially as far as his finances are concerned. When he told Mueller not to cross this "red line", he meant it, and Mueller has apparently listened to that "order" to a large extent. Instead, he has passed that field of inquiry on to the SDNY, who are relentlessly "following the money." If the feds don't get him, the State of New York will.

Justin Amash, who yesterday became the first Republican to call for Trump's impeachment, has had a big effect on the Democrats, with the possible exception of Speaker Pelosi. Let's hope he has also had an effect on some Republicans.

Tonight, Rachel Maddow again asked, "Where is Robert Mueller?" He has not been heard from in weeks, although the House Judiciary Committee is said to be negotiating with him on a date and format for his testimony. We can't afford to wait much longer to hear from *him*, McGahn, Hicks, Donaldson, etc. so we can get the process of impeachment underway in earnest.

Our Secretary of Housing and Urban Development, Ben Carson, once again demonstrated how utterly unqualified he is for that position, when he was questioned by a pair of Congresswomen today. He was unable to answer several basic questions about his job and was totally unfamiliar with some of the acronyms which anyone in that field should know. It completely humiliated him, but it is difficult to feel sorry for someone who should not have accepted a job for which he is not qualified.

Trump is planning to issue pardons for several men who are serving time for war crimes, such as machine-gunning civilians. He is thinking of doing it on Memorial Day, which makes his action all the more reprehensible. He is getting very harsh backlash, so maybe he will reconsider.

The Enemy Within: A Chronicle of the Trump Administration

Trump set up a meeting with Pelosi and Schumer today to talk about infrastructure, but he had no intention of discussing that subject. It was just a ploy to get together with them to let them know that he will not be doing *any* work on anything as long as he is under all these investigations. In other words, he is removing himself from being president before he is physically removed by impeachment. By contrast, neither Nixon nor Clinton had any problem continuing to sign bills into law while investigations were being conducted on them.

His meeting lasted less than five minutes, after which he went out onto the White House lawn where he told the reporters what he had told the Congressional leaders. Then he added the laughable claim, "I don't do cover-ups," in response to Pelosi's earlier comment that he was obviously engaged in a determined cover-up. Perhaps it has not occurred to this most inexperienced of all US Presidents that by refusing to do the work he was elected to do, he is providing yet another valid reason to remove him from the office.

Schumer's response to both the obvious staging of this sham and the comments that Trump made, was: "It would make your jaw drop." Meanwhile, there are election-security bills that the House has proposed that Mitch McConnell will not even bring up for a vote by the Senate.

One piece of progress on the Mueller-report-front is that the DOJ has now agreed to release a copy of it to the House Intel Committee with the redactions related to counter-intelligence removed.

An internal IRS memo has come to light that spells out why they MUST turn over any returns requested by the House Ways and Means Committee. New York State has offered to give Trump's state returns to Congress. These would contain pretty much the same data as the federal returns. And then we have a federal judge ruling that the Deutche Bank must comply with the subpoena for Trump's financial records. It's all coming

Book Two (09/2018-11/2019)

apart for the President's determined stonewalling of both the Mueller report and the tax returns.

Today, Congresswoman Alma Adams of North Carolina questioned Treasury Secretary Mnuchin about his reasons for failing to obey the law and give up Trump's returns. Like nearly every Republican who has been in that kind of "hot seat" before him, he had no answers, or refused to answer, including when she asked him the simple yes or no, "Did you tell Commissioner Rettig not to release Trump's tax returns?" She just got the usual talking points about the nuances of the law.

A poll on the question, "Should Robert Mueller testify before Congress and the public?" got this result—73% YES, 20% NO. Time to speak up, Mr. Mueller!

Trump's Justice Department has filed seventeen counts of violation of the Espionage Act against WikiLeaks founder Julian Assange, who is currently being held in the UK on rape charges. The DOJ wants him extradited to answer for *their* charges, which are nothing less than a grievous assault on our First Amendment right of freedom of speech and of the press. Assange is a convenient scapegoat since he is widely hated in America for assisting the Russian hackers by using WikiLeaks to disseminate the stolen data, and he may be a very bad man if he is indeed a rapist. But Trump is using him to take another outrageous blow at our most basic right and another huge step toward dictatorial power, in spite of the ironic fact that WikiLeaks *helped him get elected* with what they did. Hacking and stealing information is a crime, but publishing such information, once it is obtained, is *not*. Journalists make their living by digging up this kind of information and bringing it to light so the public can learn the truth. This is the most grievous move yet in Trump's war against what he calls "the enemy of the people." The DOJ may have a difficult time getting PM Theresa May to extradite Assange, since she may be on the verge of resigning over her Brexit failures.

The Enemy Within: A Chronicle of the Trump Administration

Since Speaker Nancy Pelosi accused Trump of a cover-up, there has been an escalating war of words between them, in which Trump has completely lost his cool (after persuading several members of his staff to praise him for his "coolness"). His rantings toward not only Pelosi but against everyone in the Justice Department who have been investigating him from the very start of his presidential campaign, are now in the "batshit crazy" category. He has Barr ramping up the investigation into everyone involved in the opening of the probe that led to the appointment of a Special Prosecutor, including our intelligence agencies. He is accusing several named people, such as Comey and McCabe, of treason and reminded us that the penalty for that is execution. If this type of rhetoric prompts one or more of his brain-dead cult followers to act on this threat, Trump should be immediately removed from office via the 25th Amendment, and then charged with inciting violence. The man is so desperate that he has become very dangerous.

As to Pelosi, he went as far as bringing back an old, doctored video of Nancy making a speech, in which she was made to appear to be drunk or incoherent. In response to Trump's repeat of his "stable genius" claim, Pelosi suggested, "maybe his family should conduct an intervention to save him."

Trump today referred to his former Secretary of State, Rex Tillerson, as, "Dump as a rock", and "not fit to be Secretary of State." But *you* picked him for that post and praised him often while Tillerson held that post, so what does that say about you, Mr. President.

Mueller has agreed to testify to Congress, but in private except for an opening statement he would deliver to the public. Both parts of his presentation should be very interesting and extremely important!

Book Two (09/2018-11/2019)

As part of his war on the investigators and the motive for the original Russia investigation, Trump has granted the power to release cherry-picked items of classified information to his *"Roy Cohn"*, Attorney General William Barr. This is an unprecedented and dangerous move which could compromise operatives and methods of our intelligence agencies, but Trump is not concerned with our national security--only with his own legal problems. By his recent actions, he has created a *real* witch-hunt, with Barr's help, waging a war against the FBI, etc. in the process. Trump seems determined to push the boundaries of all of our norms and will eventually reach a breaking point that even some of his Republicans in Congress can no longer stomach.

We now know, or have been reminded, that Former CIA Director John Brennon informed President Obama about Russian plans to attempt to interfere with our 2016 election, using an "eyes-only" brief on data he received via one of our spies in Russia, who is now being put in danger by Barr's new probe. Brennon labels this move by Trump and Barr "outrageous", and a serious breach of classified data safety.
CIA Director Dan Coats says "they will supply appropriate data." In other words, he will be selectively diligent in what he gives up.

The court has denied the attempt by Trump to block Mazars from releasing his financial documents a few days ago, and this decision is being appealed, as expected, to the D. C. Court of Appeals. Ironically, it turns out that the Chief Judge on that court is none other than Merrick Garland. Yes, that's right, the judge whose nomination to the Supreme Court by President Obama was blocked by Mitch McConnell for a year until the 2016 election. There is a real slice of Karma for you.

A Missouri judge has struck down that state's new anti-abortion law, as *unconstitutional.* No big surprise there.

The Enemy Within: A Chronicle of the Trump Administration

Sarah Huckabee Sanders has been AWOL now for about a month, appearing only on *Fox News* programs to lend a hand to their Trump propaganda agenda. She finally reached a limit I guess, to how many humiliating lies she was expected to spew for the boss. She certainly isn't going to do much about repairing her extremely tarnished image by being a Fox spokeswoman.

Theresa May has now resigned from her position as UK's Prime Minister, as expected. They seem to have no idea where to go from here.

Over this long weekend, Trump made a state visit to Japan to honor their new Emperor, Naruhito. He and the Emperor exchanged gifts, and Trump's gift to the Japanese leader included a large autographed photo of Trump's most admired person, *himself*. Once again, his pathological narcissism was on full display. There were several other ways that Trump continued his string of embarrassments in front of foreign dignitaries, including wishing Japanese sailors upon a docked ship a happy Memorial Day.

Next month he gets to visit England, including the Queen in her palace, where he will probably wish them all a fabulous 4th of July. He made a speech in which he said that he was not disturbed by North Korea's recent launch of several short-range missiles which could easily reach Japan but not the US so "they are nothing to worry about." Then he used that speech to attack his most feared opponent in next year's election—Joe Biden. Another norm down the drain—the one that says "you do not make political comments about other Americans when you are not on American soil." But the new reality we are living in today is that the GOP will *never* criticize or contradict *anything* that this disgraceful president says or does.

Book Two (09/2018-11/2019)

Maybe this story is old news, but I just heard about what Trump's long-time friend and beer-buddy, Howard Stern (former raunchy, off-the-wall disc-jockey, talk-show host and wanna-be comedian) has to tell us about Donald's real motive in running for president. Stern reveals that Trump campaigned for president as a publicity stunt to raise his ratings (and maybe his salary) for his *Apprentice* show. He never expected or wanted to actually be elected. We may not be able to determine whether this story is true or not, but it certainly fits with Trump's behavior both during the campaign and since being elected. It was his completely unorthodox approach to campaigning that won over so many people who were not at all satisfied with the way government was ignoring their needs, and figured, "What have we got to lose?" Well, now we *know* what we had to lose.

We have lost the respect of both our allies and our adversaries as a result of the policies and actions of a president who came into his new job completely ignorant of the structure of our government, the separation of powers between the three equal branches, and the limitations on the president's power that result from that balance. We have lost any chance of progress in our society as a result of complete stagnation in our legislative branch. We have lost respect for the rule of law, and respect for our most important and revered government agencies like the FBI, CIA, etc. And we are getting dangerously close to losing our freedom of speech and freedom of the press.

We have also lost a two-party system that can work together to compromise and get things done for the good of the country. We now have a two-*tribe* system which is constantly at war with itself and puts its own survival of the tribe ahead of what is best for America. Cheating, and the anything-goes attitude are now the new norms. Important government positions are awarded strictly on who you are loyal to, not on what your qualifications are.

The Enemy Within: A Chronicle of the Trump Administration

We began the difficult process of turning things around via the blue wave of 2018. We must continue to turn it in 2020 if we are to survive as a great democratic world power. It is fitting that we use this Memorial Day, to remember those who died defending our democratic way of life, to steel our resolve and do whatever it takes to prevent that way of life from being diminished by the creep toward authoritarianism. Right now, we are faced with more than a *creep* in that direction—we are faced with a leader that is charging like a bull at it. That is a *real* national emergency.

Mitch McConnell once again showed his true colors and allegiance today. When the Senate Republican leader announced proudly that the Senate will not ever *consider* removing Trump, no matter *what* evidence of how any crimes is presented by the House in their bills of impeachment, their total disdain for the rule of law, the Constitution and the American People were on full display, and they will have to live with the enduring shame of their actions for the rest of US history.

The Trump administration is stepping up its efforts to block attempts to fight Climate Change by creating a review panel whose sole purpose will be to undermine the scientific evidence and arguments that prove that our planet is in serious danger. They want to restrict the time period over which projections are made as to the ongoing negative effects of fossil fuel emissions, to go only as far as 2040. But the *real* calamity awaits us a little further into the future than that. This attitude is created, not so much by doubts about the conclusions, as it is to give support to the coal and other industries that are contributing to the problem, but are also contributing a ton of money to Republicans.

The Texas Secretary of State, David Whitley, who led the Trump-directed probe into voter fraud in that State, and failed to find any evidence of fraud whatever, has now resigned as a result of voter backlash against his action.

Book Two (09/2018-11/2019)

Senator and presidential candidate Kamala Harris says she is in full agreement with Republican Congressman Amash, who is the only one in his party, so far, to call for impeaching Trump.

Retired General Michael Hayden added his voice to the clamor with the following message: "If this is who we are, or who we are becoming, I have wasted 40 years of my life. Until now, it was not possible for me to conceive of an American President capable of such an outrageous assault on truth, a free press or the first amendment."

Today, we heard from Robert Mueller for the first time since he turned over his report to AG Barr and saw its contents completely distorted by his boss as part of the ongoing crusade by the Republican Party to cover up Trump's criminal behavior. He spoke for about ten minutes and began by reiterating what he said about the report and repeated the main thrust of the report that "If the investigation had exonerated the president, we would have said so, but it does not." He also said, "There was *insufficient evidence* to charge a broader conspiracy." He did not say that there was *no evidence*. Then he said that, "Charging the President with a crime was not an option we could consider." This is because of the DOJ policy that tied his hands—not because they did not have the evidence to do so.

This statement directly contradicts Barr's claim that he asked Mueller several times if that policy was the reason he was not indicting, and that Mueller repeatedly said that it *not* the reason. This was a bald-faced *lie*. I find this to be one of the two most significant parts of Mueller's talk today. The second one was his strong confirmation of Russian interference in the 2016 election and a stern warning that they will undoubtedly try to do it again in 2020.

My problem with the rest of his statements is that they are phrased in language in which the average citizen could fail to fully appreciate the seriousness of what he was saying. He had the opportunity to emphasize, using "conversational English", the fact that if Trump had not been president, he could have been indicted for obstruction, if not for collaboration with a foreign power to get elected. Instead, he made it clear that Congress should not expect him to say anything to them that is not in the report—in other words, "don't waste your time and mine."

Once again, he is unwilling, not unable, *unwilling* to come out strongly and let the American People know exactly what kind of president they have, and how much AG Barr has misrepresented what was specified in his report. But Judiciary Committee Chairman Nadler and/or Intel Committee Chairman Schiff should subpoena him, if necessary, to sit down with them and say what needs to be said in words that all Americans can absorb. This would provide Congress, hopefully including the Senate, with the ammo and motivation to do what needs to be done.

Rebert De Niro, who likes to play the role of Mueller on SNL, read the following address to the Special Counsel: "You've characterized the report as your testimony, but you wouldn't accept that reason from anyone your office interviewed…the country needs to hear your voice. Your actual voice…this is the report your country asked you to do, and now you must give it authority and clarity…you said that your work 'speaks for itself.' It doesn't. It may speak for itself to lawyers and lawmakers who have the patience and obligation to read through the more than 400 pages of carefully chosen words and nuanced conclusions…"

It goes on a bit from there, but you can tell that De Niro had the same reaction that I and, I'm sure, thousands of others who listened to Mueller's talk, had.

He used this appearance today to announce his resignation from the Department of Justice and return to civilian life, so fear of losing his job is not the answer to the disturbing

Book Two (09/2018-11/2019)

question: Why are you playing Mr. Milquetoast with this corrupt gang, Mr. Mueller?

But, in spite of my assessment of a weak performance on his part, most political analysts, including some at *Fox News*, found it to be a good counterpoint to Barr's erroneous interpretation, and fairly damaging to Trump. It did lay down the challenge to Pelosi, and the Democrats in general, to take the ball and run with it. That is their duty now, possible backlash be damned! Senator Cory Booker says that "Robert Mueller's statement makes clear; Congress has a legal and moral obligation to begin impeachment proceedings immediately." And he added, "History is going to look back at this moment…" Nadler says that they *will* be opening an impeachment inquiry. If this president is not worthy of impeachment, it is difficult to imagine what level of wrongdoing it would take. And we haven't even received the tax returns and all the financial records yet. Before this summer is over there will be quite a few more logs placed in the impeachment fire.

As a disheartening sidelight to the main event of the day, Mitch McConnell made it quite clear that his Senate has no intention of bringing any anti-election-interference bill to the floor for a vote. He, Trump and the bulk of the GOP are *hoping* for a repeat of that 2016 interference, because they know that it would be their only way get Trump re-elected.

As an amusing sidelight, Trump accidentally admitted that Russia helped him get elected. He said, "I had nothing to do with the Russians getting me elected." You don't often hear a lie and an admission in the same sentence.

In Mueller's adherence to fairness in his farewell speech yesterday, he avoided listing any of the evidence of obstruction against the President, following the guideline that if you are not going to indict you do not accuse, because the accused will not get his day in court to defend against the accusation. Now Barr and Trump himself are taking advantage of that fairness by making it sound like "proof" that he *had* no evidence. They are not playing by any rules, so it's time to take the gloves off, Mr. Mueller.

Today, Trump asked a reporter, "How can you impeach when there was no crime?" A classic case of "selective hearing." Someone should read part two of the report to you Mr. President, and pay attention for a change. Several Trump voters were interviewed after Mueller spoke, and they expressed surprise, some were "shocked", to find out that the report did *not* exonerate Trump like they were led to believe by the Attorney General.

The GOP is strangely silent since Mueller's speech, with the one exception of Congressman Justin Amash, who spoke out in favor of impeachment earlier in the week and doubled down on his feeling today. It is appalling that the Republican Party, which has been speaking out so strongly for decades against the Russian dictatorship and the North Korean menace, continues to throw its full support behind a president who warmly embraces them both.

Senator Eric Swalwell, says that they need to closely examine Trump's financial and tax records, and include the crimes they are certain to find therein as part of their impeachment hearings.

Congressman Mike Quigley, Democrat from Illinois, says that "we need to educate the public as to the contents of the Mueller Report and the lie that Trump keeps repeating, that it shows he committed no crimes. Meanwhile, start impeachment proceeding *now.*"

Amidst all this chaos, it is important to remember that the most important "misdeed" of all of those this president is guilty of, is the fact that he is failing to, in any way, address the danger

Book Two (09/2018-11/2019)

that the Russians will interfere again in 2020 and, if undeterred, may succeed in reelecting Trump. Imagine what a disaster *that* would be.

On MSNBC tonight, Rob Reiner stated that the Mueller Report contains the biggest collection of criminal evidence ever seen against a President of the United States. He will be broadcasting a video exposing that evidence as listed in the report, for each of the two major volumes (one on collusion with Russia, and one on obstruction). He strongly feels that we need public Congressional hearings on that report, along the lines of what was done in the Nixon case.

Columnist Charles Sykes proclaims that the old conservative principles, that the Republicans have always championed, no longer are in play under Donald Trump's administration. That fact has been obvious for quite a while.

Democrat from California, Congresswoman Katie Porter held a Town Hall gathering for her constituents, where the number-one concern was for healthcare. But she also got lots of questions about impeachment that were generated by Mueller's recent farewell speech, where they heard for the first time that Trump was in no way exonerated by that report, as implied by AG Barr and spread by *Fox News*.

The number of House members that are in favor of starting impeachment inquiries, if not actual hearings, has now climbed to fifty-one.

It is the height of irony and hypocrisy that when Obama was president and attended a baseball game on his visit to Cuba, he was vilified by the right-wing, but Trump can visit Russia and North Korea and be all chummy with the two dictators who lead those countries, and it's all just fine.

The Enemy Within: A Chronicle of the Trump Administration

Trump is going tariff-happy again and is threatening to impose a five percent tariff on ALL goods coming from Mexico, until that country does something to reduce the influx of immigrants coming over our southern border. As a result, the stock market took another plunge, as it does every time Trump takes this sort of action. He still has no concept of how tariff's work, and who gets hurt by them.

Impeachment discussions are raging on several fronts here at home while Trump and family are spending this weekend paying a state visit to the UK, where he will once again visit the queen and no doubt, once again embarrass us with his usual uncouthness. On his way, he decided it would be a good way to set up this visit by referring to Duchess Meghan Merkle as "nasty." Way to make an entrance Donald!

He will be greeted by even bigger protest crowds than he saw the last time he went there, including that now famous Trump-baby blimp. The Mayor of London had some pretty unflattering things to say about Trump as he was on his way across the Atlantic, so of course Trump had to retaliate in his usual tweet fashion, containing childish insults.

Presidential candidate Beto O'Rourke says that Trump's Mexico tariff will only make the immigrant problem worse. He says impeachment is a *must*. Democrat Congressman from Mississippi, Bennie Thomson, says his visits and talks with his constituents find them practically screaming for impeachment of the president. From *Mississippi* of all places!

But Pelosi continues her slow-walk toward that move. She needs to make it clear that she only wants to wait until they get some more ammunition via witness testimony, and review of his financial and tax records. And speaking of tax records, why is nothing being done about Mnuchin's continued refusal to hand them over? Meanwhile, Trump is calling "impeachment" a dirty, filthy, disgusting word.

Book Two (09/2018-11/2019)

The federal judge in the Mike Flynn case is trying to determine how long his sentence should be (and has been for quite a while now), so he has asked the prosecution for a transcript of a phone call between Flynn and Russian Ambassador Kislyac. He has been *refused* that information by the prosecutors, who say that it is "not relevant." The judge will explode. This is not their call to make!

Reports of severe overcrowding in detention centers at the southern border show that the situation is getting steadily worse. Conditions are abominably inhumane, unsanitary and downright illegal!

The Enemy Within: A Chronicle of the Trump Administration

Book Two (09/2018-11/2019)

June, 2019

June 3

Convicted child-pornographer George Nader, who was one of the people who attended meetings in Trump Tower and the Seychelles Islands, described in my March 19, 2018 entry, was arrested today as he deplaned at JFK airport. He apparently thought that he was shielded by the immunity he received in his plea deal with Mueller's team in exchange for his cooperation with them as to those meetings.

But new child-porn was found on his cell phone during a previous detainment and this was not part of the deal. He is typical of the type of people that the Trump campaign team associated with, throughout his quest for the presidency (and since).

Conservative political analyst Bill Kristol has formed a group called *Republicans for the Rule of Law,* composed of those who have decided they have had enough of the way Trump has demeaned the Presidency and the Republican Party. They have been passing out highlighted versions of the Mueller Report to all the lawmakers of Congress, to make it easier for them to find the damning paragraphs where the evidence against Trump can be found.

In an interview with *Axios,* Jared Kushner was unable or unwilling to answer questions about the culpability of the Saudis in journalist Khashoggi's murder.

Michael Wolff, author of the book, *Fire and Fury Inside in the White House,* has written a new one titled *Siege: Trump Under Fire.* He says that in researching this one, he was

The Enemy Within: A Chronicle of the Trump Administration

convinced of two things about our president; "He is crazy", and "He is willing to destroy democracy."

Actor Jeff Daniels, who plays Atticus Finch in the Broadway play version of *To Kill a Mockingbird,* told Lawrence O'Donnell tonight that, "We can't go on like this. The GOP is on the Titanic."

Boris Johnson, the odds-on favorite to replace Theresa May as England's Prime Minister, not only refused Donald Trump's request for a meeting with him, he also published several comments about the visiting president, which included the phrase, "his stupefying ignorance." This, in spite of the fact that Trump broke international protocol by endorsing him for the Prime Minister position. Of course, Trump would like everyone to ignore this fact, just as he would like everyone to believe his lie that the protesters were a small part of the mass of people who were actually cheering him.

Hope Hicks and Annie Donaldson are both following Trump's order and are defying the subpoenas to testify before the House. They join a steadily growing list of people who are breaking the law in this way, and so far, are getting away with it. This *has* to change, and no doubt will—eventually.

The Democratic committee chairmen are threatening to hold them in contempt. Barr is one of them so threatened, and he is offering to meet with them if the Democrats remove that threat, but Chairman Nadler says, "NO."

What about Secretary Mnuchin? Senator Erik Swalwell is calling for impeaching all of them.

The House has scheduled a meeting to discuss Trump's obstruction case (now up to eleven instances).

Trump has attacked and threatened AT&T, the parent company of CNN, in an attempt to get the news channel to back off in their criticism of the President. This is another strike against the first amendment and another impeachable offense.

Book Two (09/2018-11/2019)

Today the House passed a bill to protect the Dreamers, and did it by a very wide margin, but it has no chance on getting approved by the Senate or the President.

Thirty-seven children had to wait for over eleven hours in hot vans to be re-united with their parents, thanks to the botched procedure by the incompetent people in charge of this whole fiasco. And yet, they were the *lucky* ones.

Twenty Democratic presidential candidates have qualified through polling and/or fund-raising to participate in the first debate. Accommodations have been made for ten on each of two nights, but there is likely to be more of them added to the list before that time gets here.

After making his usual fool of himself in the UK, Trump paid a visit to Ireland where he had a meeting with its Prime Minister, Leo Varadkar. True to form, our consistently embarrassing leader could not resist the opportunity to push his anti-immigration border wall by comparing his problem with Ireland's "wall problem", in a complete misunderstanding of the nature of that nation's long history of clashes between the Catholics and the Protestants, which was finally settled without the need for a wall. In watching the televised press conference that these two attended after their meeting, you could see by the expression on Varadkar's face, as Trump was talking about their discussion, that he was utterly flummoxed by what he was hearing.

Jerry Nadler pressed Nancy Pelosi to allow his Judiciary Committee to begin impeachment proceedings. Senator Elizabeth Warren devoted her entire hour-long interview with Chris Hays on his *All In* Town Hall meeting tonight, pushing for the same thing. Bill Weld, who is challenging Trump for the Republican nomination next year, says that it is time for Nadler to begin an "inquiry" into impeachment as a prelude to actual hearings on the subject, noting that over 1000 federal prosecutors have signed on to a petition calling Trump's actions "criminal."

Pelosi's concern that the public is not yet on board with impeaching the President because recent polls show that less than fifty percent say "do it now", is understandable. But we need to remember that when they began those proceedings against Nixon, he had just been elected by an overwhelming margin and had an approval rating of 65 percent. All this changed dramatically as the impeachment hearings progressed. *This* president lost the popular vote and his approval rating has dropped since the election.

The clamor of objection to Trump's attack on the First Amendment via his pressure on AT&T, as mentioned above, is heating up considerably. This is being viewed as a breach of Trump's pledge to "preserve, protect and defend the Constitution" that he made during his swearing-in ceremony.

Former Acting Solicitor General Neal Katyal on Bryan Williams' *Eleventh Hour* tonight provided video proof that AG Barr has done a complete reversal of his opinion when it comes to whether a prosecutor, such as Robert Mueller, should or should not display the evidence of a crime when the person charged is not going to be actually indicted for that crime, as in the cases of Hillary Clinton and President Trump. Then Katyal went on to reveal that many employees of the Justice Department "are aghast" at Barr's behavior in regard to his devotion and defense of the President.

Seventy-five years ago today (June 6), the invasion of Normandy, France, by allied forces from the greatest armada in human history, supported by naval gunfire and parachutists landing behind the enemy lines, marked the beginning of the end for Nazi domination of Europe. Our president stood in front

Book Two (09/2018-11/2019)

of the grave markers of hundreds of the brave men who died on that day and, although he read a prepared speech commemorating the event, he followed it up with an impromptu attack on Nancy Pelosi and Robert Mueller, instead of paying homage to the fallen heroes before him. The younger generation today cannot appreciate what was accomplished here unless they have seen movies like *The Longest Day* and *Saving Private Ryan*. Watching these films gives you a much better appreciation for what these men went through, than any history class or book.

In a surprise move, Michael Flynn fired his legal team today, as an audio version was made public of the phone conversation between Trump lawyer John Dowd, and one of Flynn's lawyers during the time preceding his plea agreement. Here is that somewhat stammering conversation, which is a clear case of witness tampering. "Hey, Rob, uhm, this is John again. Uh, maybe, I-I'm sympathetic; I understand your situation, but let me see if I can't…state it in…starker terms. If you have…and it wouldn't surprise me if you've gone on to make a deal with, and, uh, work with the government, uh, I understand that you can't join the joint defense, so that's one thing. If, on the other hand, we have, there's information that…implicates the President, then we've got a national security issue, or *maybe* a national security issue, I don't know…some issue, we got to…we got to deal with, not only for the President, but for the country. So uh…you know, then—then you know, *we need some kind of heads up,* and if it's the former, then, you know, remember what we've always said about the President and his feelings toward Flynn and, that still remains."

John Dowd resigned months ago as Trump's personal attorney, and now the person and his cohorts on the other end of that phone call have been fired. Rats deserting (or getting removed from) the ship.

The Enemy Within: A Chronicle of the Trump Administration

Colorado Senator and presidential candidate Michael Bennet cautions against rushing too quickly into full-fledged impeachment hearings, but says we should start an inquiry into the President's behavior as presented in the report. The Democrats are nearing unanimity in their opinion on impeachment. Bennet also blames Senate Leader Mitch McConnell for the lack of progress on every front.

Fridays are usually the busiest Trump news day of the week, but not this time. As he arrived home from his customarily disastrous trip abroad, things were sort of catching their breath here at home. Here are the few developments worth mentioning.

Under all sorts of pressure from Congress, including many Republicans, Trump decided to put his tariff threat against Mexico on hold, at least for a while. He also revamped his proclamation that we would be going back to the moon sometime in the next five years. He did this in a very surprising, and somewhat amusing, tweet which read: "For all the money we are spending, NASA should NOT be talking about going back to the Moon—we did that 50 years ago. They should be focused on the much bigger things we are doing, including Mars (of which the Moon is a part), Defense and Science!"

First of all, it was Trump who raised the idea of returning to the Moon, recently backed up by VP Pence—not NASA! Second, what do those last three words of the tweet have to do with the subject at hand? Third, when he says that the moon is part of Mars, is he really that ignorant about our solar system, or is he that bad at expressing what he is trying to say? I will give him the benefit of the doubt and assume he meant to say that we need to get to the moon so that we have a jumping off place from which to get to Mars, which *is* NASA's plan for some time in the next couple of decades.

In either case, this whole subject, at this point in his troubled administration, seems to be nothing more than another one of those shiny objects Trump likes to toss out there as a distraction to what is really serious at this time.

Book Two (09/2018-11/2019)

On the currently red hot abortion issue, the state of Missouri has reached a new low in their determination to make it as difficult as possible for women to exercise their right to choose, that Roe v. Wade gives them. They have not only managed to close all but *one* abortion clinic in that state, but they have now passed a law which forces women to undergo a completely unnecessary preliminary pelvic exam, in addition to the one normally given just before the procedure is done. Women all over the country are protesting the way this issue is being "manhandled".

The 1976 Hyde Amendment, which banned federal funding of abortions, forces women to pay for the procedure themselves. Joe Biden has been on record for quite some time as supporting that law, but due to the extreme tactics being used by the GOP to reverse Roe, he has now changed his attitude on the subject. The question this raises is, was this mind-slip heartfelt or purely political? I'm sure he will get a lot of questions about it over the coming year. Meanwhile, he remains the far-ahead frontrunner for the Democratic nomination.

On Saturday night *All In*'s host, Chris Hayes, held one of his Town Hall meetings—this one featuring presidential candidate Mayor Pete Buttigieg. He was again very impressive in the way he handled questions from the audience, with comfortable ease, eloquence, and specifics on some very good ideas on all the issues that were brought up. He has a very likable personality to go with that package. So far, he and Kamala Harris are my favorite candidates to put up against Trump next year.

Then, on Sunday, Hayes did the same type of show with Elizabeth Warren, who did very well also. The audience seemed to agree with everything she had to say. Either one of these two candidates should have no trouble defeating Trump soundly in 2020. Both are moving up in the polls, closing the gap between them and Biden, who has been hurt a bit by his abortion-stand problem.

Trump tried to reduce the degree of embarrassment he brought upon himself when he was pressured by his Republican cohorts to think twice about his Mexico tariff threat. He played off his surrender by trying to sell the lie that he and the Mexicans had reached a "secret agreement" as a result of his threat, but the Mexican President was quick to point out that they already had the agreement Trump was referring to, for several months, and there was no "secret agreement." You went from bad to worse, Donald.

When Nancy Pelosi was asked this weekend about her stand on the question of impeaching the President, she said, "I want to see him in prison after were defeat him in 2020." No concern about how much more damage he can do between now and then? Trump, of course, made his usual counterpunch by calling her "nasty", and "vindictive."

The House Judiciary Committee is planning hearings, starting Monday, on the contents of the Mueller Report. It will include testimony by Watergate star witness John Dean, who has the best experience in this matter of obstruction crimes.

Some Republican Congressmen and Senators have admitted that they have not bothered to read the report, and don't really care what is in it. In other words, a far as Trump is concerned, "anything goes."

It has become apparent to me that the best one-word description that can be given to describe Trump's words, actions, policies, attitude and behavior in general, is the word, "uncivilized." He is closer to belonging in the species Neanderthal, than the species Homo-sapiens.

June 10-16

Book Two (09/2018-11/2019)

On Monday the House Judiciary Committee held the first of what will be a lengthy series of hearings leading to the impeachment of President Trump. Over the course of four hours, they heard from three expert legal witnesses to explore questions pertaining to obstruction of justice. They also heard from John Dean, who discussed the parallels between the Nixon/Watergate case and the Trump/Russia case. Dean said, "It is quite striking and quite startling to me, that history is repeating itself, and with a vengeance." Exactly what I have been pointing out throughout this chronicle.

Attorney General Barr has capitulated, under the threat of being held in Contempt of Congress, and agreed to begin handing over the underlying documentary evidence behind Mueller's presentation of wrongdoing in his report. As to hearing from Mueller himself, the Republicans seem to want to hear from him as much as the Democrats do, so what's the problem?

Committee Chairman Nadler says that they are prepared to hit every one of the witnesses who are now defying their subpoenas to testify, or produce documents (such as Trump's tax returns), with Contempt-of-Congress charges.

Barr's concession includes access to counter-intelligence information from Mueller's report that he has been refusing to release. The Committee is also demanding 302 reports that FBI agents make out whenever they monitor a grand jury witness, and it looks like they will get them. They also want all the "memos-to-file" that many people in this administration have written, to keep in their own file, when they have been asked or ordered to do something that they know is improper or illegal.

Next, they will be going to court directly, since Barr won't do it, do obtain transcripts of grand jury proceedings on relevant cases. The document/data/testimony floodgates are opening up, which will add considerable fuel to the growing impeachment fire.

The Enemy Within: A Chronicle of the Trump Administration

Back in the Nixon scandal, Republican Congressman Caldwell Butler, in one of the impeachment hearings, earned an historic name for himself when he made an impassioned and courageous speech, the highlight of which was his statement that Watergate was "their shame" and that "Republicans have a special duty to condemn the President's conduct." Two interesting things about this man is that he rode into his Congressional seat on the coattails of Nixon's landslide election, and that after calling for Nixon's impeachment, Butler was *reelected* to Congress. Politics does not always win over patriotism! At least, it wasn't so pervasive before Trump.

Historian Lawrence Tribe says that it would be a good idea to impeach Trump, even without Senate backing, because it will at least educate the public as to his criminal behavior and the evidence of it, and in so doing, change public opinion dramatically.

Not even counting the whole Russia/collusion/obstruction mess that has consumed the Trump presidency from the day he took office, there have been a host of other corruption problems involving his appointments to cabinet and lesser positions that would have sunk any president in the past. Tonight, Rachel Maddow spelled out the details of a *new* one which cropped up a few days ago, involving his Secretary of Transportation, Elaine Chao.

She was told that she must divest herself of her control of a company named Vulcan Materials, which produces the types of paving used on roads. She said she would do so, and was therefore confirmed for the position. But she has made no effort to do it, and has been using her position to enrich her company, and herself, for months. In addition to that, she has tried to arrange for a visit to China for her family for the purpose of making behind-the-scenes illegal deals with the Chinese. But there is also the fact that she happens to be the wife of Senate leader Mitch McConnell, who has been profiting greatly, along with his spouse.

Book Two (09/2018-11/2019)

The frosting on this cake of corruption is the ironic and absurd fact that Mitch oversaw her Senate confirmation hearing! This case exceeds any of the previous forced resignations that resulted from misuse of funds, etc. that have occurred over the two and a half years of the Trump presidency. At least twenty appointments have left this administration for one reason or another, and ten cabinet positions are still being filled by "Acting" personnel.

The Democrats in the House voted 229 to 13 to authorize their leaders to enforce in court all of the subpoenas which have been issued and are being resisted. The top targets are AG Barr, Commerce Secretary Wilbur Ross, former White House attorney Don McGahn, former Trump Aide Hope Hicks and Annie Donaldson, McGahn's Chief-of-staff. The vote also grants the power of the committee chairmen to go to court to seek legal enforcement. The gloves are starting to come off now—at last.

Tomorrow, Donald Trump Jr. is scheduled to return to testify before the Senate Intelligence Committee, when he will be grilled about the contradictions between his previous testimony and that of people like Michael Cohen, as to how much he and his father, the President, knew about certain meetings with Russians and other related subjects.

The latest polls show that every Democratic candidate leads Trump in a one-on-one match-up for the 2020 election. Here are the margins for the leaders (so far): Biden by 13 percentage points, Sanders by 9, Harris by 8, Warren by 7, Booker and Buttigieg by 5. Even the *Fox News* poll is very bad news for Trump, and it is obvious he is feeling it by the way he is attacking Biden at every opportunity.

President Trump's long-standing penchant for shooting himself in the foot sprang forth with a vengeance today.

The Enemy Within: A Chronicle of the Trump Administration

Apparently he is so misled by Barr's inaccurate assessment of Mueller's report (that there was no evidence of collusion), that he decided it was a god idea to tell the world that he would welcome any opportunity to repeat that crime of accepting opposition research (dirt) on his political opponent in 2020. He went so far as to say that FBI Director Wray is wrong when he states that anyone who gets an offer of such help from a foreign power needs to call the FBI and report it. So, he thinks he knows the law better that the Director of the premier law-enforcement arm in the country.

David Laufman, former Chief of the Counter-intelligence Branch of the Burrough, says he was "dumbfounded" by Trump's call for foreign information, in light of what was stirred up by his plea to Russia in 2016. This new Trump faux pas is enough, by itself, to deserve impeachment.

The House has proceeded with the issuing of Contempt of Congress charges against both AG Barr and Commerce Secretary Wilber Ross. In Ross's case, it is over documents related to his plan to include that citizenship question on the census form. After Barr conceded to turning over the evidence that supports the obstruction case against Trump, the President invoked "executive privilege" to further block its release, so Barr is backing off his recent concession. This fight is not over yet.

Intel Committee Chairman Adam Schiff says that they may subpoena FBI Director Christopher Wray for the Counter-intelligence materials that were included in the Mueller Report but were redacted.

Trump calls the latest polls that show him trailing nearly everybody, "Fake News." Of course, what else can he do about it?

Trump's statement that he would gladly accept information about his political opponent in 2020 from a foreign power if it were offered, was too much even for many members of his own party. Mark Warner, Republican Senator from Virginia, introduced a bill which would require anyone receiving such an offer to call the FBI about it. That law already exists, but Warner's bill would strengthen it. Mitch McConnell immediately blocked that bill. In the meantime, Trump realized what a stupid thing he has done and tried, lamely, to walk it back.

Chuck Schumer, the Democratic minority leader in the Senate made the following statement in response to Trump's latest gaff: "This one is a new low. It's OK for a foreign power to interfere? You don't have to report to law enforcement? That's welcoming foreign powers to interfere, and as my friend from Virginia (Warner) said, the president's own FBI Director said it's going to happen again in 2020. 'But let's cover it up, because it might have an effect that we like,' say our Republican friends. Today is a new low for this Senate, for this Republican Party here in the Senate, and for this democracy. It is truly outrageous that this unanimous consent request, which should bring all of us together, is being blocked by our Republican friends."

Democratic presidential candidate, Senator Michael Bennet, calls this "…the most unpatriotic administration in history." Mitt Romney calls Trump's intention to welcome such foreign help "unthinkable." Even Republican and passionate Trump lackey, Lindsey Graham, says "that is not OK." Federal Election Commissioner, Ellen Weintraub, strongly rebuked Trump for claiming he would do something that is a *crime*.

Mitch McConnell's wife, Elaine Chao, has started selling off her shares in that road paving company she controls, and cancelled a scheduled trip for her family to visit China, in an effort to reduce the heat on her and Mitch. Good luck with that,

Elaine, but it is probably a case of locking the barn door after the horses have all fled.

Secretary-of-State Mike Pompeo made a speech today in which he jumped all over Iran for attacking two of our oil tankers in the Gulf of Oman, without any proof that it was Iran. He sounded like he was preparing us for the prospect of a war with that very dangerous nation.

Trump just sold a very expensive property in California for which he paid $7 million, to an Indonesian politician, for $13.5 million, once again profiting from being President.

A new Special Counsel has stated that Kellyanne Conway should be fired for repeated and unprecedented violations of the Hatch Act. And we will finally see the departure of Sarah Huckabee Sanders at the end of this month. It is unclear at this time whether she got tired of facing all the criticism she faced because of her constant lies for Trump, or if Trump fired her because she has not been holding up very well under the pressure lately. You will surely *not* be missed, Sarah.

The twenty Democratic candidates for president who have qualified for a spot in the first debate have been selected. Only three did not make it.

The big story today is the confrontation we have now had thrust upon us by the attack on our two tankers, combined with Trump's determination to blame Iran, without any proof, and with conflicting opinions on the part of those who were there. His rhetoric could propel us into a war that would greatly exceed what we have gone through with Iraq and Afghanistan. Iran says it will pull out of the nuclear arms treaty in ten days. Then the gloves will really be off.

The *New York Times* reports that our intelligence agencies are so leery about Trump's coziness with Putin that they are very hesitant to share any information with the President as to what kind of surveillance they are doing on Russia, because they are afraid he will leak it to our long-time adversary, maybe even intentionally. They now consider him as a Russian agent. This is a case of the so-called "deep-state" working for the benefit of our country.

Several high-ranking government officials now are in a position where they have to choose between resigning in protest, or for the sake of our country staying in place to do what they can to reduce the damage Trump is causing.

Sixty Democrats and one Republican in the House are now in favor of impeaching Trump. Ex-GOP Judiciary Committee member David Cohen says, "We should begin impeachment proceedings now." The pressure continues to build. The debate about whether to impeach or not needs to be changed to the question of *when*, not *whether*. We *do* need to take the time to hear from key witnesses like McGahn and Mueller and get as much evidence as possible before actually filing the bill, but preliminary hearings should have started already.

Secretary of State Pompeo made a very lame attempt to explain away and/or excuse Trump's massive gaff of admitting he would be quite willing to repeat his acceptance of dirt from a foreign power, continuing to act as Trump's toady while further destroying his reputation.

Trump held an interview with *ABC News*' George Stephanopoulos, in which one of the most outrageously dishonest things he said (among many) was that he would be glad when his financial data finally was released because it was 'fantastic" and he was proud of it. One word from him and all the blockades he has been throwing up for over a year to *block* their release would vanish.

The Enemy Within: A Chronicle of the Trump Administration

Here is another sample on a different topic: "There's never been a time in the history of our country where somebody was as mistreated as I have been."

But the most outrageous lie that Trump uttered several times in this interview was that he had read the entire Mueller Report. He is not even able to digest his one page daily briefing, having the attention span of a gnat, and he expects anyone to believe he could get through a 400+ page book? And then he uses that dishonest claim to assert that Mueller found NO evidence of either collusion or obstruction—another gross falsehood which he keeps repeating, no matter who points out to him how incorrect he is.

Those really bad poll numbers that were recently leaked by his own internal pollsters have resulted in Trump severing ties with the whole crew. A classic example of "shooting the messenger."

Elizabeth Warren has overtaken Sanders in the latest polling, and is now in second place behind Biden. The first debate later this month should be a blast.

The Trump administration is now threatening to launch a retaliatory attack on Iran for its alleged attack on our two tankers in the Gulf of Oman. Mike Pompeo says that Trump has the power to order such a strike without the OK of Congress. He is wrong! This is leading to a disastrous war!

In December of 2015, the Russians hit Ukraine with a cyber-attack which caused a nation-wide blackout. The United States has since then been on guard against such an attack by both beefing up its defensive software and preparing a counter-offensive if it needs it.

The latter was revealed in that NYT report that has Trump going berserk. Here is his latest tweet on the subject: "Do you believe that the Failing New York Times just did a story stating that the United States is substantially increasing cyber-attacks on Russia? This is a virtual act of Treason by a once great paper so desperate for a story, any story, even if it is bad for our country. Also, NOT TRUE! Anything goes with our Corrupt News Media today. They will do or say whatever it takes, with not even the slightest thought of consequence! These are true cowards and without doubt, THE ENEMY OF THE PEOPLE!"

The *consequence* that he fears here is what his ally, Putin, will do, and demand that *Trump* do, in response to this action.

FEC Commissioner Ellen Weintraub spelled out the seriousness of Donald Trump's statement about repeating his willingness to accept foreign informational aid. Here is what she said: "Let me make something 100% clear to the American public and anyone running for public office. *It is illegal* for any person to solicit, accept, or receive *anything* of value from a foreign national in connection with a U. S. election. This is not a novel concept. Any political campaign that receives an offer of a prohibited donation from a foreign source should report that offer to the Federal Bureau of Investigation."

What do you think the chances are that Trump will listen to, let alone heed, that warning?

Trump knows how vital the state of Florida will be for his re-election chances, so he held another pep rally in Orlando today. Instead of offering them any future policy plans or crowing about the good economy, he continued to rail about Clinton and the news media, and said that "the Democrats are trying to destroy our country." By the end of his speech, many empty seats could be seen, since his followers have heard all this before, many times. *The Orlando Sentinel* newspaper, normally staunchly conservative and endorsing Republicans, printed an editorial in which they said that they cannot endorse Trump, because "we have to do better."

Trump continues to play to his base by making matters even worse than it already was, with the border camps looking more and more like WW2 Nazi concentration camps. He also announced that he is using ICE to round up and deport *"millions of illegal aliens"*, many of them to be grabbed up while their children are at school. A new method of family separation. He has no clue how impossible, as well as outrageous, an operation of anything close to that scope would be.

Patrick Shanahan has been our Acting Secretary of Defense for over six months now with no move toward confirmation. It was revealed today that he and his family have a history of domestic violence which culminated in his son's using a baseball bat on Patrick's wife. Shanahan has been defending his son's action, so things must have been pretty hostile between man and wife.
He has now withdrawn from consideration for the permanent post of Secretary of Defense, after his attempts to hide the above problem failed. Senator Chris Murphy, Democrat from Connecticut, says that Trump's inability to fill vital posts is leaving our country in a state of weakness.

Another Democratic Congressman, Dan Kildee from Michigan, has joined the ranks of those calling for the start of an impeachment inquiry, saying, "Nobody is above the law." He is joined by Congresswoman Katie Porter, who after hearing from her constituents in that Town Hall gathering mentioned a few days ago, decided that the time has come.

Dr. Bandy Lee, who coordinated and produced the book, *The Dangerous Case of Donald Trump,* plans to hold a Town Hall meeting sometime in July, to discuss Trump's mental state with the public. I hope it is widely broadcast because the public really needs to know.

The Trump administration, particularly Secretary of State Mike Pompeo, is escalating the tension between the US and Iran by tying them to Al Qaeda and the Taliban. Iran has fueled that tension by shooting down an American drone. Trump is

Book Two (09/2018-11/2019)

deliberately leading us into a very costly war as a means of distracting from his legal, Constitutional and political problems.

Former Trump Aide (his closest one), Hope Hicks, testified today before the House Judiciary Committee and refused to answer virtually every question she was asked, including the location of her office within the White House. She is claiming "complete immunity" by virtue of her closeness to the President—a concept which has no legal standing, and will not hold up in court, which is where she and anyone else who attempts to claim it, will find themselves. This includes the very important case of Don McGahn, who has also invoked this nonexistent ploy and whose case is already being considered by the court.

A UN report has been issued which places the responsibility for the Khashoggi murder squarely on the Saudi regime. Trump will no doubt continue to ignore that issue.

The doctors in the Planned Parenthood Clinic in Missouri have decided to refuse to perform those very unnecessary extra pelvic exams on women who come to them for an abortion, which was recently ordered through a new Missouri State law. Dr. David Eisenberg says: "There is no medical reason for them." They are risking being shut down as a result of their defiance. Democratic candidate Kamala Harris says that if she is elected she will see that any state laws inhibiting abortion have to be reviewed by the Justice Department.

Joe Biden used the word "boy" when discussing the difference between working across the Congressional aisle in *his* day and trying to do so now. Some of his rivals for the nomination jumped on it for being racially insensitive, as a way to slow down his momentum in the polls. This is just a case where an older man's insensitivity to the level of political correctness today, and the intentional overreaction by his younger, more in-tune opponents trying to take advantage of an opening. Anyone who is curious about how the word was used should just Google it and decide for yourself.

Trump is finally going to get his big parade when Independence Day arrives next month. He will no doubt consider it to be in his honor.

President Trump met with Canada's Prime Minister Justin Trudeau on Thursday, and when they sat down side by side to answer the press's questions about the meeting, our 'stable genius' president embarrassed us once again. In a somewhat incoherent and ignorant way, Trump backed away from his bellicose attitude toward Iran. He allowed that it was probably a mistake on the part of some stupid Iranian commander that our drone had been shot down, rather than on an order by the Iranian government. But then he went to elaborate that the drone was fortunately not manned, as it might have been. It sounded like he had just had it explained to him that this is what a "drone" is—unmanned. The look on Trudeau's face said all we needed to know about what he thought of this news. Later, we found out that Trump had ordered an air strike on Iran as retaliation, but had cancelled it just before that news conference. Thank you, Justin, thank you so much!

Bill Weld, Trump's GOP nemesis, says: "Trump is clueless about what to do about Iran, and is being influenced by Bolton and Pompeo."

The media was given a transcript of the testimony by Hope Hicks before Congress yesterday. She arrived at this hearing accompanied by five lawyers, one of whom objected to nearly every one of the questions put to Ms. Hicks over the course of several hours. The committee has all these unjustified objections on record for use in the upcoming court case that is likely to follow.

Book Two (09/2018-11/2019)

The US Department of Agriculture (USDA) employs a large team of scientists to examine, study and report on any actions, manmade or natural, that have an influence on our farmers. This administration has ordered this whole team to be relocated to an office in Kansas City, as a means to influence their report on climate change, which is opposed to the Trump policies. Trump has also greatly cut their budget. The scientists have unionized and are fighting back.

The GOP has been dragging their feet as to extending the 9/11 First Responder Compensation Fund. This is a particularly shameful way to treat these heroes.

Candidate Cory Booker's umbrage about Biden's use of the word "boy" is unjustified in the context of which it was used, and appears to be just a ploy to slow up Biden. They discussed this issue in what seems to have been a civilized phone call.

Three more Democratic Congressmen have now called for the start of an impeachment inquiry. The pressure continues to mount.

Another women from Trump's past has come forth with an accusation that she was not just sexually molested, but actually raped! A TV commentator/advisor and author named E. Jean Carroll told her story to the *New York Magazine*, who published it. She was on Lawrence O'Donnell's show Friday explaining in detail how she ran into Trump in a high-class women's dress shop named Bergdorf Goodman, in the mid-1990s. He was asking advice about lingerie near one of the dressing rooms, when he suddenly forced her into the room, pinned her against the wall, pulled down he clothing and forced himself inside her. Her struggles were finally enough to squirm out of his hold and escape. Trump, of course, immediately denied her story and claimed that he had never even met the woman. That was instantly disproven by a photograph showing them together at some point prior to the described incident. Ms. Carroll says she still has the clothing that she wore that day, unwashed, hanging in a closet. Shades of the Lewinski "blue dress."

The discussion is still heating up regarding the deplorable and unsanitary conditions in those "detention centers" holding children at the southern border. They have been months without soap, toothpaste or toothbrush, clean clothing, toys, books, or any contact with parents or relatives. This has become the greatest shame, other than slavery, ever borne by our once great country! When the subject is raised with Trump, he blames the whole debacle on Obama. This is not just another lie, this is outright insanity. Everyone knows that this whole mess began with the "zero-tolerance" policy of Trump and Stephen Miller.

Under extreme pressure, even from his fellow Republicans, Trump has decided on a two-week delay while he tries to negotiate a solution with the Democrats, before implementing his new campaign to round up and deport thousands of illegal immigrants. A few months ago they had a deal involving them. It was called the DACA deal, which Trump agreed to, until his extreme-right buddies at Fox ridiculed him about it.

Trump has made several comments over the past few months about extending his time as president beyond his second term (assuming he will have one). This pipe-dream of his has the Democrats in Congress worried about what he might do, if and when he loses in 2020 and contests the results over a claim of voter fraud or some other half-baked scheme. Hopefully, he will not even get that far.

June 24-30

In denying E. Jean Carroll's accusation that she was raped by Trump, the President scoffed, "she's not my type." He is so stupid, insensitive, or both, that he does not even realize that this is tantamount to admitting that he would only rape women of a certain type—in this case that would include any woman

Book Two (09/2018-11/2019)

who he is attracted to. Not a very convincing counter-argument, Donald.

The latest reports on the deplorable conditions in those child-detention centers in Texas have resulted in one of the largest ones having their kids relocated outside a different city and housed in a large tent camp in the desert. I doubt they will get any better treatment there, and it will probably be a lot hotter.

The Washington Post has written a scathing op-ed piece about their treatment. Here is a section of it: "This is a humanitarian crisis of Trump's making. A president who panders to his base by seizing billions of dollars from other programs to build a "big, beautiful wall" also panders to his base by cruelly treating brown-skinned migrant children like sub-humans. Do not look away. This is the reality of Trump's America. Deal with it."

There is only one way open for the public to "deal with it"— by backing impeachment, and if that fails, voting him out.

The twenty Democratic candidates are going into this week's debates (Wednesday and Thursday) with Joe Biden still far out in front with 38% to Sanders' 19% and Warren's 13%. Everyone else is in single digits. They are all aware that this coming week will be "make or break" for several of them.

There has been a disturbingly lengthy span without any major developments in the Trump saga, but the drought ended with a double bang this Tuesday.

First, Robert Mueller has finally reached an agreement with the House Committees and will honor the subpoena they were forced to issue in order to get him to sit down for a public hearing. On July 27 he will first answer questions put to him by Adam Schiff's Intelligence Committee, followed by a similar session with Jerry Nadler's Judiciary Committee, both in public sessions. Following that, the members of the Mueller team will meet behind closed doors with both Committees to answer more sensitive questions which might involve national security or grand jury data.

The country has been waiting for several weeks to hear from the Special Counsel, and the ten minute address he recently gave was helpful but was nowhere near enough. Those who cannot tune in to hear him speak during a work day will undoubtedly have several opportunities to hear replays, and it is *vital* that everyone take the opportunity to hear the truth from the man who spent two years *gathering* the truth.

As a sidelight to this subject, Trump attorney Jay Sekulow claims that Trump showed "no obstructive intent" in regard to those ten episodes of apparent obstruction listed in the Mueller report. No, he was just trying to objectively *not-look* at both sides of the issue.

The second bombshell was the ruling by a federal judge that Congress has every right and reason to pursue charges of violations of the Constitution's emoluments clause, of which there are dozens if not hundreds. This ruling includes the ability to go after Trump's financial documents. This could lead to yet another area of problems for the President--one which has been waiting in the shadows since day one.

Senator Lindsey Graham *used* to have nothing but bad things to say about Donald Trump, using all the derogatory terms that Mitt Romney used during the 2016 campaign. *Now,* Trump can do no wrong in Graham's eyes. In response to a question about the latest sexual abuse accuser, Graham said, "He denies it. That's all I need to know." Do you think he would be so trusting if he were commenting on a Democrat?

Trump is now falsely claiming that Obama had a worse policy of child-parent separation when he was the president. The truth is that the only time kids were removed during that period was if they were being abused by the parents.

Book Two (09/2018-11/2019)

ICE employees used to criticize Obama for politicizing his policy on illegal migrants. But several of them are now expressing that they miss his structure and consistency as opposed to Trump's utter chaos.

Under Trump, the Supreme Court has become much more politicized and partial to conservatism. The whole objective of this court since its inception was no maintain impartiality. The Congress seems to be helpless in trying to do anything about the fact it could become even worse before this administration ends.

Watching the first ten Democrats who are running for the presidential nomination debate each other in an attempt to gain some recognition and some kind of advance in their poll numbers, was a frustrating experience. The panel of moderators, which included one of my favorite TV hosts and Trump critics, Rachel Maddow, was unable to control the desperate enthusiasm of the candidates as they did their best to get as much air time for themselves as possible.

They were supposed to be restricted to 60 seconds to answer each question and 30 seconds to rebut another's answer, but *no one* was following that guideline. They kept right on talking, no matter how many times the moderator said "Thank you" as a way of saying "Your time has expired."

This chaos is sure to be duplicated tonight when the other ten take the stage, unless the producers and moderators work out a way to control each speaker by simply turning off his or her microphone. Perhaps a warning that this is what will happen will go a long way toward reducing the rudeness level. It is difficult to say if there were any "winners" or "losers" tonight. The watching public will not get much out of these debates until the number of candidates is whittled down quite a bit.

About a third of those kids who were relocated to another camp have been returned to the one from which they were removed because it its deplorable conditions. It is said to have been cleaned up quite a bit, but if no improvements have been made in the quantity and quality of the *staff* who are in charge of their care, it won't take long for things to return to the Hell that they were. The House is about to vote on an emergency funding bill to help clean up the mess that the Trump policies have created. Meanwhile, the "Acting" Border Control Chief, John Sanders, has resigned, probably in disgust.

The Senate now seems eager to get Robert Mueller to testify to that half of Congress when he gets through with his current date with the House. That should be even more interesting to watch, if it is also open to the public. I doubt it will happen.

Donald Trump has had a favorite whipping boy (Obama) and favorite whipping girl (Clinton) since his campaign in 2016. But he has another that he seems to detest almost as much, and that is the now deceased war hero, Senator John McCain. This is true largely because of McCain's deciding vote that stopped Trump's attempt to destroy the Affordable Care Act. Today, as he was complaining about how some of his Republican Senators have been treating him, he included an unnamed reference to McCain. Here is the quote: "We needed 60 votes to repeal the ACA, and we had 51 votes. And sometimes, you know, we had a little hard time with a couple of them, right? Fortunately, they're gone now. They've gone on to greener pastures—or perhaps *far less green pastures*. But they're gone. They're gone, Bill. I'm very happy they're gone." Every day, he seems to be trying to set a new low as a human being. I doubt that even this is as low as he will get.

Night two of the Democratic debate was not quite as chaotic as night one, and a lot more significant, as it went a long way toward affecting the standing of at least two of the contestants. Senator Kamala Harris and ex-vice-president Joe Biden got into it a bit over Joe's attitude and recent remarks about segregation and school bussing. He has been mischaracterized, in my opinion, as to his intent and meaning for those remarks, and his

Book Two (09/2018-11/2019)

opponents have been quick to take advantage of his "faux pas." Fair or not, Harris came off as the winner in this one and Biden the loser, and I believe the next poll will reflect that.

All the candidates were more willing to take on Trump tonight, than was the earlier group of ten. We should see a pretty large reduction of the field of candidates before the next debate is scheduled. Here is my prediction for the top five: Biden, Sanders, Warren, Harris, and Buttigieg.

Trump is now in Japan for another G20 conference, where he gets a chance to cozy up to his favorite dictators, Vladimir and Kim.

The month ended with another of those Fridays which have become the lightest day of the week on Trump news lately, where they used to quite often be the heaviest. Strange! Here is a summation of that three-day span.

Thursday night's debate among the second group of ten Democratic candidates for the presidential nomination turned out to be by far the most watched program of its kind in US history. This is a very good sign for the country, and a very bad sign for President Trump.

The Supreme Court has made two very significant rulings—one good and one bad for our future. The good one was that the administration is blocked from putting the citizenship question on the upcoming census form. They realized that this question would inhibit thousands, if not millions, of people from filling out the form, thus greatly skewing the resulting count of our population.

The bad one, from the Democrats' point of view, was that they refused to rule on the question of gerrymandering—allowing the Republican-controlled states to continue drawing district lines that give them the advantage.

The Enemy Within: A Chronicle of the Trump Administration

Trump's performance at the current G20 conference was just as embarrassing to himself and to the country as his previous ones were. His kissing up to the big three of the dictator crowd—Putin, Kim Jung Un and Mohammed Bin Salman—was disgustingly unpatriotic. He and Putin held another private powwow for at least two hours with no follow-up on the subjects discussed. He even joked, in front of the cameras, about Putin's interference in our election. Then with a nod and a wink, wagged his finger at his pal and said, "Don't do it again."

Trump topped the trip off with the major accomplishment of being the first president to step over the boundary into North Korea. They then discussed the current state of their previous agreements and the sanctions from which Kim is hoping to get some relief. It's all *talk* at this stage, and shows no sign of reaching any workable agreement.

Ivanka Trump participated in the G20 meeting and, as usual, she intruded herself into situations and conversations for which she had no business being a part. For this, she has been getting a ton of negative comments throughout social media. It looks like her father s grooming her, as well as Don Jr. to keep the presidency in the family. He seems to think he will find a way to extend his stay in office beyond the expected two terms. There are no limits to his delusion.

Trump's immigration policies and rhetoric have stoked his base to the point where we are now engaged in a new phase of the Civil War. So far, it has been a cold war. Let's hope we can keep it cold.

Two of E. Jean Carroll's confidants have stepped forward to describe when and how she informed them of Trump's attack upon her. She is the *nineteenth* woman to accuse Trump of unwanted sexual actions, if anyone out there cares about such action any more. The Trump supporters, including those in the US Senate, sure don't give a damn.

Paul Manafort was brought to New York to face charges against him, similar to, but even broader than, the ones for which he is now in prison.

And now we wave goodbye to our least favorite White House Press Secretary, as Kellyanne Conway departs and attempts to find work with someone willing to hire the second worst liar in the country.

The Enemy Within: A Chronicle of the Trump Administration

July, 2019

July 1-7

The week and the month started out unusually quietly, as far as Trump administration news is concerned. Most of it was a continued analysis of what has been going on, with very few new developments. The spotlight continues to get brighter every day on the outrageous conditions that both children and adults are being subjected to in those concentration camps along the Texas/Mexico border. Several members of Congress, including Alexandra Ocasio-Cortez and presidential candidate Joaquin Castro, have forced their way into the actual caged enclosures where the children are sleeping on cement floors and rarely get a chance to bath. They have questioned some of them to get their stories firsthand, and have been told about the way they are treated by attendants who are obviously anti-immigrant to the point of telling thirsty kids to drink from the toilet. Jerry Nadler says, "Border Agency Chiefs should be prosecuted for their treatment of these babies and youngsters."

The United States Department of Agriculture (USDA) has been and *is* working diligently to fight the climate change threat, using scientific statistical information dissemination, and trying to promote green policies. But the Trump administration has been working since day-one to quash its effort and inhibit the data dissemination, in its ongoing determination to placate and kowtow to the coal industry. This includes the previously mentioned forced relocation of the entire office of the USDA to Kansas City, which will cause the loss of many employees.

The Enemy Within: A Chronicle of the Trump Administration

Trump is planning a big military parade down Pennsylvania Avenue on July 4, which will include the use of heavy tanks. He has conceded to have them placed so as to minimize damage to the road. He considers this event to be a tribute to *him*—rather than a celebration of our nation's birthday.

The furor over the inhuman (worse than inhumane) conditions being exposed more each day, that both children and adults are being forced to endure in those Nazi-style concentration camps in Texas, keeps getting hotter by the day. The Inspector General of The Homeland Security's Office has released a scathing report describing those barbarous conditions, which includes *eighty-eight* adults having standing-room-only in a locked caged-in area designed to accommodate *forty-one*, and being held for twenty days when the law says they can be held for no more than six. This was observed in a camp in Brownsville, Texas, and it is nothing less than torture. This is on top of what we already have learned about the unsanitary and cruel treatment of hundreds, if not thousands of children. The new report calls this situation "a ticking time bomb."

Protestors of this disgrace have been gathering across the country chanting, "Close the camps." The only thing that distinguishes these camps from Hitler's is the absence of gas chambers. The problem is that the administration has no clue as to *what to do* with the migrants if they *did* close the camps. Border Control officials are calling the reports, "unsubstantiated." They are following Trump's policy of calling red, green, up is down and the moon is made of green cheese. Hey, it has worked pretty well for him so far.

The issue of Trump's tax returns, being stubbornly held by Treasury Secretary Steve Mnuchin, has been on the back burner for far too long. But we finally got some movement today. The House Ways and Means Committee's suit has made it to the court's docket and a decision should be

Book Two (09/2018-11/2019)

announced soon. Of course, it will be appealed to the next level and probably to the Supreme Court after the appeals court rules against Trump, so we won't get a decision until after the 2020 election, in all likelihood.

The post-debate polls show that Joaquin Castro got a healthy bump from his performance, but the big news is that Kamala Harris has pulled to within two points of Joe Biden. She gained thirteen points while Joe lost eight. It's starting to get very interesting already.

NBC's *Meet the Press* host, reporter Chuck Todd, asked President Trump what he considered to be the worst mistake he has made so far in his presidency. Trump replied, "Picking Jeff Sessions for Attorney General." Obviously, this response was because he was unable to get Sessions to rid Trump of Special Counsel Mueller. Sessions' Chief of Staff, Jody Hunt, has provided a lot of information to Mueller about what was going on between the AG and the President during that period. Hunt is now running the Judicial Division of the DOJ. After the Supreme Court ruled against the addition of the citizenship question to the census form, Hunt informed the court in writing that they would start printing the forms, without that question on them, immediately because they were already a day past the July 1 deadline to do so. Then Trump tweeted that this issue was not yet settled because he intended to work around that ruling by presenting a better argument to the court. Hunt and Assistant Attorney General Josh Gardner were summoned by a DC court to explain where things stood in this matter in view of Trump's tweet. Gardner assured the judge that they would ignore that tweet. The judge decided to give Trump's lawyers until this Friday to present a new and better argument for the inclusion of the citizenship question, but meanwhile the forms are already being printed without it. This is shaping up to be a possible court vs President crisis.

Trump's response to the report about the conditions in our concentration camps was, "Tell them not to come." That is the whole object of the intentional cruelty isn't it, you heartless POS!

Trump's very expensive (estimated $92 million) July 4 parade was cancelled not long ago because of the expense, but his ego and need for recognition won out and now we are about to be treated to a spectacle that a very large portion of the country will boycott and give him an embarrassing image similar to his inauguration crowd size.

On the July 4th holiday, the only Trump news of the day was his big ego-parade and accompanying speech to the crowd around the Lincoln Memorial. Advance ticket sales for a space in that area were so low that ticket sellers resorted to giving them away during the last couple of days, and practically begging people to show up for his speech. They did not want another embarrassingly small crowd size like the one for his inauguration. Trump's attempt to fire up his base included a tweet in which he said, "You may even see a close fly-over by *Air Plane One.*" Of course, he meant to say, *Air Force One,* the actual code name for the plane reserved for exclusive use by the American President. What made this faux pas even more humorous is the fact that *Air Plane One* is what Putin calls *his* plane.

The parade could not have gone worse for Trump. It rained throughout most of the day, causing Melania some embarrassment when her white dress got soaked and she was not wearing a bra. This provoked somewhat of a Twitter and Facebook rampage. The weather further reduced an already sparse crowd. Trump's speech was judged boring by most who bothered to watch it, except for

Book Two (09/2018-11/2019)

an even more amusing gaff than yesterday's *Air Plane One*. When he was paying tribute to those heroic patriots who gave us our independence, he included the description of how "they took over the airports." Most grade school students would know that during that period of our history, planes and airports did not exist yet. The depth of this man's ignorance knows no bottom, apparently.

Former Assistance Director for Counter-intelligence at the FBI, Frank Figliuzzi, is accusing Attorney General Barr of being a co-conspirator with Trump in covering up the contents of the Mueller Report.

On Rachel Maddow's show tonight she reminded us that all the Intelligence Officers and FBI officials who were in place at the time that the Russian interference investigation began, have been relentlessly attacked and undermined and are no longer in their positions. She had former FBI General Counsel James Baker on as a guest tonight. He is concerned that present and future agents will now be inhibited or intimidated in reporting what they find to be dangerous signals that need to be examined.

Republican Representative Justin Amash, who recently backed impeachment of Donald Trump, has now publicly left and rebuked the Republican Party, because he feels they are too complicit and condoning of Trump's numerous improper actions.

A former Border Control employee has described how new recruits were trained to treat the immigrants harshly and use pejorative labels for them and *to* them. Those recruits who failed to do this did not last long in the program. All part of Trump's "discourage them from coming here" campaign.

The Enemy Within: A Chronicle of the Trump Administration

Iran announced that they are starting to increase the levels of uranium enrichment beyond the limits that were imposed by the treaty that the US and Europe had succeeded in getting them sign, and which Trump pulled our country out of as one of his first "accomplishments."

On December 3 of last year, we learned about the very shady deal that sex-offender and close friend of Donald Trump, Jeffrey Epstein got away with in his last court proceeding, with the help of our current Labor Secretary, Alex Acosta. Today, he was arrested for sex trafficking. I guess old habits die hard. Trump, of course, still refers to Epstein as "a great guy."

We now have evidence that the Trump reelection committee has already begun a new disinformation campaign against some of the most popular Democrat candidates, especially the current leader of the group, Joe Biden, and rising star Kamala Harris.

Biden has, somewhat reluctantly, issued an apology to anyone who was offended by his recent remarks about school desegregation, and about the Republicans he had to work with at that time. His poll numbers continue to drop a bit and Harris is closing in.

July 8-14

This week starts off with one of the heaviest Trump news days in a while. We start with a problem we thought had been settled by the court and conceded by Trump—the census question dispute. Trump must have received some negative feedback from his right-wing followers for his concession, because he suddenly reversed himself and with the support of *his* Attorney General, William Barr, threw a big monkey wrench into the dispute by declaring that they were coming up with a new argument to present to the courts for the inclusion of that hot-button citizenship question. The team of lawyers who had been working for him on that case had all gone on vacation, thinking the matter was settled. They were called back and then replaced by a new team from the DOJ consisting of attorneys who are all inexperienced in this type of legal complexity. Barr says that he has found a way to justify the addition of that question, but he is not telling us what he has in mind. It is interesting to note that Chief Justice Roberts labeled their first reason, (to enforce the voting rights act), "contrived."

Barr has had the good sense to recuse himself from any involvement in the new Epstein case, citing his past friendship with that child molester, when they both worked for the same law firm. Epstein faces up to forty-five years in prison if convicted of the new charge, which is basically the same one he was charged with before, and dodged with the help of Labor Secretary Alex Acosta, who is now being pressured to resign his cabinet post. Senator Tim Kaine is one of those calling for that resignation. Meanwhile, Epstein's defense team tries to soften the crime by referring to the teenage-girl-victims as "prostitutes."

The *New York Times* and the *El Paso Times* have each filed their own reports on the horrible conditions in the border camps. Trump's spokesmen continue to lie whenever they try to defend what is going on down there, and they do so in the face of all the eyewitness reports and the Inspector General's written report.

Trump's original head of the EPA, Scott Pruitt, and his replacement, Andrew Wheeler, have been very busy rolling back every environment-protecting regulation that was in place when Trump took office. There have been *eighty-three* of those regulations rescinded so far. MSNBC's commentators have been replaying Trump's many promises he made during the campaign about how he was, "the champion of clean water and clean air, and our country already had the cleanest in the world." He *is* the champion of one thing, for sure--that is the ability to say one thing and then do exactly the opposite.

Representative Eric Swalwell became the first Democratic presidential candidate to drop out of the race tonight, citing insufficient fund-raising from the first debate. More will surely follow soon. Pete Buttigieg won't be one of them because he has raised more cash than anyone, including Biden. The latest poll shows that Biden is maintaining a ten point lead over Trump in a two way race. Trump's approval rating has risen a bit, to 44%, but his *disapproval* rating is still at 53% overall, and at 57% on his immigration policies.

The US Women's soccer team won their fourth World Cup title today. As they celebrated in the locker room after the game they were asked if they would go to the White House if invited by Trump. There was a resounding NO, followed by chants of "Fuck Trump." Not very ladylike, but honest and understandable.

Attorney General Barr has reversed himself about recusing from the Epstein case described yesterday. But he says he *will* remain uninvolved in the review of Epstein's previous case where he received that ridiculously light sentence with Alex Acosta's help. Legal minds doubt he can recuse from one and not the other. This change of plan was not announced by Barr himself. He had one of his clerks do it for him. Shameful! This thing is shaping up to be a huge mess for all concerned, including Trump. The fact that Secretary Acosta cut the anti-sex-trafficking budget by 80% since becoming Labor Secretary is something that Congress is going to want to question him about.

Book Two (09/2018-11/2019)

House Judiciary Committee Chairman Jerry Nadler is about to issue subpoenas to a dozen new witnesses. Here is the list of those who must now decide if they are going to honor the law or heel to Trump's "resist" order: Jared Kushner, Michael Flynn, John Kelly, David Pecker, Cory Lewandowsky, Rod Rosenstein, Jeff Sessions, and several lesser known people.

There is a new report about an immigrant-holding camp in Yuma, Arizona. In addition to all the now familiar atrocities involving sanitation, discomfort, unsafe conditions, overcrowding, etc. etc., *this* report focuses on sexual abuse toward teenage girls by attendants. One of them would pull down pants or pull up tops, and grope the girl while he and his watching pals would laugh. This offense is coupled with retribution punishment for those who dared to complain. If an attendant was decent enough to report these abuses to his superiors, his report was summarily round-filed. But someone finally got the news out somehow.

Mike Flynn has stopped cooperating with the prosecution and now awaits his sentence, which probably means he is expecting a pardon from Trump.

Labor Secretary Acosta's attempts to explain his decision to give Epstein such a sweetheart deal back in 2008 was loaded with misinformation, to put it politely, according to several legal experts. He tried to make it sound like he was the hero in that case, because the prosecution was going to let Epstein go Scott free. All he did was make matters worse for himself, and it won't be long before another of Trump's "best people" are forced to resign.

The Enemy Within: A Chronicle of the Trump Administration

Democratic National Committee staffer Seth Rich was murdered two years ago today. His death has become fodder for some bizarre conspiracy theories among the far-right fruit-cakes. *Fox News,* and people who thrive on it, are pushing the absurd idea that it was Rich who intentionally leaked Clinton's emails to the Russians—not the Russians who hacked them. This is not just crazy. It is shamefully sullying a man's reputation in order to shift the blame from the real culprits in the biggest heist in our history. WikiLeaks founder Julian Assange is one of those pushing this theory, hoping to take some of the heat off himself.

Just as it appeared that Trump was going to defy the Supreme Court's ruling against the addition of the citizenship question on the census form and create what could become a Constitutional crisis, he caved for the second time on the same issue. He now has decided that they can develop the information he is seeking about the extent of the undocumented immigrant problem, by using already existing records of various types. In the announcement of this decision, he made it sound as though he was issuing an executive order to create something new—trying to lessen the impact of the humiliation of losing another major battle. AG Barr and Commerce Secretary Ross were at his side when he made this statement of capitulation, and Barr then took the microphone to *congratulate* Trump on his "victory." The man just can't seem to stop his shameless self-demeaning behavior when it comes to his new friend and ally, Donald Trump.

Trump is targeting ten cities in his new campaign of using ICE troops to raid and deport illegal aliens, some of which have been living here for years and will have kids in school when they are dragged out of their homes. Several of these cities are refusing to cooperate in assisting ICE

Book Two (09/2018-11/2019)

with local police. Candidate Kamala Harris was on Rachel's show tonight and expounded on Trump's shameful policy of instilling fear into all immigrants, whether they are already here, or planning to come.

Jeffrey Epstein is asking the judge in his case that he be released on house arrest instead of locking him up. His victims will be terrified if he is granted that much freedom.

A State Department analyst who worked on climate change data-gathering has resigned over Trump's blockage of data dissemination that the analyst helped produce to bring the danger to the attention of the populations and the governments of the world.

The House Judiciary Committee has begun issuing those twelve new subpoenas mentioned a couple of days ago. They have gone out to Kushner and Sessions, for starters.

While the United States has been floundering lately, both technologically and economically, under the chaotic administration of Donald Trump, China is on the verge of surpassing us, with an all-out surge of advances in both of these arenas.

Rachel can add another swamp creature to her ever growing departure board of people who have left the Trump administration either by resigning or being fired. It was only a matter of time, and it came quicker than with most, before Labor Secretary Alex Acosta would join the list. He is not quite gone yet, but will be at the end of this month. That list is now over fifty-five names long—I've lost count. This is surely one record that Trump has set that will never be broken, but not one to be proud of. Acosta's replacement, Patrick Pizzella, is said to be *even worse*.

The Enemy Within: A Chronicle of the Trump Administration

Robert Mueller's testimony to Congress has been postponed until July 24. But he has agreed to give them more time than previously planned. The details of his staff members' testimony are still being worked out.

Vice President Pence visited two of the southern border camps today in McAllen Texas, to see for himself what the conditions are like for the migrants who are caged-up there. He stood outside the enclosure and stared blankly at the throng of men pleading with him for help, and letting him know that they have been there for at least forty days. Later, Pence said he was not surprised at the overcrowding, but felt that conditions were not as bad as reported and that they are being provided with all the necessities. Four hundred men in a room that gives them standing room only! The only necessities they have access to is foul air to breath, rancid water to drink and enough food to avoid starvation. After he got back and reported to the president, Trump said, "They are well run and clean." So everything is just fine, America, no need to get all hot and bothered. Meanwhile, dozens of protests against this barbaric treatment have been going on across the country.

Epstein's request for house arrest instead of jail until his trial, was denied because he has been trying to bribe some of the victims.

Trump has added a new weapon in his war against immigrants. He has ordered a drastic reduction in the number of asylum-seekers who may *even apply* for that safety.

July.15-21

Today, Trump reached a new low in his decency as a human being and a new high in his willingness to proclaim his blatant racism. In a blistering attack on a group of four freshman Congresswomen, Alexandria Ocasio Cortez,

Ilhan Omar, Rashida Tlaib and Ayanna Pressley, the president told them, among other things, to "go back to the crappy countries where they came from." In addition to being the height of unAmericanism, it was also ironic since three of the four were born in this country and the other is a naturalized citizen of the US. Needless to say, this created a maelstrom of criticism from every fair-minded section of the country. He continues to placate his racist base at every opportunity in his effort to hang on to that 35 to 45 percent of the voting public that is still sticking by him no matter what he says or does. And of course, the Republicans have nothing to say on the subject.

The neo-Nazi who rammed his car into the crowd at Charlottesville and killed Heather Heyer got a sentence of life plus 419 years, and deserved every year of it.

On her show tonight, Rachel Maddow replayed Hillary Clinton's comments during the campaign predicting that Trump planned to deport masses of immigrants, separating families in the process. She was obviously right on the money!

The uproar caused by Trump's tweets against his new rivals in the House, was the main topic in the Trump war today. It prompted the House of Representatives to pass a resolution condemning Trump's words by a vote of 246 to 187, with only four Republicans voting for the resolution. The resolution was a lengthy list of reasons why they were offended and appalled at such comments coming from a US president. In the text, there were several quotes from past presidents, including GOP hero Ronald Reagan, who spoke eloquently about how immigrants were a great source of pride and benefit for this country.

The Enemy Within: A Chronicle of the Trump Administration

In a rally today, Trump continued to dig his own political grave deeper, as he escalated the racism debate that he created through his attack on the Congresswomen of color, once again stoking the passions of his rabid followers, which amounts to fomenting what could become a new civil war. At the very least, he is encouraging the already violence-prone crowd to attack individuals whom they see as "enemies of America", thanks to the way their leader has painted them. So far, the Republicans have done and said very little to criticize this kind of rhetoric, but that restraint is showing signs of wearing thin and he is playing with fire.

The judge in the Cohen case is about to unseal the up-until-now withheld testimonial documents in the hush-money case, which could reveal new details about Trump's involvement in the crime for which Cohen is now serving time. This crime in which he is identified as "individual one" should be enough by itself to justify impeachment. On the other hand, this unsealing was done because the Southern District of New York, which has had Trump and his whole organization under investigation for more than a year, has closed that probe with no explanation. Smells like AG Barr's hand on the scales. His non-recusal from this case in very suspicious.

In tandem with the Resolution to Condemn, Congressman Al Green has filed a bill of impeachment against the president. This is the third or fourth such bill that has been filed by various lawmakers. I think these are just rehearsals for the real one. One of these days, maybe Pelosi and the House in general will start taking the idea seriously.

Seeing how big the backlash has been about his shameful delight in his crowd's new chant of "send her back", referring to Muslim Congresswoman Ilhan Omar,

Book Two (09/2018-11/2019)

Trump tried to shift the blame to his followers and claim that he actually tried to *stop* them from chanting. The fact that his actions and words are almost always on tape for all the world to see never deters him from lying about it.

Those newly unsealed documents reported yesterday show just how deeply Trump, Hope Hicks, Sarah Sanders, and others were involved in the negotiations to pay hush-money to the women Trump had affairs with. But the inhibiting factor in prosecuting him for this crime, even after he is no longer POTUS, is the question, did he realize that this was a crime? It seems that quite often, his immense ignorance of almost every subject becomes an asset that gets him off the hook. But didn't most of us grow up learning that "ignorance of the law is no excuse?"

Conservative columnist George Will was a guest of Lawrence O'Donnell on his show, *The Last Word,* tonight. They were discussing the latest Trump rampage against his new rivals in the Congress. Mr. Will had just published an op-ed piece in which he stated the following: "I believe that what this president has done to our culture, our civic discourse…you cannot unring these bells and you cannot unsay what he has said, and you cannot change that he has now, in a very short time, made it seem normal for schoolboy taunts and obvious lies to be spun out in a constant stream. I think this will do more lasting damage than Richard Nixon's surreptitious burglaries did."

It is encouraging that *some* Republicans have chosen to start stating the obvious. Meanwhile, Congresswoman Omar was welcome back to her home state of Minnesota by a huge cheering crowd, much to the chagrin of the president.

House Judiciary Committee Chairman Jerry Nadler has written to Hope Hicks requesting that she appear to explain

The Enemy Within: A Chronicle of the Trump Administration

her claim that she had no knowledge of Trump's hush-money payments to the porn stars, when the just-released Cohen documents indicate otherwise.

Attorney General William Barr and Commerce Secretary Wilbur Ross have been found in Criminal Contempt by a vote of the House today. Of course, this is nothing more than an embarrassment to these two gentlemen, the way things are being handled under this administration.

The president is awkwardly and inconsistently trying to word-wiggle his way out from under the weight of all the uproar caused by his outrageously bigoted remarks about the four young recently elected Congresswomen, now known as "the squad", whom he decided are among his worst enemies. He sat in the oval office and told reporters that he tried to stop the crowd's chant of "send her back", by quickly starting to speak again to cut off the chant. The tape showing him smugly glancing around at his adoring followers for a *full thirteen seconds* before he spoke again, is being aired repeatedly by several channels. His attitude toward that gathering has changed from day to day as he tries to walk a fine line between shifting blame off himself and avoiding pissing off the people he depends on to keep him in office. The GOP is in a virtual state of panic, trying to walk a similar fine line between not appearing to agree with such racist behavior, and alienating the leader of their party and the following that they need to keep on their side if they hope to keep their seat in 2020. They are like a family that has a mad uncle in the attic and don't know what to do with him. When confronted with reporters in the hall, asking what they think of Trump's behavior, their struggling responses would be laughable if the situation were not so serious.

House Oversight Committee Chairman Elijah Cummings is demanding answers from the Southern District of New York as to why they are ceasing their investigation of the Trump Organization, and if they were in any way influenced by AG Barr.

George Nader, who has been previously prosecuted for the same type of crimes as Jeffrey Epstein, has again been charged with sex trafficking. They are like a club of perverts.

The nominee to be our new Secretary of Defense, Mark Esper, was grilled at length today by Massachusetts Senator Elizabeth Warren, as to whether or not he would recuse himself and sever ties with his financial interests, which would constitute a conflict of interest. His answers were grossly unsatisfactory and evasive.

Border Control official Kevin McAleenan was put on the hot seat by Alexandria Ocasio Cortez and Elijah Cummings, as to the conditions which have been allowed to exist and continue in those infamous camps on the southern border. He was visibly and understandably sweating.

Washington Post Assistant Editor David Maraniss says that the Republicans who question Mueller when he testifies next week, had better be careful how they frame their questions or they may not like the answers. If Mueller says what I think he *should* say during this hearing, this could be one of the biggest anti-Trump bombshells we have seen yet (emphasis on *yet*).

Washington State Governor and presidential candidate Jay Inslee says that the GOP members of both houses of Congress, but especially in the Senate, are cowering in fear of Donald Trump and his supporters, which inhibits them from speaking out against his latest (and long-term) displays of abject racism.

It seems that nearly everyone is talking about how Trump has virtually swallowed up the Republican Party and made it unrecognizable. He is being compared to George Wallace repeatedly, but he is worse than Wallace, because Wallace never tried to hide *his* racism.

Senator Lindsey Graham calls AOC and her "squad" communists and anti-Semitic. Anything to disparage the targets that Trump has chosen to zero in on because of their criticism of him and their surging popularity.

This seems like a good point to stop and pose some questions to which we are still awaiting answers from our House of Representatives.

Dear Congressmen, since you are now the only branch of our government that is in a position to be able to take action against the blatant criminal disregard for the law that we are seeing in the form of defiance of subpoenas etc., etc. please tell us: Why is there no progress being made to enforce the release of Trump's tax returns? Or the pervasive long-term violation of the Constitution's emoluments clause? Or the illegal racial remarks from Trump that are tearing our country apart?

If even one of those remarks had been made by any employee of any organization in our country, that person would have been fired immediately. The superiors would not have a choice. But the Republicans are fine with it? What we have now is a viral infection running rampant through the Republican Party that is much worse than the "cancer growing on the Nixon Presidency."

July 22-28

As we begin the week that could become one of the most significant of the Trump administration's battle to stay in power, if not *the* most significant, speculation is swirling about how much Mueller will say in his testimony beyond a dry reading of what he has put in his report. The DOJ's Associate Deputy Attorney General, Bradley Weinsheimer, wrote a letter to Mueller telling him he should not go beyond what was in his report, showing that they and Trump are quite concerned about how much the former Special Counsel will voice his own opinion about how the basic facts should be acted upon. On Wednesday, he will be spending most of the day answering questions put to him by both Democratic and Republican House members, first from the Judiciary Committee, and then from the Intelligence Committee. He will begin with an opening statement, which may be the most interesting and most important part of his testimony, and the country will be watching it on live TV. If there was ever a *must-see* TV program, this is it.

On Tuesday, we will get sort of an opening act by FBI Director Chris Wray, who will appear before the Senate where he will be questioned by Democratic presidential candidates. That too, should be both fascinating and informative.

Iran is claiming to have captured seventeen US spies, and they are already saying that at least some of them will be executed. Trump is saying that they are lying—that there was no such capture. Secretary of State Pompeo has no comment on the subject. Tensions continue to escalate daily with the seizure by the Iranians of a British tanker. Meanwhile, Trump is talking about putting a quick end to the war in Afghanistan by using nukes to completely destroy the country. All of this is a direct result of Trump's unilateral withdrawal from the treaty that Obama made with Iran which stopped their headlong quest for nuclear power. Now, they are free to charge, full steam ahead, to advance that very dangerous program.

There are huge protests going on in Puerto Rico against Gov. Ricardo Rosselló, who is embroiled in a scandal over hundreds of pages of leaked text messages that contained misogynistic and homophobic language, and in the way he has attacked his political opponents. They are demanding his resignation.

In addition to the uproar Trump's racist rants have caused here in this country, global leaders like Canada's Trudeau and Germany's Merkle are speaking out against him.

Trump has a new favorite TV channel, now that *Fox News* can no longer be depended upon to approve and praise his every action and statement. It is named *Sputnik* and is partially staffed by journalists connected with the Kremlin. *And he accuses our Congresswomen of being un-American.*

Today, FBI Director Chris Wray, a Trump appointee, testified before Congress. The most important thing that he said in that hearing was that Russia is right now using every capability they have to set up for a repeat performance of their interference in the 2016 election when 2020 gets here.

Trump is now actually bragging about having unlimited power to do whatever he wants to do, granted by Article Two of the Constitution, which spells out the power of the Executive branch of our government. The problem is, it does nothing of the sort. Once again he is lying about the most important aspect of his job. I do not believe that this time it is because of ignorance.

Book Two (09/2018-11/2019)

He is also continuing to lie about the Mueller Report. He is still claiming it found "no collusion, no obstruction." Anyone who bothers to watch tomorrow's Mueller testimony will learn how untrue that claim is.

Today, the long-awaited and highly anticipated testimony of Robert Mueller before two house committees, Judiciary in the morning and Intelligence in the afternoon, finally came to pass, and the whole country had a chance to see, hear, and evaluate the findings contained in his voluminous report. Once again, the former Special Counsel failed to live up to the hopes, if not the expectations, of the two thirds of the country that wanted him to take off the kid gloves that he was in the habit of wearing as a member of the Department of Justice, ruled by their procedures and guidelines. No longer under their employ and a private citizen free to speak his opinion, he had the perfect opportunity to set the record straight and correct the dishonest false interpretation of his report that was presented by his last boss, Attorney General Barr. Most people would have welcomed the opportunity, not only to present the facts, but expose the corrupt pro-Trump bias of an Attorney General who is supposed to be the top lawyer for the country, not for one person named Trump. But Mueller is not "most people." He is a Company man, or in this case, Bureau man to the core, even though he is no longer employed there.

With Trump shouting "no collusion, no obstruction" at every opportunity, Mueller gave a very subdued, measured, and inconclusive presentation of the facts, and nothing but the facts, that were in his report. It is true that those facts put the lie to Trump's claims of total exoneration and made it clear that the only reason that Trump was not indicted for several counts of obstruction of justice was the DOJ's ridiculous and (hopefully due to be soon expunged), "rule" that you must not indict a sitting president. He pointed out that in three sample cases of obstruction (out of the ten he listed in the report) Trump met all three of the required ingredients of obstruction: 1. Commission of an obstructive act; 2. The obstruction act was connected to an official proceeding; 3. The act was carried out with corrupt intent.

But in the first of the two hearings, the benefit that the country and in particular, the Trump critics, may have gained by this expose was perhaps completely overshadowed by Mueller's weak, hesitant, at times confused and somewhat incoherent answers and comments. He seemed to be poorly prepared, and many times could not remember what was in his own report. He kept thumbing through it to find the passage that he was being questioned about, could not seem to understand many of the questions, had to have them repeated on many occasions, and seemed nervous and flummoxed much of the time. It is clear why he had been so reluctant to concede to making this appearance.

Of course, the Republican members of the committee did their best to add to his misery by framing their rapidly spoken questions in very complex sentences. Florida's Democratic Representative, Debbie Mucarsel-Powell, was the last one to question the witness and did the best job of it, in my opinion.

The afternoon session, with Adam Schiff's Intelligence Committee, went considerably better than the morning one did, largely thanks to Schiff's opening statement, which set the tone for the discussion about the actual reason for the investigation in the first place, and what the Trump team's role was in Russia's interference. The questions from Schiff and the other Democrats were more on point, and easier for Mueller to answer.

This hearing *should* have been the early one, with the one on the subject of obstruction following it, which *is*, after all, the order in which the events took place. As it was, Mueller's performance in the first hearing probably

Book Two (09/2018-11/2019)

caused many viewers to tune out without seeing the much more effective second hearing.

One of the most important of the missed opportunities was when the subject of collusion with Russia was being discussed. The whole issue here is whether or not the many contacts that existed between the Trump people and Russians leading up to the 2016 election, constituted the crime of *conspiracy*. There is a lot of confusion about whether the word "collusion" is a synonym for "conspiracy." The difference is that conspiracy is a crime and collusion is not (but it should be). As I have discussed previously in this book, collusion is in the same category but at a lighter or lower level than conspiracy. All those meetings with the Russians for the purpose of getting "dirt" on Clinton were more than just unethical—they were *collusion*, with the understanding of a quid pro quo agreement being part of the "arrangement." Mueller's response to Schiff's questions about these numerous contacts made it clear that this went far beyond just unethical and unpatriotic behavior.

The biggest surprise of the day was probably when Schiff asked the question, "Do you believe that knowingly accepting assistance from a foreign power to win an election is an unethical thing to do?" Mueller's answer was, "Yes, *and a crime*." Mueller also agreed with Schiff's observations that Trump's behavior and business dealings with Putin constituted ammunition for potential blackmail opportunities, such as Trump's continued desire to build a greatly lucrative Trump Tower in Moscow.

As this was going on, which included emphasis on Russia's *ongoing* efforts to create inroads into our electoral process, Mitch McConnell was blocking two bills from the House to beef up our defenses against such activity by our long-term nemesis.

The Enemy Within: A Chronicle of the Trump Administration

There is now evidence that Russia has the ability to actually modify electronic ballots in many of the states of our country. Trump and the Republicans in Congress are not only unwilling to do anything about this, but actually welcome it with open arms because it is the only way that Trump could win re-election. The *Senate* Judiciary Committee has released a report about the election interference problem. Three Democratic members say that it does not present the case strongly enough. Mueller's testimony made it very clear how serious the threat is and MUST be taken seriously before we have the voice of the people taken away from us completely. So far, Senate Leader McConnell has blocked a total of *eight* bills designed to help protect us from invasion via ballot falsification, and the president still won't even agree that Russia interfered in the 2016 election.

On O'Donnell's *Last Word* tonight, guest Joyce Vance, US Attorney for the northern district of Alabama, pointed out that when Mueller was asked if the pervasive lying by Trump's associates during his investigation hampered his ability to get at the truth, her answer was not only affirmative, but she said that the lying was the main linkage between part one of his report (the Russian interference) and part two (the obstruction). She also alluded to the fact that Mueller revealed that Trump's written answers to the questions he had been asked, were incomplete, untrue, or ignored altogether.

Legal expert Neal Katyal says that the state of New York could indict the president because the DOJ's policy does not apply to *state* charges. Very interesting! He also said that the statute of limitations on indictment would have its time-span interrupted during the president's time in office, so winning a second term would not run it out and save him.

Book Two (09/2018-11/2019)

Don McGahn is the next big target for the House, and his defiance of the subpoena to testify will soon be settled in court. It's about time to do this in a lot of cases.

The sentiment to open at least an *inquiry* into Trump's impeachment has now grown, in light of Wednesday's testimony, but Pelosi still seems determined not to move on the issue before hearing from McGahn and others. It makes it seem as though the Democrats are divided, but only on the question of WHEN, not on WHETHER.

The impeachment process has begun! On Friday, the House took the first step by opening what amounts to an impeachment inquiry, although some are reluctant to call it that yet. They are referring to it as an "impeachment investigation". Their opening filing, which was signed off by Speaker Nancy Pelosi, will give them more leverage with the courts to provide vital, but redacted and withheld, grand jury transcripts. The number of Democratic Representatives favoring impeachment has now grown to ninety-eight, with seven more added since Mueller's testimony. Unfortunately, they all now depart DC for a six-week vacation break.

The Washington Post has labeled Senate Leader Mitch McConnell "a Russian asset", and dubbed him, "Moscow Mitch", because of his unwillingness to take *any* steps to even try to prevent them from stealing the election again in 2020. Unusually harsh language, but well-deserved.

Over the weekend, the semantics of the label "investigation' versus the more official word "inquiry" was roundly discussed by all levels of interested parties. It might make a difference if the issue goes as far as the Supreme Court. As to how far to take the action, it is felt by Pelosi and the other so-called foot-draggers, that it is essential that they get Don McGahn's testimony and things like Trump's tax records, before they will have their best case on which to proceed. As anxious we are to get justice for our nation, this is the best approach. In the meantime, I predict that there will be at least one more bombshell revelation to take place in the next few months.

The Chairman of the House Oversight Committee, Elijah Cummings, is the Democratic Representative of the Maryland district that includes the city of Baltimore. He has been an outspoken critic of the president and one of the first to be in favor of impeachment. As Chairman of Oversight, he has subpoenaed Trump for a variety of White House documents, including emails of Ivanka and Kushner. So Trump has added him to his list of top enemies, and has viciously attacked both him and the "rat-infested city of Baltimore" in a series of tweets that have furthered enflamed the cries against his blatant racism. White House Chief-of-Staff, John (Mick) Mulvaney, is trying to defend Trump by denying any racist overtones in Trump's criticism of Cummings and his city. Another case where they try to convince us that black is white. Many are now asking, what is the breaking point for the Republicans on Trump's racism and criminality? Apparently there is none.

Trump is really pissed at *Fox News* for airing their own poll that shows Biden leading him by a whopping ten points. Sheppard Smith responded to Trump's rampage by showing him how accurate their polling has been in the recent past. Even *Fox News* has a couple of honest commentators.

The Supreme Court has ruled in Trump's favor on his use of federal defense funds to work on his southern border wall. The lawsuit was brought by the American Civil Liberties Union on behalf of the Sierra Club and Southern Border Communities Coalition. In a five-to-four decision on party lines, the court ruled that the plaintiff "lacked sufficient standing" to bring the case. Time for someone who has sufficient standing to stand up.

Director of National Intelligence (DNI) Dan Coats is leaving his post. It is not clear whether this move is voluntary or not, but it is clear that Coats has been an outspoken critic of Trump's policies, especially in regard to his relationship with Vladimir Putin. In a cabinet meeting a few months ago, all the members went around the table showering praise on the president, except Coats, who gave an obviously "neutral" comment. He is being replaced by John Ratcliffe, another one of those completely inexperienced, unqualified people that Trump always seems to choose only because they are staunch Trump supporters and sycophants.

A Dallas-Texas-born teenaged boy was scooped up in an ICE raid and held for twenty-three days, where he lost twenty-six pounds, before finally being released. It doesn't pay to have a brown skin and a Latino name in this country these days.

Former South Carolina Representative Mark Sanford is considering a run in the Republican primary against Donald Trump, joining Mitt Romney in that elite group. Not *all* of the GOP has drunk the Kool-Aid.

The Enemy Within: A Chronicle of the Trump Administration

Book Two (09/2018-11/2019)

August, 2019

July 29-Aug. 4

As the swirling debate continues about Trump's latest racist attacks upon several Congressmen and women of color, which he insists upon doubling and tripling down on, it has become more and more obvious that he has made this the primary issue of his re-election campaign. He is betting all his marbles on this issue being the thing that will hold his base and maybe win over enough fringe voters to pull off another miracle, with Russia's help, of course.

As Trump was announcing the hard-won passage of the first-responder relief act, he could not resist lying yet again about his role on that historically tragic day. He claimed that he "spent hours down there with them." It is actually a bit frightening to see how willing he is to keep on telling lies that are so easily disproved.

McConnell has let it be known that he does not appreciate the epithet "Moscow Mitch." Hey, Mitch, if you act like a traitor, you are going to be labeled as one. That's the way it works.

The number of Democratic Representatives who favor opening an impeachment inquiry has now grown to one hundred and seven, and is increasing by the day, if not the hour.

Four Republican Congressmen have announced that they will retire rather than seek re-election in 2020. The GOP has already lost fifteen percent of its seats before the votes are cast.

The Enemy Within: A Chronicle of the Trump Administration

Tonight, ten Democratic candidates held the first half of their second debate. It was a battle between the more progressive (liberal) members and the more moderate (conservative) members. At this point, as expected, they are more focused upon each other than on Donald Trump, as each one tries to display their strengths and point to their opponents' weaknesses. One of the main areas of disagreement is health care and particularly the pros and cons of Medicare-for-all.

California Governor Gavin Newsom is pushing for a state law which would require all presidential candidates to produce their tax returns. He would like to have this law include the current president, but that may be "a bridge too far." Trump's returns *should* be finally pried lose through the courts, before Newsom's law can get enacted.

The Chairman of the ACLU is challenging the Trump administration's continued policy of child-separation at the border. The border control officials are using some very flimsy excuses to justify cases where they say it is necessary to protect the child.

On night two of the second Democratic candidates' debate, the other ten contestants took more swipes at Barack Obama and each other, particularly at front-runner Joe Biden, than they did at Trump. Hopefully, when the field is winnowed down, they will begin to get their act together and get down to the business of going after their actual enemy in this upcoming fight for a return to sanity. The TV commentators gave high marks to Warren, Booker, Sanders and Castro. Harris did not come off as well as she did in the first one. It will be interesting to see what the upcoming polls show, and who drops out now.

Another coal mine has declared bankruptcy and closed down, putting hundreds out of work. These are the people

Book Two (09/2018-11/2019)

that Trump promised he would protect during his campaign. I wonder how they feel about him now.

As we start a new month Trump held another ego-rally in Ohio today and he didn't encourage any racist chants. Instead, he gloated about how the Democrats took turns criticizing Obama and each other. That was not a smart way to conduct that debate and they better get their act together before the next one. It looks like Warren came away the closest thing there was to a winner. Lawrence O'Donnell tonight pointed out the fact that presidents do not have to be good debaters because they depend so much on the advice and assistance of the cabinet and staff. At least all of them did before Trump, but he listens to no one.

Our new Ambassador to the UN is a young lady named Kelly Knight Craft, whose husband is a huge donor to the Trump campaign. This one has even fewer qualifications for that post than the last one did. When asked what her thoughts were on climate change, she was very noncommittal.

New York's Attorney General has issued subpoenas for documents pertaining to the hush-money payments to porn stars, in their ongoing investigation into the Trump Organization. This is an area where US AG Barr has no power to interfere.

The number of House Democrats supporting an impeachment inquiry continues to grow and is nearing a majority. The latest was Congressman Eliot Engel from New York.

The Enemy Within: A Chronicle of the Trump Administration

Another Republican Representative has announced his retirement at the end of his term, bringing that total to eight this year.

California Representative Salud Carbajal became the 118th House Democrat to support an impeachment inquiry. This crossed the line into a majority of Democrats who now support it. Speaker Pelosi responded to this event by stating, "We will hold him (Trump) accountable."

Trump's pick to be the new DCI has been withdrawn due to the onslaught of criticism about that candidate's abysmal lack of qualifications for the highest intelligence agency post. Trump credits the press for vetting the man and exposing his shortcomings. He says that he likes to pick candidates out of the blue, knowing that the media will do that vetting job for him. This is the same press that he likes to call, "The enemy of the people."

The bizarre conspiracy theory group (cult) that calls itself QAnon is under investigation now by the FBI which is labeling it as "a domestic terrorist threat." This group believes that it has the support and protection of the president, so it can get away with all sorts of crimes. I wonder why they would think such a thing.

Rick Gates, an insider of the Trump campaign and key witness to many of the examples of collusion, is scheduled to be a witness in three upcoming trials, including that of Roger Stone. For this reason, his sentencing for his own crimes, the same type for which Paul Manafort is now doing time, has still not been decided upon.

The big story of the weekend was another mass shooting by a lone gunman in the southern border town of El Paso, Texas. He is a nineteen-year-old self-professed white

Book Two (09/2018-11/2019

supremacist doing his part to stoke a race war in this country.

Then on Sunday, we had another one in Dayton. Ohio, with nine more dead and at least twenty-six wounded. The shooter in this case was Patrick Crusius, a 21-year-old white-supremacist male from Allen, Texas, who surrendered immediately to the police. Trump was quick to express condolences and support for the cities. It will be interesting to see how he handles the inevitable questions about the shooters' motives and character. Will he manage this any better than he did the Charlottesville fiasco? He has now *added* to the cloud of being a contributor to the motivation of this type of action toward immigrants.

These two latest mass killings brings the total of such cases so far in the US to 251! We are not only the world leader in such violence, in *second* place is Mexico with a total of *three*. This shameful fact is strictly due to the NRA's complete ownership of a large chunk of the Republican Party--the rest of it being owned, in fairly equal shares, by giant corporations, Russia. China and Saudi Arabia. Our two-party system is no longer a case of a difference in philosophy and policies—it has become what closely resembles a case of GOOD vs. EVIL. If you think that this statement is too hyperbolic, how about—a choice between a party which is at its *lowest* ebb in the category of corruption, and a party which has become the most corrupt one in our history, thanks in large part to Donald Trump and family.

Aug. 5-11

The latest mass murders and the repercussions that they have produced for the country, for the media, for the Republican Party and for President Trump, have monopolized the news for at least these three days of this week, with no end in sight. It seems that at this time, very little else of significance is happening in the overall Trump presidency saga. There has been even more anti-NRA sentiment expressed over this latest round of violence as there was in any of the previous mass shootings, with protesting crowds chanting "do something!" to any officials who were in earshot.

Trump was finally coerced into making a speech in which he said a few of the right kind of words of commiseration without the slightest hint of sincerity or emotion, and even managed to refer to one of the incidents as taking place in Toledo instead of Dayton Ohio.

The Republicans are trying to place the blame for all the gun violence on a combination of mental illness and video games. Anything to avoid the issue of Trump's hatred-inducing rhetoric and the easy access to firearms in the country. Counties which have hosted Trump rallies, where he revels in inciting the crowd's racist sentiments, have experienced a two hundred and twenty-six percent increase in hate crimes. Blaming mental illness is especially ironic because Trump has signed bills that make it *easier* for the mentally ill to purchase firearms, and has also cut the budget on the treatment of mental illness.

Former FBI Assistant Director of Counter Intelligence, Frank Figliuzzi, wrote an op-ed in the *New York Times*, in which he stated the following: "Instinct and experience tell me we're headed for trouble in the form of white-hate violence racially stoked by a racially divisive president. He has chosen a re-election strategy based on appealing to the kinds of hatred, fear and ignorance that can lead to violence."

In spite of requests not to come, Trump went ahead and visited both El Paso and Dayton, where he encountered protest gatherings in both cities. He visited a hospital and had his photo-op with a few hospital workers who were obvious Trump admirers by the way they were all smiles and joined him in his famous thumbs up gesture. Everything he does and everyplace he goes, he always makes it all about himself, no matter how serious the occasion. Barack Obama has spoken out very forcefully against the atmosphere of hate and violence that Trump takes every opportunity to enflame. Michelle Obama is seriously considering a run for Senator of New York State. Maybe she will become the new Hillary, but with a much smaller (unjustified) cloud of distrust over her head.

We may have the first crack among the GOP on the issue of gun control, as Ohio Congressman Mark Turner has decided, in response to the groundswell of protests, to back a ban on assault rifles and large-capacity magazines.

The Trump vs China trade-war is now at the point of threatening a world-wide economic disaster.

The House Judiciary Committee has filed a law suit to force Don McGahn to heed the subpoena for his testimony.

Deputy Director of National Intelligence, Sue Gordon, is the latest one of several high-ranking officials of our intelligence community who have left or are leaving--some filing law suits against Trump as the go. Gordon is being replaced by another "acting" fill-in--retired Admiral Joseph McGuire. That vital community has been decimated lately, due primarily, either directly or indirectly, to Trump. He seems to be solely concerned about his own political and legal problems, and not about the business of leading or protecting the country.

The news media are now starting to draw comparisons between the types of gaffs that are made by various presidential candidates, such as Joe Biden—a favorite Trump target—and those made by the President on a daily basis, which are far more numerous and serious, but tend to be downplayed simply because they have become the accepted norm from him.

As we approach the anniversary of the Charlottesville fiasco, a federal judge has handed down a decision against the white-power groups which organized the protests that resulted in so much violence. He ordered them to pay the legal expenses of the plaintiffs who were victims of that violence, and has placed sanctions on their organizations. There have been at least two other legal actions won by victims of neo-Nazi or white-supremacy groups. Those groups are being gradually dismantled.

The FBI today arrested a white supremacist who was found with an AR15 and several other guns, along with bomb-making equipment, in his possession. He had been discussing an attack on a synagogue.

Private citizens have revealed videos that prove how much Trump lied about the size of Beto O'Rourke's rally crowd compared to the size of his own, during his visit to the cities affected by the shootings. They stress how much Trump was concerned about his own image, and hardly at all about the victims he was there to comfort and encourage. Perhaps that can be attributed partly to the fact that *not one* of those victims would agree to a visit from the President of the United States.

A massive ICE raid on food plants in Mississippi left scores of children in tears as they looked for their parents. Some of those parents have since been returned, but what is happening to the rest, and to those kids?

The *Wall Street Journal* reports that Deutche Bank is continuing to turn over to investigators many of Trump's financial documents.

About two thirds of those USDA employees who were being forced to relocate to Kansas City have chosen to resign instead. Today, WH Chief-of-staff Mulvaney as much as admitted that the motive for the forced move was to inhibit the fight against climate change.

This weekend Trump's violence-inspiring rhetoric has jumped up a huge notch, from appealing to the baser instincts of the racists and white supremacists, to threatening to unleash his supporters in the police, the military and the biker gangs. Here is his latest new vile and dangerous utterance along those lines.
"You know, the left plays a tougher game. It's very funny. I actually think that the people on the right are tougher, but they don't play it together. Okay? I can tell you, I have the support of the police, the support of the military, the support of the Bikers for Trump—I have the tough people, but they don't play it tough until they go to a certain point, and then it could be *very, very bad*." (Emphasis by author). This is not the first such hint of things to come.

Michael Cohen warned Congress that Trump would not allow a peaceful transition of power if he loses the next election. And he knows the man better than just about anyone else alive.

Jerry Nadler has declared that his House Judiciary Committee is now conducting an official Impeachment Inquiry into Donald Trump.

Trump himself is now predicting that "meaningful" background checks on gun purchasers will be passed by Congress. He didn't say when.

Sex trafficker Jeffrey Epstein was found dead by hanging in his cell Saturday morning. The official story is that it was a suicide, but one wonders if it could have been staged. He was facing the likeliness of spending the rest of his life in prison, so he *did* have reason to opt out. His death is being closely investigated. One wonders to what extent those efforts will be blocked by AG Barr. Meanwhile, Trump has re-tweeted a crazy conspiracy theory that implicates Bill Clinton in that death, with no substantiating evidence whatever. This case of the death of one of Trump's longest and dearest friends, who just happened to have the same taste for young women as he has displayed, is starting to smell very fishy. Look for some juicy revelations to come out of this investigation into Epstein's cohorts in the sex business.

Aug. 12-18

The Epstein "suicide" remains the biggest story of the day, as authorities are examining his life, his properties and his death. This man was under a suicide watch, so several prison officials have been reprimanded, and the Deputy Director of the Burrough of Prisons, Hugh Hurwitz, has been questioned. They are looking for any links to the co-conspirators he worked with in the sex-trafficking ring. Those people, whoever they are, should be very nervous right now. All the non-disclosure agreements he had with his cronies will be void now that he is dead, and could produce a goldmine of interesting names.

Trump has created a new rule that would penalize any immigrant that enters our country, even legally, if they are poor enough to require federal benefits. He doesn't say how

Book Two (09/2018-11/2019)

he would penalize them. I guess we will have to revise the greeting that is etched into the Statue of Liberty.

Presidential candidate and Senator Amy Klobuchar says that she has been promised by Donald Trump, on at least five different occasions, that he favors background checks on gun purchasers, but has yet to do anything about it, so don't expect him to come through now.

Jerry Nadler's House Judiciary Committee has sent a four-page letter, containing twenty-three questions, to the DOJ pertaining to the very suspicious death of Jeffrey Epstein. One of those questions was whether any White House personnel, including Donald Trump, had anything to do with the removal of the suicide watch that had been put in place on Epstein as he entered the prison. Such a decision to remove such a safeguard is supposed to be reviewed by several officials before any such move is made. This whole thing puts me in mind of the very controversial "take-out" of Lee Oswald.

My comment yesterday about revising the Statue of Liberty poem has now actually been suggested. Trump aide, Ken Cuccinelli, has submitted his new version. It reads—"Give me your tired and poor who can stand on their own two feet and will not become a public charge."

The Russians have tested a nuclear-power-driven but conventionally armed missile which exploded shortly after blast-off and radiated several towns in northwest Russia. The Russians are of course downplaying the radiation problem.

Early Trump administration departure, Anthony Scaramucci, has turned on the president. He advises the GOP to dump him to save the party.

The Enemy Within: A Chronicle of the Trump Administration

Stacy Abrams has decided against running for president, but has instead mounted a committee to combat voter interference. It is named, Fair Fight 2020. You go, Stacy! We need all the help we can get in that regard.

The latest state-by-state polls show that if the 2020 election were held today, Trump would lose the Electoral College by three hundred, 419 to 119.

Tonight Rachel Maddow enlightened us about reports out of *Time Magazine* and *The Washington Post,* on the very shady deal that Moscow Mitch has made with the Russian oligarch Oleg Deripaska. One of the major Russian companies that had been sanctioned for "…its malign activities around the globe", was a huge aluminum plant Deripaska had built in McConnell's home state of Kentucky. McConnell agreed to work to remove that particular sanction in exchange for a huge loan ($200 million) that would save the plant from its financial problems and help the economy and save jobs in that state. He also agreed to block any bills that would go against Russian interests, such as those that would work to block future attempts at election interference. They are now trying to extend this type of operation into eight more states. Mitch may resent his new nickname, but he has certainly earned it. The "enemy within" applies to more than just Donald Trump. We are saddled with the most corrupt Senate in the history of our country.

A former economic adviser to President Obama, Gene Sperling, now a contributing editor for *The Atlantic,* is warning that Trump's wild, seat-of-the-pants, fiscal policies and tariffs are very risky, not only for the US economy, but for the world economy.

The number of Democrats in the House who support impeachment has risen to one hundred and twenty-six.

The autopsy of Jeffrey Epstein showed that his hyoid bone was broken, which is highly unusual when a person commits suicide by hanging. It is an indication of manual strangulation. This case just gets more and more suspicious.

It turns out, on further investigation, that the type of deal Mitch McConnell had with the Russians for that aluminum plant is part of a broader pattern of such Russian attempts to buy influence into the economy or politics of several nations.

Trump has nominated for a judgeship in a Circuit (Appeals) Court, Steven Menashi, who advocates ethno nationalism. This is the policy of domination of one ethnic group over all others in a particular country. In other words, it is a fancy phrase for "white nationalism". Trump has already nominated many more judges than Obama did in his whole eight years in office, thanks to his being blocked in that regard by the GOP-controlled Senate.

Texas Representative and presidential candidate Beto O'Rourke has decided to stay in the presidential race despite urging by his party to run for the Texas Senate instead. I have a feeling he will regret that decision. The Democratic Party is the worse for it because we need every Senate seat we can get in order to break the GOP roadblock.

Trump has been tossing out the crazy idea of this country purchasing the Danish territory of Greenland. The question is—why? Just more Trump depravity?

The Enemy Within: A Chronicle of the Trump Administration

Trump is bragging about receiving another "beautiful letter" from Kim Jong Un. No mention of the recent rash of short-range missile tests the North Korea has conducted recently.

The NRA is suing AG of New York Letitia James, who has issued over ninety subpoenas to NRA members, including Oliver North. They want their own attorneys taking part in North's questioning.

The latest polls show that Biden leads Trump, 50 to 38 percent, Sanders leads him 48 to 39, Warren leads him by 46 to 39 and Harris by 45 to 39.

Economy experts are predicting a recession in our not distant future, caused primarily by Trump's tariffs. One sign of this is that the Dow today had another precipitous tumble of eight hundred points.

A new TV Special named *American Swamp* reports that Trump's infrastructure plan and promise have produced zero action so far.

Aug. 19-25

The House has passed a bill requiring beefed-up background checks on gun purchasers, but Trump has already reversed himself on this issue, saying, "We already have background checks and don't need any more."

Trump wants to change the law that limits to twenty days the time that immigrants and asylum seekers can be detained at the border. He wants to be able to hold them "indefinitely." This new law of his would also give ICE the sole power over the conditions of the facilities, and access to them by attorneys.

Book Two (09/2018-11/2019)

A small newspaper named *Epoch Times* has been generating a ton of Facebook propaganda promoting Donald Trump and his policies. This is an anti-Communist-China paper which is funded and controlled by a fringe, apocalyptic, religious group. One of this paper's supporters had disrupted a speech by the Chinese president when W. Bush was president and visiting him. She was arrested on several charges, but they were later dropped. Bush apologized for the interruption. Trump seems to be loved by quite a few organizations like this one, that are really way outside the mainstream—KKK, white-supremacists, neo-Nazis, etc.

Trump's latest demonstrations of pathological narcissism included self-descriptions such as: "I am the king of the Jews"; "I am the second coming of God"; and "I am the chosen one." The signs of his mental deterioration grow more concerning by the day. There is a new edition out now of the book titled *The Dangerous Case of Donald Trump*. Two of the contributing mental health experts were on Lawrence O'Donnell's show tonight. One of them labeled Trump "a raving maniac."

The leader of Denmark called Trump's proposal to purchase Greenland, "absurd." Trump pf course took umbrage with that word and ranted about it in no uncertain terms.

Mike Flynn's sentencing has been postponed again, for the umpteenth time, because he is *still* not through telling all that he knows. Rick Gates is scheduled to testify in the trial of Paul Manafort's former attorney, Greg Craig.

Congresswoman Lauren Underwood has announced her support for the impeachment of the president. She says that

The Enemy Within: A Chronicle of the Trump Administration

she bases that decision on the evidence of collusion with Russia in their election interference, rather than the evidence of obstruction, upon which most House members have based their conclusion. She complains that "…we still do not have the unredacted Mueller Report."

We are finally getting some action on the law suit to get Trump's tax returns pried loose from the Treasury Department. House Ways and Means Committee Chairman Richard Neal has filed an appeal to the judge in this case for an immediate release.

New York AG Letitia James is still going after Trump and the NRA with several law suits. Some of the NRA members are cooperating with her.

Every day now more Democratic Congressmen decide to support an impeachment inquiry, spurred by the president's recent rant about being "the second coming" etc. The total is now up to 130, most of them very concerned about Trump's mental health. Three more of them were added to the list today. Mental health expert, Dr. Lance Nodes, was on O'Donnell's *Last Word* tonight, and described Trump as being "in a psychotic-like state." His madness is being compared to "the madness of George III", portrayed in a play of that name.

Trump leaves today for another G7 meeting, where he plans to plead the case for allowing Russia back into that group—still playing the role of Putin's puppet.

Huge fires are consuming much of the Amazon jungle, reducing our planet's ability to produce the oxygen that allows the Earth (and us) to breathe. But according to Trump and many Republicans, global warming is a hoax.

Book Two (09/2018-11/2019)

Newark, New Jersey is experiencing a lead-poison water problem rivaling that of Flint Michigan. This one is caused by old, eroding lead pipes that conduct the water to homes. The city is in a state of emergency requiring massive delivery of bottled water for drinking and cooking.

The latest polls show that Trump's approval rating is at 36% and his disapproval rating is at 62%. It would take a drastic reversal to give him any shot at re-election without an outright steal even greater than in 2016.

This weekend, Trump's ill-advised trade wars and their drastically negative effects on our economy, including huge stock market losses and bankrupting many farmers, are creating alarm among many of his own aides as well as the leaders of other nations at the G7 summit. A sense of panic is becoming pervasive all around. To add to this atmosphere, he has gone as far as *ordering* US companies in general to cease trading with China. This is another one of those powers he thinks he has, but does not. It is just another example of how crazed he has become. Anthony Scaramucci, one of Trump's earliest-to-leave aides, says Trump is "having a total mental breakdown—he is a full-blown lunatic." Ron Reagan Jr. on Chris Mathews' *Hardball* program says, "It's only getting worse. No previous president would get away with what Donald Trump does."

Trump's attempt to speak for Russia's readmission to the G7 and make it the G8 again got a very negative public response from European Council President Donald Tusk. Then he decided not to even attend a meeting among the members on the subject of climate change. He provided no reason for his absence other than a lie about it being scheduled later that day, when it had actually already taken place. We know the reason, of course. The subject is one he has no interest in. He is one of the many ostriches with head in the sand.

His latest harebrained idea is to use nuclear bombs to "disrupt or destroy" hurricanes. Not only would that not have the desired effect, it would probably exacerbate the force of the storm, to say nothing of the resulting radioactive fallout.

Democratic Congressmen and women have been hearing from their constituents that they are heavily in favor of the impeachment of Trump, even in a lot of RED districts.

Aug. 26-Sept. 1

During this unusually long time period with fewer than usual entries about this never-ending saga, my wife Ruth and I moved from one location in Florida to another closer to the beach, just in time to be faced with an oncoming hurricane. Between the move and the storm, we were without internet or TV service for several days, so I could not keep abreast very well with the news. Fortunately, there were no new big developments occurring in the Trump saga during this period. Here are a few relatively minor tidbits I managed to gather during this span.

With no internet or TV connection set up in the new home yet, we hooked up an ancient DVD player that we should have heaved a long ago but, fortunately held onto for no explainable reason. So we used that device to 2One of the DVDs we watched was a movie named *Thirteen Days*. It was a very realistic and accurate account of the way the Kennedy administration handled the Cuban missile crisis in 1962. It was a terrifying reminder of just how close the world came to a global nuclear holocaust during that two-week period, and how the will and courage of the Kennedy brothers to refuse to give in to the aggressive demands of the joint chiefs to take actions that would have ignited a holocaust, saved us all. I kept picturing in my mind how things would have turned out with someone like Donald Trump leading the nation during that crisis. I truly believe that, even if Trump were three times smarter and three times more experienced politically and diplomatically than he is, his narcissism alone would have prevented him from finding the path to the compromise that JFK achieved. We have been extremely lucky (so far) that neither of our very powerful and ambitious adversaries have taken advantage of our vulnerable position.

Here are the few things that I was able to get from my meager observation opportunities.

The media has had a field day over the fact that many of Trump's statements made at the recent G7 conference were composed of his usual incomprehensible, incoherent or irrelevant gibberish. He looked like a fool once again among intelligent and informed people.

Trump has ordered ICE to track down migrant children who are on expensive life-support machines, disconnect them and deport them and their families, dooming many of the kids thus affected. The level of his biased cruelty knows no bounds at all.

Trump now trails Biden by *sixteen* percentage points.

The Enemy Within: A Chronicle of the Trump Administration

Book Two (09/2018-11/2019)

September, 2019

Sept. 2-8

The main point of discussion these days is the effect Trumps' trade war with China is having on our economy. We seem to be heading inexorably toward a recession, which would certainly put an end to any chance that Trump could win re-election in 2020. The Midwest farmers, most of whom voted for him in 2016, are being badly hurt, many to the point of bankruptcy, by his policies and are turning against him. Senator Amy Klobuchar says, "The world is watching and what they're seeing is chaos."

Public outrage has caused Trump to back away from his new policy of taking migrants off life support and deport them.

Trump's latest emoluments violation is telling Pence, who was making a trip to Ireland where he has relatives, to stay at Trump's resort on the west coast of the country, instead of at a hotel in Dublin. That involved expensive flights across the country and back, at taxpayers' expense, and at the same time it put more money in Trump's pocket. They are now scrambling to find excuses for this outrage.

The House Judiciary Committee is about to start holding hearings in their investigation into Trump's hush-money payments and his lies about it.

Trump's latest indication of mental problems is his erroneous warning to the people of Alabama that they were in the path of a huge hurricane, when no weather map of Dorian's course showed it heading that far from the east coast. When his error was pointed out, he tried to explain his error. He took one of the earliest weather maps and used a black sharpie to draw his own extension into a path toward Alabama, adding insult to injury in the most childish fashion. Why is there no one in the White House these days who have the guts to try to save him from himself? Oh yeah, that's right. They have all resigned or been fired.

Trump is appropriating $30 million from various military projects and school buildings to put toward building his border wall. If this is not illegal, it should be. Congress has the power to stop this if they wanted to.

Congress is back from their summer vacation and are ready to pursue their investigations on several fronts into the Trump administration's legal problems, including some court dates.

All the Democratic candidates for 2020 are making climate change their number one issue, while the GOP continues to ignore the problem.

First, Trump did his best to avoid and delay imposing the sanctions against Russia for invading Ukraine. Then he tried, at two consecutive G7 meetings, to get Russia admitted back into that club. Now he has put on hold all financial assistance to Ukraine, at Putin's bidding. He is once again proving that he is Putin's puppet and an agent in the White House.

Trump's attempt to raid military funds to finance his wall is meeting stiff Congressional and legal resistance. The Republican Senators who have backed Trump's reallocation effort are losing a lot of their political funding and are facing stiff opposition in 2020.

The Trump administration is responding to the Democratic candidates' stand on climate change by coming up with outlandish and downright silly criticisms of their proposals.

A new addition to the issues being investigated by the House Oversight Committee is VP Pence's recent trip to Ireland, where he landed on the *west* coast and stayed at Trump's resort in Doonbeg, instead of landing at his destination in Dublin on the east coast, thus putting more cash into Trump's coffers—another clear violation of the Constitution. Pence could be charged as an accessory to this offence.

Politico reports that a C-17 is the latest of a stream of military aircraft which have landed at a small airport near Trump's resort in Scotland, which is bailing Trump out of the financial problems this property has been facing since the election.

Trump's approval rating now stands at 39% compared to a disapproval rating of 57%.

Sept. 9-15

The Washington Post reports that Trump has been pressuring Ukraine officials to dig up and report dirt on Joe Biden, whom Trump fears most as an opponent in 2020. He is using the threat of cutting off military aid to them as an inducement. This smacks of extortion or bribery.

Four states have decided to cancel their 2020 presidential primary, to avoid the bad optics of having what is now a group of three Republican opponents to Trump's nomination, with Representative from Florida, Mark Sanford now declaring to run against Trump.

The Enemy Within: A Chronicle of the Trump Administration

In North Carolina's ninth district, you may recall, there was a massive voter fraud uncovered which nullified the election in that district in 2018. A special election will be held this Tuesday so we will see if the "blue wave" is still rippling.

In an effort to try to save face for Trump in regard to his childish Hurricane Dorian weather map debacle, Commerce Secretary Ross told Neil Jacobs, Director of the National Oceanic and atmospheric Association, a Division of the National Weather Service, to back up Trump's forecast of the course of the hurricane, or be fired. A probe into this move is underway.

Refugees from the Hurricane Dorian disaster in the Bahamas were on a ferry to the USA when they were stopped and informed that unless they had a valid visa they would not be allowed to enter this country. Typical Trump policy!

We have just learned that in 2017, the US extracted one of our top spies in Russia, who had close access to Putin, because the CIA feared for his safety in view of the casual way the Trump administration treated classified information. He is now living in New York under the watchful eye of our FBI, for his protection.

The House Judiciary Committee is preparing to vote tomorrow on a proposal to initiate an official Impeachment Inquiry. Its biggest problem will be where to focus among the multitude of violations Trump has presented them with.

John Bolton, our third National Security Adviser (after Mike Flynn and H. R. McMaster), has resigned. Trump says that he was fired because of many differences of opinion, but Bolton strongly disputes that claim, and says he will be writing a blistering book that will be even more embarrassing for Trump than the several that have come out already. We are now in the dangerous position of having only the voice of Secretary of State Pompeo to try to reason with this fly-by-the-seat-of-his-pants President.

Michael Flynn's sentencing date, already postponed several times to give him more time to cooperate with the prosecution, has been set for *December 18*. He has replaced his legal team with a female conspiracy theorist. Weird!

Today is the eighteenth anniversary of the terror attack on the twin towers and Pentagon.

Several of Bolton's staff members have decided to leave with him, making our National Security Dept. an empty shell, which Trump in having a very difficult time filling. No one seems to want the job, and can you blame them. He feels he is his own best advisor and may not ever fill that position. Scary!!! Bolton has proclaimed his intent to write a tell-all book in which, "I will have my say in due course." This book is slated for next summer, just in time to have maximum impact on the election, and could make all the other tell-all books look mild. Many commentators are saying that he should speak out *now,* instead of a year from now, and they are right.

Michael Cohen is still cooperating with the Attorney General and the State Prosecutor of New York, in their ongoing case against the Trump Organization for tax fraud and illegal hush money payments.

This Thursday evening the remaining ten Democratic candidates held their third debate. It was far more orderly and interesting than the first two. The three leading in the polls, Biden, Sanders and Warren, were in the center of the row. Biden and Sanders got their fair share of the two hours, but Warren was given no questions and was pretty quiet for the first hour. She came alive in the second hour and seemed to at least hold her own. I have a feeling that she will slip back a bit in the next poll. The feistiest moment came when Julian Castro accused Biden of contradicting himself on the question of whether his proposed new Medicare for all health insurance plan would be compulsory of not. He asked Joe if he forgot what he has said two minutes ago, implying that he was reaching the age of forgetfulness. Fact checkers made Castro the forgetful one or perhaps not really grasping what Joe said. Senator Kamala Harris made a very forceful opening statement blasting Trump on several issues. She may have gained a bit. I imagine the next debate will contain three or four fewer contestants.

Trump has rolled back another of Obama's anti-pollution laws, this one affecting the cleanliness of our water supplies. It is the 85th such reduction or removal of the laws put in place by Obama and his predecessors, to help reduce the pollution problem.

Trump has been holding back funds slated for military assistance to Ukraine in its ongoing battle with Russia, but today a group of Senators, both Republican and Democrat, pushed him to free those funds up. We shall see if he complies.

The House Judiciary Committee has now voted to formalize their impeachment inquiry, which is the first step in the impeachment process. It establishes a set of rules as to how they will proceed to investigate the charges, what witnesses to call, etc.

The Trump controlled DOJ has refused to release grand jury information pertaining to any of the Trump associates who have been put on trial and anyone subpoenaed by House committees.

Sept. 16-22

Back in early October of last year, I summed up the highly controversial confirmation of Brett Kavanaugh as the new Supreme Court Justice, by pointing out that the investigations into his behavior with women were ongoing and would catch up with him in due time. Well, the chickens are now coming home to roost, as the *New York Times* has reported that their reporters have been tracking down and interviewing several people who confirmed of corroborated the charge that Kavanaugh sexually assaulted Deborah Ramirez. The sham investigation that was conducted by the Republican-controlled Congress during his confirmation fight failed to do anything like what these reporters have done, and we all knew it was a cover-up at the time. It looks like Justice Kavanaugh may be impeached before Trump is.

While he was trying desperately to find someone to replace Bolton as the National Security Advisor, Trump claimed that he has a list of fifteen people lined up to be considered. He says, "Everyone wants the job because they know how easy it is to work for Trump. I make all the decisions." Does he not know that the fact he makes all the decisions is exactly why no one wants the job. He doesn't listen to anyone, so it is a waste of time.

Saudi Arabian oil fields were bombarded by missiles this weekend and the Saudis are blaming Iran for the attack. Trump seems to be agreeing with them about who is to blame before any evidence is produced to prove who launched them.

The Enemy Within: A Chronicle of the Trump Administration

The US Air Force has openly stated that Trump's reallocation of funds from their budget to build his wall, has seriously undermined our national security.

As expected, Warren gained ground in her battle for the nomination, but surprisingly, Sanders and Harris fell back a bit, according to the post-debate poll.

The sparsity of Trump-related news we have had of late came to an end today with a triple bang. First, Adam Schiff, House Intel Committee Chairman, revealed that he just learned about a memo sent to the Inspector General of National Intelligence, by an anonymous whistleblower in the intelligence community, warning of a serious breach of security going on in the White House. Schiff requested a copy of that warning memo from our new DNI, Joseph McGuire, and was denied by McGuire, who stated that he was prohibited from releasing it to anyone by "a higher authority." There is no higher authority than the DCI other than the President. Schiff is demanding that McGuire come in and talk with his committee by this Thursday. There is an obvious cover-up going on here by our beleaguered POTUS. The question is, of what?

Second, the New York AG has subpoenaed eight years of Trump's tax returns as part of their case against the Trump Organization. What took them so long? Barr and his DOJ will not be able to stop this action by a *state* government.

Third, Trump is buying into the Saudis' claim that it was Iran who bombed their oil facilities, and is actually asking the king what they would like him to do about it. He is apparently willing to go to war with Iran if his Saudi buddies want him to. Who is running this country?

Politico reports that Trump's advisors are desperately seeking "an escape hatch" out of the Trump tariffs on

Book Two (09/2018-11/2019)

China, because they know how devastating they have been and will be on our country, especially in the Midwest. They have already cost about 300,000 jobs and this will increase to anywhere from 400k to 900k if they continue. This will almost certainly lead to a recession, or worse.

 The big event of the day was the five hour questioning of Trump's former campaign manager Cory Lewandowsky, by members of Jerry Nadler's House Judiciary Committee. When this was over, the impression among TV commentators was, "What a disgraceful circus, a clown show." The GOP members of the committee managed to reach a new low in their shameless obstruction of any attempt to conduct a normal, truth-seeking hearing. The Democratic members were pitifully unprepared and incompetent in asking the right questions or dealing with Lewandowski's evasiveness and dishonesty. The only one who seemed to know how to handle such a witness was experienced prosecutor Barry Berke. He pinned Cory down nicely with a prepared clip of him making the statement attributed to him in the Mueller report. This is one about whether or not Trump ever told him to go to AG Sessions and give him Trump's dictated statement instructing him to say that the Mueller investigation was unfair and that Trump was not guilty of any wrongdoing. Cory did his very best to avoid admitting to any such event, but he was making a liar out of himself doing it. Representative Sheila Jackson Lee of Texas said that Lewandowski should have been held in contempt of Congress. In almost every case his response to a question was, "I have been instructed by the president not to answer any questions about internal White House conversations." The claim of executive privilege is not valid in this case, and this answer, by itself, is another case of obstruction, both by Lewandowski and by Trump. Nadler opened this hearing by labeling Trump's orders to his aides to avoid answering any and all questions, "a cover-up, pure and simple."

Acting DNI McGuire has refused the request to appear before Schiff's committee on Thursday and refused to submit a copy of the whistleblower's memo about wrongdoing in the White House. A subpoena will be forthcoming but will no doubt be ignored. It is time to turn up the heat on these lawbreakers with heavy fines or imprisonment!

The federal court of appeals in New York has ruled that the case against Trump for emoluments involving Trump's hotels is valid and may proceed, overruling a lower court ruling that the plaintiffs "had no standing."

In spite of persistent pressure from both the public and the Democrats in both houses of Congress, Mitch McConnell still refuses to bring any gun control legislation to a vote until he gets approval from Trump. The entire Senate has ceded all of their coequal power to the executive branch.

Latest polls show that Warren has just about overtaken Biden in the presidential nomination race, with Sanders and Harris losing ground. This may become a two person race sooner than expected.

The *Washington Post* has reported that they have learned that the gist of that whistleblower's complaint to the Inspector General of the Intelligence community was a phone call that Trump had with a leader of an unnamed foreign power in which he made an unspecified promise to that leader, which the whistleblower deemed to have serious national security implications. The call was made on August 12 of this year, and logs show that Trump had a phone conversation with Putin on that day. That informant is now at risk, so there is a serious question as to whether he will now come forward, in light of IG McGuire's reluctance to cooperate with Congress's request for the memo or a meeting. This development may turn out to be one of the biggest blows to the Trump presidency so far.

Former prosecutor Barry Berke, who was the only questioner in the hearing with Lewandowsky yesterday who was able to make him squirm, says that the former Trump campaign chairman committed perjury during the meeting and should have been charged with Contempt of Congress in any case, because of his contemptuous attitude throughout the entire proceeding.

The whistle blower story has been revealed to be about calls to Ukraine instead of Russia. Indications are that it involves the Trump administration's attempt to get that country to investigate Biden and his son for dirt that Trump could use in the 2020 campaign. As mentioned in my report of 9/7-8, Trump threatened to withhold funds that were being provided to that country to help in its ongoing battle with Russia, if they did not comply with his request. The White House and the DOJ (Barr) are pulling out all the stops to bar any access to either the accusing memo or the writer of it or access to the Inspector General who has the memo, from seeing the light of day. It must be pretty explosive for them to use such blatant cover-up methods. They are also threatening the whistle blower, which is illegal in itself. This new bombshell could be the straw that breaks the GOP's support of Trump and its resistance to impeachment.

Rudy Giuliani and the other Trump lawyers are now trying to tell us that a president cannot even be investigated for ANY crime, much less indicted. In other words, he is above the law. This is in direct contradiction to what our

The Enemy Within: A Chronicle of the Trump Administration

Constitution was designed to prevent. They are using this preposterous argument in their suit with the AG of New York in her case against the Trump Organization and family. NO CHANCE!

The whistleblower and his memo continue to be the hot topic today, and will be for quite a while, I believe. Inspector General Michael Atkinson differs with Acting DNI Joseph McGuire on the issue of obeying the law and turning that hot memo over to the House Intel Committee Chairman, Adam Schiff. The key question is, "Did Trump's conversation with Ukraine's President amount to bribery of a foreign power?" Attempts are being made to persuade the unknown whistleblower to come forward and talk with Schiff's committee. Schiff says that they will sue the DNI if necessary to obtain that memo.

If either event takes place, it will be extremely significant. It is interesting to consider that the GOP's major issue for many years has been *national security*, but *this* issue, with its dire national security implications, has received nothing but their usual stonewall protection of Trump.

Meanwhile, Trump is calling for an investigation into Biden and his son over their activities in Ukraine in recent years, when Hunter Biden was a board member of a Ukrainian gas and oil company. This is the very subject that Trump was raising with President Zelenskyy* (about eight times, according to the transcript of one of their phone conversations).

*The double y is not a typo. He really spells his name that way.

A mammoth, globe-wide protest demonstration about climate change was held today, mostly by young people who were led by a young Swedish girl named Greta

Thunberg. The younger generation, once again, as they did on the gun-control issue, have taken the lead to try to wake us all up to the calamity that lies ahead if we continue to do nothing. As long as Republicans control the Senate, nothing is exactly what they will do.

Sept. 23-29

This weekend there were only three topics being heavily discussed on the TV airwaves. One was the continuing drama over Trump's phone conversation with the Ukrainian president in which he is alleged to have attempted to bribe Zelenskyy to investigate and accuse Hunter Biden and his dad, Trump's most feared rival for 2020, of illegal actions with a Ukrainian gas company. Several more Democrats have joined the rising voices for impeachment because of the severity of this action. Democrats from all over the country are expressing the frustration with the lack of action on the part of the party leadership in this ongoing war against the most corrupt and inept administration in our history. The GOP has of course been virtually silent on the new scandal, with exception of Congressman Amash and Trump's competitors for the nomination, Mitt Romney and Bill Weld.

The second topic was a continuation of the demand for action on the climate change crisis, spurred by that huge global protest march. Chris Hayes' show *All In* was devoted to coverage of this vital issue. It is about time that the pressure be turned up on the ostrich-like Republican Party, led by the leading denier, Trump. Unfortunately, it may already be too late to any more than delay the inevitable. The scientists are now saying that we will be feeling major changes by 2030.

The third topic is the fact that Warren now has a two point lead over Biden and is still surging. Biden will unfortunately lose ground over the Ukraine hoopla, deserved or not. Joe had better go on the offensive right now if he doesn't want to be done in by Trump's ploy. It looks like we will be down to a three person race before long.

The obvious offer of a quid pro quo ($40 million in military support for dirt on Joe Biden and son, and a visit to the White House) made by Trump to Ukrainian President Zelensky, has made a very strong impact on many Democrats, and even a few Republicans, who were on the fence about impeachment, The common feeling is that this offense by Trump is "beyond the pale" for an American president, and is impeachable on its own—worse than the Russian collusion. The event that ties the quid to the pro is the fact that Trump ordered his acting chief of staff, Mick Mulvaney, to put a hold on those funds to Ukraine just a few days before he made those phone calls to Zelenskyy looking for political help. Trump and Giuliani have themselves confirmed about seventy five percent of what has been learned about the complaint. Trump has vacillated back and forth between saying "I did it" and "I didn't do it." He seems to be completely confused about what he should or should not say, because he does not seem to know that what he did was a violation of his oath. But if that is the case, why all the furious efforts to conceal?

Nancy Pelosi says, "Bring the whistleblower in to talk with Congress or we will open impeachment proceedings." She plans to make an announcement tomorrow. This could be it!

Nancy has finally had enough! She made a short but very formal address to the nation this afternoon, in which she announced that several House committees will be devoting their energy to investigating, itemizing offenses and filing bills of impeachment against Donald Trump.

Book Two (09/2018-11/2019)

Things were already underway to some extent, but now they will go full steam ahead, officially. No more slow-walking. I may not have to write a third volume of this book.

Trump has agreed to release the whistleblower's complaint to Congress and to the public, calling it "a perfect call.". Trump has also said he will release transcripts of the July 25 phone call to the Ukrainian president, where he repeatedly asked for help in the form of an investigation of Biden and son. Surprising, and suspicious as to motive. Will they be accurate and genuine? It looks like Trump is now welcoming impeachment because he thinks a Senate acquittal is good for his re-election chances.

Schiff has been in contact with the whistleblower's lawyer, seeking his agreement to testify. Maxine Waters, Chair of the Financial Services Committee, says that "things will move along very quickly now." The acting DNI, Joseph McGuire, will appear before Congress on Thursday, to explain why he refused to release the complaint memo.

So there will be considerably more impetus for impeachment forthcoming in the next few days, and the pressure on the Republicans in the Senate will continue to mount until the public reading of the several bills of impeachment, listing Trumps crimes, puts the cherry on the cake and makes it very difficult for them to explain a NO vote to the voters, not to mention how they will be portrayed in the history books.

Trump is not the only person in trouble over the Ukraine shakedown. Giuliani, Pence and Barr are all very much involved in the bribery, as liaisons between Trump and Zelenskyy or in the cover-up of it, or both. Numerous

The Enemy Within: A Chronicle of the Trump Administration

White House personnel were also identified as participating in the concealment of the whistleblower's memo by placing it in a server reserved for top secret material only, which has only "code-word" access. The fact that they were so bent on concealing it is proof that they knew it contained evidence of wrongdoing.

Acting DNI McGuire threatened to resign if he were not allowed to speak freely in his upcoming meeting with Schiff's committee tomorrow. This is a good sign that maybe he is not a willing part of the cover-up. We will soon see.

We now know that Trump also pressed Zelenskyy to back the false theory that Russia was not the one who hacked the 2016 election. There is no end to what he will do for his puppet-master.

Acting DNI McGuire was questioned by members of Schiff's House Intel Committee. He was asked to explain why he held back the complaint memo until given the OK to release it by Trump, the *subject* of the complaint. His reply was that he needed to make sure that he was not divulging anything that came under the heading of executive privilege. This *would* make sense if the subject of the complaint were not the *president himself.* McGuire was repeatedly questioned about why he went first to the White House and then to the DOJ, which is controlled by another suspect in this whole drama—AG William Barr. It's safe to say the man did not come out smelling like a rose.

Trump's reaction to all this furor was to rail against the whistleblower and whoever fed him the information contained in his complaint, likening that person to a spy, and longing for the good old days when spies were executed. He just seems unable to refrain from making things even worse than they already are for his presidency.

Giuliani says that he should end up being the hero in this whole scandalous affair, which is both laughable and disgusting at the same time. I guess Rudy has joined Trump on some other unseen planet. There are only two heroes in this drama, and they are the unnamed whistleblower and the Inspector General of Intelligence, Atkinson, who deemed the complaint credible and important.

Trump's call to Zelenskyy is being referred to as "the smoking gun" for the impeachment trial, and there will now surely be a trial, by the members of the US Senate. During the testimony of DNI McGuire, and since then, Republicans have had little, if anything, to say in defense of that damning phone call. Presidential historian John Meacham says that, "This is the first of many more bombshells." The only thing he got wrong there is that this is far from the first of such bombshells. The impeachment bills should address each and every one of them—not just this latest one.

Those House committee chairs who are now a team preparing for impeachment, are about to issue subpoenas for Secretary of State Pompeo's ambassadors and deputies to testify before them.

Trump Special Envoy to Ukraine Kurt Volker has abruptly resigned after finding that he was mentioned in the whistleblower's complaint memo. The rats are going to noticeably speed up their departure from the sinking ship.

Fox News has largely turned against Trump these days, which should have some impact on those stubborn Trump supporters who feed off everything that Fox has to say. If they go all the way over, it will surely be the death knell for Trump.

The Enemy Within: A Chronicle of the Trump Administration

Schiff says he has arranged for a meeting with the willing male whistleblower, to be pinned down soon. This could be even bigger than Mueller's testimony.

Trump is on an insane rampage with an absurd accusation that Schiff inserted words into that explosive call to Zelenskyy. You have to be really bonkers to lie about something that has been confirmed and will be even *more* so shortly. He says he wants to meet the whistleblower. He may have his chance to before this issue is over.

There has been an incredible thirteen point swing in favor of impeachment since the whistleblower story came out. The numbers are now 55% in favor and 45 % opposed.

Beto O'Rourke becomes the first presidential candidate to call for Trump's resignation. No doubt he won't be the last. That option will look better and better to Trump if the Senate Republicans start to turn on him. Which way will he deal with the least amount of humiliation? The second one to resign the office, or the *first* one ever removed by impeachment and Senate conviction?

The Democrat team leading the impeachment inquiry has subpoenaed Rudy Giuliani for any and all documents in his possession pertaining to the Ukraine scandal. He says he has not decided yet if he will comply. It is way past time for the Democratic leadership to take legal action against those who think they can ignore these legal demands.

Secretary of State Pompeo has been traveling all over the globe trying to enlist aid to pursue this administration's crazy conspiracy theory about the origins of the Mueller investigation. He should be spending his time trying to get out from under the cloud he has placed over himself involving the Ukraine call's contents and cover-up.

Book Two (09/2018-11/2019)

Trump's tweet rhetoric has grown increasingly off-the-wall aggressive against the whistleblower and Congressman Adam Schiff. It gets more and more obvious that he is becoming even more unstable than usual.

I will conclude this explosive chapter in the Trump saga by displaying the significant "smoking gun" passages of that phone call between Trump and the Ukrainian President. Keep in mind that Trump had very recently ordered a block on the military aid the US had voted to provide Ukraine to combat the ongoing Russian invasion.

Trump: I will say that we do a lot for Ukraine. We spend a lot of effort and a lot of time. Much more than the European countries are doing and they should be helping you more than they are. Germany does almost nothing for you. All they do is talk and I think it's something that you should really ask them about. When I was speaking to Angela Merkel she talks Ukraine, but she doesn't do anything. A lot of the European countries are the same way so I think it's something you want to look at, but the United States has been very very good to Ukraine. I wouldn't say that it's reciprocal necessarily because things are happening that are not good, but the United States has been very very good to Ukraine.

Zelenskyy: Yes you are absolutely right. Not only 100%, but actually 1000% and I can tell you the following; I did talk to Angela Merkel and I did meet with her. I also met and talked with Macron and I told them that they are not doing quite as much as they need to be doing on the issues with the sanctions. They are not enforcing the sanctions. They are not working as much as they should work for Ukraine. It turns out that even though logically, the European Union should be our biggest partner but technically the United States is a much bigger partner than the European Union and I'm very grateful to you for that because the United States is doing quite a lot for Ukraine. Much more than the European Union, especially when we are talking about sanctions against the Russian Federation. I

The Enemy Within: A Chronicle of the Trump Administration

would also like to thank you for your great support in the area of defense. We are ready to continue to cooperate for the next steps. Specifically we are almost ready to buy more Javelins from the United States for defense purposes.

Trump: *I would like you to do us a favor though because our country has been through a lot and Ukraine knows a lot about it. I would like you to find out what happened with this whole situation with Ukraine, ... The server, they say Ukraine has it. There are a lot of things that went on, the whole situation. I think you're surrounding yourself with some of the same people. I would like to have the Attorney General call you or your people and I would like you to get to the bottom of it. As you saw yesterday, that whole nonsense ended with a very poor performance by a man named Robert Mueller, an incompetent performance, but they say a lot of it started with Ukraine. Whatever you can do, it's very important that you do it if that's possible.*

A little later Trump said,

"There's a lot of talk about Biden's son, that Biden stopped the prosecution (of a Ukrainian oil and gas company on which Biden was a board member, by firing Ukraine's top prosecutor—completely unsubstantiated) *and a lot of people want to find out about that, so whatever you can do with the attorney general would be great. Biden went around bagging that he stopped the prosecution, so if you could look into it, it sounds horrible to me."*

And this is the quid pro quo that is so incriminating to anyone who knows that such a request is strictly against the Constitution and US law. The coming month will go a long way toward determining the fate of the Trump administration. If he continues his thoughtless, self-destructive rants he will only succeed in speeding up the already rapid shift in our population's attitude towards his pending impeachment, which in turn will influence the attitude of those Republicans in the Senate upon whom Trump's fate depends.

Book Two (09/2018-11/2019)

October, 2019

Sept. 30-Oct.6

Mike Pompeo now admits that he was in on that fateful call between Trump and Zelenski, after previously saying that he knew nothing about it. He has been subpoenaed by Schiff and is not sure if he will honor it or not. Schiff says that the Secretary must recuse himself on anything related to that call, for conflict of interest.

Trump's latest suggestion for slowing down the "invasion of immigrants" is to either build a moat filled with alligators and snakes, or shoot them in the leg, or both.

The pressure is really taking its toll on Trump, more so than ever, as he had the most bizarre, profane, lie-laden series of rants yet, including one during a press meeting with the President of Finland, Sauli Niinistö, sitting beside him. After one particularly outrageous claim by Trump, Niinistö could not suppress a chuckle or two. His main defense against the incriminating Ukraine phone call is to attack Adam Schiff for making things up, and the whistleblower for being a partisan spy. He insists that his call was "perfect" and "beautiful." I think that there is a good chance that his complete ignorance of our laws and of our Constitution may lead him to actually believe what he is saying in this case, and maybe several others.

Later, in a separate encounter with his arch enemy, the press, he could not even answer a reporter's question, "What did you ask the Ukrainian President for." He talked about everything but the question. Someone must have warned him to avoid that subject, although it is too late because he has already "confessed" to the crime.

The Enemy Within: A Chronicle of the Trump Administration

The Washington Post reports that VP Pence was also aware of the problem with this deadly phone call, both during it and in its concealment. He not only pressured Zelenskyy in person about the Bidens, at Trump's request, but also has been traveling to other countries eliciting the same type of political help that Trump did. He is now in as much jeopardy as Giuliani and Barr. His defense, that he knew nothing about this subject, is a blatant lie.

Just to make sure that everyone understood how intent he was about getting himself impeached, Trump stood on the White House lawn today and once again called on Ukraine to investigate the corruption of Joe Biden and his son Hunter. Then, to add some frosting on the confession, he did the same thing with China as his abettor. He really does not believe there is anything wrong with this. Talk about helping to dig your own grave! We have still not seen the full text of that damning phone call, which is still locked up in that top secret server.

Kurt Volker, former US special representative to Ukraine, resigned last week amid the whistleblower scandal. Today, he became the first witness to testify in the House Democrats' impeachment inquiry of Donald Trump. He did so for over nine hours for three House committees, but behind closed doors, so we only have a few hints as to how that went. We have learned that he and another Special Envoy were sent to Ukraine by Trump a day or two after Trump's call to Zelenskyy, for the very same purpose—to push them for an investigation.

Another whistleblower came out today, this one from the Treasury Department, to reveal that someone interfered with the standard income tax audit that is conducted on all new presidents (interesting—in more ways than one). Who wants to go next?

Book Two (09/2018-11/2019)

Giuliani admits that he was the one who sent that strange packet of conspiracy data to the Congress. He doesn't explain why.

In response to subpoenas and from the testimony of Volker yesterday, dozens of text messages have been received by the House, which back up and expand upon the whistleblowers complaint. As a result, the guilt has now spread out to include VP Pence and others in the cover-up of the Ukraine shakedown. There are a lot more such texts waiting to be examined. We have just seen the tip of the iceberg.

The quid pro quo part of the offense was quite obvious with Trump's statement during the call, "I would like you to do us a favor though." But no quid pro quo was even necessary for Trump's solicitation of dirt on Biden to have been a crime. Federal Election Commission Chairwoman Ellen Weintraub today made it very clear that this is a crime, quid pro quo or not, with the following reading of the law: "It is illegal for any person to solicit, accept, or receive anything of value from a foreign national in connection with a U.S. election…Anyone who solicits or accepts foreign assistance risks being on the wrong end of a federal investigation." So the quid pro quo aspect is just adding the additional felony of extortion/bribery to the main one. The Trump defenders keep ignoring that crucial fact every time they argue about what is blatantly obvious and self-confessed.

Several important witnesses are scheduled to testify before Congress in the coming week. And now a second whistleblower on the Ukraine scandal has come forward to support the first one. We will probably be hearing from *both* shortly as soon as arrangements can be made to protect their identity,

Today, Trump lost a huge court battle when a New York judge ruled that his tax returns must be turned over by his New

York bank in response to the House subpoena. It should not be long now before we learn what he has been so desperate to hide.

As he threatened to do recently, Trump ordered the withdrawal of all our troops from Syria, without consulting any of his advisors or his allies. This will leave the Kurds at the mercy of their arch enemies the Turks. Only a few days ago Trump was on the phone with the president of Turkey, Recep Tayyip Erdogan, whom Trump seems to regard as a friend of his. Now one of our main bastions against ISIS is about to be too busy trying not to be exterminated, to be of any help with our most immediate enemy. This rash move also strengthens Iran. Even many of the president's GOP supporters are criticizing this move.

Monday, Oct. 7-Sunday, Oct. 13

Even Senator Lindsey Graham, who went from being one of Trump's strongest critics when he was a candidate for president, to being one of his most ardent supporters as president, is being quite critical of Trump's withdrawal from Syria, as have several other Republicans, both in Congress and not. This very rash and unwise new policy seems to be an attempt to mollify the Turkish president for a perceived slight he felt when Trump suddenly withdrew his invitation to the White House, and declared, "If Turkey does anything that I, in my unmatched wisdom, consider to be off limits, I will totally destroy and obliterate the Economy of Turkey (I've done it before)." His "wisdom" is unmatched alright, but not in the direction he perceives it to be. How about what the Turks are already doing, beginning the day you ordered the withdrawal?

Trump donor and appointee Gordon Sondland, former Ambassador to the European Union and current representative of our state department in Ukraine, is at the center of both the Ukraine shakedown project and the cover-up of it. He was at Trump's elbow, along with Rick Perry and the aforementioned Kurt Volker, during that damning call. They can all shed even more light on the scope of the project if they can be persuaded to talk. Sondland has been deposed by Congress.

True to form, Trump ordered Sondland not to appear, so now he is being subpoenaed.

Attorney General and Trump lapdog William Barr has been ridiculed by a federal judge when he tried to sell the Trump defense that Justice Sirica got it wrong when he ruled in the Nixon case that a president can't be subpoenaed.

Senators Harris and Blumenthal of the Senate Judiciary Committee have sent a letter to all of Trump's cabinet members demanding that they preserve ALL documentation of any kind.

Turkey has already begun its attack on the Kurds, killing hundreds on the first day. Trump's Senate supporters are very angry about it, and not just with the Turks.

Latest polls say that 51% of the voters now are in favor of Trump's Impeachment. Quite a few of his critics have still not quite reached that point yet.

Two associates and clients of Ruddy Giuliani were arrested as they were about to board a plane to leave the country with one-way tickets. Igor Fruman and Lev Parnas were apparently heavily involved in the shadowy Ukraine quid pro quo deal. This has opened Rudy up to some extensive investigation.

Trump suffered several courtroom losses today. For one, a DC appeals court ruled against him in his battle with the House Oversight Committee on the issue of his tax forms release. Then, a different court ruled against him on his border wall appropriations fight and his immigrant "indigent" rule that would require the asylum seeker to be able to support himself or herself.

The Enemy Within: A Chronicle of the Trump Administration

Sheppard Smith, who has been quite critical of Trump for a while now, abruptly left *Fox News* saying he has seen enough of the channel's defense of the indefensible. Why would a decent man like him ever work for *Fox News* to begin with?

Fiona Hill, President Donald Trump's former top Russia adviser, will explain to Congress when she testifies on Monday, the 14th, that she was unaware of some aspects of the escalating Syrian problem, according to a source close to Hill who spoke to her Thursday. Hill has been subpoenaed and is working with her lawyer on logistics. She officially departed her role in August, though she had handed over most of her responsibilities in July, but was involved as Rudy Giuliani was making public pronouncements about Ukraine. She has kept a low profile in recent weeks in England with her mother.

But the biggest bomb to fall on Trump since the first whistleblower came out, is a lady named Marie Yovanovitch, a former U.S. ambassador to Ukraine who was abruptly ordered back to the US a few months ago. She testified Friday and told lawmakers that she was "incredulous" that the government had cut short her term as ambassador, "based, as best as I can tell, on unfounded and false claims by people with clearly questionable motives." Below, I have reproduced, verbatim, most of her opening statement, which I believe will be the "coup de gras" of the Trump presidency. She has made herself the Joan of Arc of the fight against this attempt to subvert our entire Constitution.

"Thank you for the opportunity to start with this statement today.

"For the last 33 years, it has been my great honor to serve the American people as a Foreign Service Officer, over six Administrations—four Republican, and two Democratic. I have served in seven different countries, five of them hardship posts, and was appointed to serve as an ambassador three times—twice by a Republican President, and once by a Democrat.

Book Two (09/2018-11/2019

Throughout my career, I have stayed true to the oath that Foreign Service Officers take and observe every day: "...that I will support and defend the Constitution of the United States against all enemies, foreign and domestic;" and "that I will bear true faith and allegiance to the same." Like all foreign service officers with whom I have been privileged to serve, I have understood that oath as a commitment to serve on a strictly nonpartisan basis, to advance the foreign policy determined by the incumbent President, and to work at all times to strengthen our national security and promote our national interests.

... (personal background)

"From August 2016 until May 2019, I served as the U.S. Ambassador to Ukraine. Our policy, fully embraced by Democrats and Republicans alike, was to help Ukraine become a stable and independent democratic state, with a market economy integrated into Europe.

Ukraine is a sovereign country, whose borders are inviolate and whose people have the right to determine their own destiny. These are the bedrock principles of our policy. Because of Ukraine's geostrategic position bordering Russia on its east, the warm waters of the oil-rich Black Sea to its south, and four NATO allies to its west, it is critical to the security of the United States that Ukraine remain free and democratic and that it continue to resist Russian expansionism.

"Russia's purported annexation of Crimea, its invasion of Eastern Ukraine, and its de facto control over the Sea of Azov, make clear Russia's malign intentions towards Ukraine. If we allow Russia's actions to stand, we will set a precedent that the United States will regret for decades to come.

... (history)

"The Revolution of Dignity, and the Ukrainian people's demand to end corruption, forced the new Ukrainian government to take measures to fight the rampant corruption that long permeated that country's political and economic systems. We have long understood that strong anti-corruption efforts must form an essential part of our policy in Ukraine; now there was a window of opportunity to do just that.

... (discussion of Ukraine's corruption)

"But change takes time, and the aspiration to instill rule-of-law values has still not been fulfilled. Since 2014, Ukraine has been at war, not just with Russia, but within itself, as political and economic forces compete to determine what kind of country Ukraine will become: the same old, oligarch-dominated Ukraine where corruption is not just prevalent, but is the system? Or the country that Ukrainians demanded in the Revolution of Dignity—a country where rule of law is the system, corruption is tamed, and people are treated equally and according to the law?

"During the 2019 presidential elections, the Ukrainian people answered that question once again. Angered by insufficient progress in the fight against corruption, Ukrainian voters overwhelmingly elected a man who said that ending corruption would be his number one priority. The transition, however, created fear among the political elite, setting the stage for some of the issues I expect we will be discussing today.

"Understanding Ukraine's recent history, including the significant tension between those who seek to transform the country and those who wish to continue profiting from the old ways, is of critical importance to understanding the events you asked me here today to describe. Many of those events—and the false narratives that emerged from them—resulted from an unfortunate alliance between Ukrainians who continue to operate within a corrupt system, and Americans who either did not understand that corrupt system, or who may have chosen, for their own purposes, to ignore it. It seems obvious, but bears stating, that when dealing with officials from any country—or those claiming connections to officialdom—one must understand their background, their personal interests, and what they hope to get out of a particular interaction before deciding how to evaluate their description of events or acting on their information.

Book Two (09/2018-11/2019)

"To be clear, Ukraine is filled with many citizens and officials who want the very things we have always said we want for the United States: a government that acts in the interests of its people; 'government of the people, by the people and for the people.' The overwhelming support for President Zelenskyy in April's election proved that. And it was one of our most important tasks at the embassy in Kyiv to understand and act upon the difference between those who sought to serve their people and those who sought to serve only themselves.

"With that background in mind, I would like to briefly address some of the specific issues raised in the press that I anticipate you may ask me about today.

I arrived in Ukraine on August 22, 2016 and left Ukraine permanently on May 20, 2019. Several of the events with which you may be concerned occurred before I was even in country. Here are just a few:

• The release of the so-called "Black Ledger" [A ledger kept by Manafort while he was intimately involved with the corrupt president of Ukraine and several oligarchs, before the revolution produced the election of Zelenskyy.] and Mr. Manafort's subsequent resignation from the Trump campaign;

• The Embassy's April 2016 letter to the Prosecutor General's Office about the investigation into the Anti-Corruption Action Center or AntAC; and

• The departure from office of former Prosecutor General Viktor Shokin.

"Several other events occurred after I was recalled from Ukraine. These include:

• President Trump's July 25 call with President Zelenskyy;

• All of the discussions surrounding that phone call; and any discussions surrounding the reported delay of security assistance to Ukraine in summer 2019.

•As for events during my tenure in Ukraine, I want to categorically state that I have never myself or through others, directly or indirectly, ever directed, suggested, or in any other way asked for any government or government official in

Ukraine (or elsewhere) to refrain from investigating or prosecuting actual corruption. As Mr. Lutsenko, the former Ukrainian Prosecutor General has recently acknowledged, the notion that I created or disseminated a "do not prosecute" list is completely false—a story that Mr. Lutsenko, himself, has since retracted.

- Equally fictitious is the notion that I am disloyal to President Trump. I have heard the allegation in the media that I supposedly told the Embassy team to ignore the President's orders "since he was going to be impeached." That allegation is false. I have never said such a thing, to my Embassy colleagues or to anyone else.
- Next, the Obama administration did not ask me to help the Clinton campaign or harm the Trump campaign, nor would I have taken any such steps if they had.
- I have never met Hunter Biden, nor have I had any direct or indirect conversations with him. And although I have met former Vice President Biden several times over the course of our many years in government, neither he nor the previous Administration ever, directly or indirectly, raised the issue of either Burisma or Hunter Biden with me. [Burisma is the oil and gas extraction company that Hunter Biden was associated with]
- With respect to Mayor Giuliani, I have had only minimal contacts with him—a total of three that I recall. None related to the events at issue. I do not know Mr. Giuliani's motives for attacking me. But individuals who have been named in the press as contacts of Mr. Giuliani may well have believed that their personal financial ambitions were stymied by our anti-corruption policy in Ukraine.
- Finally, after being asked by the Department in early March to extend my tour until 2020, I was then abruptly told in late April to come back to Washington from Ukraine "on the next plane." You will understandably want to ask why my posting ended so suddenly. I wanted to learn that too, and I tried to find out. I met with the Deputy Secretary of State, who informed me of the curtailment of my term. He said that the President had lost confidence in me and no longer wished me to serve as his

ambassador. He added that there had been a concerted campaign against me, and that the Department had been under pressure from the President to remove me since the summer of 2018. He also said that I had done nothing wrong and that this was not like other situations where he had recalled ambassadors for cause.

"I departed Ukraine for good this past May. Although I understand that I served at the pleasure of the President, I was nevertheless incredulous that the U.S. government chose to remove an Ambassador based, as best as I can tell, on unfounded and false claims by people with clearly questionable motives. To make matters worse, all of this occurred during an especially challenging time in bilateral relations with a newly elected Ukrainian president. This was precisely the time when continuity in the Embassy in Ukraine was most needed.

"Before I close, I must share the deep disappointment and dismay I have felt as these events have unfolded. I have served this nation honorably for more than 30 years. I have proudly promoted and served American interests as the representative of the American people and six different presidents over the last three decades. Throughout that time, I—like my colleagues at the State Department—have always believed that we enjoyed a sacred trust with our government.

"We make a difference every day on issues that matter to the American people—whether it is war and peace, trade and investment, or simply helping with a lost passport. We repeatedly uproot our lives, and we frequently put ourselves in harm's way to serve this nation. And we do that willingly, because we believe in America and its special role in the world. We also believe that, in return, our government will have our backs and protect us if we come under attack from foreign interests". [And here is the crème de la crème.]

"That basic understanding no longer holds true. Today, we see the State Department attacked and hollowed out from within. State Department leadership, with Congress, needs to take action now to defend this great institution, and its

thousands of loyal and effective employees. We need to rebuild diplomacy as the first resort to advance America's interests and the front line of America's defense. I fear that not doing so will harm our nation's interest, perhaps irreparably. That harm will come not just through the inevitable and continuing resignation and loss of many of this nation's most loyal and talented public servants. It also will come when those diplomats who soldier on and do their best to represent our nation, face partners abroad who question whether the ambassador truly speaks for the President and can be counted upon as a reliable partner. The harm will come when private interests circumvent professional diplomats for their own gain, not the public good. The harm will come when bad actors in countries beyond Ukraine see how easy it is to use fiction and innuendo to manipulate our system. In such circumstances, the only interests that will be served are those of our strategic adversaries, like Russia, that spread chaos and attack the institutions and norms that the U.S. helped create and which we have benefited from for the last 75 years.

"I am proud of my work in Ukraine. The U.S. Embassy, under my leadership, represented and advanced the policies of the United States government as articulated, first by the Obama Administration and then by the Trump Administration. Our efforts were intended, and evidently succeeded, in thwarting corrupt interests in Ukraine, who fought back by selling baseless conspiracy theories to anyone who would listen. Sadly, someone was listening, and our nation is the worse off for that.

Thank you for your attention. I welcome your questions."

And thank you, Ms. Yovanovitch, for having the courage to tell it like it is to those who need to listen, and act accordingly.

Oct. 14-Oct.20

The week began with Dr. (PHD) Fiona Hill testifying to the House committee for over nine hours. Ms. Yovanovitch was an impossible act to follow, but Hill impressed the lawmakers so much that one of them said as he left the hearing room, "That

Book Two (09/2018-11/2019)

was the best witness I have ever seen." She not only confirmed everything that her fellow envoy had said on Friday, but also filled in a lot of details.

Meanwhile, while Hill was so busy, Trump finally realized what a stupid mistake he had made, due to the outrage of even his Senate supporters, when he pulled the troops out of Syria, that he tried to stuff the genie back in the bottle by putting sanctions on Turkey and getting on the phone with the Turkish leader to try to get him under control. No effect!

The parade of Ukraine-related officials who defied Trump's block and appeared before Congress to tell what they knew about the illegitimate negotiations that Trump, Giuliani and crew were conducting, continued on a daily basis. On Tuesday, it was George Kent, deputy assistant secretary at the State Department. On Wednesday it was Michael McKinley, who recently resigned as top adviser to Secretary of State Mike Pompeo, over his bosses actions during the past few weeks. On Thursday it was top Ukraine diplomat Gordon Sondland. They all had nothing but praise for Friday's star witness Marie Yovanovitch.

Our former National Security Advisor, war hawk John Bolton, when asked about his role, if any, in the Ukraine quid pro quo sandal, said, "I won't be part of that drug deal", and "Rudy Giuliani is a hand grenade."

On Tuesday evening twelve Democrat presidential candidates debated on the same packed stage, and all were in agreement,--the president must be impeached and removed from office for the salvation of our democracy. The new front-runner, Elizabeth Warren, came under attack by most of her competition, and the consensus was split as to how well she handled it. The standouts of the night were Pete Buttigieg and Amy Klobuchar. It will be interesting to see what the next polls show. We need to get down to about half this many candidates before the next debate. My bet is that they will include: Warren, Biden, Sanders, Harris, Buttigieg and Klobuchar.

Giuliani, Pence, the Pentagon, and the Office of Management and Budget all claim that they will not comply with their subpoenas to appear, or produce the requested documents. It is past time to start charging these people, who are thumbing their nose at the law, with contempt of Congress and arresting them. The SDNY has its sights set on Giuliani even more since his two cohorts, Lev Parnas and Igor Fruman, were arrested. Rudy needs a good lawyer. He may turn out to be the most important "flipper" yet.

Trump's latest self-inflicted and probably fatal wound, his turning tail from Syria, has caused such a furor even among his own party, that he felt forced to phone Turkey's President Erdogan and practically beg him to call off his troops who were on a quest to wipe out the Kurds. He did manage to get Erdogan to call a temporary cease fire while they tried to work something out, but that is not working very well, as sporadic fighting and shelling is still going on. Then Trump sent the following threatening letter to Erdogan.
"Let's work out a good deal! You don't want to be responsible for slaughtering thousands of people, and I don't want to be responsible for destroying the Turkish economy – and I will. History will look upon you favorably if you get this done the right and humane way, It will look upon you forever as the devil if good things don't happen. Don't be a tough guy. Don't be a fool! I will call you later."
It is no surprise that the Turkish president did not react kindly to this juvenile attempt at high-level bullying.

The combination of several different pressures has brought Trump to the point of complete meltdown, as evidenced by his behavior in a hastily-called meeting at the White House of about twenty-five assorted White House, Congressional and

Book Two (09/2018-11/2019

military personnel. Trump entered the room, slammed down a stack of documents, and proceeded to lash out at everyone and everything like a petulant third-grader, resulting in everyone walking out of the meeting very prematurely. At one point during this brief meeting, Pelosi stood up, pointed at Trump, and said, "All roads with you lead to Putin." A camera caught this scene and it shows Trump looking like a scolded schoolboy, while the other attendees, especially the military ones, slumped into their chairs looking embarrassed. Several participants later said the he is "spiraling out of control." He may end up in a mental institution instead of prison. Every day now, events and words give Trump's supporters in Congress more reason to re-evaluate their level of allegiance to him. It is hard to see how the dam cannot continue to hold much longer. Scaramucci says that he believes that at least twenty Republican Senators are ready to flip on Trump in the impeachment vote. My estimate of the chances of that happening has risen from about ten to twenty percent, to more like fifty to sixty percent. The fear of impeachment and probable subsequent imprisonment, has made him more unbalanced and more dangerous than ever. It looks like Trump will face one of three possible fates: resign, be the first president to be removed via impeachment, or be removed via invocation of the 25th amendment.

On Thursday, Trump's Chief-of-staff, Mick Mulvaney, answering a reporter's question about the Ukrainian deal, admitted that, *"Sure there was a quid pro quo, politicians do that all the time. Get over it."* He then got his ass chewed out by Trump, so had to come back later in the day and try to walk it back—not very successfully. There has been an immense amount of puzzlement as to how a savvy guy like Mulvaney could make such a blunder. I think it is simply a case of, what kind of quid pro quo he was talking about? It is true that politicians at all levels use the art of "give and take" when negotiating a deal. That is how very important treaties are made.

The Enemy Within: A Chronicle of the Trump Administration

There is nothing wrong with the basic concept of a quid pro quo, *except when one of the things being bartered is unethical or illegal, or the trade is being coerced.* That is the point that both Trump and Mulvaney seem to turn a blind eye to. Soliciting or accepting help from a foreign power for aid of any kind in an election is prohibited by the same emoluments clause that prohibits him from profiting from his many properties, and when you use extortion to get what you are seeking, you more than double the offense.

Also on Thursday, Representative Elijah Cummings passed away after a long battle with various problems which produced complications. The TV airwaves were largely devoted to tributes to him and to a review of his life and service.

Pelosi and four other Congresspersons made a sudden trip to Jordan to try to introduce some sanity into the Syrian-Turkish-Kurd fiasco that Trump has created. It is unclear as to the effect, if any, except for Trump's fury over her "interference".

Trump topped off a very bad week by adding a huge new emoluments offense to the mountain of such offenses already stacked up against him. He claimed that, after considering a dozen possible locations for the next G7 meeting, scheduled for somewhere in the USA, he decided that the most appropriate place to host it was his own resort in Dural Florida. His "generous offer" to only charge for coverage of his costs, in no way lessens this outrageous money grab.

Out of the blue, Trump decided to trash one of his favorite military targets, former CIA Director John Brennon, calling him "vastly overrated." Brennon was quick to respond with some witty remarks that put Trump in his place. A short time later, another military legend, Trump's short-time Secretary of Defense, James Mattis, gave his own opinion of how badly this president has miss-played just about every foreign policy decision he has made during his three years as our Commander-

Book Two (09/2018-11/2019)

in-Chief. To make it a trifecta of blows from his ex-military appointments, General Barry McCaffrey, strongly condemned Trump's Syria cut-and-run.

On Saturday afternoon, after two full days of condemnation, from pretty nearly everyone on the planet, Trump caved in once again and retracted his plan to hold the G7 conference on his own property. Will he ever learn to think a bit before he decides to take rash action or shoot his mouth off?

The latest poll shows that 63% of Americans believe Trump must cooperate with the impeachment investigation.

Oct. 21-27

Every time you think that our president has sunken as far as he can possibly go in his complete disrespect and disregard for the Constitution he swore to protect, preserve and defend on January 20, 2016, he manages to find a way to sink even lower. Today, irked by having to back down on his plan to further pad his bankbook by hosting the G7 conference at his Dural Florida resort, he called the emoluments clause "illegitimate" and "invalid." Then he added that the impeachment section is equally invalid. If he had his way, he would rewrite the document to his own liking. But he is finding out that he does not have that power—he is not the king! How can the Republican Senators fail to see how dangerously dictatorial he has become?

The State Department investigation into Clinton's email use has concluded, finding "no deliberate miscommunication found." Case finally closed.

On Tuesday, William Taylor, the very experienced diplomat who replaced Marie Yovanovitch when she was recalled from Ukraine by Trump, testified all day before Schiff's committee. His opening statement alone, which was even more revealing than hers, was enough to make it unnecessary to even go into a question and answer session, except to give the Republican lawmakers a chance to try to diminish the impact, if they could. The quid pro quo was an open and shut case already, but Taylor put the frosting on the cake. This has become much more than just your average "smoking gun." Here are some of the highlights which followed a lengthy description of this diplomat's experience in service to our country.

"...As the Committees are aware, I said on September 9 in a message to Ambassador Gordon Sondland that withholding security assistance in exchange for help with a domestic political campaign in the United States would be 'crazy'. I believed that then, and I still believe that.

"...Ukraine is special for me. And Secretary Pompeo's offer to return as Chief of Mission was compelling. I am convinced of the profound importance of Ukraine to the security of the United States and Europe for two related reasons: First, if Ukraine succeeds in breaking free of Russian influence, it is possible for Europe to be whole, free, democratic, and at peace. In contrast, if Russia dominates Ukraine, Russia will again become an empire, oppressing its people, and threatening its neighbors and the rest of the world.

"...I worried about what I had heard concerning the role of Rudy Giuliani, who had made several high-profile statements about Ukraine and US policy toward the country. So during my meeting with Secretary Pompeo on May 28, I made it clear to him and the others present that if the U.S. policy toward Ukraine changed, he would not want me posted there and I could not stay. He assured me that the policy of strong support for Ukraine would continue and that he would support me in defending that policy.

"...But once I arrived in Kyiv, I discovered a weird combination of encouraging, confusing, and ultimately alarming circumstances.

"...I found a confusing and unusual arrangement for making U.S. policy toward Ukraine. There appeared to be two channels

Book Two (09/2018-11/2019

of U.S. policy-making and implementation, one regular and one highly irregular. As the Chief of Mission, I had authority over the regular, formal diplomatic processes... At the same time, however, there was an irregular, informal channel of U.S. policy-making with respect to Ukraine, one that included then-Special Envoy Kurt Volker, Ambassador Sondland, Secretary of Energy Rick Perry, and as I subsequently learned, Rudy Giuliani. I was clearly in the regular channel, but I was also in the irregular one to the extent that Ambassadors Volker and Sondland included me in certain conversations. ...On June 27, Ambassador Sondland told me during a phone conversation that President Zelenskyy needed to make clear to President Trump that he, President Zelenskyy, was not standing in the way of "investigations." I sensed something odd when Ambassador Sondland told me on June 28 that he did not wish to include most of the interagency participants in a call planned with President Zelenskyy later that day. ...By mid-July it was becoming clear to me that the meeting President Zelenskyy wanted was conditioned on the investigations of Burisma and alleged Ukrainian interference in the 2016 U.S. election. It was also clear that this condition was driven by the irregular policy channel I had come to understand was guided by Mr. Giuliani. "...In the same July 19 phone all, they gave me an account of a July 10 meeting with the Ukrainian officials at the White House. Specifically, they told me that Ambassador Sondland had connected "investigations" with an Oval Office meeting for President Zelenskyy, which so irritated Ambassador Bolton that he abruptly ended the meeting, telling Dr. Hill and Mr. Vindman that they should have nothing to do with civilian politics. He also directed Dr. Hill to 'brief the lawyers." Dr. Hill said that Ambassador Bolton referred to this as a 'drug deal' after the July 10 meeting. Ambassador Bolton opposed a call between President Zelenskyy and President Trump out of concern that it 'would be a disaster'.

" ...On July 25 President Trump and President Zelenskyy had the long-awaited phone conversation. Strangely, even though I was Chief of Mission and was scheduled to meet with President Zelenskyy along with Ambassador Volker the following day, I received no readout of the call from the White House. The Ukrainian government issued a short, cryptic summery.

"...On August 16, I exchanged text messages with Ambassador Volker in which I learned that Mr. Yermak had asked that the U.S. submit an official request for an investigation into Burisma's alleged violations of Ukrainian law, if that is what the United States desired. A formal U.S. request to the Ukrainians to conduct an investigation based on violations of their own law struck me as improper, and I recommended to Ambassador Volker that we 'stay clear.'

"...My concerns deepened on August 22, during a phone conversation with Mr. Morrison [Tim Morrison, who helms the National Security Council's Eurasia desk]. I asked him if there had been a change in policy of strong support for Ukraine, to which he responded, 'it remains to be seen.' He also told me during this call that the 'President doesn't want to provide any assistance at all.' That was extremely troubling to me. As I had told Secretary Pompeo in May, if the policy of strong support for Ukraine were to change, I would have to resign."

"...During this same phone call with Mr. Morrison, he went on to describe a conversation Ambassador Sondland had with Mr. Yermak at Warsaw. *Ambassador Sondland told Mr. Yermak that the security assistance money would not come until President Zelenskyy committed to pursue the Burisma investigation....This was the first time that the security assistance—not just the White House meeting—was conditioned on the investigation.*"

These excerpts from Taylor's testimony are more icing on the cake of the "smoking gun."

The Democrats are focusing on the "abuse of power" charge so far in their impeachment inquiry. I hope they are including *all* of the cases where he has abused his power, not just the Ukraine shakedown.

Book Two (09/2018-11/2019

On Wednesday, we met the Deputy Assistant to the Secretary of Defense, Laura Cooper, the first Pentagon official to defy Trump's order to refuse to comply with any and all subpoenas. She was in a committee hearing room testifying before the House Intel Committee, composed of Republicans as well as Democrats, when a group of twenty or so Republican Congressmen, led by Florida's Matt Gaetz, forced their way into the hearing room and disrupted the proceedings, causing a several hour delay. Some were carrying cell phones, which were prohibited in the top security SCIF where the hearing was being held. They were soon forced to obey the law and leave. They should face legal action, but they won't. This was a juvenile and disgraceful stunt, a scene straight out of the movie, *Animal House,* done at the behest of the panicking president. They say they did this in protest against "the unfair secret and exclusive manner in which the Democrats have been holding the recent string of testimony hearings, but no such hearings are held without representation from *both* sides being present and asking the questions.

In the courtroom where Giuliani's henchmen, Lev Parnas and Igor Fruman, were being processed, arguments being made by their lawyers once again entered the world of the absurd and downright crazy. Under prodding by the incredulous judge, they confirmed their belief that a president is immune from even *investigation* or apprehension for ANY crime, up to and including mass murder. This is exactly what Trump believes—the man in control of the nuclear codes and that all-important red button. Anybody sleeping well these days?

Ambassador Sondland is now in legal jeopardy for perjury, after being convincingly contradicted by Taylor about his knowledge of the shadow policy being run in Ukraine.

The Enemy Within: A Chronicle of the Trump Administration

Trump has just lost another court case about the so-called "immunity" for his tax returns. Of course they keep on moving to the appeals courts, and will probably end up in the Supreme Court where Chief Justice Roberts will have the deciding vote.

On Thursday, Trump's number one lawyer/supporter/puppet, our shamefully biased Attorney General William Barr, has now opened an official criminal investigation into the "oranges" (as Trump pronounces it) of the Russia investigation and subsequent Mueller report. With the assistance of U.S. Attorney John Durham, he has started traveling around the globe, beginning in Italy, looking for government officials of other countries who might have some sort of ammunition to support his crazy conspiracy theory, without any success of course. There seems to be nothing this man won't stoop to in support of his boss, the phony president. If any other law-enforcement official tried to open a criminal investigation without evidence or cause of any kind, he/she would be reined in by their superiors. But who reins in the Attorney General of the U.S. other than the President? And what do you do when it is the President that has "suggested" such an investigation?

The Democrats say they will begin holding *public* impeachment hearings in which some of the explosive witnesses will be recalled, sometime in November. This will certainly be "must watch TV."

Senator Lindsey Graham says that he has studied the transcript of the call between Trump and Zelenskyy, and "It is ok with me." He may be sorry he said that at some point down the line.

While the Turkish and Russian leaders get together to discuss a fair way to carve up their newly won territory in Syria that they gained as result of Trump's troop pull-out, Trump goes on TV to brag about "what a huge victory he just pulled off that no previous administration could achieve." Our former

Book Two (09/2018-11/2019

allies against ISIS, the Kurds, meanwhile are yelling "betrayal" as they are fighting for their lives.

On Friday, Trump suffered his most important court defeat yet, when Federal Judge Beryl Howell ruled that the impeachment process underway by the House Democrats was *not* "invalid" as the Republicans tried to claim. She also ruled that the grand jury data in the Mueller investigation must be released to that inquiry. This was the administration's last gasp attempt at defense, as they are completely unable to challenge the facts that Trump has stacked against him, on several fronts.

Many cities across the U.S. have announced that Trump owes them very large bills for his rallies and other types of visits. Good luck trying to collect, folks.

Giuliani's latest humiliation comes from two "butt-dialed" phone calls which were recorded and contained some embarrassing and maybe incriminating words.

Today, it was Thomas Reeker, American diplomat and career foreign service officer with the Department of State who currently serves as Acting Assistant Secretary of State in the Bureau of European and Eurasian Affairs, who testified all day before the House impeachment investigating committee. He no doubt provided even more corroboration to those who have gone before him and dug Trump's legal hole a little deeper.

There is a new tell-all book coming out soon, by the anonymous author of the now famous *New York Times* op-ed article by the same unknown writer. It is titled *A Warning,* and the author seems to be someone who was pretty high in the White House. My guess is—John Kelly, who has said that the day he left the White House as Trump's COS, he "warned" him not to hire a yes-man to replace him or he would be impeached.

The Enemy Within: A Chronicle of the Trump Administration

We woke up Sunday morning to the news that our Special Forces had conducted a night raid on a tunnel in Syria and succeeded in taking out the current leader (at Osama Bin Laden's level) of ISIS, Abu Bakr al-Baghdadi. Trump addressed the nation at 9:30 A.M. to brag about this accomplishment, as though it was all his doing, giving some praise to the brave men who conducted the raid but no credit to the intelligence agencies who tracked Baghdadi's movements, and who were not even kept in the loop about the raid. They, in turn, said that this raid was a success not *because* of Trump, but in *spite* of his foolish troop pullout move.

Trump says that he will keep enough of our troops in Syria to guard the oil, because "to the victor belong the spoils." This confirms our country's motive for being there in the first place.

Trump and Ivanka attended a World Series game today and when the camera showed them on the big screen, he was roundly booed amid chants of "Lock him up." Only in America, and only for this unprecedented President.

November, 2019

Oct. 28-Nov. 3

The week began with new White House press secretary Stephanie Gresham, making one of the most laughable statements yet by one of Trump's mouthpieces. Speaking about former COS General John Kelly's upcoming new book, she said that Kelly, "…was not equipped to deal with the genius of someone like Trump."

On Tuesday, Schiff's committee took the testimony of yet another witness to the shadow policy going on in Ukraine at the time that the now infamous July 25 phone call was made. A national security expert advisor to the National Security Council assigned to Ukraine, *current* Director Lt. Colonel Alexander Vindman, who was actually on that call, released an opening statement that was just as damning as those from Yovanovitch, Hill and Taylor, and *this man is risking his job to speak up.* Like the others, the actual question and answer period, **conducted by both Democrats and Republicans***,* was closed to the public, but I'm sure we will learn some additional highlights from that testimony. The Republicans in Congress will have no luck at trying to muddy the background or reputation of this witness, and have run out of ways to try to defend this president. They gave up trying to dispute the facts of the case a while ago and argued against the "process". Then the judge ruled the process legitimate, so the only thing they have left is to try to impugn the witnesses, but these recent witnesses are far above reproach. They are some of this nations heroes, even before they defied a presidential order to keep their mouth shut. Pelosi has announced the plan to take an official vote of the House on Thursday, on the adoption of the plan format for the impeachment of President Trump.

The Enemy Within: A Chronicle of the Trump Administration

Among Vindman's testimony were the very damaging revelations about edits made to the summary of the July 25 phone call, done to omit some comments about Biden and son—more evidence for the cover-up. Vindman says, "I am not the whistleblower", so the Republicans on the committee spent most of their question-time trying to get him to name who was, unsuccessfully. In his opening statement, released to the public, was his alert to two levels of State Department officials that he was very concerned about what he had heard on that phone call between Trump and Zelenskyy.

It seems that not only were most of our intel community kept out of the loop about the raid to kill the ISIS leader, Trump's COS Mulvaney was not even aware of it until it was under way. He must be still in Trump's doghouse since that weird and embarrassing press conference admission about the quid pro quo.

The Democrats are preparing to present their resolution which defines their procedure for the upcoming impeachment vote—this Thursday. It defines the rules that will control this process, giving equal time to both parties for comments and questions. It is basically the same wording as the roadmap which was used in the Nixon and Clinton cases. History in the making and to a large extent, repeating itself.

Meanwhile, there are *two* forest fires raging in California (again), forcing many homes to be evacuated while many more are being destroyed. This is what our future looks like all over the world unless we can turn back the tide of climate change, formerly referred to as "global warming."

On Wednesday, Christopher Anderson and Catherine Croft testified before the House Committee. They further corroborated the testimony of the previous witnesses like Vindman, Taylor and Yovanovitch. Anderson was a senior State Department official working in Ukraine under Kurt

Volker. In all this testimony over the past two weeks, the only discrepancy pointed out so far involves pro-Trump statements by Sondland that are contradicted by Taylor and Vindman and may lead to perjury charges.

John Bolton has been asked to testify. He says that he will not do it voluntarily, but *would* obey a subpoena. One will likely be forthcoming.

On Thursday, yet another witness defied Trump's block. NSC official Tim Morrison testified after resigning from his job the previous day as an additional statement against the Trump administration. Morrison did this on the day that a hugely historic vote was taken by the full House of Representatives on whether to accept the resolution spelling out the rules and procedures to be followed during the filing of bills of impeachment. That passed by a vote of 232-196, with no Republicans voting for it and two Democrats voting against it. Thus, a major step forward was taken in the long, careful process of putting a US president on trial.

On Friday's *All In* show, Chris Hayes showed a dozen or so video clips of Trump's Congressional allies stating that there was "no quid pro quo" in Trump's disputed phone call with Ukraine's President Zelenskyy, but if there had been, they all agreed they would have a *different* opinion of the case. Hayes then proceeded to list nine different pieces of evidence that it was indeed a case of quid pro quo; evidence which included the testimony of nearly every witness before the House committee over the past two weeks.

Last week, Tim Ryan dropped out of the presidential race (most people were not even aware that he was in it), and now Beto O'Rourke has given up the quest as well. The field has finally begun to shrink.

The Enemy Within: A Chronicle of the Trump Administration

Rick Perry, Trump's former Secretary of Energy, has been subpoenaed to testify to Congress next week. Odds are, he will resist. He, together with Sondland and Volker, have been given the name. "The Three Amigos". Next Monday, John Eisenberg, the main lawyer for the State Department embassy group in Ukraine that we have become so acquainted with lately, will appear to provide *his* version of what went on with that infamous phone call. John Bolton has agreed to a hearing next Thursday, if subpoenaed. That could provide the cherry on top of the icing on the cake that has already been provided by the recent parade of witnesses.

Pelosi says that open hearings *will* begin next week. At that point, things begin to get *really* serious.

The court has released a ton of documents from the grand jury discussions made during the Mueller probe, and they have provided quite a bit of new information for the House committees to consider.

Trump has been talking about having an FDR-like fireside chat, to read the full transcript of the phone conversation with Zelenskyy that has him in such a big vat of hot water. This would be very interesting to listen to, but I doubt very much that he will actually go through with it. Someone will surely convince him of how self-incriminating that would be. Even *he* cannot be that stupid.

On Sunday, he went on one of his patented tweet rampages and attacked every one of his perceived enemies, including the heavily decorated Lt. Colonel Vindman, using seventy-five tweets or retweets. He called Adam Schiff a shifty freak. He does this every time he feels the walls closing in a little tighter.

Nov 4-10

This week began with two significant developments, one good and one bad. The good one, for everyone but Donald

Trump, was the release of the full transcripts of several of the witnesses from the Ukrainian embassy who testified over the past two weeks. Among the most revealing of them were those showing the real reason that Marie Yovanovitch so suddenly left and returned to the US. The early morning call she received telling her to take the next plane home, was *not* because she was being discharged from her position. It was a warning that her life was in danger. She had already been subjected to several threats from people close to the president and from Trump himself, at least indirectly—all because she was showing her unwillingness to participate in the shadow campaign to pressure Zelenskyy to do Trump's bidding.

The bad one was the reluctance for any of the witnesses who were scheduled to testify *this week* to appear. Schiff says they will include this obstruction as another article of impeachment.

Rudy Giuliani is still, while under serious investigation for his part in the Ukraine scandal, continuing to push Ukraine for its cooperation with Trump's demands.

One of the two Giuliani associates who are out on bail right now has agreed to cooperate with the prosecution. Rudy should be very worried. Lev Parnas was paying Rudy's very large salary that he was not charging Trump for being his lawyer. Where was the money actually coming from?

A New Federal Appeals court has ruled against Trump about release of his tax returns. He loses again. The judge also questions the rule about not prosecuting a president. He is not the first judge to express that opinion.

Trump, with the vocal support of Rand Paul, is demanding the release of the identity of the original whistleblower, even though he or she has been corroborated by many of that person's associates. This demand is nothing more than threat to intimidate anyone else who might consider such action in the future, and is against the law put in place to protect whistleblowers.

On Tuesday, several states held off-year elections for state and local offices. These proved to be one of two blows President Trump was dealt on the same day. The first one was when Ambassador Gordon Sondland, realizing that he was in peril of a perjury charge for stating in his testimony the other day that he was unaware of any quid pro quo being offered, decided that his memory has been refreshed and he would like to amend that statement and agree with the other ten or so witnesses who testified otherwise. He specifically says that "...there was a bribery of Ukraine and it is an impeachable offence." Thus, Trump's only supporter on the issue among that group is now on the other team.

The other blow was even more damaging to the GOP in general. The blue wave seen in 2018 produced another one almost as big. Two states had the most striking results. Virginia's state house was completely turned from red to blue for the first time in many years; and Kentucky elected a Democrat, Andy Beshear, for Governor, upsetting the incumbent who been ahead by five percentage points until Trump came to Kentucky last week and practically begged his supporters not to let him down by voting for the Democrat. He made that vote all about himself instead of the candidate, because he had won that state by thirty points in 2016. But his plea actually cost Governor Matt Bevin his five point lead and he lost by less than a percentage point. He has refused to concede yet, and a recount may be held, but even if the result is switched, the indicator is that Mitch McConnell should be very afraid.

Perhaps the biggest worry for the GOP is the trend, throughout the nation, of suburban voters, who had been for some time now generally voting Republican, to now be voting quite heavily the other way.

Book Two (09/2018-11/2019)

Wow! There *is* a depth to which Bill Barr will not stoop in his support of the president, after all. The *Washington Post* reports that Trump asked Barr to call a press conference to tell the country that he sees nothing criminal in any of Trump's actions, and that Barr actually refused. I wonder how Trump is dealing with this rebuff from his "Roy Cohn".

Lindsey Graham has an interesting new way to try to defend Trump against the extortion charge. He says that he does not think that Trump and his team were competent enough to come up with that kind of scheme. This has to be the champion of all back-handed compliments.

The last witness before they become open to the public testified on Wednesday in a closed session. It was Pompeo Aide David Hale, the third-highest official at State, who is expected to tell lawmakers that Secretary of State Mike Pompeo and other senior officials determined that backing Marie Yovanovitch would imperil the military assistance slated for Ukraine, according to the Associated Press. He will say that the hesitation to support Yovanovitch stemmed from concerns among the officials about how Trump lawyer Rudy Giuliani, who had been pressing to have her removed, would react.

The first returning witness to come back in and *discuss for the public* the statements that he made behind closed doors a few days ago, will be William Taylor, scheduled for next Wednesday. Today, his closed door testimony transcript was released and discussed. It revealed several interesting things. He will be followed a day or two later by Alexander Vindman. Of all the witnesses who were part of the recent two-week parade of nightmares for Trump, these two men were the most damaging to him. We can only hope that a huge percentage of the voting public take the time to pay attention to what these men have to say.

The Enemy Within: A Chronicle of the Trump Administration

Roger Stone's trial is now underway and that also contained some juicy info pertaining to his and Trump's communications with WikiLeaks. He is facing several charges, all of which can net him jail time. His defense claims that he lied because the truth looked bad for Trump.

Chief of Staff Mulvaney was subpoenaed to appear before Schiff's committee on Thursday but declined the "invitation", for which he could have been arrested. But Schiff's strategy now is to simply add these refusals, which are at the direction of the president, to the bill of impeachment on obstruction.

Rachel Maddow devoted her show tonight to reading some excerpts from the new book by Anonymous titled "A Warning." They were more than interesting—they were scary! The previous tell-all books by authors who managed to obtain unprecedented access to the inner workings and attitudes of the White House were mild compared to this one. The extent to which the staff members would go to protect our democracy from the rash and dangerous intentions of this completely incompetent president was amazing.
 Here is a taste of one of those excerpts, which confirms what we have been told by several others about Trump's appalling unreachability and lack of interest in learning anything.

"Two traits are illustrative of what brought the Steady State together [the name this inside group trying to contain Trump gave themselves]: the president's inattentiveness and his impulsiveness. ,,, But coming to terms with these characteristics for the first time had a powerful impact on the people serving the administration. ...Nor should they bring summaries to the Oval Office. If they must bring paper, then PowerPoint was preferred because he is a visual learner. Okay, that's fine, many thought to themselves, leaders like to absorb information in different ways. Then officials were told that PowerPoint decks had to be slimmed down. The president couldn't digest too many slides. He needed more images to keep his interest—and fewer words. Then they were told to cut back on the overall messages (on complicated issues such as military readiness or the federal budget) to just three main points. Eh, that was still too much. Soon, West Wing aides were exchanging "best practices" for success in the Oval Office. The most salient advice? Forget the three points. Come in with *one* main point and repeat it—over and over again, even if the president inevitably goes off on tangents—until he gets it."

A person with this amount of learning ability should not be the president of *anything*. I can't wait for this book to become available to the public. I hope we eventually find out who the author is.

The first two witnesses to give their open testimony before the House committee are William Taylor and George Kent. They will be followed by Marie Yovanovitch.

On Thursday the transcripts of Kent's and Fiona Hill's testimony in the *closed* hearing were released, and it exposed a lot of dialog very damaging to Trump's flimsy defense. Much of Hill's was read by Rachel Maddow tonight—fascinating! One Republican questioner tried his best to draw something out of her about possible evidence of *Ukrainian* interference with the 2016 election, but she completely destroyed every attempt.

Their testimony revealed how much pressure was applied to Zelenskyy to meet Trump's demands, and how close he came to acquiescing to them, before the first whistleblower's memo was outed and caused him to back up.

At Trump's latest ego-rally, most of his supporters were wearing tee-shirts that read, "READ THE TRANSCRIPT". The Democrats in Congress are talking about passing out their own tee-shirts that say, "YES! READ THE TRANSCRIPT". Trump's backers and his critics seem to differ about just what that full transcript will say. Trump's supporters seem to believe their master when he claims that the call "was perfect", but anyone who can read and understand English and who actually has read it, knows that even the sanitized version that we have been allowed to see contains indisputable proof of a combination of the felonies of bribery and extortion, depending on how much pressure was applied to accept the quid pro quo being forced on Zelenskyy. He says he felt no pressure, but the testimony of the call itself and those who heard it say otherwise.

Nov. 11-17

Last week was very bad for the Trump presidency, and this one will be much worse. On Wednesday, Kent and Taylor will be questioned in hearings which will be publicly aired. And on Friday we will hear from Yovanovitch, who led off the parade of whistleblower corroborators with her mind-blowing opening statement. Any viewers of these hearings who are just now trying to catch up with what has been going on, are going to be in for a series of shocks. We should not expect these open hearings to have very much of an impact on the forty percent who die-hard Trump supporters, because they are under the influence of "group think." That is the tribalism that makes it very difficult for a member of a group that includes family members, friends and neighbors who are of like mind, to admit that he or she has been persuaded to change their mind on such an emotional subject. Most of them are too stubbornly brainwashed to even think about altering their convictions.

The Republicans, for the most part, have given up the fruitless task of trying to mount a defense against the charges (two of them—solicitation of the cooperation of a foreign power to provide assistance in the 2020 election, *and* extortion/bribery of that power to provide that assistance). So they are now resorting to claiming that these crimes do not rise to the level of *impeachable.*\

This raises once again the question of, just what did the framers of our Constitution have in mind when they used the phrase, "*high crimes and misdemeanors?*" The president's behavior most certainly is far more serious than a *misdemeano*r. So the question remains, how high a *crime* (pair of crimes) is it?

Book Two (09/2018-11/2019)

Well, let's compare it to the crime that the jury in the Clinton impeachment felt was not high enough—the sexual indiscretion with an intern and the fact that he lied about it. One could easily come to the conclusion that this was pretty bad, but maybe not bad enough. Now compare it to the charges against Nixon, for which the Senate *was ready to remove him*, if he did not save them the trouble and resign. He was charged with being behind a break-in of the Democratic Party headquarters to steal political information, then lying to cover it up. Ask yourself, all you Trump supporters; do you consider those charges to be "higher crimes" than the extortion crime that they have on Trump? And that is without adding all the other crimes they could and hopefully will include, such as emoluments violations like no one has ever seen before, directing the crime for which Cohen is now in prison, ten incidents of obstruction listed in the Mueller report in which he desperately tried to hide his collusion with the Russians to influence his election, just to name the most egregious (*highest*). If Trump's behavior is not high enough, what the Hell would it take, mass murder? But in our case, the guessing game should not be necessary, because the *entire* phrase that spells out the judging point is, ..."treason, *bribery* and other high crimes and misdemeanors". Trump's quid pro quo was at least bribery, and most legal experts consider it to be extortion, which is even more serious. It is time to *take* it seriously, GOP!

The week starts off with an observance of Veteran's Day. Trump made a fairly lengthy speech to commemorate the day, and for a change he stuck pretty much to the script that a very good speechwriter had written for him, without going off on one of his usual nutty tangents.

The last witness before they become open to the public testified on Wednesday in a closed session. It was Pompeo Deputy David Hale, the third-highest official at State, who is expected to tell lawmakers that Secretary of State Mike Pompeo

The Enemy Within: A Chronicle of the Trump Administration

and other senior officials determined that backing Marie Yovanovitch would imperil the military assistance, according to the Associated Press. He will say the hesitation to support Yovanovitch stemmed from concerns among the officials about how Trump lawyer Rudy Giuliani, who had been pressing to have her removed, would react.

The first returning witness to come back in and *discuss for the public* the statements that he made behind closed doors a few days ago, will be William Taylor, scheduled for next Wednesday. Today, his *closed* testimony transcript was released and discussed. It revealed several interesting things. He will be followed a day or two later by Alexander Vindman. Of all the witnesses who were part of the recent two-week parade of nightmares for Trump, these two men were the most damaging to him. We can only hope that a huge percentage of the voting public take the time to pay attention to what they have to say.

Roger Stone's trial is now underway and that also contained some juicy info pertaining to his and Trump's communications with WikiLeaks. He is facing several charges, all of which can net him jail time. His defense claims that he lied because the truth looked bad for Trump.

Chief of Staff Mulvaney was subpoenaed to appear before Schiff's committee on Thursday but declined the "invitation", for which he could have been arrested, but Schiff's strategy now is to simply add these refusals, which are at the direction of the president, to the bill of impeachment on obstruction.

Rachel Maddow devoted her show tonight to reading some excerpts from the new book by Anonymous titled "A Warning." They were more than interesting—they were scary! The previous tell-all books by authors who managed to obtain unprecedented access to the inner workings and attitudes of the White House were mild compared to this one. The extent to which the staff members would go to protect our democracy

Book Two (09/2018-11/2019)

from the rash and dangerous intentions of this completely incompetent president were amazing. Here is a taste of one of those excerpts, which confirms what we have been told by several others about Trump's appalling unreachability and lack of interest in learning anything.

"Two traits ae illustrative of what brought the Steady State together [the name this inside group trying to contain Trump gave themselves]: the president's inattentiveness and his impulsiveness. ,,, But coming to terms with these characteristics for the first time had a powerful impact on the people serving the administration. ...Nor should they bring summaries to the Oval Office. If they must bring paper, then PowerPoint was preferred because he is a visual learner. Okay, that's fine, many thought to themselves, leaders like to absorb information in different ways. Then officials were told that PowerPoint decks had to be slimmed down. The president couldn't digest too many slides. He needed more images to keep his interest—and fewer words. Then they were told to cut back on the overall messages (on complicated issues such as military readiness or the federal budget) to just three main points. Eh, that was still too much. Soon, West Wing aides were exchanging "best practices" for success in the Oval Office. The most salient advice? Forget the three points. Come in with *one* main point and repeat it—over and over again, even if the president inevitably goes off on tangents—until he gets it."

A person with this amount of learning ability should not be the president of *anything*. I can't wait for this book to become available to the public. I hope we eventually find out who the author is.

As Congress and the American People were gearing up for the start of the historic impeachment hearings, Trump was saying that he was considering firing the Inspector General of the intelligence community, because he was the one who received, approved and passed on the memo from the original whistleblower who set this whole impeachment process in motion. Just the threat of this action is another case of abuse of power. If he goes through with it, it could be an additional article of impeachment. He is also making the very questionable move of hosting Turkish President Erdogan at the White House. Since Trump pulled our troops out of Syria, Erdogan has not been a very good ally of the US with his immediate all-out assault on the Kurds.

The latest Iowa polling shows that Buttigieg has moved up eleven points to take a slight lead over Biden and Warren. His weakness seems to be among the African American vote.

As scheduled, on Wednesday Ambassador William Taylor and Deputy Assistant Secretary George Kent testified in an open hearing before the Democratic impeachment committee and Republican members of the Intelligence and Judiciary committees, who represented the defense of the president. This group included a late addition; Congressman Jim Jordan, who has been one of the most fervent Trump defenders. Jordan and others tried their best to paint these two highly respected and extremely experienced veterans of the State Department as "never Trumpers" with zero success. The only defense they could offer for Trump's attempt at extortion was that he didn't succeed in getting what he wanted and the Ukrainians got the aid that they had been expecting and was allocated for them. But that aid was not released until the lid of the extortion plan had been blown off. The attempt to extort, like any other attempted crime, is still a crime. And we still heard a lot of that old attempt to discredit the whistleblower by continuously calling it all "hearsay", even after so many people who were in a position to know exactly what took place corroborated that memo sent to the Inspector General that started this whole bonfire. The desperation is just dripping off these pathetic lackeys.

Book Two (09/2018-11/2019)

There was a new important phone call between Trump and Zelenskyy brought out today. Georg Kent was sitting at an outdoor cafe with colleagues when Sondland made an unsecured cell phone call directly to Trump and discussed the status of the "deal". Taylor said that the call was placed from a restaurant where Sondland was eating lunch with a couple of aides. This call was overheard by all three in the restaurant and it made it clear that Trump cared more about those "investigations" than about the welfare of Ukraine. Now Sondland will be called back once again to explain why he did not mention this call in his testimony. This cannot be good for Sondland or Trump.

Mueller's public testimony—low-key as it was—changed public opinion to some extent. Today's testimony should do even more damage to Trump's stubborn support. And they are just getting started. Friday, Marie Yovanovitch will do at least as much.

In the Roger Stone trial, Rick Gates testified that Trump was informed by Stone about the WikiLeaks impending email release much earlier than Trump has been claiming. Steve Bannon said that Stone was Trump's "access point" to WikiLeaks.

On Thursday, Pence Aide Jennifer Williams testified before Schiff's committee. It was supposed to have been John Bolton, but he is still waiting for a federal judge to tell him it is alright to defy Trump's order not to appear, in spite of being subpoenaed.

On Friday, two weeks after her closed testimony, Marie Yovanovitch returned to be questioned in an open hearing broadcast on TV for the nation to see and hear this highly experienced, very intelligent, courageous woman, who had been and is still being unfairly maligned by our now panicking president. She spent many hours calmly and thoroughly answering every question put to her by both Democrat and Republican Congressmen. A few of the latter tried their best to trip her up or rattle her, but they were unable to even come close. When the session was finally over, late in the afternoon, she received a standing ovation from her "audience".

It began with opening statements from chairman Schiff, followed by ranking GOP member Devin Nunes and then the former Ambassador. Nunes' remarks were his usual array of pitiful blather that contained nothing even close to a defense of Trump. Their only attempt at a defense of the president was that no investigation was opened by Zelenskyy and the aide was released, so harm, no foul. In other words, "My client's knife attack on this victim didn't kill him so you can't charge his attacker with murder."

After her opening, which was basically the same comprehensive one she gave two weeks ago, Yovanovitch described the events surrounding her abrupt departure from her position as Ukraine Ambassador, and left no doubt about the level of intimidation she felt from the president, Rudy Giuliani and Donald Trump Jr. that made her feel that her life might be in danger. She made it abundantly clear that she was forced out and replaced by an inexperienced Trump supporter because she stood in the way of Trump's efforts to get the Turkish President to get to agree to his "request" to make a public announcement that he would be opening investigations into Burisma corruption involving the Bidens, *and* Ukraine's 2016 election interference to help Clinton—not Russian interference to help Trump.

Another aspect of her testimony pertained to several attempts to report these pressures she was receiving--from Rudy Giuliani and the trio which has come to be referred to as "The Three Amigos"-- EU Envoy Gordon Sondland, Special Envoy Kurt Volker and Energy Secretary Rick Perry--to Secretary of State Pompeo, for which she received nothing but what she called "deafening silence." It has become increasingly obvious that

Book Two (09/2018-11/2019)

Pompeo is involved in at least the cover-up of these crimes, if not a coconspirator.

During the course of this testimony, Trump decided that this would be a good time to send out another couple of tweets adding to both the slurs and the intimidation of this outstanding woman. In so doing, he stupidly provided Chairman Adam Schiff with another article of impeachment to add to the list.

Ironically, while all this was going on, Roger Stone was found guilty on all seven counts against him, which included lying and *witness intimidation*.

Later in the day, a new witness testified behind closed doors. This was David Holmes, a State Department Aide, who had been one of those who were sitting in a restaurant, the day after that infamous call between Trump and Zelenskyy, when Gordon Sondland placed that newly discovered phone call to Trump. It was placed using an unsecured cell phone which was almost certainly being monitored by Russian intelligence as well as being within earshot of other patrons in the restaurant. Holmes was able to confirm everything that Taylor had described on Thursday and flesh it out with several additional details. So much for "hearsay". What they heard was Sondland assuring Trump that Zelenskyy "loved" Trump and was going to do anything that Trump asked him to do. [The only thing that stopped him from delivering, was the revelation by the whistleblower.]

Later in the week, there was another off-year election held in the State of Virginia in which the Democrats took over both houses of the state legislature for the first time in decades, in spite of Trump's usual appeal for help.

To round out the week: a) the transcript of Williams, Pence's Aide, was released to the public and added even more information damaging to Trump, Giuliani and Pence; b) Trump had an unscheduled examination because he was experiencing chest discomfort; c) Buttigieg surged ahead by six points in the latest Iowa poll; d) a new candidate was added to the list of Democrats for president—former Governor of Massachusetts, Deval Patrick. They seem to be added as fast as they drop out of the race. This coming Wednesday we will see the next debate.

Nov 18-24

This week was even more devastating to Trump, Pompeo and Giuliani than the previous two weeks have been. Nine witnesses were scheduled to give their open testimony, starting with Pence Aide Jennifer Williams and Colonel Alexander Vindman on Tuesday morning and former NSC Aide Tim Morrison and Ambassador Kurt Volker in the afternoon. They were followed by Ambassador Gordon Sondland on Wednesday morning, and Laura Cooper and David Hale in the afternoon. In each case, the opening statement by minority leader Devin Nunes was both laughable and shameful. He keeps displaying a clear indication of the desperation level Trump's defenders now find themselves in.

On Tuesday it became clear that the "hearsay" defense has been completely obliterated by several people who were in on the crucial conversations. They are now relying on trying to impugn the reputation of the witnesses and pushing debunked conspiracy theories. It is even more impressive that the first two witnesses are Republicans appointed by Trump, and called to testify by the Republican Congressmen. They made it clear that the "three amigos were being guided by Rudy Giuliani.

All these witnesses were very straightforward and supportive of the others who had disputed the defensive claims of "no quid pro quo", except Morrison, who was rather evasive, still trying his best not to anger the president. Of the four, Vindman was the star and even elicited applause at one point.

Book Two (09/2018-11/2019)

On Wednesday Gordon D. Sondland, Mr. Trump's envoy to the European Union, took up most of the day in his third appearance, and was every bit as explosive as expected under his circumstances (trying to avoid a perjury charge). He told the House Intelligence Committee that he reluctantly followed Mr. Trump's directive. He testified that the president instructed him to work with Rudy Giuliani, Mr. Trump's personal lawyer, as he pressured Ukraine to publicly commit to investigating former Vice President Joseph Biden and his son Hunter, *and* a debunked theory that Democrats conspired with Ukraine to interfere in the 2016 election. The picture of a secret irregular cadre of people applying pressure to President Zelenskyy was blown up and replaced by the fact that it was a "main stream" policy to perform this illegal act, conducted by the entire upper echelon of our government including, Trump, Pence, Barr and Trump's Chief of Staff Mulvaney. His very words were: "They were all in on it."

Wednesday late afternoon and evening we heard from Pence Aide Laura Cooper and State Department's third in command, David Hale. Hale discussed the smear campaign against Yovanovitch and "how wrong" it was. Cooper discussed the fact that Zelenskyy was aware of the freeze on his aide money when he was being pressured by Trump, contrary to what the Republicans were asserting.

On Thursday, Dr. (PHD) Fiona Hill and David Holms returned to give their open-to-the-public testimony. Hill was not only the star of the day, she was a virtual tie with Yovanovitch for star of the *entire set* of impeachment hearings. Her northern England accent only served to give flavor to her brilliant presentation of the facts as she saw them first hand, working closely with all the other Ukraine embassy diplomats who testified in the past few weeks. One of her most impressive warnings was to the Republicans on the committee, not to swallow the Russian-invented conspiracy theories about

Ukraine being the source of 2016 election interference instead of Russia. The bulk of her experience has been in dealing with Russia, so she has the "chops" to back up what she says.

Holmes provided more details about what he overheard in that July 26 call from the outside café from Sondland to Trump, when Sondland assured the president that "...he (Zelenskyy) will do anything you want. He loves your ass."

This probably wraps up the parade of witnesses, unless they eventually manage to get John Bolton or Don McGahn to come forward. Schiff's closing remarks at the end of the day indicated that he feels they have more than enough now to proceed with the preparation of the bills of impeachment. Everything depends on how strongly they can present those bills and how the American public will react to that presentation. Unless there is a sizable groundswell of public demand for the conviction of Trump, there is no chance that this Senate will vote to remove him.

Friday, November 22, was the fifty-sixth anniversary of the JFK assassination, and nobody even noticed, it seems.

On Saturday evening, dozens of documents were released by the State Department, showing that Rudy Giuliani's smear campaign against Yovanovitch involved both Pompeo and Trump. The House committee has been asking for these documents for a while now. It took a FOIA suit by a civilian group to get these released.

Giuliani associate Lev Parnas' lawyer has told the House committee that his client has valuable information about the Trump extortion attempt on Ukraine and it involves Devin Nunes—the leading Trump defender in the House. Parnas says he helped Nunes gain access to Ukraine to try to push the investigation into the Bidens. He seems to be trying to cut a deal. The question is, does he really know anything? In any case, Nunes is now a new subject of at least an ethics investigation for his part in the conspiracy to get Ukraine to launch an inquiry into the Bidens.

Ken Starr, an attorney who headed up the investigation of those associated with President Bill Clinton during his impeachment investigation, says that after that Sondland testimony the Republican Senators need to seriously consider taking a walk down to the White House to advise Trump to resign. We can only *hope* they have that much regard for the country.

Secretary of the Navy Richard Spencer was forced to resign this weekend by the Secretary of Defense (on orders from Trump?), because he disputed Trump's interference in the Navy's decision to strip a Seal of his commission and trident pin for the infraction of posing for a photo beside an enemy's corpse. That presidential interference would have a large detrimental effect on the military's code of disciplinary conduct. Just another case of Trump acting on impulse without consulting anyone about the possible ramifications.

Just what we needed! Another Democratic candidate for the presidential nomination. And another billionaire trying to buy that position. Former New York City mayor Michael Bloomberg has decided to make a late entry to the race, bypassing the early targets of Iowa and New Hampshire and going all out for Super-Tuesday, starting with $31 million worth of advertising, with a whole lot more where that came from.

Nov. 25-30

We begin this final week of Trump coverage in this second volume of my Trump chronicle with a very important ruling by a federal judge that continues Trump's lengthy string of court loses. D. C. Judge Ketanji Brown Jackson ruled in the case of White House lawyer Don McGahn that he cannot be blocked by an executive order from the president from obeying the

The Enemy Within: A Chronicle of the Trump Administration

subpoena to testify before the House Judiciary committee. In a multi-page ruling the judge essentially confirmed the president is not a king and cannot override a coequal branch of government. This is a momentous ruling that will have far reaching and long lasting effects for such cases, and might result in not only McGahn testifying, but could bring in Bolton as well. The catch, however, is that the judge also ruled that witnesses cold refuse to answer via either fifth amendment or executive privilege.

The case will no doubt be appealed by the GOP in order to buy time which Schiff's committee is not willing to spend. We will see.

Navy Secretary Richard Spencer, who was forced out of his position by Trump because he refused to obey the President's attempt to pardon a war criminal, sent a strong letter to Trump on his way out. Here is the main section of that letter.

"As Secretary of the Navy one of the most important responsibilities I have to our people is to maintain good order and discipline throughout the ranks. I regard this as deadly serious business. The lives of our Sailors, Marines and civilian teammates quite literally depend on the professional execution of our many missions. And they also depend on the ongoing faith and support of the people we serve and the allies we serve alongside.

"The rule of law is what sets us apart from our adversaries. Good order and discipline is what enabled our victory over foreign tyranny time and again. ... The Constitution and the uniform code of Military Justice, are the shields that set us apart and the beacons that protect us all. Through my Title Ten Authority, I have strived to ensure our proceedings are fair, transparent, and consistent, from the newest recruit to the Flag and General Officer level. Unfortunately it has become apparent that in this respect I no longer share the same understanding with the Commander I Chief who appointed me, in regards to the key principle of good order and discipline. I cannot in good conscience obey an order that I believe violates the sacred oath

Book Two (09/2018-11/2019)

that I took in the presence of my family, my flag and my faith to support and defend the Constitution of the United States."

So here we have yet another blow against the misconception that Trump is a great supporter of our military, and they of him.

There has been a new release of documents, including emails, from the office of Management and Budget (OMB). This is the department that controls the receipt and disbursal of funds voted on by Congress, such as that $250 million that was allocated for the military defense of Ukraine against the Russian invasion. When Trump put a hold on that money, with the now obvious attempt to use it as a carrot to force Zelenskyy to do his bidding, several employees of the OMB realized that this was not proper and probably illegal. Two of them resigned as a result—one of them from the legal office of that department.

The co-founders of Fusion GPS, which published the Steele dossier, were on Chris Hayes' *All In* program on Tuesday. Their most startling comments were about how convinced they are that Russia will be interfering in the 2020 election, just as they did before, but smarter.

Trump has essentially thrown Rudy Giuliani under the bus by his comments in the past few days distancing himself, as he always does when he feels the spotlight badly shining on him. Rudy responded that he is not worried because he "has an insurance policy." This portends a possible flip on his part, if the current investigations he is under get too hot.

Pete Buttigieg has surged into the lead in the latest nationwide poll of presidential candidates. Warren continues to fade, mainly because of her proposal for Medicare-for-all. This has got to be hurting Sanders as well.

Ambassador Sondland and Trump were in agreement, around the time of Sondland's testimony, to the effect that on

The Enemy Within: A Chronicle of the Trump Administration

September 9, two days before the hold on the Ukraine support funds was lifted, they were on a call during which Trump declared, "I want nothing! I want no quid pro quo." Investigators have been unable to find any evidence at all that such a call took place. Another Sondland and Trump lie. This call was already suspect because it sounded so scripted.

Neal Katyal was on MSNBC Wednesday evening describing his new book titled *Impeach*, in which he lists the evidence of several crimes that can be used in bills of impeachment against Trump. He emphasized the crime of bribery, which is one of the specific crimes mentioned in the Constitution as impeachable. But once again there was little attempt to distinguish between bribery and the more serious crime of extortion, the one of which Trump is *really* guilty.

On Thursday, my wife Ruth and I were invited to join one of Ruth's long-time lady friends, her gentleman-friend, and a few members of his family, for Thanksgiving dinner. As was no doubt happening all over this great country of ours, everyone studiously avoided the subject of politics, lest it result in an explosive difference of opinion on the subject of Trump's upcoming impeachment. I kept wondering if the others at the table were feeling the tension as much as I was. This is what Donald Trump's three years of divisiveness have done to America. On the ride home, Ruth and I agreed that, in view of the fact that next year Thanksgiving will come only a few days after the election, the tension will probably be just a strong, if not worse, no matter what the result of the voting will be. We will be celebrating it alone next year.

Trump paid a surprise visit to our troops in Afghanistan, which would have been a little feather in his cap had he not spoiled it by making an address to a gathering of the service men in which he spent the entire time boasting about how much he had improved the economy and strengthened the nation since

Book Two (09/2018-11/2019

he took office—something we should all be thankful for. He cannot resist making everything about himself.

As the month of November ended, the furor over Rudy Giuliani's role in the Ukraine snake pit that now threatens the Trump presidency more than any of his other crimes, continues to broil. The NYT reports that the SDNY has enough evidence against him to indict him any day now, not only for the Ukraine fiasco, but also for his alleged illegal financial dealings over there. Then we will see just how loyal he is willing to remain to his boss, the President.

The first House hearing to present the evidence for Trump's impeachment will be this coming Wednesday, He has to decide soon whether he will accept Schiff's offer to appear before them personally, with a lawyer, either for the first hearing or for the entire procedure.

The Ukrainians say that they may decide to go ahead with those investigation that Trump was seeking, now that they have the support money that was allocated for them months ago. If they do, that completes the quid pro quo.

It is now clear that we still have at least a couple of months to go before the impeachment trial of Donald J. Trump reaches a decision. This book has already reached what I feel should be the capacity of any six-by-nine paperback, so I will reluctantly wrap it up for now with a few thoughts of what I believe we should, and hopefully will, see in the indictment from the House as they present their case against the 45th President.

The first, and primary bill will contain the charge consisting of a combination of the following offenses: abuse of power; bribery/extortion; obstruction of justice to impede the investigation into these crimes, which all come out of his attempt to force Ukraine's President to help him by smearing his chief rival, Joe Biden. There will follow bills charging: A) the ten episodes of obstruction into the Special Counsel's investigation into Russia's interference in the 2016 election, that were itemized in the Mueller report; B) directing his personal attorney Michael Cohen to pay off women with whom he had extramarital relations which would have had a negative impact on his campaign for president; C) massive violations of the Constitution's emoluments clause prohibiting the use of his office to enrich himself.

Unless there is a sudden and extensive wave of patriotism among the Republican in the Senate, Trump will not be removed from his office. He will be, however, further tainted by the airing of the impeachment trial, which will further reduce the already tiny chance that he could win reelection, no matter which Democrat wins the nomination. Along with Trump will go several Republicans running for reelection, including McConnell, Nunes and others who have been his most fervent defenders.

At this point, I am undecided as to whether or not I will write a third book in this series. Putting between three and five hours every day for the past three years into this description and analysis of a very depressing subject has taken its toll on both the mental and physical condition of this soon-to-become eighty-eight-year-old body. I will continue, for now, keeping notes of the most significant developments, and I will decide at some point, depending upon how the Senate vote goes on Trump's removal, whether I have the will to go at it for another year. Meanwhile, I will work on producing eBook versions of this book for your kindle.

Book Two (09/2018-11/2019)

Epilog

December 1-18

In the few days since I attempted to wrap this book up, the impeachment hearings have entered their official stage when the articles are drawn up and presented. After much debate among the Democrats as to how much and how many should be presented, they made what I believe was the worst choice—to go light and simple, so as not to be confusing to our sadly uninformed general population of voters. They put forth only two articles instead of the four that were screaming to be use: 1. Abuse of power (non-specific and ambiguous); 2 Obstruction of Congress (using only Trump's ban on any testimony from government employees).

In the first article, the abuse of power referenced only his attempt to pressure Zelenskyy to open those two investigations he sought—one to benefit him in the 2020 election, and one to benefit Putin by deflecting blame for the 2016 election meddling to Ukraine. No mention of the word "bribery" or the word "extortion", which would have been both justified and much more specific than "the abuse of power".

In the second article, they failed to include the ten counts of obstruction of justice that Mueller itemized in his report, and pointedly said that the only reason he was not indicted for those crimes was because of the DOJ's rule against indicting a president. He left it up to the Congress to take that step, and they did not.

It is bad enough that they gave Trump a pass on the hush money payment crime that sent his crony Cohen to jail, and they gave him a free ride on his excessive use of his office to enrich himself in continuous emoluments violations. But they did not even fully load the gun on the articles that they did use. They shot blanks! *They blew it!* Nancy Pelosi, how could you? As a result, the hearings that they hoped would at least have some effect on the public to help defeat Trump in the next election, probably had as much, if not more, the reverse effect of what they were going for.

I watched the vitriolic, closed-minded and hypocritical speeches practically screamed by the Republicans defending Trump as they branded the whole process "unfair", "illicit", "invalid", and "a personal vendetta against the President from the day he was elected". It was the most disheartening thing I have ever watched. It became clear that the current form of the Constitution's impeachment section can never work as it was hoped that it would by the founders. Two major flaws need to be corrected to make it effective. First, the definition of "high crimes and misdemeanors needs serious clarification with several more specific examples. Second, after the House presents articles of impeachment, the Senate should be able to present its own side of the case, but the trial should be conducted by a jury that is as politically impartial as possible, just as civil trials are very selective about jury selection. This would be a difficult problem to solve, but necessary to remove the current partisanship control that has pervaded every one we have ever encountered.

On Wednesday, December 18, the House voted 230-197 on article 1, and 229-198 on article 2, to impeach Donald J. Trump. They did so knowing it was a foregone conclusion that he would be acquitted by the Mitch McConnell-controlled Senate. Mitch has readily admitted that he will not be an impartial juror and will follow Trump's lead all the way.

Before voting, there were several more hours of debate during which many speakers from both parties were given a chance to voice their opinions about this whole process and whether or not the articles, as presented, were convincing evidence of impeachable crimes. I watched as Republican after Republican took the golden opening that these weak articles presented them, and claimed that they listed NO crimes. Of course, abuse of power *is* a crime and obstruction of Congress *is* a crime, but not as obvious and understandable to an ignorant public as bribery and obstruction of justice which brought down Nixon. So, as I knew they would, the president's defenders were able once again to obscure the facts of the case. Opportunity lost. A much more effective presentation would have been made if the used "Abuse of Power" as a blanket category under which to list the specific crimes that demonstrated that abuse.

Now Pelosi is negotiating with McConnell over the rules to be used for the trial in the Senate. These rules *should* be established by Chief Justice Roberts, who will be presiding over the case, not by Mitch McConnell who has admitted that he is not an impartial juror. Virtually anything can happen from this point.

The End (maybe)

Acknowledgements

First, I would like to credit and praise all the news commentators and journalists of MSNBC, but particularly Rachel Maddow and Lawrence O'Donnell, who provided about eighty to ninety percent of the information contained in this book. This has been a very different way of researching a book, but then it is a different type of book—one based on daily activity instead of history. Critics could correctly say that the information-source is one-sided, but when the other side is represented by the likes of an Entertainment Channel (*Fox News*) and other right-wing conspiracy and propaganda outlets, there is no good alternative. The type of guest speakers and interviewees that appear on MSNBC on a nightly basis is the best indication of the veracity of what is being reported. They purvey the exact opposite of "fake news".

Second, I would like to express my gratitude (and condolences) to my loving wife Ruth for her willingness to be my sounding board and proof-reading collaborator for the past three years, even though her level of interest in politics is far less feverish than mine.

Book Two (09/2018-11/2019)

Bibliography

Anonymous………………………….*A Warning*
Cohn, David & Isikoff, Michael...*Russian Roulette*
Lee, Bandy………………………….*The Dangerous Case of Donald Trump*
McCabe, Andrew……………….....*The Threat*
Mueller, Robert………………………*The Mueller Report*
Newman, Omarosa…………………*Unhinged*
Wolff, Michael…………………………*Fire and Fury Inside the Trump White House*
Woodward, Bob……………………...*Fear: Trump in the White House*

Made in the USA
Columbia, SC
31 August 2022